Effective Teaching in Elementary Social Studies

Fourth Edition

Tom V. Savage
California State University, Fullerton

David G. Armstrong
University of North Carolina, Greensboro

Merrill
an imprint of Prentice Hall
Upper Saddle River, New Jersey   Columbus, Ohio

Library of Congress Cataloging-in-Publication Data

Savage, Tom V.
    Effective teaching in elementary social studies / by Tom V. Savage
and David G. Armstrong.—4th ed.
        p.   cm.
    Includes bibliographical references and index.
    ISBN 0-13-082622-7
    1. Social sciences—Study and teaching (Elementary)—United
States.   I. Armstrong, David G.   II. Title.
LB1584.S34   2000
372.83′044—dc21   99-21213
                                                            CIP

Cover photo: Index Stock Photography, Inc.
Editor: Bradley J. Potthoff
Editorial Assistant: Mary Evangelista
Production Editor: Mary M. Irvin
Design Coordinator: Diane C. Lorenzo
Text Designer: Carlisle Publishers Services
Cover Designer: Mark Shumaker
Production Manager: Pamela D. Bennett
Director of Marketing: Kevin Flanagan
Marketing Manager: Megan Shepherd
Marketing Coordinator: Krista Groshong
Production Management and Editorial Supervision: Carlisle Publishers Services

This book was set in Transit 511 by Carlisle Communications, Ltd. and was printed and bound by
R. R. Donnelley & Sons Company. The cover was printed by Phoenix Color Corp.

©2000, 1996 by Prentice-Hall, Inc.
Pearson Education
Upper Saddle River, New Jersey 07458

Photo Credits: British Information Service, p. 77; Canadian Tourism Commission, p. 14; Scott
Cunningham/Merrill, pp. 12, 86, 205, 250, 259, 313, 327, 451; Embassy of Finland, p. 145; F.A.O. Food
and Agriculture Organization, p. 115; Israel Tourism Ministry, p. 120; Korea Tourism Corporation, p. 103;
Library of Congress, pp. 31, 36; Anthony Magnacca/Merrill, pp. 69, 173, 227, 235, 366, 419; New Mexico
Department of Tourism, p. 157; New York State Department of Commerce, p. 58; Norwegian Information
Service in the United States, p. 60; PhotoDisc, pp. 52, 135; Barbara Schwartz/Merrill, pp. 180, 193, 300, 340;
Silver Burdett Ginn, p. 398; Simon & Schuster/PH College, pp. 8, 126, 154, 163, 383; Terry Tietz/Merrill,
p. 98; Tourist Organization of Greece, p. 11; United Nations, pp. 1, 16, 21, 145; US Department of
Agriculture, p. 109; Anne Vega/Merrill, pp. 173, 214, 245, 262, 283, 291, 357, 423, 429, 465, 471, 487;
Virginia State Travel Service, p. 202; Washington DC Convention and Visitors Assn., p. 69.

10 9 8 7 6 5 4 3 2 1

ISBN: 0-13-082622-7

Prentice-Hall International (UK) Limited, *London*
Prentice-Hall of Australia Pty. Limited, *Sydney*
Prentice-Hall of Canada, Inc., *Toronto*
Prentice-Hall Hispanoamericana, S. A., *Mexico*
Prentice-Hall of India Private Limited, *New Delhi*
Prentice-Hall of Japan, Inc., *Tokyo*
Prentice-Hall (Singapore) Pte. Ltd., *Singapore*
Editora Prentice-Hall do Brasil, Ltda., *Rio de Janeiro*

preface

As we enter the twenty-first century we look back in amazement at the enormous changes that have occurred during the twentieth. We can be certain that the rate of change will only accelerate, and wonders that we have not yet considered will become commonplace. It is also clear that the roles of citizens of the world will become increasingly demanding and complex. Ethical, moral, and social questions will accompany each advance in science and technology. The consequences of the decisions of people in one part of the world will be felt by others living far away.

Citizens of the twenty-first century must have knowledge, problem solving skills, and an ethical base for their decisions. We believe that good social studies instruction beginning in the early primary grades must help young people develop sophisticated thinking skills and understanding that will assist them in making difficult decisions in the future. To do any less poses enormous risks. Simplistic instruction that demands little more than simplistic recitations of arid facts and past events will not do. Young people need to develop multiple perspectives for viewing problems, understand broad ideas that can be applied to new circumstances, and develop the moral and ethical character to stand firm in the face of injustice.

It is because we believe so strongly in the importance of social studies that we have written *Effective Teaching in Elementary Social Studies.* We believe that this subject must be an important part of the education of all children. Teachers in the elementary grades need to understand the purposes of social studies and possess knowledge of methods that make the subject vital and interesting. Because of the interrelated nature of knowledge and the complexity of decisions that are required of citizens, social studies can no longer be identified as simply history and geography. Definitions of the social studies curriculum must be expanded to include a wide range of subjects and topics, including multicultural, gender, environmental, and global issues.

A complex subject such as the social studies places heavy demands on teachers. Not only must teachers have a fundamental grasp of history and social sciences; they must also know how to help pupils learn decision-making and problem-solving skills and how to challenge them to go beyond merely acquiring knowledge to formulating values and beliefs. Teachers must also be knowledgeable in how to infuse new technologies into the social studies program. Schools must accommodate the needs of an increasingly diverse student population, including a large number of students who have a primary language other than English. These students must not miss important social studies learning simply because of language barriers. We addressed these challenges as we wrote this text.

Previous editions of *Effective Teaching in Elementary Social Studies* have been used successfully in undergraduate and graduate social studies courses. It is designed primarily for use in elementary social studies methods courses, as a source for discussion in advanced curriculum classes, and as a personal reference for elementary school teachers. Users of earlier editions have stated that it is practical, readable, and user-friendly. We have tried to keep these considerations at the forefront in this edition.

NEW TO THIS EDITION

The fourth edition features several changes:

- National standards in those areas critical to social studies instruction have been included.
- More emphasis has been placed on fundamental approaches to instruction, with the addition of chapters on the acquisition of information and the construction of knowledge.
- The content in the technology chapter has been updated and the emphasis changed to help teachers use the Internet and the World Wide Web.
- Each chapter includes addresses of sites on the World Wide Web so that readers can find rich resources and expand their understanding.
- A section on the uses of charts and graphs has been added.
- The previous section on a selection of themes has been dropped, and content from that section has been integrated in other chapters.
- The topic of authentic assessment has been added to Chapter 13.

TEXT FEATURES

Each chapter of the fourth edition of *Effective Teaching in Elementary Social Studies* includes the following:

- *Chapter Goals* to help focus attention on intended outcomes for each chapter
- *Graphic Organizer* to show the relationships among chapter topics and facilitate comprehension
- A *Case Study* to prompt readers to think about a significant issue discussed in the chapter
- *Special Features* including (1) boxed items that pose questions and challenge readers to think about issues and (2) other figures and activities to enrich understanding
- *Web Check* providing addresses of sites on the World Wide Web so that readers can find additional resources and pursue topics of interest
- *Key Ideas in Summary* to pull together and reinforce important chapter content
- *Chapter Reflections* prompting readers to reflect on chapter content and changes that might have occurred in their thinking as a result of reading the chapter

- *Extending Understanding and Skill* to help readers extend and enrich their understanding of the chapter content
- *References* that direct readers to sources of information used in the preparation of the manuscript

ORGANIZATION

Content has been organized for flexible use. We recognize that each instructor has an organizational preference. To accommodate these preferences, the information in each chapter can be used independently of that in other chapters.

The first five chapters of the text focus on what we define as the *foundations for social studies.* The focus is on understanding the purposes of the social studies and the social studies curriculum. We know that many students enter a social studies course with an incomplete or fragmented understanding of the content sources of the social studies curriculum. Therefore, we have included chapters that give an overview of the content sources, national standards that have been adopted for several of the subjects, some of the key ideas from the subject, and some sample teaching ideas.

Chapters 6 through 11 focus on a variety of instructional approaches that can be used to teach a variety of content to social studies students. Chapters 12 and 13 continue the emphasis on instruction with a focus on planning and assessment. We have placed the planning chapter somewhat later in this edition because students have reported that planning is easier once they have a better understanding of the purposes of social studies and the instructional alternatives from which they might choose. We have purposefully placed the planning and assessment chapters together in the hope that readers will understand that planning and assessment need to be related. Assessment plans should be developed along with unit planning so that the major outcomes are assessed.

Chapters 14 through 16 provide information that supports the teaching of social studies. We know that the elementary curriculum includes a variety of important curriculum topics. The only way the variety of demands can be accommodated is by integrating the curriculum. Chapter 14 provides information to help the reader understand how social studies and other curriculum topics can be integrated. Chapter 15 provides information on technology that can be used to enrich the social studies program. The final chapter provides information to help teachers support social studies learning for limited-English-proficient (LEP) pupils.

ACKNOWLEDGMENTS

Any work is the product of many influences. A number of individuals have provided important contributions to the fourth edition of *Effective Teaching in Elementary Social Studies.* We wish to acknowledge those individuals who have used previous editions and have shared their suggestions with us. We are also indebted to the students in our classes, who continue to share with us their hopes, desires, and needs. It is their inspiration that keeps us working to try to develop a better text. We thank the reviewers of the manuscript for their comments and insights: Gloria T. Alter, Northern Illinois University; Greg Bryant, Towson University; John J. Chiodo, The University of Oklahoma; Sandy Jean Hicks, University of Rhode Island; Susan Kent, Ohio State University at Newark; and James B. Kracht, Texas A & M University. We want to thank the helpful staff at Merrill/ Prentice Hall, especially Brad Potthoff and Mary Evangelista, for their patience and assistance in developing and publishing the manuscript. Finally, we want to recognize the important contributions of our wives, Nancy and Marsha. They provided us with useful professional advice and assistance, and they exhibited remarkable patience when we struggled during the writing process.

TVS
DGA

Discover Companion Websites
A *Virtual Learning Environment*

Technology is a constantly growing and changing aspect of our field that is creating a need for content and resources. To address this emerging need, we have developed an online learning environment for students and professors alike—Companion Websites—to support our textbooks.

In creating a Companion Website, our goal is to build on and enhance what the textbook already offers. For this reason, the content for each user-friendly website is organized by topic and provides the professor and student with a variety of meaningful resources. Common features of a Companion Website include:

For the Professor

Every Companion Website integrates **Syllabus Manager™**, an online syllabus creation and management utility.

▶ **Syllabus Manager™** provides you, the instructor, with an easy, step-by-step process to create and revise syllabi, with direct links into Companion Website and other online content without having to learn HTML.

▶ Students may log on to your syllabus during any study session. All they need to know is the web address for the Companion Website and the password you've assigned to your syllabus.

▶ After you have created a syllabus using **Syllabus Manager™**, students may enter the syllabus for their course section from any point in the Companion Website.

▶ Class dates are highlighted in white and assignment due dates appear in blue. Clicking on a date, the student is shown the list of activities for the assignment. The activities for each assignment are linked directly to actual content, saving time for students.

▶ Adding assignments consists of clicking on the desired due date, then filling in the details of the assignment— name of the assignment, instructions, and whether or not it is a one-time or repeating assignment.

▶ In addition, links to other activities can be created easily. If the activity is online, a URL can be entered in the space provided, and it will be linked automatically in the final syllabus.

▶ Your completed syllabus is hosted on our servers, allowing convenient updates from any computer on the Internet. Changes you make to your syllabus are immediately available to your students at their next log-on.

For the Student

▶ **Topic Overviews**—outline key concepts in topic areas

▶ **Electronic Blue Book**—send homework or essays directly to your instructor's e-mail with this paperless form

▶ **Message Board**—serves as a virtual bulletin board to post—or respond to—questions or comments to/from a national audience

▶ **Web Destinations**—links to www sites that relate to each topic area

▶ **Professional Organizations**—links to organizations that relate to topic areas

▶ **Additional Resources**—access to topic-specific content that enhances material found in the text

To take advantage of these resources, please visit the *Effective Teaching in Elementary Social Studies* Companion Website at www.prenhall.com/Savage.

contents

Chapter   4   *Content Sources: Economics, Sociology, Anthropology, and Psychology   103*

Chapter   5   *Multicultural and Gender Issues   145*

Chapter   8   *Inquiry and Thinking Skills*   235

Chapter   9   *Group Learning*   259

Chapter 13   *Assessing Learning*   *383*

lesson ideas

chapter 1

Defining the Social Studies

This chapter will help you to:

- point out the importance of the social studies component of the elementary curriculum,
- describe and explain the three basic purposes of social studies,
- explain what is meant by "citizenship education,"
- list some topics that are typically covered in the K–8 social studies curriculum,
- identify relationships between the purposes of social studies and the topics often taught at each grade level, and
- explain how teachers' attitudes affect pupils' motivation.

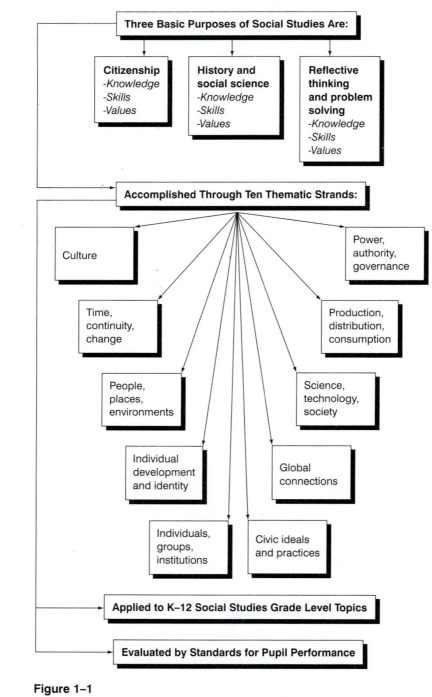

Three Basic Purposes of Social Studies Are:

Citizenship
-*Knowledge*
-*Skills*
-*Values*

History and social science
-*Knowledge*
-*Skills*
-*Values*

Reflective thinking and problem solving
-*Knowledge*
-*Skills*
-*Values*

Accomplished Through Ten Thematic Strands:

Culture

Power, authority, governance

Time, continuity, change

Production, distribution, consumption

People, places, environments

Science, technology, society

Individual development and identity

Global connections

Individuals, groups, institutions

Civic ideals and practices

Applied to K–12 Social Studies Grade Level Topics

Evaluated by Standards for Pupil Performance

Figure 1–1
Defining the social studies — graphic organizer.

Case Study

WHAT IS THE RELEVANCE?

Pat Taylor, a new sixth-grade teacher, was preparing her new class for their first social studies lesson of the year. She announced, "Today we are starting our study of social studies." She heard a groan from the class. Pat persisted. "Who can tell us what we learn in social studies? Susan?"

"Well, we learn about things that happened a long time ago."

"Good. Billy?"

"We have to memorize names, dates, capital cities, lots of boring stuff like that."

"So you think social studies is boring?" Pat asked.

Several heads nodded in agreement. "Sure, who cares about that stuff? Why do we need to know when the battle of the 'Little Big Horn' was fought?" Janelle said.

"Yeah," Mary added. "Why do we need to know that corn is grown in Iowa, or that Helena is the capital of Montana? We don't live in those states."

It was obvious that there was widespread agreement that social studies was a boring and not especially important subject. Pat's stress level began to rise. She had not enjoyed social studies when she was in school. Privately, she agreed with what her pupils were saying. She thought to herself, What do I tell them? How do I motivate them? What is the purpose of social studies? I'll have to think about some way to convince them this information is important. If I don't I'll have problems all year.

What Is Your Response?

1. What is the purpose of social studies? How would you respond to these learners' comments and questions?
2. Is social studies relevant to the lives of learners? How can it be made relevant and important?
3. Is social studies one of the *essential* or *core* subjects in the curriculum? Why or why not?
4. To what extent do you agree with the young people in Pat's class?
5. What do you think would happen if a teacher does not believe that the subject is important?

INTRODUCTION

Individuals entering teaching face complex issues. Debates about education have become a daily feature of our national life. Politicians have discovered education as a useful campaign topic. News media regularly report on what appears to be poor performance by United States' learners on tests designed to make international comparisons. Parents seek a larger voice in establishing school policies. The intensity of this attention ensures that people preparing to teach in the 21st century will enter an exciting world where debate, pressures for change, and demands of justification for "what the schools are doing" will be a commonplace of educators' professional lives.

The school social studies program will draw its share of attention. Some questions we can expect include:

- What is the role of social studies in the elementary school program, and is this role defensible?
- If we agree this content *should* be taught, is there any justification for regarding social studies as a required core subject? Or, should social studies be relegated to the status of an academic frill, nice to have, but not really necessary?
- What should pupils be able to demonstrate as a result of their exposure to social studies instruction? How do we know whether or not they are succeeding?
- How much time should be devoted to teaching social studies content as compared with such subjects as language arts and mathematics?

Some educators fear that debating these questions will have a negative impact on social studies as a core subject in the curriculum. This is nonsense. Social studies has survived as an important academic subject area even though we have had decades of debate on questions such as those noted above and on others that are much more narrow in scope. For example, the professional literature in the field features years of arguments focusing on the question of whether social studies ought to be a unified field of study or a study of separate disciplines such as history and geography (Whelan, 1997). Divergent opinions on controversies surrounding social studies have energized, not weakened this subject area. We see no reason to feel that debates in the future will have any other outcome.

If you want to know where we stand with respect to the general issue of the importance of social studies, we are happy to let you know that we are unabashed supporters of the importance of social studies instruction in the education of every individual. We believe that a huge body of compelling evidence supports this view. After years of reflection and consideration of the evidence, that is now our position. We also understand that not everyone accepts our view.

For example, we certainly agree that much of what has been called social studies is dull, boring, and of questionable significance. This is reflected in many reports of learner attitudes toward social studies. Several surveys have found that social studies ranks close to the bottom of the list of subjects elementary pupils like (McGowan, Sutton, & Smith, 1990). Much of this reputation, we believe, results not from social studies content, but rather from teacher uncertainty regarding the purposes of social studies and how the subject is often taught. (See Figure 1–2.)

If pupils do not see a school subject as particularly interesting or significant, they will more likely engage in inappropriate and off-task behavior. As a result, social studies lessons can become a part of the day that is dreaded by both learners and teachers. This situation can be avoided if you have a clear understanding of the purposes of social studies and how the subject can be taught in ways that interest and engage your young people.

In summary, as a teacher you will be called upon to defend your program. If you do not have a clear understanding of all areas of the curriculum, including social studies, others may make decisions that can be detrimental to the solid education of future citizens.

Research indicates that teachers spend more time teaching those subjects they enjoy. If you are to be successful in establishing a social studies program, you need to consider your attitude toward and feelings about the social studies.

THINK ABOUT THIS

1. What are your memories of social studies when you were in elementary school?
2. What methods were most prevalent? Which ones did you enjoy?
3. How do you think this previous experience will influence your teaching?
4. How do you feel about social studies now? Do you think it is an important subject?
5. Do you agree that an uninterested teacher will have uninterested learners?
6. What do you think you need to learn in order to be a successful social studies teacher?

Figure 1–2
You and the social studies.

Teachers report that many youngsters are not greatly motivated to learn social studies content. This situation is not a function of the content; it results from teaching approaches that may not be well suited to building pupil interests. As you continue to work with this text, we invite you to engage in critical reflection regarding the purposes, the curriculum, and the instructional methods of social studies in the elementary and middle schools. This kind of engagement can give you the tools you will need to discuss the role of the subject, understand its purposes, and design and deliver instruction in ways that will satisfy both you and the young people in your classrooms.

DEFINING SOCIAL STUDIES

How do we define *social studies?* Educators give a number of answers to this question. Although the subject has been taught in school for decades, there still is no consensus about what should be included (Barr, Barth, & Shermis, 1977). Sometimes this lack of definitional consensus has led to proposals to abandon the term *social studies* altogether and to replace it with more familiar academic labels, such as *history, geography,* or *civics.* For example, the California guide for teaching this part of the school curriculum is titled *History—Social Science Framework.*

Ross (1997) defines social studies as the preparation of young people with the knowledge, skills, and values necessary for active participation in society. This emphasis on developing future citizens has been a recognized goal of American education since colonial times. While the preparation of young people for active participation in society certainly involves studying history and the social sciences, it implies a complex outcome that goes beyond simply requiring young people to master the content of those subjects.

To provide opportunities for active engagement with the kinds of problems faced by adult citizens, some social studies educators advocate the use of important human dilemmas to guide social studies programs. Table 1–1 presents some examples of these dilemmas together with related focus questions. Supporters of this approach believe social

Table 1–1
Common human dilemmas and social studies focus questions.

Dilemmas	Selected Focus Questions
Stability vs. Change	What is worth preserving in society? What needs to be changed? How do we adapt to change while preserving what is good?
Individual Freedom vs. Community Rights	When do the rights of individuals conflict with the needs of society? How do we decide when individual rights or societal needs should be given priority? What is the proper relationship between an individual and government? What is the role of laws and rules?
Reacting to Diversity	How can we live in harmony with people who are different? When should diversity be encouraged? When should conformity be encouraged? How can we overcome irrational prejudice and discrimination?
Providing for Wants and Needs	How can we organize economic production to meet the most needs and wants? Who should decide what is produced? What is the role of government in controlling the marketplace?
Controlling Population Growth	What are the consequences of continued population growth? What can be done to reduce the rates of population growth? How does one reconcile personal choice, religious freedom, and views of morality with population control? What places in the world are most in need of population control?
Using the Environment	Who should decide how the environment and resources are to be used? How can we utilize resources of the earth wisely? How do we ensure that future generations will enjoy a quality of life at least equal to our own?
Technological Change	How do we use technological changes to our advantage? What happens when ethics and morality conflict with technological advances? Who should control the application of technology to our lives?

studies lessons should help young people grow into socially responsible adults who can adapt to changing social conditions (Cherryholmes, 1992). This suggests the need for social studies instruction that helps learners develop attitudes and skills that will enable them to adapt and construct new knowledge necessary to cope with future challenges.

Though individual conceptions of social studies vary, they universally recognize that this part of the school curriculum focuses on people. Social studies lessons help us understand people both in the present and in the past with all their fascinating diversity. Who are we as individuals and as a nation? How did we get this way, and where are we going? How do I understand those around me? What are my responsibilities to others and to the environment around me? How do I make decisions that impact the lives of people? These are some of the key questions that need to be addressed.

These questions can be addressed a number of ways. They can be addressed through the study of history and the social sciences or through the study of enduring human dilemmas. If we maintain our focus on people and these important questions, the potential for making social studies an interesting and significant topic is apparent. These are questions that are of vital concern to all of us. We are all motivated to search for meaning and significance in our lives and to understand those who live in the world with us. There are few things that are more interesting than the incredible diversity of people and the choices they have made and continue to make as they search for meaning and significance.

There is general agreement that three basic themes help organize the multiple purposes of social studies education (Ross, 1997). These include (1) citizenship; (2) the transmission of facts, concepts, and generalizations from history and the social sciences; and (3) the promotion of reflective thinking and problem solving.

The leading national association of social studies education professionals is the National Council for the Social Studies (NCSS). In *Expectations for Excellence: Curriculum Standards for Social Studies,* social studies is defined as follows (NCSS, 1994).

> Social studies is the integrated study of the social sciences and humanities to promote civic competence. Within the school program, social studies provides coordinated, systematic study drawing upon such disciplines as anthropology, archaeology, economics, geography, history, law, philosophy, political science, psychology, religion, and sociology, as well as appropriate content from the humanities, mathematics, and natural sciences. The primary purpose of social studies is to help young people develop the ability to make informed and reasoned decisions for the public good as citizens of a culturally diverse, democratic society in an interdependent world. (p. 3)*

This definition includes all of these elements noted by Ross (1997). It emphasizes the promotion of citizenship through the integration of social sciences and humanities and by giving learners the tools to make reasoned and informed decisions. Note that this definition does not limit subject matter content to the social sciences. Content drawn from any subject that (1) has a focus on the human experience and (2) will assist pupils in becoming better informed citizens and decision makers can be used logically in the school social studies program.

Citizenship Education

Although there is widespread agreement that citizenship education is a key element and a major justification for social studies education, there is much less agreement concerning the definition of citizenship and the purposes to be achieved by instruction guided by this focus. What exactly is *civic competence,* and what is *good citizenship?* Is the purpose to promote stability through the values and behaviors of the traditional, dominant society? Is the purpose to develop learners as critics of American society by examining controversial topics (Ross, 1997)? Is it the inculcation of patriotism? Is it unquestioned obedience to the laws of society? Is it acceptance of the status quo? Is it voting in elections? Is it active involvement in public affairs?

Though views about the purposes of citizenship education vary, three common threads run through many discussions of this issue. First, there is general agreement that young

*From *Expectations of Excellence: Curriculum Standards for Social Studies* by the National Council for the Social Studies, © 1994. Reprinted by permission.

A major purpose of the social studies is to develop an understanding of our heritage and the rights and responsibilities of citizenship.

people need to be encouraged to commit to such core American values as democratic decision making (National Council for the Social Studies Task Force on Curriculum Standards for the Social Studies, 1994). Second, it is widely acknowledged that citizenship education lessons should encourage pupils to critique present ways of doing things (Leming, 1989). Third, it is expected that good citizenship education programs will produce young people who will leave school with a predisposition to become actively involved in public affairs.

Are these realistic expectations for elementary school learners? Some research suggests that even fairly young pupils are quite aware of important social problems (Berman & La Farge, 1993). Young people are much more aware of "what is really going on" than many adults suppose. Some authorities believe that elementary social studies teachers need to take advantage of this sensitivity. Pupils need to be taught cooperation and conflict resolution, respect for diversity, and the importance of attacking issues in ways that will make a difference (Berman & La Farge, 1993).

Sanford Horwitt, a director of a national citizenship education project, is concerned that many young people view citizenship obligations too narrowly. Regarding this issue, he commented, "Young people have an impoverished notion of citizenship. . . . Basically, they think it's not breaking the law, and that's all" (Taylor, 1990, p. 7). Part of our responsibility as social studies teachers is to give our learners a much broader and deeper understanding of citizenship responsibilities.

History and Social Science Education

In addition to citizenship, the 1994 NCSS definition of *social studies* includes an important emphasis on content from academic disciplines. Though some content in social studies programs is drawn from many fields, programs today continue to place particularly heavy emphasis on information drawn from history and such social science disciplines as geography, political science, economics, sociology, anthropology, psychology, archaeology, and law. For this text, we have chosen to label the academic content component of the social studies program *history and social science education.*

Effective citizenship rests on a solid knowledge base. History and the social sciences (and some other subjects that sometimes provide social studies content) have developed information and successful methods of investigation. These have the potential to enrich lives and to help pupils increase their ability to make the kinds of rational decisions expected of good citizens.

Though we have chosen the term *history and social science education,* the academic content of the social studies program is not limited to history and the social sciences. Any subject that deals with human behavior can provide good content for social studies lessons. When we look for lesson content, our object is to find information that can help pupils understand their world. We are not guided to select content because it is associated with a particular academic subject, such as history or geography, but rather because it may have potential to help our learners learn significant things about the world "as it is" and "as it might be."

Reflective Thinking and Problem-Solving Education

Citizens in democratic societies need to be good thinkers. Adults are called on to respond to pressing problems of all kinds. Decisions they make influence their own lives and those of others in the community, state, and nation. Hence, reflective thinking and problem-solving education are another key component of the elementary social studies program. Lessons associated with this focus help pupils master techniques that are useful to them as they attempt to solve problems. (Specific problem-solving approaches are introduced in Chapter 8, "Inquiry and Thinking Skills.")

In summary, social studies has a specific responsibility to promote citizenship education. This is exercised through lessons drawing content from history and social sciences. This content often is organized and presented so as to facilitate the development of learners' reflective thinking and problem-solving abilities.

COMMON EMPHASES WITHIN SOCIAL STUDIES PROGRAMS

For each broad social studies purpose there are three emphases that need to be identified: knowledge, skills, and values (see Figure 1–3). *Knowledge* refers to specific facts and understandings a person needs to know. *Skills* refer to processes of gathering and using knowledge. *Values* are attitudes and beliefs individuals use to justify their actions. When these three areas are combined with (1) citizenship education, (2) history and social

	Citizenship Education	History and Social Science Education	Reflective Thinking and Problem Solving
Knowledge			
Skills			
Values			

Figure 1–3
Matrix of social studies purposes.

science education, and (3) reflective thinking and problem solving, a clearer picture of the content of social studies emerges.

Emphases Within Citizenship Education

Knowledge
Young people should be exposed to knowledge related to the American heritage; the Constitution; the Bill of Rights; political processes followed at the local, state, and national levels; and other basic information an educated adult citizen is expected to know.

Skills
Elementary school pupils need to be taught processes associated with rational decision making. They need to learn how to negotiate and compromise, to express their views clearly, and to work productively with others.

Values
Citizens do not make decisions only on the basis of information. They also consider social and personal values. Learners need to be exposed to values associated with democratic decision making and those that collectively support the operation of our nation's local, state, and national governments.

Emphases Within History and Social Science Education

Knowledge
The academic disciplines, including history and social sciences, are repositories of information that give us powerful insights into human behavior. This kind of information comprises an important part of the elementary social studies program.

Skills
Elementary social studies programs introduce skills that academic content specialists use as they gather and assess the importance of information. Many specialists use variants of the scientific method as they seek to verify and modify hypotheses. These same skills often are useful to learners as they begin to confront the kinds of personal and public dilemmas that adults face in their daily lives.

The study of history brings students into contact with the great accomplishments of human civilization.

Values

Certain values are implicit in how academic content specialists go about their work. For example, they are predisposed to prize knowledge based on data more than knowledge based on intuition or feeling. Learners in the elementary program need to understand how values affect what individuals believe to be real or important.

Emphases Within Reflective Thinking and Problem-Solving Education

Knowledge

Young people need to learn basic information about how rational decisions are made. Introducing them to procedures useful for bringing problems into focus and attacking them in a systematic, step-by-step way are important concerns of this part of the social studies program. As they learn how to identify relevant information and to use it to solve problems, pupils acquire techniques for organizing and evaluating data and for formulating and testing hypotheses.

Skills

Pupils' capacity for engaging in serious reflection and problem solving improves when they have opportunities to make decisions about real issues and to experience the consequences of these decisions. In the lower grades, problem-solving skills are developed as learners work with issues important to individuals and families. More mature elementary learners use these skills to work with a broader range of social and political problems affecting communities, states, the nation, and the world.

Many problems in a democratic society require collective decision making. Hence, part of the elementary social studies' skill-development program focuses on helping

Reflective thinking and the search for solutions to pressing social problems help make social studies meaningful and valuable to students.

pupils to work productively in groups. This allows learners opportunities to engage in the kind of give-and-take discussion that characterizes adult group decision making.

Values

Instruction in this area is designed to help pupils develop a commitment to approaches to reflection and problem solving that are based on rational thinking. It is hoped they will come to prize decisions that rest on evidence and logic and that they will resist jumping to conclusions based on unexamined assumptions or restrictive biases. Helping pupils develop a tolerance for diverse views is another important part of the values dimension of reflective thinking and problem-solving instruction.

*   *   *

The major social studies purposes of (1) citizenship education, (2) history and social science education, and (3) reflective thinking and problem-solving education and the subcategories under each—(a) knowledge, (b) skills, and (c) values—frame the overall elementary social studies program. Well-balanced programs provide some learning experiences directed to each of these areas. However, it is not likely that all will receive equal attention at each grade level. At some grade levels it is usual for some areas to receive more emphasis than others.

Figure 1–3 illustrates the major purposes of the social studies program. Each cell of the matrix indicates an important emphasis. This can be helpful as you define purposes for your social studies program. You can identify purposes in each cell related to the specific content you are teaching. For example, if you are teaching fifth grade you can ask, "What are the citizenship, history/social science, and reflective-thinking knowledge, skills, and values that need to be included?

TEN THEMATIC STRANDS IN SOCIAL STUDIES

The National Council for the Social Studies publication *Expectations of Excellence: Curriculum Standards for Social Studies* (1994) defines ten themes or strands that ought to permeate the social studies regardless of how they are organized. These ten themes provide additional clarification as you define social studies. These strands provide some specific citizenship and history/social science that should permeate the K–12 social studies program. In addition, they are useful in identifying performance expectations that can serve as benchmarks for learner progress. The ten thematic strands follow.

Culture

The theme of culture focuses on the fact that humans create culture. Culture is dynamic and constantly changing as we encounter new situations and ideas. Some cultures change rapidly and others change slowly. There are a variety of unique cultures across the Earth that can help us better understand ourselves and others who inhabit this planet. In the early grades, pupils can begin to understand the concept of culture by studying traditions and folkways of different families and communities. In later grades the study of culture can extend to investigating the traditions, folkways, and beliefs of people who lived in the past as well as of those who live in different parts of the world.

Time, Continuity, and Change

This theme is a central one in the study of history. Individuals need to develop an understanding of the sequence of events through time. It is also important to understand that although there is some continuity to human existence, change is inevitable. The world around us is in constant change and we change as well. Learning how to understand and cope with change can be one of the most challenging tasks we face.

Children in the primary grades have difficulty comprehending sophisticated concepts of time. At this level they need not develop sophisticated timelines but can simply understand that something happened long ago. Young children have a fascination with the past and are captivated by good stories about what happened "long ago." Change can be related to changes in their own lives. They can note how they are changing as they grow and learn, how their family changes, and how the world around them changes throughout the seasons of the year.

People, Places, and Environments

This theme has roots in geography. This theme helps pupils learn about the diversity of environments across the earth and how different groups of people interact with those environments. It emphasizes the importance of spatial concepts of location and spatial interaction. Because of improvements in communication and transportation, we have daily interactions with different parts of the world. We eat food and wear clothes that were made far away. We live in communities with people who came from distant places. The nightly news brings us information about events occurring in faraway places. Intelligent

Studying the rich tapestry of cultures around the world helps us understand and appreciate diversity.

decisions require that we have knowledge of where things are located, why they are there, and how we are interdependent with them.

Young pupils can begin to understand concepts of place by noting the location of features in their neighborhood and school. They can note the special locational requirements of things such as stores, schools, and parks. Changes in the local community can help them understand how people relate to and change their environment.

In the later grades, pupils can begin to locate things on maps, identify regions and locational patterns, and learn how to plot interactions between different regions. They can also engage in reflective thinking about the impact of human habitation on the environment.

Individual Development and Identity

The most interesting topic for many people is themselves. We are interested in who we are, how we are changing, and what we will become. We are also fascinated by other people and are curious about why they behave the way they do. This theme, drawn primarily from the subjects of social psychology and anthropology, addresses these interests. It also prompts us to investigate how our culture influences how we perceive ourselves and how people throughout the world meet their needs in a variety of ways. In addition, this theme incorporates ethical issues relating to what is right behavior and to developing a respect for individual differences.

Young children like to play "grown-ups" and imagine what they will become as adults. This curiosity can be channeled to help them consider how individuals learn, develop, and change. They can observe differences in people in their own families and begin to develop a positive self-image as they learn that each person is unique and has special abilities.

In later grades learners begin to encounter personal issues of identity. They seek to understand who they are. This personal concern and search for identity can be a good motivational component for implementing this strand. As learners investigate contemporary as well as historical figures, they are often surprised to discover that their heroes went through periods of identity crisis. If young people in the middle grades can learn that growth and development and the search for personal meaning and identity are common, they may find less reason to seek acceptance through antisocial means such as gangs.

Individuals, Groups, and Institutions

As a part of our personal growth and identity, we are influenced by a number of groups and institutions. Human beings are social creatures who naturally seek out membership in groups. These groups strongly influence the norms, values, and behavioral expectations of their members. Affiliation with groups helps us feel accepted and provides us with a sense of power. It is important for learners to understand the powerful role of groups and institutions in their lives. They need to understand the role of institutions such as school, church, and governments as well as less formal groups such as clubs and gangs.

Young children can develop an understanding of this theme as they begin to identify all the groups they belong to. They can reflect on how these groups influence their behavior and their thinking. In addition, they can begin to explore the power of groups as they study how people with common interests join together to get something that all desire.

Older pupils can study how institutions and groups change over time and what happens when there is a values conflict between and among groups to which they belong. They need to understand how groups and institutions promote conformity. They need to consider how they might help to bring about needed changes in groups and institutions.

Power, Authority, and Governance

Power is a central concept in political science. Who has it? How is it obtained? How is it used? Developing civic competence requires an understanding of this concept. This leads to a comparison of different forms of government and political systems. Different systems answer these questions about power in different ways. The rights and responsibilities of those in authority as well as individual citizens are other key emphases. This theme relates directly to the study of values and ethics. What are the values that we consider so important that they should be made into law and enforced on all members of society? What do we mean by a rule of law, and what can be done when a law is considered unjust? What is a just society, and what are the roles of majority and minority groups?

Although these issues may seem abstract for many young learners, in reality even younger elementary pupils have had considerable direct experience with different forms

In order to meet the basic need of food, these people have gone to great lengths.

of power. Parents have power over their children because of their age and experience. They generally do not exercise this power democratically. Teachers are given power because of their position. Sometimes larger children exercise power over smaller ones.

In the early grades, many life experiences can be used to help learners develop personal knowledge of their rights and responsibilities. These lessons can also help them develop an appreciation of what constitutes appropriate uses of power and authority. Pupils can begin to explore the importance of law by helping make rules for the classroom and by participating in conflict resolution when conflicts arise.

In middle grades learners are capable of developing a more comprehensive understanding of the interactions among rights and responsibilities and power. Lessons can help them explore local and state governments and how they make decisions. They can begin to participate in elections and assess the importance of citizen participation. They may have the opportunity to consider alternative ways to influence the local government and respond to injustice.

Production, Distribution, and Consumption

This theme is drawn primarily from economics. As people attempt to respond to a world where wants are unlimited and resources are scarce, they have to make decisions on what to produce and how to get it to those who want or need it. Different economic systems encourage people to make decisions differently about what is to be produced and who is to get it. Lessons organized in support of this theme place heavy emphasis on such key concepts as wants, needs, goods, services, trade, money, specialization, and transportation.

Learners in the early grades can begin to address this theme by distinguishing between needs and wants. What is it that they really need, and what are those things they merely want? They learn that they may not get everything they want because their parents have limited resources. As a result, they have to make decisions about which needs and wants will be satisfied. Another focus of early-grades instruction related to this theme is how money works as a medium of exchange.

Older pupils can begin to explore more complex topics and begin to engage in economic reasoning. Lessons frequently focus on such topics as goods, services, unequal distribution of resources, factors of production (land, labor, and capital), specialization, and trade. Many of these learning experiences begin by having youngsters investigate the local community and the goods and services produced there. They plot how goods are brought into the community from other places and which goods are sent to other places.

Science, Technology, and Society

Technology is a powerful influence on our lives. Its many applications raise important questions. For what purposes should technology be used? What changes will result from the application of technology? Who will benefit and who will be harmed? How does the application of technology relate to our fundamental beliefs and values? For example, a number of years ago one of us attended a conference where a scientist was discussing technology. He ended his remarks with the statement that we now have the technological capabilities to perform some astounding feats. However, his concern was whether these astounding feats were really worth doing. As social studies teachers, we would be remiss if our lessons did not help young people grapple with some important cultural and ethical questions raised by the application of technology.

In the early grades a beginning step is to help our learners develop an awareness of the impact of technology on our lives. They can study the influences of such common technologies as electricity and transportation. Lessons can help them appreciate the changes that have taken place in the lives of people as these technologies have improved and been applied.

As young people move into the middle grades, they can begin to explore both the positive and negative consequences of technology. For example, what are the consequences of building a new highway in the community? What will be the impact on the environment? What will happen to the people who live in the community? How will their lives change? Addressing these issues will help pupils learn the importance of reflective thinking and decision making.

Global Connections

It is no longer possible for citizens of any nation to live their lives unaffected by what goes on elsewhere. Recently we have had numerous examples of how economic difficulties in one part of the world impact all other parts of the world. Diseases occurring in one area quickly spread to other places. Wars and hostilities in little known corners of the world soon become important issues for all governments. Volcanic eruptions in a distant place influence climate all around the globe. These realities underscore the folly of a social studies program that fails to help young people appreciate the increasingly interconnectedness of our world.

Pointing out global connections to young people in our classrooms is an easy and natural task. Children observe daily television broadcasts from distant places. The labels on the clothes they wear reveal connections to other places. In the primary grades some relatively common activities such as making and eating food from other countries can begin to develop an awareness of global connections. Pupils can plot the origins of various everyday items in order to note the interdependence we have with other parts of the globe.

Learners in the middle and upper grades can begin to explore the complex interactions between various states in the United States and between nations of the world. In many classes there will be pupils who have traveled to other parts of the world and have information to share about the connections between different parts of the world. One creative teacher made arrangements to have a stuffed animal travel on an airliner with a request for people to send postcards from the various places the stuffed animal visited. Over time huge numbers of cards arrived from all over the world. The activity excited the young people in this teacher's class and motivated them to learn more about other peoples and places.

Civic Ideals and Practices

Understanding the civic ideals and values that guide our nation is a critical part of the social studies program. While it is important for learners to know how and why our government works the way it does, lessons with these emphases are not enough to produce sophisticated civic understandings. If we are serious about developing civic competence, then we have to provide opportunities for learners to *practice* these ideals and practices. Citizenship education is not complete unless it culminates in civic participation.

We need to take actions that allow pupils even in the early elementary grades to be involved in examining the values and ideals that guide these actions, such as establishing classroom and school rules. They can participate in setting rules and confront issues such as conflict between rights of different learners. We can use good children's literature as a vehicle for helping young people understand these important values and ideals.

As learners mature, we can encourage them to become involved in activities such as school governance and to participate in civic projects at the local level. Our purpose here is to help young people appreciate their rights and responsibilities as citizens of a community, state, and nation.

*   *   *

As you begin your preparation for teaching social studies, these ten themes or strands can help you decide what to teach and how to evaluate learners. These themes need to be implemented at various levels of complexity throughout the grades. One of the ways to do this is to consider how these themes can be implemented in the content identified in the social studies curriculum for each grade level.

THE GRADES K TO 8 SOCIAL STUDIES CURRICULUM

Traditionally, the elementary social studies program was organized around the idea of *expanding horizons*. The rationale for this pattern was that pupils should first study what is familiar and concrete to them and then move outward to less familiar and more abstract topics. For example, in the primary grades, programs focused on families, schools, neighborhoods, and local communities. In the middle and upper grades, topics expanded to include emphases on the state, nation, and world.

There have been challenges to the expanding-horizons organization. Critics point out that children have widespread contacts with people and places at very young ages. As a result, they are much more aware of patterns of life beyond their own communities than were children who grew up before the television age. From their earliest years, television brings images of patterns of living into children's homes that may be quite different from their own. Films, too, expose young people to different places and cultures. Information young people glean from their exposure to the media and the growing interdependence of the world's peoples have influenced the organization of the school social studies program. Thus, some contend that restricting study to the neighborhood and local community is unnecessarily limiting. In addition, critics point out that some programs focusing on the family reinforce stereotypes of families that are not in tune with the family life experienced by many children.

Today, children do not simply study their own schools, families, communities, and neighborhoods. As the National Council for the Social Studies Task Force on Scope and Sequence (1989) reported, "Social studies programs have a responsibility to prepare young people to identify, understand, and work to solve the problems that face our increasingly diverse nation and interdependent world" (p. 377).

Another criticism of the expanding-horizons approach is that it delays study of the world outside our own hemisphere. This limitation is of real concern given the increasing interdependence of our world.

In many parts of the country, modifications to the social studies curriculum have been made in response to concerns about the traditional expanding-horizons approach. The study of neighborhoods and communities from around the world and throughout time have been included in some primary grade programs. For example, the *History–Social Science Framework for California Public Schools* (1987) identifies the first-grade topic as "A Child's Place in Time and Space." In addition, "World History and Geography: Ancient Civilizations" is the focus of the sixth-grade program.

In its report, the NCSS Task Force on Scope and Sequence (1989) identified titles of courses that are common in many school districts throughout the United States. The group found a number of different patterns in grades 6, 7, and 8. As a result, the report identified three alternative sequences for these grade levels. These are illustrated in Figure 1–4.

Subsections that follow discuss grade-level offerings in social studies as described in the report of the NCSS Task Force on Scope and Sequence (1989).

Kindergarten: Awareness of Self in a Social Setting

The purpose of social studies instruction in kindergarten can be summed up in one word: *socialization*. Lessons teach young children about themselves and about patterns of

The National Council for the Social Studies Task Force on Scope and Sequence (1989) identifies three alternative sequences for grades 6, 7, and 8.

Alternative One
Grade 6: People and Cultures: Representative World Regions
Grade 7: A Changing World of Many Nations: A Global View
Grade 8: Building a Strong and Free Nation: The United States

Alternative Two
Grade 6: European Cultures With Their Extension Into the Western Hemisphere
Grade 7: A Changing World of Many Nations: A Global View
Grade 8: Economics and Law-related Studies (one semester of each)

Alternative Three
Grade 6: Land and People of Latin America
Grade 7: People and Cultures: Representative World Regions
Grade 8: Interdisciplinary Study of the Local Region

THINK ABOUT THIS

1. What do you see as the advantages and disadvantages of each option?
2. Which option do you prefer? Why?
3. Which option seems to be the best "fit" with the K–5 social studies program?

What is the curriculum sequence in your area? How does it compare with the curriculum described in this chapter?

Figure 1–4
Alternative curriculum sequences for grades 6, 7, and 8.

behavior that are expected at home and at school. Pupils are encouraged to master basic rules governing social relationships.

Grade 1: The Individual in Primary Social Groups— Understanding School and Family Life

In grade 1, socialization experiences begun in kindergarten continue. Some basic social studies concepts are introduced. For example, different categories of people who work in the school can be used as examples to provide pupils with a rudimentary understanding of the idea of "division of labor" (NCSS Task Force on Scope and Sequence, 1989). Pupils might be asked to find out where their grandparents live. This information could be used to help build an initial understanding of concepts such as "urban" and "rural."

Grade 2: Meeting Basic Needs in Nearby Social Groups— The Neighborhood

Using the neighborhood around the school as a context, the second-grade program introduces the study of communication, transportation, production, consumption, and ex-

Changes in transportation have allowed the development of global connections with many fascinating places.

change of goods and services. These topics typically are introduced in lessons that help pupils understand how people in neighborhoods and local social groups in other countries go about meeting their needs.

Grade 3: Sharing Earth and Space With Others—The Community

The social studies program in grade 3 concentrates on the learner's local community. Lessons emphasize the interdependence of cities and communities in the state, nation, and world. Among issues considered are change and growth in communities, and the governments, history, and locations of communities.

Grade 4: Human Life in Varied Environments—The Region

In grade 4, pupils are introduced to the concept of *region.* Frequently lessons feature an in-depth study of the home state as an example of a region. World geographic regions often are introduced. Lessons afford opportunities to compare and contrast these world regions with characteristics of the home state and with one another.

Grade 5: People of the Americas— The United States and Its Close Neighbors

The title of this course, particularly as it pertains to the "close neighbors" of the United States, reflects more a hope of the NCSS Task Force on Scope and Sequence than an accurate reflection of present practices. Today, most grade 5 programs are heavily oriented to the study of the history and geography of the United States. Often, Canada and Latin America receive sparse attention. It is hoped that as time goes by, more fifth-grade programs will spend ample time on Canada and Latin America, particularly on how these areas interact with the United States.

Grade 6: People and Cultures—Representative World Regions

The focus of instruction at grade 6 is on representative peoples and cultures of both Latin America and the Eastern Hemisphere. Learners are encouraged to become familiar with important cultural contributions of people in these areas of the world. Interdependence among nations is a frequent theme in lessons. A persistent problem at grade 6 has been the tendency of some teachers to cover too many topics without developing any in depth. Better programs focus on a small group of nations that are presented as examples of particular world areas. This allows for a more detailed study of topics related to the selected nations. This kind of arrangement produces more substantive learning than a more general "cover everything" approach.

Alternative emphases at grade 6 include the following:

- European cultures and their extension into the Western Hemisphere
- Land and people of Latin America

Grade 7: A Changing World of Many Nations—A Global View

The content of the grade 7 program often ties in closely to what is taught in grade 6. (However, there are important local variations. For example, in some places, a state history course is taught in grade 7.) The major intent is to increase learners' awareness of the world, especially the world outside the Western Hemisphere. Physical geography and place location receive considerable attention. Learners are introduced to historical information about certain places to grasp the idea that conditions change over time. Distinctions are drawn between nations of the developed and developing world.

An alternative emphasis at grade 7 is "People and Cultures: Representative World Regions." This emphasis tends to be favored in school districts where the grade 6 program has been restricted to a study of Latin America.

Grade 8: Building a Strong and Free Nation—The United States

The primary objective of the grade 8 program is to introduce learners to the economic and social history of the United States. Political history receives less attention. The idea is to engender interest in our country's history by focusing on lives of people, especially ordinary people. Lessons also often emphasize the role of the United States in world affairs and the idea of interdependency among nations.

Alternative emphases at grade 8 include the following:

- Economics and law-related studies
- Interdisciplinary studies of the local region

ORGANIZING YOUR PROGRAM

One useful approach to help you identify the specific content to be taught at a given grade level is to organize a chart placing the ten strands identified in the standards on one side of the chart with the content taught at each grade level on the other. Such a chart is found in Figure 1–5.

When using Figure 1–5 to decide what to emphasize in your social studies program, you identify the topic for the grade level you will be teaching and then try and plan so you can include each of the ten strands. For example, if you will be teaching kindergarten, the usual topic will be on an awareness of self. How can you then include content that will focus on culture, time, continuity and change, people, places and environments, and so on, within the context of developing an awareness of self? As you fill in boxes on the chart, the curriculum content for your program comes into focus.

Remember, however, to make sure that you keep the common emphases of citizenship, history, social science education, and reflective thinking in mind. Basic knowledge, skills, and values will also need to be included.

ESTABLISHING STANDARDS FOR PUPIL PERFORMANCE

Once you have a clear understanding of the content of the curriculum, performance standards need to be considered. Throughout the last decade one of the major efforts in education has been to establish performance standards for different subjects in the curriculum. It is a part of a large effort to determine what young people at a particular grade level should know and be able to do. Performance standards accomplish several important purposes.

One important purpose of performance standards is to establish benchmarks for learner progress. Having some general indication as to what learners should be able to do at different levels of education can help us as we go about the important business of deciding on the curriculum and the instructional approaches for our pupils. Having a clear set of guidelines can keep us on track and help us revise our programs so that they better serve the needs of the learners. In addition, these standards can be used as a basis for diagnosing what learners already know so that we can build on their previous knowledge and design appropriate instruction. (See Figure 1–6.)

Finally, in an age of considerable scrutiny of education, teachers are being held accountable for what pupils learn. Performance standards provide us with a way of gathering and organizing data that indicate the extent to which learners are mastering important content. If we are to maintain social studies as an important component of the instructional program, we must be able to demonstrate that we are accomplishing worthwhile goals.

The best available source of information related to performance standards for school social studies programs is the publication *Expectations of Excellence: Curriculum Standards for Social Studies*, prepared by the National Council for the Social Studies Task

	Culture	Time, Continuity, Change	People, Places, Environments	Individual Development and Identity	Individuals, Groups, Institutions	Power, Authority, Governance	Production, Distribution, Consumption	Science, Technology, Society	Global Connections	Civic Ideals, Practice
Kindergarten: Awareness of Self										
Grade 1: School and Family Life										
Grade 2: Neighborhood										
Grade 3: Community										
Grade 4: Region										
Grade 5: United States										
Grade 6: World Regions										
Grade 7: Global View										
Grade 8: United States										

Figure 1–5
Organizing the content of the social studies program.

	Early Grades	Middle Grades
Culture	Describe similarities and differences in the way people and groups meet common human needs and concerns	Provide reasons why individuals and groups respond differently to their social and physical environments
Time, Continuity, and Change	Identify examples of change, state cause-and-effect relationships, and construct simple timelines	Identify and use key concepts such as change, conflict, and causality, and identify patterns of historical change and continuity
People, Places, and Environments	Locate and define various landforms such as mountains, valleys, plateaus, rivers, oceans, islands, and continents	Estimate distance, calculate scale, and identify geographic relationships such as spatial distribution patterns and regions
Individual Development and Identity	Describe personal changes that occur over time related to physical development and personal interests	Describe ways that gender, ethnicity, nationality, and family composition contribute to personal identity and individual uniqueness
Individual, Groups, and Institutions	Define important people and institutions in our neighborhood and community	Define key-individuals and important institutions, such as government, school, and church, which influence the state and the nation
Power, Authority, and Governance	Give examples of how the government helps provide for the needs and wants of people	Describe different types of governments and how they acquire, justify, and use power
Production, Distribution, and Consumption	Define needs, wants, production, and consumption	Describe how supply and demand, cost, profit, price, and incentives influence what is produced in a market economy
Science, Technology, and Society	Identify examples in which science and technology have changed the lives of people in areas such as homemaking, transportation, work, and communication	Identify possible positive and negative consequences and conflicts that might arise from the introduction of scientific or technological change
Global Connections	Identify specific examples of language, art, music, and other cultural elements that have their origin in other places and cultures	Define issues that have global implications such as health, environmental quality, security, and economic development
Civic Ideals and Practice	Provide examples of the rights and responsibilities of citizens	Identify and examine the origins and influences of key ideals of the democratic republican form of government such as individual human dignity, rule of law, liberty, justice, and equality.

Figure 1–6
Sample performance standards for social studies.

One of the purposes of this chapter is to prompt thinking about your beliefs and commitments regarding social studies education. Take a minute to reflect on the following questions.

THINK ABOUT THIS

1. Choose a grade level that interests you. Review the content normally taught at that level. What ought to be the priorities in teaching social studies at that grade? How would you incorporate citizenship? Reflective thinking? Problem solving? History and social science education?
2. Brainstorm what you know about the learners at this grade level. What challenges does their age present in teaching social studies to them? Do you think they should be introduced to controversial aspects of society? Do you think they are capable of reflective thinking and decision making? Why or why not?
3. What are some purposes for teaching social studies that you could use for planning at your grade level?
4. What might be some ways you could apply the ten thematic strands at your grade level?

Figure 1–7
Refining your beliefs and commitments.

Force on Curriculum Standards for the Social Studies (1994). It identifies suggested performance standards for different grade levels for the 10 themes discussed above. These performance standards can be used as benchmarks or indicators of what learners should be able to do as a result of social studies instruction.

Figure 1–6 presents a chart of sample performance standards based on those suggested by *Expectations of Excellence: Curriculum Standards for Social Studies.* It should be noted that there are many possible standards that could be included for each level. We have chosen only one to provide you with an example of performance standards. The standards suggested are for the broad categories of early grades and middle grades. They would need to be modified for a specific grade level or situation. You may wish to obtain the above publication in order to get a complete listing of the suggested performance standards.

The need for informed citizens has never been greater. Powerful programs in social studies are needed to meet this enormous challenge. Teachers are needed who have a clear grasp of the purposes of studying social studies and an understanding of how to achieve them. It is the intent of this text to assist you in becoming one of these teachers. (See Figure 1–7.)

WEB CHECK

Note: Electronic addresses of sites on the Web change frequently. If the listed URL fails to work, use a standard search engine to locate the new address of the site.

- National Council for the Social Studies
  URL—**http://www.ncss.org/online/home.html**
  This is the home page of the largest association that promotes the teaching of social studies. You can obtain useful information about social studies, some lesson plans, and information about professional development opportunities.
- ERIC Clearinghouse for Social Studies/Social Science Education ERIC/Chess
  URL—**http://www.indiana.edu/~ssdc/eric_chess.html**
  This is a nationwide depository for social studies materials that includes curriculum guides, instructional units, journal articles, and bibliographies.
- Social Studies Sources
  URL—**http://education.indiana.edu/~socialst/**
  This site, maintained by Indiana University, directs users to information related to general history, government/politics, geography/culture, world history, U.S. history, news sources, and cultural diversity. There are also links to news groups and other resources of interest to social studies teachers.
- Social Studies Education Network
  URL—**http://busboy.sped.ukans.edu/~soess/index.html**
  This site, maintained by the University of Kansas, provides links to Web sites featuring lesson plans and an on-line lesson planning tool. In addition, there is a discussion forum on topics related to teaching social studies content.
- Archives of Personal Experience and Related Resources
  URL—**http://www.libertynet.org/zelson/publish/list.html#projects**
  This site features an extensive listing of Web locations with content related to the fascinating topic of oral history. This is a "must visit" site for teachers interested in incorporating oral history lessons into their social studies programs.

KEY IDEAS IN SUMMARY

1. Social studies lessons provide pupils with tools they can use to make decisions about pressing personal and social problems. There are disagreements about what components should be present in a good social studies program. Some people want a strong emphasis on content from the academic disciplines to ensure that all young people leave school with a common core of knowledge. Others want social studies programs to focus on controversial issues and to help pupils to become reflective thinkers and individuals committed to active participation in democratic decision making. Whatever perspective is reflected in a given program, teachers face risk. Regardless of what they do, some people will challenge their priorities. Social studies teachers must have a clear personal conception of the social studies and be prepared to engage in responsible debate with people holding different views.

2. There is a consensus that preparation for citizenship is one important purpose of the social studies. Widely accepted emphases include focuses on (a) history and social science education and (b) reflective thinking and problem-solving education.

3. There are three important subemphases associated with the major social studies program focuses of citizenship education, history and social science education, and reflective thinking and problem solving. These are (a) knowledge, (b) skills, and (c) values.

4. The National Council for the Social Studies has identified ten strands or themes that ought to run throughout the social studies curriculum. These themes are based on the purposes of social studies: promoting citizenship, historical and social science knowledge, and reflective thinking. They include (a) culture, (b) time, continuity, and change, (c) people, places, and environments, (d) individual development and identity, (e) individuals, groups, and institutions, (f) power, authority, and governance, (g) production, distribution, and consumption, (h) science, technology, and society, (i) global connections, and (j) civic ideals and practices.

5. The sequence of topics in the social studies curriculum is often based on what has been called the *expanding-horizons* approach to curriculum. Although that pattern has been criticized, it still exerts a powerful influence on the organizational structure of many elementary social studies programs. The National Council for the Social Studies Task Force on Scope and Sequence made the following recommendations for the curriculum content in grades K through 8: (a) Kindergarten: Awareness of self in a social setting; (b) Grade 1: The individual in primary social groups—understanding school and family life; (c) Grade 2: Meeting basic needs in nearby social groups—the neighborhood; (d) Grade 3: Sharing Earth and space with others—the community; (e) Grade 4: Human life in varied environments—the region; (f) Grade 5: People of the Americas—the United States and its close neighbors; (g) Grade 6: People and cultures—representative world regions; (h) Grade 7: A changing world of many nations—a global view; and (i) Grade 8: Building a strong and free nation—the United States.

6. When deciding on the content of your social studies program, you need to consider combining the curriculum content suggested for a given grade level with the ten strands or themes suggested in the standards developed by the National Council for the Social Studies. Joining these two elements provides specific guidance for your planning of social studies units and lessons.

7. Performance standards help establish benchmarks for what pupils at different levels should know or be able to do. These benchmarks keep us focused on important social studies outcomes and provide a basis for demonstrating to ourselves and others that pupils are learning and making progress. *Expectations of Excellence: Curriculum Standards for Social Studies* provides some suggestions for performance standards for the early grades and middle grades (National Council for the Social Studies Task Force on Curriculum Standards for the Social Studies, 1994). These suggestions provide excellent guidance as you define expectations for learners and establish benchmarks for your program.

CHAPTER REFLECTIONS

Directions: Now that you have completed the chapter, reread the case study at the beginning. Then answer these questions:

1. How would you now respond to the pupil questions posed in the case study?

2. Have your responses to the questions changed? If so, in what ways, and why?

3. Can social studies lessons be made to connect to lives of elementary pupils? What would you do to make a topic you might teach relevant to your learners?

4. What do you see as the central purposes of social studies instruction?

5. How can you apply the ten themes or strands to the grade level that interests you?

6. What do you think you still need to learn that will help you to make social studies more interesting and meaningful to pupils?

EXTENDING UNDERSTANDING AND SKILL

1. Choose a curriculum guide for a grade level of your choice. Compare the content of this guide with the grade level content suggestions of the National Council for the Social Studies. Is it similar or different? To what extent are the emphases of (1) citizenship education, (2) history and social science education, and (3) reflective thinking and problem-solving education represented in the guide? Which of the ten strands or themes seem to be included? Which ones seem to be omitted?

2. Choose a topic that you might teach at a grade level of your choice. Write a short paper presenting at least one example of how you might include each major social studies purpose (citizenship education, history and social science education, and reflective thinking and problem-solving education).

3. Combine the ten themes suggested in the standards and the curriculum topic for the grade level of your choice. Develop at least three or four performance standards that could serve as benchmarks for pupil achievement.

4. Interview several children in a grade level you would like to teach. Ask them what they like and dislike about their social studies lessons. Summarize their comments in a short paper. Make particular note of those things they like. Suggest how you might build on their ideas to make your own social studies program more appealing to your pupils.

5. Take time to reflect on your views about the importance of social studies and about your interest in the subject. Are your feelings positive or negative? What is the source of your feelings? How might they interfere with or help you as you teach social studies content to elementary pupils? What might you do to develop more positive attitudes and feelings toward the social studies? Share your views with others in your class.

REFERENCES

BARR, R. D., BARTH, J. L., & SHERMIS, S. S. (1977). *Defining the social studies.* Arlington, VA: National Council for the Social Studies.

BERELSON, B., & STEINER, G. (1967). *Human behavior: An inventory of scientific findings.* New York: Harcourt, Brace & World.

BERMAN, S., & LA FARGE, P. (1993). (Eds.). *Promising practices in teaching social responsibility.* Albany, NY: State University of New York Press.

CHERRYHOLMES, C. (1992). Knowledge, power, and discourse in social studies education. In K. Weiler, & C. Mitchell (Eds.), *What schools can do: Critical pedagogy and practice* (pp. 95–115). Albany, NY: State University of New York Press.

History–social science framework for California public schools: Kindergarten through grade twelve. (1987). Sacramento, CA: California State Department of Education.

LEMING, J. S. (1989). The two cultures of social studies education. *Social Education, 53* (6), 404–408.

McGOWAN, T. M., SUTTON, A. M., & SMITH, P. G. (1990). Instructional elements influencing student attitudes toward social studies. *Theory and Research in Social Education, 18* (1), 37–52.

NATIONAL COUNCIL FOR THE SOCIAL STUDIES TASK FORCE ON CURRICULUM STANDARDS FOR THE SOCIAL STUDIES. (1994). *Expectations of excellence: Curriculum standards for social studies: Bulletin 89.* Washington, DC: National Council for the Social Studies.

NATIONAL COUNCIL FOR THE SOCIAL STUDIES TASK FORCE ON SCOPE AND SEQUENCE. (1989). In search of a scope and sequence for social studies: Report of the National Council for the Social Studies Task Force on Scope and Sequence. *Social Education, 53* (6), 376–385.

ROSS, E. W. (1997). The struggle for the social studies curriculum. In E. W. Ross (Ed.), *The social studies curriculum: Purposes, problems and possibilities* (pp. 3–19). Albany, NY: State University of New York Press.

TAYLOR, P. A. (1990). A national morale problem— Americans feel increasingly estranged from their government. *Washington Post National Weekly Edition,* (14 April–20 May), 6–7.

WHELAN, MICHAEL. (1997). History as the core of social studies education. In E. W. Ross (Ed.), *The social studies curriculum: Purposes, problems and possibilities* (pp. 21–37). Albany, NY: State University of New York Press.

chapter 2

Content Sources: History and Geography

This chapter will help you to:

- identify the role of history and the social sciences in the social studies curriculum,
- describe the unique perspectives of history and geography,
- identify selected concepts and generalizations from history and geography that can be incorporated in the elementary social studies program, and
- develop social studies lessons that focus on content from history and geography.

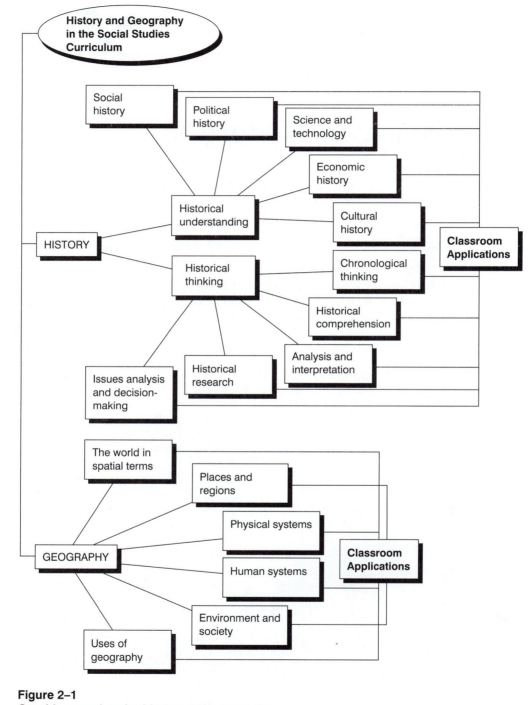

Figure 2–1
Graphic organizer for history and geography.

Case Study

TOO MANY SUBJECTS, TOO LITTLE KNOWLEDGE

Juan Isaguirre is scheduled to student teach next semester. He is assigned to a fourth-grade classroom. As is typical of a university student at this point in his professional development, Juan is both excited and apprehensive as he thinks about his readiness for student teaching. In discussing his feelings about student teaching he made the following comments:

> It's really intimidating to think about all the subjects I'm supposed to teach. I'm more worried about some subjects than others. I mean, in some cases, I can pretty well identify courses I have taken that will help me. The math I have completed at the university is far beyond what I will need to know to teach fourth grade. I'm not really worried about the content I will be expected to teach in arithmetic.
>
> On the other hand, I'm a bit concerned about the social studies. I know social studies is primarily history and geography with some political science. I've had a lot of history at the university. But there is so much to cover and so many facts to learn. How do I select what to teach? Also, I can't see how the many facts I've learned in those classes transfer to teaching fourth graders. Are they really interested in what happened long ago in some far-off place? I guess I don't see the point. As for geography, I had only one course. That was an intro course that focused primarily on the physical environment. I can see how I can use some of that in science, but is there something else I'm supposed to cover in geography? I guess the focus is on learning the names of state capitals, continents, rivers, and mountain ranges. How do you keep the pupils interested? I feel weak in geography. I've had several political science classes, so I guess I'm okay there. I can describe the political system, and how elections work. Again, what is most important for fourth graders to learn about our political system? I know there are many things to cover in a short time. I'm not really sure I know how to go about selecting the content I can teach in the limited amount of time that is available—this is a real worry.

What Is Your Response?

Think about Juan's concerns. Then, briefly respond to these questions:

1. One problem Juan identifies is his own lack of preparation in one of the academic areas (geography) from which content for elementary social studies lessons is often drawn. How do you feel about your own depth of academic preparation in academic subjects related to social studies? If you sense any inadequacies in these subjects, what might you do?
2. Juan defines the social studies as primarily history and geography. How do you react to his definition? Do you agree?
3. Another problem that concerns Juan is the issue of selecting content. What ideas do you have for selecting content for inclusion in the elementary classroom?
4. Juan is also concerned about the interests of fourth-grade pupils and whether the information he learned is really something that will be useful to him. How would

you respond to this concern? How would you relate social studies content to the interests of the pupils? What is the function of university classes in preparing you for teaching the subject in the elementary school? Is it to present you with content to be translated and then taught in a simplified version to young children?

5. Some critics of elementary social studies programs assert that teachers cannot possibly know all of the content they need in order to teach. They argue that elementary learners would be better served if the several areas of social studies were abandoned and replaced with content focusing on a single subject such as history or geography. If this were done, these critics allege, teachers would have a better chance to develop some academic depth in the subjects they were asked to teach. What do you see as the strengths and weaknesses of this idea?

INTRODUCTION

The focus of social studies is on human behavior—past, present, and future. It is unrealistic to expect elementary social studies programs to expose pupils to everything that might be taught about this vast subject. Teachers must make content choices. Which choices are correct? There is no single answer to this question. What is clear is that rapidly changing conditions in our society are making these decisions more difficult (Risinger, 1992). In making choices, social studies teachers consider questions such as these:

- What do pupils need to study to learn how to participate effectively in society?
- What examples of human behavior are most effective for teaching people how to live together and solve difficult social problems?
- What content is most useful for helping individuals understand their cultural heritage and decide what needs to be retained and what needs to be changed?
- Out of the wide array of human cultures, past and present, which ones should be studied in the elementary school?
- What content is important for individuals as they try to make sense of the personal and social worlds outside the classroom?

These questions have no simple answers. Individuals have responded to them in different ways, depending on their own particular sense of what is important. Answers to these questions have been made even more difficult for teachers who must deal with learners from highly diverse cultural and ethnic groups. Meeting needs of today's pupils requires teachers to draw on content that has potential meaning for people who bring extremely diverse cultural and social perspectives with them to school each day.

Recent events have demonstrated the need for American citizens to develop a comprehensive and connected understanding of human affairs. The memorization of names, dates, and other isolated facts drawn from a single culture is not sufficient for young people who are growing up in an increasingly interdependent world. Citizens of the United States today must understand that their decisions may have implications for people living thousands of miles from our shores and that decisions made abroad often have significant effects on the United States. This new world reality requires social studies that is global and inclusive in its outlook. As the National Commission on Social Studies in the Schools (1989) pointed out, these challenges require people whose thinking is broadly based: "Individuals do not think well if they do not understand their own history, appreciate political and cultural diversity, and understand the economic and sociological realities of a changing world" (p. xi).

This statement hints at the importance of information drawn from history and the social sciences. Specialists in these fields have identified concepts and developed generalizations that help us to explain the complexities of our world. In the elementary social studies program, information from these fields helps pupils to better understand the world and themselves. To be useful, information from history and the social sciences needs to be integrated and applied to important practical problems. The information needs of future citizens cannot be met through the study of a single subject. That is, it no longer suffices to study history alone, or geography alone, or economics alone. These and other social science disciplines need to be combined into a systemic and interrelated study of peoples (National Commission on Social Studies in the Schools, 1989).

This chapter and the two that follow provide a brief introduction to history and the social sciences, and suggest how you might use content from these disciplines in planning and implementing sound elementary social studies programs. This is not meant to imply that these are the only content sources elementary social studies teachers use. Teachers often also draw on information from music, art, religion, philosophy, and even the physical and biological sciences. However, it probably is fair to say that more elementary social studies content comes from history and the social sciences—geography, economics, political science, sociology, anthropology, and psychology—than from other sources.

The focus of this chapter is history and geography. History and geography are often considered the foundations of the social studies. Together they deal with time (history) and space (geography).

HISTORY

Some people consider the terms *history* and *social studies* to be synonymous. It is not uncommon to read articles in the media dealing with social studies where the focus is primarily on history. When social studies is mentioned to many people, they immediately assume that the focus is on teaching history. The importance of history in elementary social studies is reflected in many ways. For example, American history is the featured subject of the grade 5 curriculum almost everywhere in the United States. History is mentioned in the third goal of Goals 2000: Educate America Act (1994). Often, state history is the focus of fourth-grade programs. In addition, some states, such as California, have a major focus on history throughout their state frameworks.

History has played and continues to play such a dominant role in the elementary social studies curriculum for several reasons, not least because it has long been viewed as an important element of general citizenship education. For example, the *National Standards for History* (National Center for History in the Schools, 1996) states that "knowledge of history is a precondition of political intelligence" (p. 1). The authors of the standards contend

Relating the past to the familiar, such as school, helps promote interest in history and the basic theme of change.

that one cannot be an informed, discriminating, participating citizen without historical knowledge and historical inquiry. Many people have assumed that systematic study of the origins of our nation and key events in our history will socialize young people to accept values critical for the maintenance of our democratic tradition. This assumption explains why history is potentially one of the more controversial subjects in the social studies curriculum.

Considerable controversy and publicity accompanied the initial publication of the *National Standards for History.* Many of the critics (some of whom had been supportive of the move for national history standards) criticized the standards because they felt the standards de-emphasized the American experience and the values of democracy in favor of a more multicultural, non–Western emphasis. As a result the original standards were rewritten.

As a teacher you need to be sensitive to the fact that there are those who view history with political and patriotic fervor. They will be attentive to what is taught and will be quick to criticize if they do not believe that history is furthering these values. Therefore, you need to have a clear understanding of the purposes of history in order to formulate a solid rationale for your choices and actions.

Another reason for learning history cited in the national standards is that it contributes to the development of the "private individual" as well as the "public citizen." In this context, history is seen as the key to self-identity. It is through history that one's connectedness with all of humankind is noted. Through history we see where we fit in the stream of time and begin to appreciate how those that have lived in the past influence us and how we will influence generations that follow.

Other individuals point to the integrative potential of history as another part of the rational for teaching history. These individuals believe that history as a subject lends itself well to integrating content from the various social sciences and from the humanities. A focus on history, some say, promotes learning efficiency. The unifying element of time can draw together content from many separate subjects and help pupils recognize the interrelatedness of many different kinds of content. The national standards note that history is an integrative field focusing on human activity in at least five different spheres: social, scientific/technological, economic, political, and cultural.

Real historical understanding requires that students engage in historical thinking. Historical thinking involves getting students to raise questions as they read historical documents including journals, diaries, textbooks, and historical fiction. Helping pupils improve their thinking skills through the study of history requires teachers to think carefully about the particular history they are teaching to pupils. Sometimes this point is not widely appreciated. For example, in the *History–Social Science Framework for California Public Schools* (1987) there is emphasis on history as a "story well told" (p. 4). While certainly well-written history often presents a good story, the real issue for teachers and their learners should be on *whose* story is being told, the *accuracy* of the story, and the *intended purposes* of the story. There are many well-told stories that can be told. Some of these stories are inaccurate and are intended more to promote myths rather than reveal truth.

No historical account is true in any absolute sense. Knowledge of past events must be reconstructed from artifacts and surviving accounts. The historian must make judgments about what to include and what to omit. His or her values come into play when such choices are made. For example, a historical account written by a person who sees class struggle as the most important theme in human affairs will write an account of settlement of the American West that differs from one written by someone who sees technological change as the dominant theme.

Lesson Idea 2–1

RESOLVING CONFLICTING ACCOUNTS OF EVENTS

Grade Level:	5–6
Objectives:	Learners can (1) identify bias is historical accounts, and (2) state the importance of identifying bias in materials they read.
Overview:	To help pupils recognize bias and different perspectives on a single event, it is helpful to present them with two or more conflicting accounts of the same event and have them identify and explain discrepancies.
Procedure:	***Learning Set*** Ask pupils if they have ever had two different people tell them about the same thing, and each one's story was very different. Ask them why they think this happens.

Presentation: Place a chart on the board with two columns, one marked Account 1 the other Account 2. Head the chart "The Burning of Washington in the War of 1812." Give the pupils Account 1 and have them read it.

Account 1

Victorious troops of the crown swarmed into Washington. With huzzahs all around, torches were passed. Officers led their men on a block by block campaign to torch the rebel capital. Officers of the general staff believe that this action will soon break the back of the American resistance. There is talk that before the year is out these rebel colonies will be rightfully returned to the crown. American resistance is said to be crumbling. Loyal subjects of the king are said to be waiting in Canada for the signal to return south and reestablish proper colonial governments (Report filed by a corre-spondent of the London Gazette.*)*

When all have read the account, fill in the chart with students' answers to the following questions: Was the burning viewed as a positive event? What was the reason? How were the troops viewed? How were the Americans viewed? What words are used to describe each side? Give the pupils Account 2 and have them read it.

Account 2

The British barbarian showed his true colors today. Consistent with the pattern of 25 years ago when American rights were trampled into the ground, the undisciplined British troops took Washington today with unprincipled savagery. With little regard for the safety of women and children, they went on a rampage that resulted in the burning of most of the buildings in Washington. American troops, shocked by the brutality, are rallying. Determination has never been higher. All look forward to taking a revenge that will forever free this continent from the tyranny of the British. (Report filed by a correspondent of the New York Review.*)*

Use the same questions, reversing the nationality as appropriate, and fill in the chart under Account 2. After completing both sides of the chart, lead a discussion using the following questions:

1. How are the accounts similar?
2. How are the accounts different?
3. How do you explain the differences?
4. What do you think the reaction would be from people who would read each account?

5. Can you identify a recent incident where a similar thing happened?
6. What do you think this means you should do when you read or hear an account of an event?

Closure: Ask the class, "What did we learn today? Why is what we have learned important?"

When they encounter history, pupils should be taught to approach it much as they approach a mystery. They need to think about the author's perspective, and they must be provided with other opportunities to develop critical thinking skills. Good history teaching sensitizes pupils to the idea that all people do not experience the same event in the same way. Helping pupils think about issues of perspective as they study historical content can nurture the development of a worldview that recognizes and appreciates multiple realities.

The History Curriculum

The *National Standards for History* presents standards that can be used in deciding what to teach and how to teach the historical dimension of the social studies. The standards are organized into two categories, historical understanding and historical thinking. The history curriculum is generally organized around topics. For example, United States history is usually the topic of study in the fifth grade. The two categories are to be integrated as these topics are taught.

Historical Understanding
The history curriculum is generally organized around topics such as the Revolutionary War, the westward movement, and the Age of Enlightenment. The standards for historical understanding are intended to give some guidance concerning what is to be covered within the topics. The standards are intended to be taught in ways that engage students in the lives, aspirations, struggles, accomplishments, and failures of real people (National Center for History in the Schools, 1996).

The standards for historical understanding are organized around five spheres of human activity. One standard focuses on *social history*. Through the study of social history students develop a deeper understanding of society, including different and changing patterns of family structures, of men's and women's roles, and of childhood and children's roles, and relationships between groups within society and movements such as class conflict, immigration, migration, and slavery.

Another standard emphasizes *political history*. Political history investigates the history of government and governmental institutions and the struggle to achieve and preserve basic human rights. This should be studied beginning with the local community. Then lessons expand to include topics associated with the state, nation, and various societies throughout the world. The intent is to help pupils understand the core principles and values of American democracy that unite us as a people. Lessons focus on people and events that have exemplified these principles and the struggles to bring rights guaranteed by these principles to all Americans.

Visiting living historical sites is a useful way of engaging students in learning about cultural history.

The study of the *history of science and technology* is addressed in another standard. In meeting this standard students develop a deeper understanding of the scientific quest to understand the world we live in. This study should encompass efforts to improve everything from producing food and caring for the ill to transporting goods and advancing economic security. Understanding of the work people have done and the scientific/technological developments that have propelled change are central to the study of history and can be of great interest to students.

Economic history is another emphasis in the standards. This area looks at the economic forces that have influenced the quality of people's lives, the structuring of society, and the course of human events. The economic relationships that have developed have had major impacts on society, politics, and all other spheres of human activity.

Cultural history is the last area addressed by the historical understanding standards. This area includes the study of religion, philosophy, art, music, and popular culture.

Studying these topics through literature, sacred writings, oral traditions, and other historical narratives helps reveal the aspirations and achievements of all societies and helps deepen understanding of the human experience.

What do these standards imply as you select and organize your curriculum? These standards are so broad that they may not give the individual teacher much guidance in choosing specific content to be taught. They are valuable in pointing out some emphases that should be present. They point out that history is not just the study of presidents and generals. It is not just the memorization of a set of facts. Rather, the study of history includes the study of common people, their aspirations, hopes, and dreams as well as their failures. Topics such as production of food, transportation, and caring for the ill are also legitimate topics to be included. In addition, the study of history should look at the development of significant ideas and values included in areas such as religion, philosophy, art, and music.

As noted in the preceding brief descriptions, content from history often overlaps with topics treated in one or more of the social sciences. In history lessons, the unifying thread is human behavior over time. Concepts central to the discipline of history are *change* and *continuity*. Instruction is guided by such questions as, How have things changed, and why? and How has there been continuity over time, and why? Lesson planning that draws on content from history attends carefully to questions, concepts, and generalizations that are central to the discipline. Some of these are noted in Figure 2–2.

Historical Thinking

The second category of standards focuses on historical thinking. This is an important set of standards because it expands the definition and role of history. These standards help individuals understand that history is more than the memorization of names and dates, presidents and kings, wars and battles. The historical thinking standards emphasize that history is an active subject that requires the involvement and thinking of people as they encounter historical documents and narratives. This active involvement and thinking is of five types. Those five types are chronological thinking, historical comprehension, historical analysis and interpretation, historical research capabilities, and historical issue analysis and decision making.

The first type of historical thinking is that of chronological thinking. This type of thinking is the heart of historical thinking. This standard calls for students to be able to distinguish between past, present, and future, measure and calculate calendar times, construct and use timelines, and identify the temporal structure of historical narratives—the development of a time perspective. Understanding the temporal order of events is a key element in helping students search for patterns and relationships. However, teachers of young children need to realize that time is very abstract and young children have difficulty comprehending time concepts. They do understand the differences between long, long ago and yesterday but cannot move much beyond those broad categories.

The second type of historical thinking is that of historical comprehension. This standard calls for students to be able to identify the central questions in a historical narrative. They must take into account the historical context of events and the motives of those involved, identify the source or author of a historical narrative, reconstruct the literal meaning of a historical passage, and use a variety of sources such as maps to help clarify their understanding of historical events. This type of thinking is intended to help

The following are examples of central questions, concepts, and generalizations that are important in studying content drawn from history.

CENTRAL QUESTIONS (A SELECTION)

- Who wrote this account, and where did the writer get the information?
- What facts were omitted?
- How is language used to portray the event or person?
- Are the conclusions warranted by the facts?
- Where else could I get information about this event or person?
- What do other accounts say?

CONCEPTS (A SELECTION)

Change, continuity, chronology, multiple causation, interpretation, primary source, secondary source, era, period, innovation, validity

GENERALIZATIONS (A SELECTION)

- Continuous change is universal and inevitable.
- The rate of change in a society varies with factors such as the values and beliefs of the people and the extent of their contact with others.
- Events of the past influence the present, and present events will influence the future.
- The history of a society provides guidelines for understanding the thoughts and actions of the people as they respond to current affairs.
- The history of a nation establishes the culture, traditions, beliefs, attitudes, and patterns of living of the people.

Figure 2–2
Central questions, concepts, and generalizations associated with history.

students search for the sequence, the meaning, and the causes of events. This standard focuses attention on one of the central concepts of history, that of change.

Historical analysis and interpretation is the third type of historical thinking. The intent of this standard is to help students move to the level of being thoughtful readers of history and become critical thinkers. This standard calls for students to consider multiple perspectives of events, compare and contrast different accounts, distinguish between fact and fiction, analyze historical fiction for accuracy, analyze illustrations for historical accuracy, hypothesize about the influences of the past, challenge arguments of historical inevitability, and explain causes in analyzing historical actions. Once again, many of these dimensions of historical analysis seem to be quite abstract for young children. However, young children can begin to discriminate between fact and fiction and compare and contrast different accounts through children's literature selections. The experiences of parents, grandparents, and others in the community are other resources that can be used to help young children develop historical interpretation skills.

The fourth type of historical thinking is developing historical research capabilities. This standard calls for students to be able to develop questions from their encounters with historical artifacts and narratives, obtain data from a variety of sources, determine the credibility and authenticity of historical materials, identify bias and distortion, and construct stories and explanations. This standard also involves historical inquiry or the "doing" of history. Even at very early ages students can begin to learn to inquire about events in their daily lives and to learn how to gather data from a variety of sources. Meeting this standard can be very interesting to students, as it requires that they become active in the process of creating historical accounts.

The last standard in historical thinking is that of historical issues—analysis and decision making. This standard calls for students to be able to identify the issues, dilemmas, and problems that confronted people in historical situations. They should be able to identify problems or dilemmas, identify the causes of the problems, identify the interests and values of those involved, propose alternative ways of resolving them, and then take a position or course of action. Useful approaches for doing this involve the use of historical fiction, legends, myths, and fables. Using historical accounts and the consequences of the choices that people made can be very important in helping students consider the values and beliefs of individuals both past and present. Examples of lessons consistent with the standard are Values, Issues, and Consequences Lessons 10–5 and 10–6.

The history standards are very useful in helping teachers identify what should be taught and how to teach history. They have the potential to bring history alive and engage the students in active learning. History can become interesting to them as they learn to think using the historical perspective. It is something they can discover, not just be told about.

History-Related Classroom Activities

As suggested in the discussion of the history standards, classroom activities need to be designed which help students go beyond recalling information. Students need to begin to look at the perspectives of those who write history. They need to be taught to rethink arguments of historians, to ask questions about interpretations of facts, and to suggest alternative explanations of events (Gagnon, 1989). This suggests that elementary social studies lessons should actively involve students in the processes of historical inquiry. The following are ideas for accomplishing this purpose.

Chronological Thinking
Chronological thinking requires familiarity with many time concepts. These include "seconds," "minutes," "hours," "years," "decades," and "centuries." Time is an abstract concept. Many children, particularly those in the primary grades, have distorted ideas about time. For example, some of them believe that conditions long ago were similar to today. Others think that practically every aspect of modern life has been created within the last four or five years. Students can begin to develop chronological thinking by relating the concept to their own experiences. For example, students may be asked to mark off passing days on room calendars and to observe changes associated with changes of the seasons. To help students gain improved understanding of time and change, a time line chart is useful. Such a chart might include information about (1) birth dates of members of the class and their families, (2) dates of significant events, (3) dates of inventions, and (4) dates when presidents served. An example of a time line chart is provided in Figure 2–3.

Decades	1990	1980	1970	1960	1950	1940
Birth dates (family members, friends)						
Important						
Inventions						
Presidents						
Other items of interest						

Figure 2–3
My personal timeline.

The time line chart personalizes human events. They become more interesting to pupils when introduced in a context that includes birth dates of relatives who were alive when certain events occurred. Information on the chart often prompts pupils to ask their relatives about some of the events listed.

Historical Comprehension

Historical comprehension involves helping students view the past in the context of that specific era. They need to view events through the eyes of those who were there. It must be remembered that the history standards emphasize helping students see their roots and a sense of personal belonging. In addition, history is not just the study of the extraordinary events and leaders but also the study of common people and their experiences. One approach to meeting the history comprehension standards in the early grades is viewing people as resources for learning history.

For example, learners may be asked to interview older people who were alive when certain events occurred and who can describe "what it was like." Parents and grandparents are good human resources. When they interview several people about a common past event, learners sometimes are surprised that everyone does not remember it in the same way. Such conversations are valuable for helping them learn that events can be interpreted in different ways and that historical inquiry requires consideration of information from multiple sources. An example of a lesson focusing on historical comprehension is one focusing on family origins and traditions.

The local community is an excellent resource for lessons focusing on historical comprehension. Communities have important historical residues including buildings, people, cemeteries, museums, and statues that can be used for historical inquiry (Armstrong & Savage, 1976). Pupils are familiar with local communities. As a result, lessons built around local community resources often have more motivational appeal than those focusing on distant places that have few, if any, ties to learners' personal experiences. They can begin to view the past through the experiences of people in their own community and learn that history not only is contained in textbooks but is revealed in parts of their environment. These types of lessons focus on posing questions about things that are observed in the environment and then seeking answers to the questions. For example, one of the authors enjoyed great success in getting a group of initially unmotivated fifth and sixth graders interested in social studies by starting with some questions about origins of street names and buildings in the urban community where they lived.

Lesson Idea 2–2

FAMILY ORIGINS AND TRADITIONS

Grade Level:	K–2
Objectives:	Pupils can (1) learn how to interview a family member, (2) identify how change and continuity have taken place, and (3) share information with the class.
Overview:	This lesson may take place a few days before some or all students celebrate almost any recognized holiday or commemorative event. During any holiday season it is useful to make sure that all pupils are included. This lesson addresses historical comprehension by getting students to look at past events through the experiences of people who were there. It helps make history alive and meaningful for young children and also provides an opportunity for pupils to begin appreciating the diversity of cultures and change and continuity.
Procedure:	*Day 1: Learning Set* Discuss the upcoming holiday season and ask pupils about some of the different things they do during the holidays. State that different people have different holidays and different ways of celebrating the holidays. Tell them to talk with their parents and/or grandparents about how they celebrated holidays when they were young. On chart paper, record some of the questions they might want to ask. Discuss the questions and select five or six. Write these on a questionnaire along with some directions to the parents to enlist their help in discussing the questions and completing the questionnaire along with the children.
	Day 2: Discussion When the questionnaires have been returned, place pupils into groups of four and have them share their information with each other. Change the groups three or four times so that class members experience a variety of responses.
	As a group, construct a chart listing the changes that have taken place in the celebrations. Those who identified traditions

and customs brought from other countries can identify the location of that country on a map.

Closure: Ask pupils, "What did you find out about how things have changed? Do you think things will be different when you are grown up?"

_____

Thanks to Gayle Chew and Theresa Squires, Vicentia Elementary School, Corona, CA, for this idea.

Artifacts are tangible reminders of times gone by. In the classroom, they function well as prompts for historical inquiry lessons. The task is to find ways of getting the artifact to tell its story. For example, artifacts such as old photographs, objects of various kinds, letters, documents, artwork, and music can be used to stimulate thought about the ways of life of people in the past. Studying the lyrics of a song sung by immigrants lamenting their permanent separation from their native land often will "connect" to pupils more effectively than any prose narrative describing the immigrant experience. A youngster who hefts a heavy iron used by Chinese laundry workers during the California Gold Rush has tangible evidence that such a life existed. He or she also gains some important insights into the kind of fatigue laundry workers must have experienced after having spent 10 or 12 hours on their feet doing this kind of work.

Historical Analysis and Interpretation

An important part of historical analysis and interpretation is having pupils develop some independence and begin to search for clues on their own. They can learn that looking for clues to historical interpretation can involve more than just reading about an event. In fact, popular culture often provides insights into the feelings, motives, and beliefs of the people. Music is one dimension of popular culture that children find interesting. Lesson Idea 2–3 uses the lyrics of a song to help them interpret a historical event.

Lesson Idea 2–3

GOD SAVE THE SOUTH

Grade Level: 5

Overview: Art and music often capture the moods, fears, values, and aspirations of many people of a culture. These forms of expression can be important sources of information in social studies classrooms for developing understanding and insight that might not be possible through standard textbooks.

Procedure: *Learning Set* Tell the class, "We can learn about history from many different places. One of those places is the songs people sing. Why do you think that might be a good source of information?"

Presentation   Say to the class, "The following is a song that was popular in the Confederacy at the beginning of the Civil War. Read the verses and see if you can find clues about how the Southerners viewed the war."

God Save the South

God Save the South!

God Save the South!

Her altars and firesides—

God Save the South

Now that war is nigh

Now that we arm to die—

Chanting our battle-cry,

Freedom or Death!

God make the right

Stronger than might!

Millions will trample us

Down in their pride—

Lay Thou their legions low

Roll back ruthless foe,

Let the proud spoiler know

God's on our side.

Words by George H. Miles

Discussion Questions:

1. What do you think it means that they ask God to protect their altars and firesides?
2. Where does that indicate they think the war will take place?
3. What does it mean that they ask God to make right stronger than might?
4. What words indicate what Southerners thought about the Northerners?
5. On the basis of this song, what do you think the attitude of the South was toward the Civil War?
6. What could we do to find out if the view presented in this song was accurate?

[Note: This song can be played to the class. It is on the tape *Civil War Songs,* by Keith and Rusty McNeil, WEM Records, Riverside, CA: 1989.]

Closure:

Ask the class, "What did we learn today about how songs might help us understand history? What did we learn about the attitude of the people in the South toward the Civil War?"

Historical analysis and interpretation include getting students to look at historical events through different perspectives. Well-written children's books are excellent tools for doing this (Savage & Savage, 1993). Works of children's literature are written in a more engaging style than school texts. They feature stories with a clear beginning and end. There are books that satisfy even very young elementary school pupils. Two good titles are *Sarah Bishop* by Scott O'Dell [Houghton Mifflin, 1980] and *My Brother Sam Is Dead* by James Lincoln Collier and Christopher Collier [Four Winds Press, 1974]. Both books provide different perspectives on the American Revolution. Similarly, an interesting view of the Civil War is presented in Irene Hunt's *Across Five Aprils* [Follett, 1964].

Biographies represent a particularly useful genre for teaching historical information. For example, Jean Fritz has written a number of well-researched biographies about famous people in American history. These biographies help students discover the motives, values, and ideas of important people in history.

Historical Research

Elementary teachers who believe that there are skills that can only be applied in secondary schools often misunderstand the history research standards. However, historical research can begin in very simple ways by getting students to construct their own historical accounts of everyday events in which they have participated. The lesson dealing with the story of what happened yesterday on the playground is one example (Lesson Idea 2–4).

Lesson Idea 2–4

YESTERDAY ON THE PLAYGROUND

Grade Level:	3–6
Objectives:	Pupils can (1) write an eyewitness account of an event, (2) identify why historical accounts differ, and (3) state different ways history can be written.
Overview:	Students can be made aware of how history can be written from different perspectives and in different ways by having them try to reconstruct an event that they all have experienced. This activity can be useful by helping them begin to understand the problems that historians face when trying to write an account, how to judge the accuracy of information, and how to organize the information into a good story. This lesson includes several components of the historical research standard and illustrates how this standard can be incorporated into the curriculum for young children.
Procedure:	*Learning Set* Begin by telling the class that today they are going to learn about a past event of great importance, lunchtime yesterday. Ask them, "What happened on the playground yesterday at lunch?" Let a few share their experiences. Then state that it is obvious that many things happened.

Day 1: Presentation   Tell the class to write some histories of yesterday on the playground. Ask them how they will need to begin and what they will need to do. You might ask if any others should be interviewed about what happened. For example, they might want to interview the teacher who was on playground duty, the secretary in the office to see if anyone was hurt or sent to the office, and pupils from other grades who might have been on different parts of the playground. They might also want to find out if anything happened before lunch that might have influenced later events. Maybe a new game was introduced in a class or perhaps some balls were flat and could not be used. Perhaps someone had an injury that prevented him or her from participating in some activities.

At this point the class can be grouped into groups of four or five to plan their research and how to write their history. As they gather data, suggest to them that they can write their history in several ways. One way would be chronologically, from 12:00 to 12:10 P.M., and so on. Another approach would be geographically: at the ball field, at the primary area, in the office, and so on. A third approach would be to organize their histories by important episodes or events.

Day 2   After the pupils have gathered data, discuss with the class what they might need to consider to make their history interesting. Have each group write its history. Some groups may want to attach drawings or photographs of the playground or playground events. When completed, the accounts can be bound as a book.

Closure: Ask, "What did you learn about writing history? What does a historian have to think about when deciding what to include? How can you use this information as you read historical accounts in our social studies book or in the library?"

How Historians Judge the Truth

Good history is not just a matter of the writer's opinion. It rests on the careful examination of evidence. As appropriate for their age, developmental level, and intellectual sophistication, elementary pupils should be introduced to the ways that historians identify and evaluate evidence. When historians consider the truth or validity of a historical document, they consider (1) external validity and (2) internal validity.

External Validity

External validity has to do with the issue of authenticity. Suppose a historian found a document that was supposed to have been written in England in the year 1610. The historian might arrange for a chemical analysis of the paper and ink to establish whether they represented types available in 1610. The words used in the document might be compared to words used in other documents known to have been written in the early 17th century.

While doing this, the historian would be trying to find words in the mystery document inconsistent with what logically might be expected in a document of this date. Detective work associated with external validity often unmasks forgeries.

Internal Validity

Internal validity seeks to determine the accuracy of information contained in a historical record. For example, it would be possible for a document that really was produced in 1610 to contain inaccurate statements. Even if the external validity tests indicate that the document was written in 1610, the historian must be careful not to accept without question everything that was written. In the search for internal validity, the historian must consider whether the person who allegedly wrote the material was really capable of doing so. For example, did the writer have an education that would account for the kinds of words and sentences found in the document? Perhaps someone else wrote the material. Why did the person write the material? Did the author have an interest in writing the truth, or was there some reason to distort some, or even all, of the information? For example, public speeches or political documents intended to be read by a wide audience sometimes are designed not so much to illuminate absolute truth as to support the case for a particular point of view. On the other hand, a letter to a personal friend or relative that was not intended for dissemination to others may more accurately reflect what the writer personally believes to be true.

In the search for internal and external validity, the historian looks for explanations that go beyond the obvious. The search is part of the excitement of the historian's craft. History is not just a matter of collecting and writing down information about the past. Rather, historians must make careful judgments about the validity and reliability of evidence. Good history is the product of disciplined thinking.

A Selection of Information Sources

Teachers look constantly for material they can incorporate into lessons that interest and excite their pupils. The following subsections describe information sources that many teachers find useful when planning social studies lessons.

National Council for History Education

During the latter half of the 1980s, concerns about the quality of history instruction led to the formation of the Bradley Commission on History in the Schools. Bradley Commission members included leading historians, history education specialists, and public school educators with an interest in history. The Bradley Commission supported many symposia, conferences, and curriculum projects.

In 1988, the Bradley Commission issued curriculum guidelines that have been widely discussed by individuals interested in improving the quality of history in both elementary and secondary schools. The commission initiated the publication of a monthly newsletter, *History Matters*. This publication often includes information of interest to elementary teachers.

In 1990, the Bradley Commission changed its name to the National Council for History Education. The organization continues to publish *History Matters* and provide other services to educators who wish to improve history teaching in the schools. For member-ship information, write to the National Council for History Education, 26915 Westwood Road, Suite A-2, Westlake, OH 44145.

National Council for the Social Studies

The National Council for the Social Studies (NCSS) is the largest national organization of educators interested in social studies education. For many years, NCSS has published *Social Education.* The Elementary Education section of this journal often includes ideas for teaching historical content to young learners. A subscription to *Social Education* is in-cluded in the basic NCSS membership fee.

NCSS also publishes *Social Studies and the Young Learner.* This professional journal is dedicated exclusively to issues of interest to elementary school teachers. For subscrip-tion information, membership information, and information about other services pro-vided by NCSS, write to the National Council for the Social Studies, 3501 Newark Street, NW, Washington, DC 20016.

GEOGRAPHY

History views human affairs from the perspective of time, and geography places human affairs in a locational context. Risinger (1992) states that "geography is the stage upon which the human drama is played" (p. 4). An idea central to geography is that each place on earth is unique. This means that an understanding of diverse settings is prerequisite to real understanding of the human condition.

Professional geographers have long been concerned that many public school programs fail to introduce students to much of what geographers do. To develop a more adequate appreciation of what should be included in sound geography-based school programs, sev-eral national organizations of geographers joined together and developed a set of stan-dards for geography. Those standards, *Geography for Life: National Geography* (Bednarz et al., 1994), were published in order to promote improved geographic education.

Geography is a subject that most people will profess to understand. However, this un-derstanding is usually inadequate at best and often a distortion of the subject. Some in-dividuals perceive geography as involving little more than teaching students to recognize locations of continents, name countries, identify landforms, and memorize state capitals. This conception of geography misses the central concepts and importance of geography for citizens.

The authors of *Geography for Life* provide several reasons for studying geography. They point out that from a practical standpoint the interconnectedness of the world makes geographic knowledge critical. Markets are now worldwide markets. Businesses must understand world markets, the location of resources, and transportation routes. In-tellectually, an understanding of geography can assist in overcoming ethnocentrism and parochialism. Understanding the exciting variety of fascinating people and places helps everyone develop an appreciation for diversity and helps us make more informed and wiser decisions. Ethically, as Earth continues to hurl through space, it is not certain that

Geography looks at the unique characteristics of places created by the interaction between people and environments.

it will continue to be a planet that will support human habitation. Understanding the interdependency of the human and physical environments provides a basis for making decisions that will be in the best interest of future generations.

Geography studies the relationships among people, places, and environments. This can be done beginning with an understanding of relationships at the local level and then moving to the global level. The focus is on patterns of spatial distribution and on interactions of phenomena as they occur across space. Studies of distribution make sense because resources, people, and other environmental features are not evenly distributed. Some places lack things that other places have. These differences prompt flows of people and resources from place to place. These flows take the forms of human migration and trade. Because of movements of people and goods from place to place, there are interactions among different places on the Earth's surface. Geographers interested in spatial interaction study relationships among different world regions, paying particular attention to factors that enhance or inhibit the volume or intensity of these interactions. (See Figure 2–4.)

The Geography Curriculum

Geography for Life points out that geography is composed of the three interrelated components of subject matter, skills, and perspectives. These components are organized into

The following are examples of central questions, concepts, and generalizations that are important when studying geography. They are useful to the elementary social studies teacher when making decisions about what to include in lessons relating to the study of geography.

CENTRAL QUESTIONS (A SELECTION)

- Where are things located? Why are they there?
- What patterns are reflected in the grouping of things?
- How are these patterns explained?
- How can things be grouped to form a region?
- How do people influence the environment? How does the environment influence people?
- What causes changes in the patterns of distribution?
- What problems does unequal distribution cause?
- What are the links and interactions between different parts of the world?

CONCEPTS (A SELECTION)

Environment, environmental perception, landform, climate, weather, latitude, longitude, elevation, spatial distribution, density, diffusion, interaction, accessibility, location, relative location, region, land use, central place, Equator, North Pole, South Pole, natural resource, area differentiation, settlement pattern, migration, rotation, revolution (of the Earth)

GENERALIZATIONS (A SELECTION)

- Human use of the environment is influenced by cultural values, economic wants, level of technology, and environmental perception.
- Each culture views the physical environment in a unique way, prizing aspects of it that may be different from those prized by others.
- More change and conflict occur near the boundaries of regions than in their interiors.
- The accessibility, relative location, and political character of a place influence the quantity and type of its interactions with other places.
- The character of a place is not constant; it reflects the place's past, present use, and future prospects.
- Innovation and change influence the accessibility and desirability of places.
- Successive or continuing occupancy by groups of people and natural processes together give places their uniqueness.

Figure 2–4
Central questions, concepts, and generalizations associated with geography.

six essential elements and eighteen standards, standards that are seen as characteristics of a geographically informed person.

Element One: The World in Spatial Terms
This theme studies the location of people, places, and environments across the face of the Earth. There are three standards related to this theme.

The geographically informed person knows and understands:

- How to use maps and other geographic representations, tools, and technologies to acquire, process, and report information from a spatial perspective.
- How to use mental maps to organize information about people, places, and environments in a spatial context.
- How to analyze the spatial organization of people, places, and environments on Earth's surface.

Element Two: Places and Regions

Each place on Earth's surface has unique characteristics because of the nature of the interaction of the cultural characteristics of people and the environment. The region is a central concept of geography. It is a grouping of an area of any size or shape based on certain common characteristics. Regions provide convenient units of analysis for studying the relationships of different phenomena. There are three standards related to this theme.

The geographically informed person knows and understands:

- The physical and human characteristics of places.
- That people create regions to interpret the Earth's complexity.
- How culture and experience influence people's perceptions of places and regions.

Element Three: Physical Systems

This theme is closely related to the physical science and ecology components of the school curriculum. Physical processes are constantly shaping the surface of the Earth. The pattern of these processes and their interaction across the Earth are fascinating topics of study. For example, how can a warm pool of water off the western coast of South America called El Niño influence snowfall in Maine and drought in Southeast Asia? There are two standards related to this theme.

The geographically informed person knows and understands:

- The physical processes that shape the patterns of Earth's surface.
- The characteristics and spatial distribution of ecosystems on Earth's surface.

Element Four: Human Systems

The Earth as the home of humans is a major thrust of geography. It is human habitation and activities that give a dynamic nature to the study of geography. Humans compete for control of the surface and resources of the Earth. They create political regions and establish boundaries. There is a constant movement of people, resources, and ideas across the surface. Understanding the factors that enhance or inhibit movement is important if we are to understand our interdependence with others. This theme has five standards.

The geographically informed person knows and understands:

- The characteristics, distribution, and migration of human populations on Earth's surface.
- The characteristics, distributions, and complexity of Earth's cultural mosaics.

- The patterns and networks of economic interdependence.
- The processes, patterns, and functions of human settlement.
- How the forces of cooperation and conflict influence the division and control of Earth's surface.

Element Five: Environment and Society

Geographers have historically been interested in human-environmental interactions. They study how physical environments influence people and how people modify physical environments. The consequences of these interactions are of critical importance. The physical environment is modified largely by the ways in which human societies value and use natural resources. This theme has three standards.

The geographically informed person knows and understands:

- How humans modify the physical environment.
- How physical systems affect human systems.
- The changes that occur in the meaning, use, distribution, and importance of resources.

Element Six: The Uses of Geography

This theme recognizes that many events of the past are not clearly understood apart from the geographic perspective. In addition, knowledge of geography is important in order for us to understand current issues and problems. Many proposals addressing current issues fall short of the mark because they fail to take into account the geographic perspective. Finding solutions to current problems such as war, immigration, and even disease requires an understanding of geography. Making informed decisions and taking actions that will impact the future also require an understanding of geography. How will cities grow? What will be the impact of new modes of transportation? How will destruction of rain forests influence our climate? These and other similar questions require an application of geographic knowledge. This theme includes two standards.

The geographically informed person knows and understands:

- How to apply geography to interpret the past.
- How to apply geography to interpret the present and plan for the future.

Geography-Related Classroom Activities

As noted in the geography standards, geography involves much more than the memorization of state capitals, mountain ranges, and continents. Good lessons in geography focus on involving students to begin "thinking geographically." This requires that students develop observation skills and prompts them to begin asking questions about the world around them. They need to ask not only "Where is it?" but also "Why is it there?" and "How is it related to other things?" Lesson Ideas 2–5 and 2–6 can be used to get students to begin thinking geographically.

Lesson Idea 2–5

WHAT KIND OF DOG IS THAT?

Grade Level: 2–5

Objectives: Students will (1) gather data from a variety of resources, (2) construct a map showing the origins of different breeds of dogs, and (3) make inferences from their maps.

Overview: Children like pets. This love of pets can be used to stimulate an interest in locating different places in the world. This activity is consistent with the geography element of viewing the world in spatial terms.

Procedures: *Materials*   It would be helpful to obtain a fairly large map of the world and place it on a bulletin board. You will also need sources of information about dogs. One excellent source is Pugnetti's *Simon & Schuster's Guide to Dogs* [New York: Simon & Schuster, 1980]. You can also find information about breeds and bulletin boards where you can ask questions on the Internet; or look for magazines, such as *Dog World,* at bookstores and newsstands.

Select 8 to 10 breeds of dogs. You can obtain good color pictures of many of the breeds from some good magazines. Cut out several pictures and mount them on a piece of colored paper.

Learning Set   Ask class members to talk about pets they have at home. Focus attention on dogs. Ask the students if they know the place, in the world, where those dogs came from. The idea is to emphasize that, like people, the local and familiar dog has important international roots.

Activity   Show the class the pictures of the dogs you have gathered. Older children can choose a breed and use reference material to see if they can find the origin of that breed. Once they have done so they can place the picture of the dog around the map and use yarn to stretch between the picture and the country of origin. With younger children, you might place the pictures yourself, give them the place of origin, and then help them find the location.

The following is a sample selection.

Breed	Origin
Boxer	Germany
Poodle	France
Chihuahua	Mexico
Shih-tzu	China
Lhasa apso	Tibet
Basenji	Egypt
Yorkshire terrier	England

With older children you can follow this up by seeing if they can make any inferences about the country just by looking at the pictures and reading about the dogs.

Closure: Conclude the lesson by asking students what they learned through this activity.

The World in Spatial Terms

An important part of beginning to think about the world in spatial terms is to use maps to locate things in the environment. There are two types of location that can be used. Absolute location refers to where a place is located in terms of some sort of a reference system, such as latitude and longitude. Relative location refers to where things are located in relationship to other things, such as transportation routes, bodies of water, or social and economic activity.

Pupils can learn to identify both absolute and relative locations by working with things in their immediate environment. For example, they might consider locations of their classroom, home, school, and community. Many teachers find it useful to use simple grid systems to introduce learners to the idea of absolute location. A simple grid might have letters A, B, C, D, and so forth along one axis and numbers 1, 2, 3, 4, and so on along the other. For example, pupils in a class might be given a simple drawing of their classroom featuring locations of individual student desks with letters and numbers along the axes. Then, the teacher might ask individual youngsters to identify the location of their desks by referencing the grid. (My desk is at location B-3, and so forth.) These simple grid lessons can be followed by more sophisticated exercises involving use of grid systems to locate places on community and state maps.

You may begin a relative location lesson by asking pupils to describe locations of several places they know in their own communities. Pupils often will talk about locations of such places as schools, markets, shopping malls, and movie theaters. Once identified, you may then ask pupils about where these places are in relation to one another. They might describe locations in terms of direction and distance from well-known locations such as rivers, parks, harbors, and major streets and highways. You may then lead them into a productive discussion of why certain places might be located where they are. Questions such as the following help pupils think about reasons some kinds of places are located either close to or far away from others:

- Why are many residential areas not located close to where factories are located?
- Would you expect lots of doctors' offices to be located close to hospitals? If so, how would you explain this pattern?
- Why are there often many gas stations near entrances and exits of major highways?
- If there were three stories in a school, would you expect to find all the drinking fountains on just one floor, or would you expect to find some on each floor? Why?

Places and Regions

Students can begin to develop an understanding for places and their unique characteristics beginning in the primary grades. Taking pupils for walks around the school or the

Understanding why and how cities grow and change is an important element of geography.

neighborhood, and asking them to identify items in the environment, is a good starting point. You might ask the following prompt questions during such a walk:

- Why do you think a school was built here?
- What things are near the school? What things are near your home?
- How is our community changing?
- Where do you think things in the grocery store come from?

As pupils grow older, asking more sophisticated questions can stimulate their curiosity about geography:

- How is our community different from other communities?
- Why is it colder in the winter in the interior of the continent than on the West Coast?
- Why are there so many vacant buildings in the old downtown area?
- What changes will take place when those new houses that are being built are finished?
- Why are deserts where they are?

Lesson Idea 2–6 illustrates how even children in the primary grades can begin to grasp the regional concept and its usefulness in organizing the world.

Lesson Idea 2–6

REGIONS

Grade Level:	Primary
Objectives:	Learners can (1) identify criteria for establishing a region, and (2) draw boundaries for a region.
Overview:	A region is an area of any shape or size that has some common characteristic. This does not mean that other activities or things do not occur in the region. For example, the Corn Belt includes many other things besides farmers growing corn. Regions do not need to be areas of vast size. They can be as small as the painting region of the classroom or as large as the continent of Asia. Pupils can begin to develop the idea of region by starting with an area familiar to them. This might include area of the room, the playground, or the neighborhood.
Procedures:	*Learning Set* Begin by stating to the class, "In our homes and in our school, there are certain places we go for certain types of activities. For example, if we want to eat, where do we go? We could call this the *eating region.* At home, if we want to sleep, where do we go? We could call this the *sleeping region.* Today we are going to go out to the playground and see if we can identify different areas or regions on the playground."

Provide groups of pupils with a simple map of the playground. Walk around the playground and discuss with the pupils a few of the different regions and the labels they could give the regions. Those might include the following:

- Tether ball region
- Soccer region
- Baseball region
- Swings region
- No-running region
- Primary-grade region
- Upper-grade region

Have each group decide where they would draw the boundaries of each region on their map. Encourage them to think of other regions they might include on their map. After returning to the room, have groups share their maps. Discuss why they drew the boundaries where they did. Ask them if the only thing that ever happens in their region is the activity they identified. Point out that people called *geographers* divide the Earth into regions. Sometimes they disagree where the boundaries of a region might be. Those regions also include many things other than the one thing identified for the region.

Closure: Ask the pupils to define a region and state what they have learned about regions. Encourage them to think about regions in the neighborhood.

Human Systems

Human systems investigate the distribution and interaction of people and places around the world. Spatial interaction refers to the interaction that occurs between and among places. Pupils can begin to understand this idea by discussing and mapping relationships between where they live and where their parents or guardians work. Primary pupils often are taught interactions between urban and rural areas. People get their milk from others who work on farms in rural areas. In turn, people on farms purchase many items from stores in urban areas. A trip to the supermarket affords an excellent opportunity for a lesson focusing on spatial interaction. Many products have labels indicating their origin. Pupils may take note of this information. Back in the classroom, the class can plot some of the locations on a large map and discuss the variety of places supermarket merchandise comes from.

One class conducted an interesting experiment that led to insights about interactions among people in different parts of the world. The class purchased a stuffed animal. A letter was drafted and attached to the animal, asking people who encountered it to write a postcard to the class telling where they had seen the animal and how the animal got there.

Geography investigates the interaction between people and the environment.

The respondents were asked to pass the animal along to someone else, particularly to someone who might be doing some traveling. A parent in the class started the activity by giving the animal to an airline flight attendant. Soon postcards began coming to the class from people all over the world. The teacher and the pupils plotted locations of the stuffed animal and its movement on a large world map. This activity greatly heightened the students' awareness of spatial interaction and stimulated their interest in learning about some of the places the animal had visited. Lesson Idea 2–7 on migration focuses on the human systems theme of geography by looking at the movement of people.

Lesson Idea 2–7

MIGRATION

Grade Level:	5–6
Objectives:	Learners can (1) locate places on a map, (2) identify movement patterns, and (3) state reasons for movement from one place to another.
Overview:	The movement of people and goods from place to place is an important feature of our world. Understanding the reasons for movement, the impact of the movement, and the patterns of movement can help pupils to understand the linkages between places and the changes that have resulted from such movement, and to predict problems that might arise as a result.
Procedures:	As a homework assignment the night before the lesson, have the pupils find out from their parents the birthplaces of their parents and their grandparents.

Learning Set Ask class members, "How many have moved?" Discuss reasons why they moved. Tell them that movement from place to place is very common and that understanding those movement patterns can help us understand different places and the advantages and problems they might have. Give each child a set of six circles with "sticky" backs, and have the child put his or her name or initials on each one. On one sticker write *father,* on another *mother.* On the other four, indicate the grandfather and grandmother on the father's side of the family, and the grandfather and grandmother on the mother's side of the family.

Divide the class into groups of five or six. Give each group a world map and have them locate the places of birth of their grandparents and parents. Have each group share its maps with the rest of the class.

Discuss the maps, using the following questions:

- Did you notice any patterns of movement in our class?
- Why do you think there were patterns?
- Why did your parents or grandparents move?

- What causes people to move?
- What problems might occur when many people from many different places decide to move to the same place?

Closure: Conclude the lesson by asking, "What did we learn about movement? What did we learn about our class? What other types of movement might be interesting to study?"

Environment and Society

This theme can be implemented by helping students investigate how humans change their environment as well as how the environment changes human behavior. As a beginning, pupils might look at the local community and seek answers to questions such as these:

- How is the local community changing?
- Are new homes being built?
- Are trees being eliminated or planted?
- What changes in the environment might take place as the result of a new highway?

Such questions afford an opportunity to tie questions associated with geography to historical information about the community. Answers encourage pupils to understand not only what is happening now but also what had existed.

A study of weather and climate is often included as a component of units focusing on human-environment interactions. Lessons help learners discover how people living under different climatic conditions interact with their circumstances to build special kinds of buildings and wear particular types of clothing. Kinds of recreational activities pursued by people in different climatic regions often also interest elementary school-children.

An important component of environment and society is an understanding that different people view the environment in different ways. What might be viewed as a worthless parcel of desert by one person might be viewed as an ideal location for a home by another or as a perfect location for gambling casinos. Lesson Idea 2–8 acquaints students with the concept of *environmental perception*.

Lesson Idea 2–8

ENVIRONMENTAL PERCEPTION

Grade Level: Primary

Objective: Pupils can state the influence of experiences on their ideas and perceptions.

Overview: Geographers interested in environmental perception believe that human relationships with the environment are not adequately explained by the world "as it is." Rather, these relationships are the result of what people *believe* the world to be. Personal experiences help shape how people view the world. For example, surveys of people in different regions of the United States have revealed great variations in opinion about the location of the best place to live. Similarly, experiences often lead to misperceptions of distance. Longtime residents of the Northeast often underestimate the distance separating western cities such as Los Angeles and San Francisco. Westerners have difficulty understanding the proximity of eastern cities such as Boston and New York. Pupils can begin to understand how their personal experiences have influenced their view of the world by focusing on elements of their own neighborhood.

Procedures:

Learning Set   Discuss with the pupils the kinds of things they can do in a park. Tell them that they are going to be allowed to design the "perfect" park. Ask the following questions and write the responses on the board:

- What kinds of things should be in the park?
- Where did you get your ideas?

Give cooperative groups an opportunity to draw a park to include the things they have identified and where they think the best place would be for the items they want to include. Then discuss the following questions:

- How do you think your ideas of a perfect park would be different if you lived in the center of a city? In a farming community? In a snowy region? In a desert region?
- Why do you think people in different places would have different ideas about what would be best?

Debrief the class, pointing out that the experiences people have influence the choices they make. What might look like a good place for a park to us might not be the same place and type of a park that someone else would choose. Asking pupils why some people prefer to go to the mountains for vacations and others prefer to go to the beach or to the city could extend this.

Closure:

Ask the class, "What did we learn about the way people view the environment? How is our view influenced by our experiences?"

The activities that we have briefly described here are samples of what can be done with geography-related content. Most of these activities require active pupil involvement. Further, they demand that learners think. Sound geography-based lessons require learners to do much more than learn locations and memorize names of capitals. That kind of boring, mindless activity has given geography instruction a bad name. The discipline of geography has marvelous explanatory powers. Good geography-based lessons both interest learners and contribute to the development of their mental powers.

A Selection of Information Sources

National Council for Geographic Education

The National Council for Geographic Education (NCGE) is the leading national professional organization for educators interested in geography. NCGE publishes the excellent *Journal of Geography*. A subscription is included as part of the annual membership fee. Many issues feature articles describing imaginative approaches to teaching geographic content to elementary school pupils. For information, write to the National Council for Geographic Education, NCGE Central Office, Indiana University of Pennsylvania, Indiana, PA 15705.

Joint Committee on Geographic Education

Members of the Joint Committee on Geographic Education were drawn from two professional groups that have long been interested in improving the quality of geographic education: the National Council for Geographic Education and the Association of American Geographers. The Joint Committee's work led to the publication, *Guidelines for Geographic Education: Elementary and Secondary Schools* (Natoli et al., 1984). As noted previously, this document includes important information regarding kinds of geographic content that should be taught at each grade level. Copies of this material are available from the National Council for Geographic Education.

Geographic Alliance Network

The National Geographic Society has become interested in revitalizing the quality of geographic education in the schools. To this end, the society has sponsored the formation of more than 40 state-based Geographic Alliances. The alliances seek additional support from state government and private sources.

Each alliance draws together professional geographers and classroom teachers. An alliance coordinator helps to organize activities and disseminate information about each state's activities. Alliances sponsor summer geographic education institutes, put on one- and two-day workshops, and support the development of high-quality instructional materials. Many Geographic Alliance activities are directed toward elementary school teachers.

For information about the Geographic Alliance Network, write to Geographic Education Program, National Geographic Society, Washington, DC 20036.

WEB CHECK

Note: Electronic addresses of sites on the World Wide Web change frequently. If the listed URL fails to work, use a standard search engine to locate the new address of the site.

- National Council for History Education

  URL—**http://www.history.org/nche/main.html**

  The National Council for History Education is the leading organization promoting the study of history in the schools. Among other things, the site features numerous helpful links to other Web addresses with useful information related to teaching history.

- History Buff Home Page

  URL—**http://www.historybuff.com/index.html**

  This site contains a searchable library of newspaper coverage of events in American history. Categories include baseball, Old West, Civil War, and crime fighters. Information is available in print, photographic, and sound form. Highly recommended.

- National Archives—American History

  URL—**http://www.thehistorynet.com/THNarchives/AmericanHistory**

  Large numbers of original items can be found at this site. There are photographic as well as print items available. Users will encounter excellent content on a wide variety of subjects related to history.

- Library of Congress—American Memory

  URL—**http://rs6.loc.gov/amhome.html**

  This outstanding site is searchable. There are audio as well as video records of all kinds available. This should be one of the "first visits" of elementary social studies teachers who are interested in exploring the range of history-related material available on the World Wide Web. Highly recommended.

- Invention Dimension

  URL—**http://web.mit.edu/invent/**

  This site includes lots of information about inventions and inventors that can be interesting to elementary school learners.

- Horus' Web Links to History Resources

  URL—**http://www.ucr.edu/h-gig/horuslinks.html**

  This site, maintained by the History Department at the University of California at Riverside, includes a marvelous set of Web links to other sites with history-related information. An excellent resource for elementary social studies teachers.

- Geographic Resources for Teachers

  URL—**http://www2.gasou.edu/facstaff/dangood/**

  This site, provided through the courtesy of Dr. Daniel Good of Georgia Southern University, offers a wealth of information of interest to teachers who wish to integrate computer technology into teaching geography-related content.

- Envirolink

  URL—**http://envirolink.org/**

  This site includes a vast amount of information about the environment and has attractive graphics.

- Altapedia Online

  URL—**http://www.atlapedia.com/index.html**

  At this site, you can download maps and up-to-date statistical information about every country in the world. Highly recommended.

- National Council on Geographic Education—Home Page
  URL—**http://multimedia2.freac.fsu.edu/ncge/**

  The National Council on Geographic Education is the nation's leading professional organization for people concerned about teaching geography. There are excellent resources related to geography curriculum and geography-related professional development opportunities available at this site.

- Geography
  URL—**http://www.eduplace.com/ss/autoact/ss_1.html**

  This site features a collection of geography lesson plans for grades K–6 compiled by Houghton Mifflin.

KEY IDEAS IN SUMMARY

1. Content drawn from history can be used to help pupils develop an appreciation for multiple perspectives on events and more sophisticated thinking skills. The National Standards for History provides guidance for teachers as they plan for history lessons. The standards include two integrated components of history, historical understanding and historical thinking.

2. The *National Standards for History* establishes criteria that can be used in identifying what history-related content to teach and how it should be taught. The National Standards are organized around five key spheres of human activity: (a) social history, (b) political history, (c) history of science and technology, (d) economic history, and (e) cultural history.

3. Historians, as they attempt to determine truth, are concerned about both internal and external validity of information sources. Procedures used to determine external validity focus on the likelihood that a document or other historical artifact could have been produced at the time it was alleged to have been produced. Internal validity procedures seek to verify the accuracy of information in the material.

4. Two professional organizations have been particularly active in developing information and sponsoring programs designed to improve the quality of history teaching. The National Council for History Education's publication *History Matters* often has articles of interest to elementary school teachers. The National Council for the Social Studies, a group with interest in promoting effective school instruction in content areas tied to history and the social sciences, also sponsors many initiatives of interest to elementary schoolteachers. Geography focuses on spatial patterns. *Geography for Life: National Standards* outlines 18 standards that define a geographically informed person. Those 18 standards are divided into six elements: (a) the world in spatial terms, (b) places and regions, (c) physical systems, (d) human systems, (e) environment and society, and (f) the uses of geography.

5. The National Geographic Society has encouraged the development of Geographic Alliances in each state. These are coalitions of professors of geography and class-

room teachers who are interested in geography. Alliances sponsor summer programs and workshops and engage in the development of geography-related classroom materials.

CHAPTER REFLECTIONS

Directions: Now that you have read this chapter, reread the case study at the beginning. Then, answer these questions.

1. How would you respond to Juan's statement about not understanding the point of teaching history in the elementary school?

2. How would you respond to Juan's question about how to select content for inclusion in the elementary school program?

3. How do you react to Juan's question about what geography should be taught in elementary social studies classes? How would you answer his inquiry about how to keep the students interested in geography?

4. What do you think you need to learn about different subjects to teach them successfully?

5. Have your ideas about what should be taught changed as a result of reading this chapter? If so, in what ways?

EXTENDING UNDERSTANDING AND SKILL

1. Review several issues of *History Matters.* Share with other members of your class some arguments in this publication for including history instruction in the elementary school program. For information about receiving *History Matters,* write to the National Council for History Education, 26915 Westwood Road, Suite A-2, Westlake, OH 44145.

2. Examine the history content in an elementary social studies textbook that is designed for use at a grade level you would like to teach. Approximately what percentages of the total content relate to (a) social history, (b) political history, (c) history of science and technology, (d) economic history, and (e) cultural history? How satisfied are you with the distribution of content across these categories? Present your findings in the form of a report to your class.

3. Prepare a position statement in which you defend history and geography as important components of the elementary social studies program. Present this to your instructor for review and comments.

4. Review geography-related content in two elementary school textbooks that are designed for use at the same grade level. How much content do the two textbooks

provide for each of these "essential elements": (a) the world in spatial terms, (b) places and regions, (c) physical systems, (d) human systems, (e) environment and society, and (f) the uses of geography? If there are important differences in emphasis between the two books, which do you prefer and why? Share your findings with others in your class.

5. Begin building resource files you can use in the classroom to teach social studies in the classroom. You might begin by searching some of the Web Check sites. Include such things as photographs, newspaper accounts, journal articles, and cartoons. Organize the material you gather so that it will be easy to find and access.

REFERENCES

ARMSTRONG, D. G., & SAVAGE, T. V. (1976). A framework for utilizing the community for social learning in grades 4–6. *Social Education, 40* (3), 164–167.

BEDNARZ, S. W., BETTIS, N. C., BOEHM, R. G., DESOUSA, A. R., DOWNS, R. M., MARRAN, J. F., MORRILL, R. W., & SALTER, C. L. (1994). *Geography for life: National geography standards.* Washington, DC: National Geographic Research and Exploration.

BRADLEY COMMISSION ON HISTORY IN SCHOOLS. (1988). *Building a history curriculum: Guidelines for teaching history.* Westlake, OH: National Council for History Education, Inc.

GAGNON, P. (1989). *Democracy's half-told story: What American history textbooks should add.* Washington, DC: American Federation of Teachers.

History–social science framework for California public schools: Kindergarten through grade twelve. (1987). Sacramento, CA: California State Department of Education.

NATIONAL CENTER FOR HISTORY IN THE SCHOOLS. (1996). *National standards for history* (basic ed.). Los Angeles, CA: University of California, Los Angeles.

NATIONAL COMMISSION ON SOCIAL STUDIES IN THE SCHOOLS. (1989). *Charting a course: Social studies in the 21st century.* Washington, DC: American Historical Association, Carnegie Foundation for the Advancement of Teaching, National Council for the Social Studies, Organization of American Historians.

NATOLI, S. J., BOEHM, R. G., KRACHT, J. B., LANEGRAN, D. A., MONK, J. J., & MORRILL, R. W. (1984). *Guidelines for geographic education: Elementary and secondary schools.* Washington, DC: Association of American Geographers and National Council for Geographic Education.

RISINGER, C. F. (1992). *Current directions in social studies.* Boston: Houghton Mifflin.

SAVAGE, M. K., & SAVAGE, T. V. (1993). Children's literature in middle school social studies. *The Social Studies, 84* (1), 32–37.

chapter 3

Content Sources: Political Science and Law-Focused Education

This chapter will help you to:

- describe the special perspectives of political science in studying human behavior,
- identify central questions, concepts, and generalizations associated with political science,
- develop social studies lessons that draw content from political science,
- find information and material useful for teaching law-focused topics,
- list the steps for using mock trials in the classroom, and
- state how local community resources can be used for teaching law-focused topics.

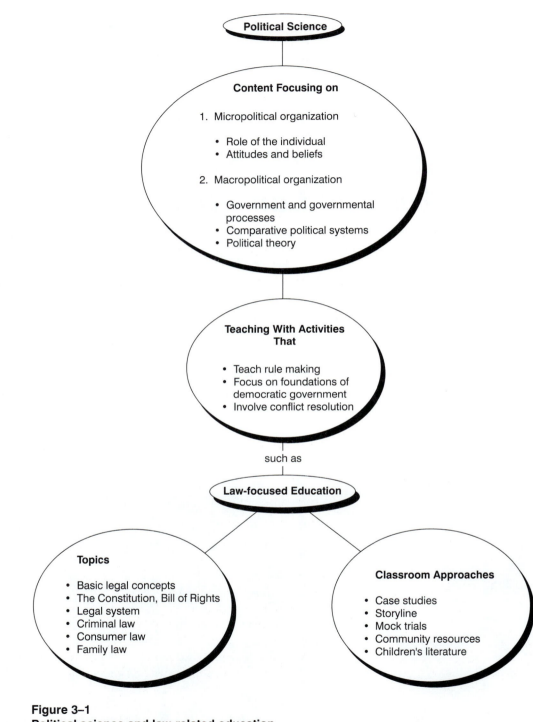

Figure 3–1
Political science and law-related education.

Case Study

WHAT IS CITIZENSHIP?

Members of the teaching staff of Glen Eden Elementary School were gathered for their first faculty meeting of the year. After a few welcome-back comments and some routine business, the principal launched into the first substantive agenda item, the social studies curriculum.

"As you are all aware," she began, "our student population has been changing in the past few years. We now have many of our pupils who are immigrants or children of immigrants. These individuals often lack an understanding of and a commitment to our form of government. If these new members of our community do not develop this understanding and commitment, our form of government and way of life could be in jeopardy.

"I am sure you are also aware that right-wing groups have been active in monitoring school programs and protesting policies and activities that they perceive to be inconsistent with citizenship and patriotism. I'm sure you are familiar with the difficulty and embarrassment caused by these protests. We want to avoid that here. We want a quiet, peaceful school year.

"Putting together these two forces, the need to educate an immigrant population in our democratic tradition, and the protests of these conservative groups, leads us to consider what should be taught in the social studies program. As you teach social studies this year, I want you to avoid controversial topics and discussions. Don't discuss problems in our government. Teach the positive accomplishments of our government so that pupils will develop a positive image of our nation and will grow to be committed and patriotic citizens. This will also ensure that no group can have any grounds for criticizing what we are doing in school."

What Is Your Response?

Read the information above and imagine that you are a teacher in the Glen Eden School. Then, briefly respond to these questions:

1. Do you agree that recent immigrants need to be taught to cherish our form of government?
2. Is avoiding discussion of controversial or negative aspects of our political system the best way to develop a commitment and understanding?
3. Should the social studies curriculum be influenced by the actions of protest groups?
4. What should be the role of the school in responding to the concerns of various groups interested in the school curriculum?
5. Do you think that social problems and some of the failures of our political system should be included in the elementary curriculum, or are such topics best left until later?
6. What would be a proper way to include controversial issues in the classroom?
7. How would you respond to the principal's remarks if you had attended this faculty meeting?

INTRODUCTION

Have you ever had a defective product that the maker refused to fix? Have you ever been frustrated while trying to read the small print on a contract or warranty? Did you ever receive a class grade that you believed was an unfair measure of your performance? Have you ever felt that you were wronged by someone to the extent that you wanted to file a lawsuit? Do reports of crime in your local community and state frighten you? Have you been made angry by some of the problems our country faces today?

Nearly everybody has had these or similar experiences. When such situations occur, people feel much less powerless when they have some understanding of how governments and legal systems work to resolve problems and conflicts. In the elementary social studies program, content designed to promote this kind of knowledge draws heavily on the discipline of political science.

Purposes of this kind of instruction include helping learners grasp how decisions are made and assisting them to understand that personal involvement can make a difference. Regrettably, many young people have inadequate concepts of the law, distorted by television and movie dramas. One result is that they begin to believe that rights are available only to others (Wasson, 1994). This perception can lead to a sense of powerlessness and frustration where violence and lawlessness are considered acceptable. This alarming condition is at the root of many contemporary problems. A growing concern about the alienation of individuals from the law has led to law-focused education and other academic programs that seek to help young people learn about authority and government.

The process of learning about the government and acquiring values and perspectives about one's role is called *political socialization*. Some early efforts to include the content of political science in the social studies curriculum were largely attempts at political socialization. The results of these attempts were not always as anticipated. For example, one state legislator once remarked that social studies had obviously failed because so many individuals were involved in mass protests against the government. For this individual, this was an obvious indication that individuals lacked patriotism. A contrary interpretation might be that the political socialization of those individuals protesting was very successful; it was just that they had developed political views that were at odds with those of the legislator.

Though political socialization has a place in school programs, today we appreciate that the discipline of political science has much more to offer the elementary social studies curriculum. In particular, political science has perspectives that can help us teach pupils about themselves and their role in a democracy. Lessons with these emphases go beyond a study of basic structures of government. For example, influences in establishing directions and goals for our society come from sources such as the Chamber of Commerce, National Rifle Association, American Medical Association, Parent-Teacher Association, trade unions, and religious groups. These are special interest groups outside what we might label *formal* government. Institutions of government account for only a part of the decisions made in the political systems.

In addition, in some places in the world, the political functions are performed by family or tribal groups rather than by some special institution that we call *government*. Focusing narrowly on government would exclude study and understanding of these alternative ways of performing political and legal functions.

The study of political science investigates how people solve conflicts and deal with controversy.

POLITICAL SCIENCE

The study of political science involves the study of controversy and disagreement. In every society there are disagreements between individuals and groups over the goals of the society, the best methods for achieving those goals, the values that ought to be made into law, enforcement of laws, and the rights of various groups and individuals in the society. Informed and well-meaning individuals disagree about these issues. As a result, each society must have a set of institutions to settle these conflicts. This set of institutions can be identified as the political *system.*

Political science is the study of this system and, where they exist, the institutions of government. Political science is concerned with the conflicts in the society, how these conflicts are resolved, who makes the decisions, and the consequences of the resolution. Figure 3–2 presents some of the central questions, concepts, and generalizations that have been used to organize the study of political science.

Political Science in the Curriculum

There are different ways these central concepts can be organized for study so that pupils begin to understand political systems and how they operate to resolve conflicts. Sorauf (1965) labeled these approaches *micropolitical* and *macropolitical.* One approach focuses

The following are examples of central questions, concepts, and generalizations that are important when studying content drawn from political science.

CENTRAL QUESTIONS (A SELECTION)

- Who decides the rules or laws?
- Are the rules or laws accepted by the people?
- What difference does it make who decides the rules?
- Who enforces the rules or laws?
- What values are reflected in the rules and laws?
- How much impact do the citizens have on the decisions made by the government?
- How does the system change?
- What happens if the system does not change in the direction that people desire?
- What is the decision-making process in different political systems?
- What alternative ways have people established for making political decisions?
- What are the consequences of different ways of making political systems?

CONCEPTS (A SELECTION)

Distribution of power, authority, equality, conflict resolution, decision making, compromise, Constitution, law, law making, rights, responsibilities, freedom, justice, due process, citizenship, state, nation, civil liberty, separation of powers, common law, legal system, democracy, monarchy, totalitarian, theocracy

GENERALIZATIONS (A SELECTION)

- Every society establishes a system of authority that makes decisions and enforces social regulations on members of the society.
- A stable political system facilitates the social and economic growth of a nation.
- Some consent of the governed is required in all governments, and without it a government will eventually collapse.
- The political system acts to help resolve conflicts when individuals and groups have competing goals and values.
- In order for a political system to survive, it must have the ability to change as values and circumstances change.
- A democratic society depends on the presence of educated and informed citizens who have a willingness to compromise and a respect for the rights of minorities and the loyal opposition.

Figure 3–2
Central questions, concepts, and generalizations associated with political science.

on the individual within the political system, and the other is concerned with the big picture or overall operation of the political system.

Micropolitical Organization
The *micropolitical* way of organizing content from political science focuses on the role of the individual in the political system. The following two key questions direct the attention of individuals approaching political science from this perspective:

- How do individual citizens influence the political system?
- What is the impact of the political system on individual citizens?

People who study micropolitical organization are concerned with the goals, beliefs, and responsibilities of individuals and how they acquire them. Each person has some understanding about the political system and the power and responsibilities of individual members of society. The attitudes and beliefs of individuals have a great influence on their political system. For example, people who believe that the individual is powerless and the system is insensitive to their needs may become alienated. When a high percentage of citizens become alienated, often political unrest results, threatening the continued functioning of the political system.

Another important element of the micropolitical arena is attention to how individuals make political decisions. People often encounter issues where different groups to which they belong favor different choices. For example, we might be involved in a situation in which our occupational group favors one solution to a problem and our religious group favors another. Resolving these competing loyalties, sorting through competing claims of truth, and making a personal decision is an important and demanding task for all of us.

In helping our pupils grasp some of these difficulties, we need to familiarize them with how various groups use persuasion techniques to influence attitudes and opinions of a majority to win support for a particular public policy. Lessons need to include information about the role of media and the use of various propaganda techniques. Citizenship education implies a need for our pupils to have the kinds of knowledge and skills required for them to sort through conflicting claims so that they may base their decisions on sound criteria.

Macropolitical Organization

Macropolitical study looks at the operation of the political system as it tries to accommodate the conflicting demands of various groups. Lessons designed to provide pupils with this perspective can be organized around the following basic themes:

- Government and governmental processes
- Comparative political systems
- Political theory

Government and governmental processes instruction emphasizes how decisions are made and how widely held values become formalized as laws. Our lessons in this area focus on how the leaders of the political system are selected and how authority and power are distributed.

Comparative political systems emphasize the way people at various times and in various places have organized themselves to make political decisions. Topics include the allocation of power, conflict resolution, enforcement, and the rights of individual citizens.

Political theory deals with the issue of how people ought to be governed to preserve the rights and freedoms of individuals while at the same time ensuring the continuation of the society as a whole. Concepts such as *justice, freedom,* and *equality* are associated with this emphasis.

GRADES K–4 AND 5–8

- What is government and what should it do? (Grades K–4 standards)
- What are the basic values and principles of American democracy? (Grades K–4 standards)
- What are civic life, politics, and government? (Grades 5–8 standards)
- What are the foundations of the American political system? (Grades 5–8 standards)
- How does the government established by the Constitution embody the purposes, values, and principles of American democracy? (Grades K–4 standards, Grades 5–8 standards)
- What is the relationship of the United States to other nations and to world affairs? (Grades K–4 standards, Grades 5–8 standards)
- What are the roles of the citizen in American democracy? (Grades K–4 standards; Grades 5–8 standards)

From *National Standards for Civics and Government* (1994). Calabasa, CA: Center for Civic Education.

Figure 3–3
Examples of key questions from *National Standards for Civics and Government (1994).*

Curriculum Content Standards

The Center for Civic Education has actively promoted the development of standards for school instruction centering on the values of political democracy. A key center publication on this topic is the *National Standards for Civics and Government* (1994). This document presents standards for three grade-level clusters: K–4, 5–8, and 9–12. Materials in this document are organized around key questions. For each question, there is a general statement about what pupils should understand. These statements are further defined by a series of behaviors that pupils who grasp the relevant content should be able to display. Figure 3–3 illustrates the basic focus questions for grades K–4 and grades 5–8.

Recently, the Center for Civic Education has been engaged in an effort to develop a document titled *Call for International Participation in Developing Education for Democratic Citizenship: A Framework.* This initiative involves educators from around the world in projects designed to summarize core learning in school programs that seek to prepare people for life in constitutional democracies (Center for Civic Education, 1997). This document should be available by the time this text is printed. For details about this project or other activities of the center, contact:

Center for Civic Education
5146 Douglas Fir Road
Calabasa, CA 91302-1467
Phone: (818) 591-9321
Fax: (818) 591-9330
Web home page: **http://www.civiced.org/index.html**

Comparing different forms of government helps students understand different ways that people have made rules and allocated power.

Political Science–Related Classroom Activities

One of our major purposes in selecting content from political science is to help learners understand the function of rules and laws. They need to realize that there are honest differences between people regarding the goals and directions of a society and the role of government.

Materials in these subsections focus on ideas for helping young people see themselves as individuals with the potential to influence political decisions. They are designed also to provide pupils with insights into how our government works. Legal controversies of various kinds have become a common feature of everyday life. To help our pupils better understand how our system handles legal challenges of various kinds, we devote an entire later section of this chapter to a political science–based instructional approach called *law-focused education.*

Making Rules

A central focus in the study of political science content is the function of rules and laws. We want pupils to understand the importance of having fair and just rules that are accepted by most people. They need to learn that rules or laws are ineffective if most people do not agree with them. Our lessons can also help learners discover the differences in the rules that come about because of the special perspectives of those who make and enforce them.

Rule making can be a meaningful activity in classrooms, beginning with the primary grades. In these early grades, lessons can be tied to the establishment of rules for the classroom or school. Having the pupils discuss who should make the rules can expand the rule-making activity that usually takes place at the beginning of the year. We might have our pupils think about how rules made by the principal or the teacher might be different from rules they make.

Some teachers have found it useful to involve pupils in developing a set of classroom rules organized into a classroom constitution that all class members sign. Not only does this help them learn important political science concepts, it helps classroom discipline by providing pupils with some ownership in the regulations. (See Lesson Idea 3–1.)

Lesson Idea 3–1

RULE MAKING

Grade Level:	K–2
Objectives:	Pupils can (1) identify reasons for and advantages and disadvantages of rules, and (2) practice making decisions about issues that have alternative solutions.
Overview:	To help individuals understand the importance of being involved in decisions and how to influence decisions. They can also recognize the specific purpose for a given decision and the values and assumptions that lead to the establishment of a rule.
Procedures:	*Learning Set* Identify a given area of the playground that the pupils enjoy using. Discuss why they like playing in that area. Then tell them that there have been some problems in that area. Several people have been injured, so the school has decided to make rules about use of the area. Several rules have been suggested. The class is going to discuss these rules and decide what to do.

Presentation   The first possible rule is to allow only the older pupils to play in the area. It is thought that this would reduce problems because the older children would not have to worry about younger children getting in the way. The younger children would have to play in another (less desirable) area of the playground. Ask the class what they think about this rule. Use the following questions to prompt discussion:

- What is good about this idea?
- What do you think the people who thought about this idea liked about it?
- Do you think this rule would solve the problem of people getting hurt?
- Why do you think the upper-grade pupils like it?
- What problems might this rule create?
- Do you think this is a fair rule?

The second proposed rule is that only those people who have demonstrated that they are good citizens will be allowed to play in this area. Buttons will be made, and those children who work hard in class and who follow the rules will be given a button by the teacher that they can wear. They can then go and play in the area, and all others will have to stay out. Someone who misbehaves will lose his or her button. Discuss this idea using the questions posed previously.

At this point have the class suggest other rules for use of the area. Have pupils think about issues of fairness and equality as they propose new rules. When they have identified a rule they agree with, they can discuss what they can do to encourage its adoption. They could decide to send a group to the student council or the principal, or discuss the issue with other classes to get their support. The point is for the pupils to begin to understand that group action can influence political decisions.

Closure: At this point, inform the class that this was only a make-believe issue. Ask them what they learned about making rules. Why might different groups propose different rules? What should people consider when making rules? What can people do when they do not like a proposed rule?

Resolving Conflicts

An important function of government is resolving conflicts between individuals and groups. Every society has individuals and groups with different ideas about the goals of the nation and how to achieve them. It is important for children to understand that disagreement does not mean that one side must be good or right and the other bad or wrong. There are honest disagreements between good and intelligent people concerning the best course of action.

We also have to help our learners understand that some people and groups try to resolve conflicts by force or violence. We can develop lessons that involve pupils in exploring the consequences of this type of conflict resolution. These situations can be compared with our system, where we try to resolve conflicts through voting and through a court system designed to uphold the ideals of fairness and justice.

Lesson Idea 3–2

CONFLICT RESOLUTION

Grade Level: 4–6

Objectives: Pupils can (1) identify steps that can be followed in resolving conflict and (2) identify the potential role of governments in conflict resolution.

Overview: One of the most important functions of government is resolving conflict among citizens. Government acts as a referee that brings conflicting groups together, sets forth rules on how to resolve these conflicts, and specifies how the decisions are to be enforced. Mock government—focusing, as appropriate to the issue, on a city council, a state legislature, the United States Congress, or the United Nations—can help pupils become more familiar with the potential conflict resolution role of government.

Procedure:

Learning Set   Present to the class a newspaper report on a current issue in the news. It is best to present one with merit on both sides of the issue. Read the article to the class and have pupils discuss their thoughts and feelings. Tell them that an important role of government is trying to resolve conflicts like this while preserving stability and order. Tell them that the class is going to establish a mock government to try to find some solutions.

Presentation: Step 1—Assigning Roles   An important part of the mock government is assigning roles to class members. It is best if the whole class can be involved. One way of accomplishing this would be to divide the class into at least three groups. One group could be assigned to gather information and to make a presentation on one side of the issue. A second group could be assigned the task of finding and presenting information on the other side of the issue. A third group would be assigned the role of the governmental body, hearing both sides of the issue and proposing a solution. This group's preparation task would be to meet as a group and try to identify the criteria that should be followed in judging the arguments and in arriving at a decision. For example, the members might identify *fairness* as an important criterion. They should also set the rules for the hearing they will conduct.

Step 2—Defining the Issue   At this stage, hold a discussion before the pupils begin to work in their groups. Focus on identifying the specific issue and the goals of the opposing groups.

Step 3—Establishing the Hearing Rules   Before the hearing is to take place, the third group needs to present its rules on how the meeting will be conducted. It needs to state how much time the two sides will be allowed to present their positions and whether they will be allowed rebuttal time. The role of the members of the government in asking questions should also be presented and a person designated to chair the meeting. The power of that person to stop arguments should also be considered. When the rules are presented to the class, the pupils can be provided with an opportunity to discuss them. The government group can then decide if it wants to change them.

Step 4—Presenting the Positions   The hearing begins and the sides present their case.

Step 5—Establishing Decision Criteria and Deciding   At this point, you and the governmental body discuss what the criteria should be in deciding the issue. Try to get the whole class involved in discussing the criteria. Pupils should also decide how they propose to resolve the issue. Will they take a vote on one side or the other or will they propose a third alternative that might then be voted on?

Step 6—Debriefing   This is an important part of the lesson and should not be overlooked. Lead a discussion of the entire decision-making process, noting how the process works in local, state, or federal government.

Closure: Ask the pupils to review what they learned about conflict resolution during this activity. Ask them to compare this approach with other possible approaches, such as one authority (a king or queen) making the decision, or solving the conflict using force.

Conflict resolution is something that pupils of all ages will confront. They are constantly facing conflicts in the playground and the classroom. They frequently lack knowledge of alternative means for resolving disputes, and they are prone to resort to fighting or other forms of violence. The basic issues of conflict and conflict resolution that confront young children in play parallel those that arise within and between nations.

We need to begin classroom discussions on the issue of conflict resolution with a focus on pupils' personal experiences. In the primary grades, discussion might center on the use and sharing of toys or materials. We can encourage class members to discuss alternative ways of resolving these disagreements. To conclude the lesson, we might involve pupils in voting on a preferred solution. In the upper grades, the pupils can be presented with conflicts that might be occurring in the local community over policies or actions of the local government. We can help pupils trace the actions of different groups as they try to resolve the conflict. In addition, older children can look at the issues of the loyal opposition in our political system and the always difficult problem of resolving international conflicts. Unfortunately, numerous examples of international conflict are available for discussion.

Basic Foundations of Democratic Government

One purpose of the social studies is providing future citizens with a basic understanding of how government works. This has been an item of considerable concern in recent years. Several studies have revealed that about one-half of high school graduates have only superficial knowledge of the institutions, principles, and processes of their government (Patrick & Hoge, 1991). Since many of the attitudes and beliefs about government begin to emerge during the elementary grades, considerable attention must be devoted to teaching the foundations of our government.

Teaching the basic foundations of democratic government requires teaching about the Declaration of Independence, the U.S. Constitution, the Bill of Rights, and other great documents of our nation. However, our approach should not emphasize rote memorization, leaving pupils with the impression that these are musty old documents with little relationship to contemporary issues. We need to teach this material in ways that illustrate the drama and the contemporary relevance of these documents. The Constitution, for example, outlines the basic values that serve as criteria for judging the actions and laws of the people of the United States.

One useful approach is to teach the relevance of these documents using case studies, that is, simplified statements of issues relating to questions of individual and societal rights, privileges, and obligations. Learners can discuss whether they believe the constitutional rights of the individuals involved were violated. As they are involved in the discussion, they usually begin to understand how difficult it is to write clear laws that are fair. They also begin to appreciate those values and laws that serve as a foundation for our nation.

Lessons focusing on our government allow pupils many opportunities for discussion of controversial issues, which we want to encourage. Attempting to avoid controversy eliminates much of the excitement and relevance of social studies instruction and can result in a cynical rather than supportive attitude toward government. In addition, we should orient instruction in this area toward interesting pupils in active participation in governmental affairs. Some lessons should encourage pupils to take some action in support of those topics that are of interest to them. This active participation might begin with letter writing and move on to other forms of involvement in efforts to resolve local or national issues.

Social studies teachers should include lessons deriving content from political science beginning with the primary grades. Understanding the function of laws, how to influence government, and the rights and responsibilities of citizens helps youngsters to become informed and to develop a commitment to active involvement in the processes of democratic governance. The activities that we have briefly described here are only a few examples of what we can do to help pupils grasp relevant and useful principles from political science. This aspect of the elementary social studies curriculum has rich potential for producing citizens who are committed to a form of government that truly provides "liberty and justice for all."

LAW-FOCUSED EDUCATION

A growing concern about the alienation of individuals from the law has led to a number of academic programs labeled *law-focused education*. The basic premise of law-focused education is that individuals who understand the laws and legal system that underpin a democratic society are less likely to feel powerless and to resort to destructive, antisocial behavior. Dissemination of information about law, the legal system, and those who are involved in it is a basic requirement of effective citizenship. The issue, then, is not whether elementary school children should learn about the law, but rather what they need to know and how they should learn it.

Law-focused education, by helping learners appreciate more fully how our legal system works, seeks to produce future citizens who will view the law and the legal system as something positive rather than negative. It is hoped that pupils who are exposed to such instruction will develop a personal commitment to working within the structure of the American system of governance. It is hoped, too, that they will more fully appreciate the roles of those who make, administer, and enforce the law.

An important component of law-focused education is helping individuals learn how they can participate and have their opinions heard.

Law-focused education programs emphasize both common values of our society that draw us together and values conflicts that divide us. Pupils are invited to examine social problems and controversial issues. Lessons are designed to help children understand that difficult problems seldom have absolutely right or wrong answers and that decisions result as much from a consideration of values priorities as from a consideration of evidence. Teaching children processes associated with legal conflict resolution is an important feature of law-focused education programs.

Goals of Law-Focused Education

A series of definite goals guide law-focused education programs in the elementary school classroom. Law-focused programs should help pupils do the following:

- Identify the basic functions of law in society.
- Develop an appreciation of the need for a society governed by law.
- Develop an ability to think critically about issues related to laws and the legal system.
- Apply problem-solving skills in proposing solutions to legal issues and problems.
- Identify societal values that guide the development of laws and legal processes.
- Accept the rights and responsibilities of a citizen.
- Develop realistic and honest views of our legal system, its strengths, and its weaknesses.

Law-focused education is not intended to turn students into miniature lawyers. Its purposes are consistent with the overall goals of the social studies. They include emphases on learning substantive content, identifying and clarifying values, and applying critical-thinking and problem-solving skills. Some basic questions related to the goals of law-focused education are the following:

- What are rules and laws?
- Why do we need rules and laws?
- Who makes the laws?
- What do I do if I think a rule or a law is unfair?
- What happens if a person breaks the law?
- What are my obligations as a citizen to follow the laws?
- How does the law protect me and my rights?
- What do I do if I feel I have been wronged?
- Why does the legal system seem so complicated?

Topics in Law-Focused Education

Historically, a limited number of curriculum topics could be considered law-focused education. In recent years, however, the list of topics has expanded dramatically and now ranges from basic legal concepts, the Constitution and the Bill of Rights, and the legal system to criminal, consumer, and family law.

Basic Legal Concepts

The intent of this topic is to help pupils understand the function of law in society. Lessons often focus on where laws come from, limitations of laws, relationships between values and laws, and a free society's need for laws. The basic concepts of fairness, justice, liberty, equality, property, due process, and power are highlighted.

The Constitution and Bill of Rights

The Constitution and the Bill of Rights are the basic documents around which our legal system is built. Pupils need to understand how these two important documents embody key legal concepts that influence our lives every day. Lessons often emphasize the relationship of these documents to situations familiar to learners. For example, they may focus on issues related to education, discrimination, and privacy.

Lesson Idea 3–3

APPLYING THE BILL OF RIGHTS

Grade Level: 5–6

Objectives: Pupils can (1) define in their own words the meaning of articles in the Bill of Rights, (2) identify contemporary applications of the articles, and (3) work together in cooperative groups.

Overview:

The Constitution and Bill of Rights are often taught in ways that lead pupils to the conclusion that they are dusty historical documents with little relevance to current issues. This lesson applies the cooperative learning approach to helping them identify contemporary applications of the articles of the Bill of Rights.

Procedure:

Learning Set   Ask the class how many have heard of something called the Bill of Rights. Ask several pupils if they know what it is, when it was written, and if it is important to know. Inform them that they are going to be involved in a project to learn about the Bill of Rights and how it applies to us all.

Presentation   Divide the class into groups of four pupils. Assign each group the responsibility for becoming an expert on one of the first ten amendments to the Constitution. Each group should be provided with a handout that includes the amendment along with some questions to guide their thinking about the amendment's meaning. The outcome of this phase of the group work is for pupils to state in their own words what the amendment means. Each of the definitions can then be placed on the top of a large sheet of paper.

The second assignment for each group is to search through newspapers and magazines to find headlines, articles, cartoons, letters to the editor, or advertisements related to the issues raised in the amendment. They are to make a collage or a poster on the large sheet of paper that contains their definition of the amendment. When these have been completed, each small group shares its findings with the larger group. They may choose to do this with a role playing of one of the items on their collage or through other creative methods.

Closure:

This procedure will take several days. At the end of each day, review the group work skills demonstrated and what was learned during that day. At the conclusion of the lessons, pupils should state what they learned about the Bill of Rights and how it applies to the present.

The Legal System

This topic focuses on how our legal system operates. Lessons with this emphasis may consider law enforcement agencies, courts, lawyers, judges, and juries. Learning experiences that emphasize the duties of police officers and the nature of and limitations on their power help pupils develop an honest and realistic understanding of the roles these individuals play in our society. Lessons focusing on what attorneys do are often featured. Children who do not understand how the system works often view lawyers as extremely powerful individuals who have all the answers. Television programs that glamorize the roles attorneys play, no doubt, influence this perception. Young people need to understand that attorneys are not magicians who can "get you off," but rather that they are professionals who must operate within limits prescribed by law.

Understanding how the legal system functions is an important outcome of law-focused education.

Young people often also have mistaken understandings of the roles of judges and juries. (See Figure 3–4 for a suggested method for identifying these misconceptions.) It is common for them to believe that judges and juries make laws. They need to understand that judges act to interpret laws made by others, and that their decisions must conform to these laws. Similarly, it is important for children to recognize that there are important limitations on what juries can do.

Criminal Law

The crime rate in the United States has become a much-discussed national problem. Serious students of this situation point out that law enforcement alone can never reduce the crime rate. A low crime rate depends on a population committed to lawful behavior. Lessons focusing on criminal law help pupils understand what constitutes a crime, why society has defined certain acts as crimes, and what can happen to individuals who choose to violate the law. Of special importance here are topics related to the typical problems youth have and to how the juvenile justice system works. Other topics of interest include trial and courtroom procedures, punishment, probation, rehabilitation, and the rights of the accused.

Consumer Law

Young people in our society have disposable income and have considerable influence in the national marketplace. As consumers, they need to know their rights and responsibilities. There are laws that protect them from fraud as well as laws that protect producers from irresponsible consumers. Some areas often covered under the heading of consumer law are advertising, contracts, guarantees, labeling, and consumer fraud. Lessons often also inform learners about options that are open to them when they find they have purchased a defective product or when they feel they have been pressured into buying something they really do not need or want.

Figure 3–4
Identifying misconceptions.

A good beginning point for teaching law-focused material is to identify children's misconceptions. Interview pupils at different grade levels to identify their understanding of the roles of police officers, attorneys, and judges. You may wish to ask the following questions.

When the interviews are complete, compare them with those of other class members. Identify misconceptions and any patterns that might relate to children's developmental level.

1. What types of things do _____ do when they are working?

2. How does a person get to be a (an) _____?

3. Where did you get your information about _____?

4. When might you need a (an) _____?

Family Law

The family is a basic unit in society, and there is a body of law that governs family relationships. Pupils tend to be very interested in issues associated with family law. Lessons related to this topic often emphasize laws governing marriage, parental responsibility, adoption, child abuse, spouse abuse, divorce, wills, and death. The personal nature of many of these issues requires us to be sensitive in our instructional approaches. We must know our pupils well and deal with the content in an honest, nonjudgmental way.

***

Law-focused education can be integrated into the social studies classroom in several ways. As with other approaches, it is important for us to consider pupils' background, interests, and developmental level in deciding how to introduce the content. Case studies and simulations have been found to be particularly effective in law-focused education programs. Many commercially prepared materials encourage the use of these techniques.

Using Case Studies

Case studies have long been used to introduce people to the law. Most law schools use this approach in teaching prospective attorneys. This method was extended to the elementary and secondary schools when law-focused programs began to appear in public school curricula. Cases prepared for use in elementary schools tend to be short, often only two to three paragraphs in length, with reading difficulty reduced to make them accessible to elementary school readers.

Sometimes cases used in elementary schools are derived from famous and important cases that have been decided by the Supreme Court. Others focus on cases heard by lower courts that feature situations particularly interesting to younger learners. The case study approach helps children to identify key issues and to make decisions about where they stand.

Selecting Cases for Classroom Use

You should follow several guidelines when selecting or creating cases to present to learners. First, the cases selected should be ones that focus on significant issues of enduring value. For example, the issue of the right to privacy was included in the Bill of Rights over 200 years ago. Although the original writers had specific events of the time in mind, the larger issue continues to be relevant, such as with cases concerning eavesdropping. Cases focusing on freedom of speech, religion, the press, and other Bill of Rights concerns continue to be litigated in our courts. These issues remain very important.

In addition to having the potential to focus on significant and enduring legal issues, cases selected for study should also be of interest to the learners and should allow for a variety of viewpoints. Legal cases centering on trivial matters that have little interest for people other than the litigants will not generate much pupil interest.

Preparing a Case

Cases prepared for classroom use are available from several commercial sources. Individual teachers often find it necessary to modify these materials to make them suitable for their own learners. There are useful guidelines you can follow when modifying a case that has already been prepared for classroom use or when developing a case from original sources.

First, basic facts need to be introduced. Language used in doing this needs to be uncluttered, jargon free, and appropriate for the learners who will be studying the case. New terms need to be identified and explained. Often it is worthwhile to apply a readability formula to any prose material to be sure that its reading level is consistent with pupils' abilities. Next, important legal issues raised in the case need to be identified. Often this is accomplished by developing a sequence of questions to which learners must respond. For example, a case focusing on the issues of privacy rights and powers of the police might feature questions such as these: Do the police have the right to stop anyone walking down the street? Do individuals stopped by the police have the right to refuse to be searched? Can the police protect citizens if they lack the freedom to go about their work as they see fit?

Some case studies begin with a narrative of events. An alternative beginning is to present a situation's events from the viewpoints of involved individuals. Lesson Idea 3–4 illustrates how this might be done.

Lesson Idea 3–4

A CASE STUDY: POLICE SEARCH

Grade Level:	5–6
Objective:	Learners can (1) apply the principles of the Bill of Rights to a hypothetical situation and, (2) state the difficulties faced by law enforcement officials in performing their role.
Overview:	Pupils are usually unaware that the police must also follow rules. Their job can be a difficult one where they must make

decisions that sometimes may lead to legal troubles for themselves. The intent of using a case study like this is to show that there is no obvious right and wrong. This can prompt intense discussion by pupils.

Procedure:

Learning Set   Ask the class, "Can anyone tell me if the police have rules they must follow? Where do they get those rules?" Inform them that one place where they get the rules is from the U.S. Constitution. One of the rules in the Constitution is the following:

> *Amendment IV: Security from Unreasonable Searches and Seizures*
>
> *The right of the people to be secure in their persons, houses, papers, and effects, against unreasonable searches and seizures, shall not be violated, and no Warrants shall issue, but upon probable cause, supported by Oath or affirmation, and particularly describing the place to be searched, and the persons or things to be seized.*

After reading this to the class, ask pupils what they think the amendment means. Clarify any difficult terms or words.

Presentation   Tell the class, "What I want us to do is apply this amendment to the following incident to see if you think the police acted correctly." Read the following event description aloud.

> *The Event*
>
> *At 1.30 A.M. on the morning of November 7, two men were seen walking down the street. Both wore dark clothing. As they walked, they made frequent stops. They seemed to be looking into houses each time they stopped. A police officer sitting in an unmarked car watched them for about five minutes. He was in the neighborhood because there had been reports of house burglaries. The officer approached the two men, stopped them, and asked them why they were in the neighborhood. Then, he proceeded to search them.*

Use the following questions to prompt discussion.

Legal Issues

- Did the officer have a right to search the two men?
- Under what conditions do you think the police should have the right to search someone?
- What right or rights do you think would be involved in a case such as this?
- If you were to write a law that would protect the rights of people and yet allow the police to do their job, what would it say?

After some discussion, ask the pupils what they might do to find out whether the police followed the correct procedure. They might propose asking a police officer or an attorney how this case might be judged by inviting him or her to class or by writing a letter.

Closure: Conclude the lesson by asking, "What did we learn today about the rules police must follow? What did we learn about how difficult or easy it is to know exactly what to do? How does this apply to all of us?"

When preparing a case for classroom use it is helpful to identify the factors that the courts take into account in deciding similar issues. Most legal issues involve a clash between two or more rights. We need to help learners understand how the courts go about balancing these rights and reaching a decision. Many commercially prepared classroom cases provide information for teachers about lines of legal reasoning that the courts have used in past cases. Although you need not present this material formally to the class, it is helpful for answering pupils' questions. If the classroom case is based on an actual court case, information about the final decision is useful. However, the decision should not be shared with class members until they have had ample time to discuss the case and to reach their own decisions. At this time, you may share the decision and use it to begin a discussion of the strengths and weaknesses of the reasoning that learners used in arriving at their conclusions.

Presenting Case Studies
The case study approach seeks to get learners actively involved in discussing a case, identifying important issues, and making decisions. These purposes are best met when you exercise indirect rather than direct leadership in the classroom. You need to motivate pupils by pointing out the importance of the case, presenting the facts of the case, making sure they understand the facts, prompting discussion and exploration of legal issues, and getting learners to think about their own reasoning and to make a decision.

Debriefing
Debriefing is an important part of lessons featuring case studies. During debriefing, learners evaluate their own reasoning. They may compare their thinking with the thinking of others, including the judge who may have decided the case in a real court of law. Make sure that the basic legal principles and issues are summarized and understood by the class members. During this time, it is important for you to keep your personal views to yourself until pupils have had ample opportunities to share their own points of view.

Teachers who use case studies frequently report that pupils find them to be motivating. Case studies do not require learners to come up with answers that are right or wrong in any absolute sense. Further, activities require them to deal with challenging and puzzling situations. Many children find these learning activities to be a welcome change from the more traditional read-and-recite fare they have come to associate with social studies lessons. A good follow-up to the use of case studies in the classroom is a classroom visit by an attorney; perhaps the attorney could be asked to discuss basic legal principles used in deciding cases similar to the ones discussed in class. In summary, the case study approach is an especially good vehicle for introducing law-focused issues to children in elementary school classrooms. It motivates pupils. More importantly, the approach has excellent potential for introducing them to principles related to the function of law in society and to their rights and responsibilities as citizens.

Lesson Idea 3–5

A CASE STUDY: HURT ON THE JOB

Grade Level:	4–5
Objective:	Pupils can (1) interpret conflicting viewpoints and (2) apply legal considerations to a hypothetical case.
Overview:	Case studies of real situations can be very motivating to pupils. The following case study, although fictional, is based on a real incident. Discussing the case helps pupils better understand their rights and responsibilities and how the law functions to protect the rights of people.
Procedure:	*Learning Set* Ask class members to share the types of jobs they would like. Ask them if they know what the boss does. Pose the following situation, "What would you do if you were working and your boss asked you to do something that you thought was dangerous?" After they have shared their ideas tell them that today they are going to study what happened in a situation like that.
	Presentation Read the following case study to them. Stop after the facts as seen by Mr. Chiu have been presented and ask them what they think about this situation. Then inform them that there are usually two sides to a situation. Read them the facts as seen by the boss. Use the questions on legal issues to conduct a discussion.

> *The Facts as Seen by Mr. Chiu*
>
> *I arrived in the United States just a couple of years ago. I came looking for a better life. I didn't have lunch money when I arrived. Finally, I found a job working in a warehouse. It was hard work. But, I was willing to do what I had to do to make money.*
>
> *One day my boss told me to get some boxes from the back of the warehouse and take them to the loading dock. I don't know how to drive the mechanical loader most of the people use to move boxes. I usually use a handcart. This day the boss was in a big hurry. He insisted that I use the mechanical loader. I told him I didn't want to, but he insisted. He told me he'd fire me*

if I didn't do it. So, I got on the loader and tried to use it. Because I didn't know what I was doing, a large crate fell. It hit me and broke my arm. Now the boss says it was my fault. He fired me. I can't pay my medical bills, and I can't get a job right away because my arm is broken.

The Facts as Seen by the Boss

Mr. Chiu worked hard for me from the minute he was hired. But, he was afraid of machinery. He always wanted to do everything by hand. I suppose this is how it is done in his native country. We tried to teach him to use our machinery, including the mechanical loader. But he wasn't eager to learn, and he always went back to doing everything by hand. On the day of his accident, we had to get out an important order in a hurry. The truck was at the loading dock and was about ready to leave. I told Mr. Chiu to use the mechanical loader to save time. When he started to operate it, he got very nervous. A box fell. It hit him and narrowly missed another employee. I have a business to run. I have to operate efficiently. Also, I can't put up with an employee who does things that might endanger the safety of others. For this reason, I had no choice but to fire Mr. Chiu.

Legal Issues

1. Who do you think was responsible for the accident?
2. Should the boss pay for Mr. Chiu's medical treatment, since Mr. Chiu was hurt on the job?
3. Did Mr. Chiu have a right to refuse to operate the mechanical loader?
4. Did the boss have a right to fire Mr. Chiu because he could not operate the machinery properly?
5. Did Mr. Chiu have an obligation to learn how to operate the mechanical loader?
6. In general, can an employer require an employee to do something that might be dangerous?
7. To what extent must employers justify their reasons for firing someone?

In using a case formatted in this way, teachers often find it useful to summarize information on both sides of the issue. This helps class members recognize that each side has reasonable arguments favoring its position.

Closure: Bring the lesson to a conclusion by reviewing the main points made by the pupils. Ask them what might be done to find out what laws may apply to situations like this. You may wish to assign additional research or invite a guest speaker to help the pupils understand the legal issues involved.

Story Line

Story line is an interesting approach to teaching social studies that fits nicely with law-focused studies, and may be adapted to younger children. The story-line method has been developed in Scotland over the past couple of decades (Barr & McGuire, 1993). Advantages of story line are that it helps integrate the curriculum and capitalizes on pupils' enthusiasm for storytelling. It is an active approach that uses students' prior learning and experience and engages them in active dialogue as they construct meaning (Barr & McGuire, 1993).

The first step in story line is informing the pupils that they are going to be creating a story together. You then may establish the time and the setting for the story based on your curriculum objectives. For example, to meet objectives related to learning about contemporary applications of law, you may choose the present as the time frame and a setting that would be of interest to the pupils. This is then communicated through a description of the time and place that helps the pupils develop an image in their minds. The following is an example of a description you might present to the class:

> Sunshine reflects off the waves as they roll toward the sandy beach. Houses are built running down the hillsides almost to the edge of the water. Many of the houses have views of the ocean and the beach. The houses are generally small, of one story. Most of the houses have small yards containing many colorful flowers. Palm trees line the narrow streets that crisscross the community. On weekends the streets tend to become crowded with cars as people come to the beach.
>
> Scattered throughout the community are several businesses, stores, a couple of schools, and a few churches. There are no large factories or buildings in the community. This is a place where people live who work in the large city nearby.

Once given this description, the class discusses the community. Pupils can discuss what they think the climate might be like and what they think might be important to the residents, and ask any questions they might have. Pupils who may have lived in or visited a place similar to this can share their experiences. The class can then create a mural or a map depicting their visual image of this place.

The next step is for the class to create some characters for their story. They can discuss some of the people who might live in this community. You might go on to break the class into small groups, with each group creating families who live here. They need to think about the names, ages, personalities, and special interests of the people in their families. Each group then introduces its characters to the rest of the class. Group members can do this by drawing pictures of their characters or even by role playing a family situation.

Once the time, setting, and characters are in place, present the class with a series of episodes based on the main points and objectives of the unit. Pupil response to these episodes leads them into the story making. For example, you might present an episode where the people coming to visit the beach leave lots of litter. The pupils can then create a story of what they would do. As they begin to construct their story, they can research litter laws and the rights of people. For example, would be it possible for them to decide that they were not going to let anyone who did not live in the community visit the beach? In this way their stories become something more than just an exercise in imagination. They are learning about the function of law as they are trying to solve the problems they face.

Other episodes you might present include disputes between people within the community or land-use issues such as what they would do if a developer bought all of the land along the beach and proposed to build high-rise buildings that would block the view of many residents. During the unit, you also can include other activities such as writing persuasive letters, role playing, conflict resolution, making speeches, drawing pictures and maps, and passing laws. The pupils write or record their stories so that they have a narrative of the life of the community. There are numerous ways to use the story-line technique. Another setting might be a family situation, where different episodes introduce aspects of family law. The essential ingredient is that the setting and the characters are constructed so that the pupils can relate to them and care about what happens. This personal involvement makes the approach a powerful and motivating one.

Children's Literature

As with many topics in social studies, children's literature can be a useful stimulus for dealing with law-focused topics. For example, *A Family Apart*, by Joan Lowery Nixon [Bantam, 1988] deals with a family that is divided because of the death of the father and the inability of the mother to provide for the six children. In the book, Chapter 4 includes a court scene that could be used to discuss some of the issues of family law.

Books such as *A Picture Book of Frederick Douglass, A Picture Book of Rosa Parks*, by David Adler [both Holiday House, 1993], and *Free at Last*, by Sara Bullard [Oxford University Press, 1993] provide examples of individuals who sought to secure rights for all people and were even willing to violate unjust laws. Other books, too, often have themes or episodes you can adapt for law-focused lessons in our elementary classrooms.

Mock Trials

The mock trial is widely used in school law–focused education programs. Mock trials are simulation activities that feature enactments of trials. Because they include an element of competition between the contending parties, mock trials frequently stimulate high levels of pupil enthusiasm. Although mock trials have been used more widely at the secondary level, they have been applied successfully at the elementary level (Hickey, 1990). Mock trials can be developed either from actual trials that have taken place or around controversial issues that, at some point, might result in litigation.

If you are interested in engaging learners in experiences based on actual trials, you can draw on an enormous volume of school materials developed by certain firms. These include complete sets of directions for mock trials based on real court cases, videocassettes, and classroom simulations. Increasing numbers of these materials are directed toward elementary school learners. An excellent general source for such materials is Social Studies School Services. For its elementary school social studies catalog, write to Social Studies School Services, 10200 Jefferson Boulevard, Room 1, P.O. Box 802, Culver City, CA 90232-0802.

Many options are available if you wish to develop mock trial lessons based on controversial issues that may not have resulted in court cases. Such lively public controversy can serve well as a focus for a teacher-developed mock trial. Because the media give heavy exposure to an issue of this type, pupils (and certainly their parents) may well be familiar with the basic situation. This gives credibility to the mock trial experience in that it focuses on something that is of clear concern to the world beyond the school classroom. In addition, by assisting learners to focus carefully on the arguments of both sides of a divisive issue, mock trial experiences help pupils learn basic information about how our legal system operates, such as information about the operation of courts and trials and the roles of participants. They also afford excellent opportunities for guest speakers from the community to come in to broaden learners' understanding. You may have good opportunities, for example, for attorneys and judges to share information with learners about how trials operate and more general aspects of our justice system.

Using mock trials in a classroom involves the three stages of preparation, enactment, and debriefing. The success of a mock trial depends on careful attention by the teacher to each of these stages.

Preparation

One of the first steps is to introduce the learners to the purpose of a mock trial. They need to know something about the focus of the trial and what they will do to prepare for it. The basic purpose of this step is to motivate students and to teach them any rules or procedures that they will need to know. You then provide basic information concerning the facts of the case, preparing and distributing facts related to both sides of the disputed issue, often in the form of a simple fact sheet. Once it is distributed, take time to check for pupil understanding and to respond to questions.

Next, identify the roles needed and assign them to individual members of the class. Typically, these roles include a judge (or panel of judges), attorneys for both the prosecution and the defense, jurors, and court assistants such as court reporters and bailiffs. Some trials require witnesses and people to play the accused person or persons.

Once you have assigned roles, give each pupil specific information about his or her role and responsibilities. Often this is done by providing each person with a sheet that summarizes the role to be played and provides some specific suggestions. You may also ask learners to do additional research in preparation for the trial. This preparation may require one or two class days. If pupils have never been involved in a mock trial before, often it is helpful to stage a short rehearsal trial. To do this, select a focus issue that will not require pupils to do much by way of background preparation. Assign learners roles. Guide students through the process, answer questions, and generally help them understand the flow of the event.

Enactment

The enactment stage involves actually running the trial in the classroom. The general sequence followed is:

- Opening of the court
- Opening statements by attorneys, with the prosecuting attorney going first and the defense attorney second
- Witnesses for the prosecution, with cross-examination by the defense attorneys
- Witnesses for the defense, with cross-examination by the prosecuting attorneys
- Closing arguments, with the defense going first and the prosecution second
- Jury deliberations
- Verdict and adjournment of the court

Certain specific statements are made by the clerk and the judge at each step of the process. You may provide these to the pupils playing these roles so the enactment more closely resembles a real court session. During the enactment, serve as an adviser and a monitor. Your basic task is to keep the enactment on track.

Debriefing

You need to monitor time carefully so ample opportunity remains for this important component of the learning process. During debriefing, focus pupils' attention on issues raised, logic used, and processes implemented. Typically, you would lead a discussion in which you solicit observations and feelings of the different participants. Ask learners about what they have learned. Often, pupils are tempted to dwell only on the verdict. Although this is an important component of the experience, discussion of the verdict should not be allowed to overshadow significant learning about the general trial process.

Mock trials require a considerable amount of class time, often a full week. The need to commit such a substantial block of time is an important drawback to their use. Realistically, most teachers find that they can conduct a mock trial only once or twice during a school year. Those who use them find the commitment of time more than repaid in terms of pupil learning and excitement.

In addition to formal mock trials, there are numerous simulations that can be used to teach law-focused content. Simulation is a very useful approach for teaching processes and decision-making skills. A number of simulations have been developed that focus on topics such as juvenile hearings, constitutional conventions, mediating conflicts, and even serving as a police officer on patrol. Chapter 9, "Group Learning," provides guidelines for using simulations in the classroom.

Community Resources

In nearly every community there are people who can be invited to school to share their insights with learners involved in law-focused activities. Such resource people include those working for governmental law enforcement and corrections agencies—police departments; highway patrols; corrections institutions; city, county, and district attorneys' offices; and all levels of courts. Representatives from these agencies are often willing to come to a classroom to talk. Their visits add an important dimension of reality to the content of law-focused lessons.

Lesson Idea 3–6

WHAT ARE YOUR RIGHTS?

Grade Level:	5–6
Objectives:	Pupils can (1) define the term *warranty,* (2) state how a warranty protects a consumer, (3) and state what to do if they believe a right has been violated.
Overview:	Social studies lessons that pupils perceive to be related to their everyday concerns are more interesting to them. This les-

son acquaints pupils with some consumer law by using a situation likely to be of interest to them.

Procedure:

Learning Set Bring a few examples of warranties to class. Ask the pupils if they know what they are. Read the following situation to the class:

> *Maria's favorite activity was riding a bicycle. She often looked at the new bikes in the store and wished that she had one. She really liked the 10-speed mountain bikes. There were several children in her family, and she knew that her parents could not afford to buy her one. One day, after looking at a new bike, she decided that the only way she was going to get one was for her to try and save enough money.*
>
> *Maria started by asking neighbors if she could help them with work around their houses. She collected aluminum cans and took them to the recycling center.*
>
> *It took a long time, but, finally, Maria had enough money to buy a new mountain bike. She talked to her father about it, and he agreed that since she had worked and saved the money, she could buy a bike. They went to the store, where they had lots of new bicycles. Maria found a red 24-inch 10-speed bike that she could afford.*
>
> *Maria was so excited about her bike that she rode it all over the neighborhood. One day, after she had the bike for one week, she was riding it down the street when she hit a bump. When she hit the bump, the right pedal broke completely off! Maria was so upset! She didn't know what to do. He brother told her that she should take the bike back and make them give her a new one.*

Discuss the situation with the class. What do you think? Would her bike be covered by a warranty? How could she find out? Under what conditions might a warranty not take care of her bike? What could she do if the people at the store told her that they would not fix or replace her bike because she had mistreated the bike?

Some of the conditions of the warranties brought to class could be reviewed to help the class decide whether the bike was still covered by a warranty.

Closure:

Ask, "What did we learn today about warranties? What does this tell us about our rights as consumers? What do we need to do when we buy a new product?" Give the class a homework assignment to find some warranties on things their family might have at home and to bring them in so that they can be analyzed and used in other lessons.

Investigating the rights of consumers and how people can be protected from fraud is an important and meaningful topic in law-focused studies.

For example, the problems of law enforcement and the decisions a police officer must make take on added significance when an actual officer who comes to the classroom explains them. Bar associations and law schools are possible sources of attorneys who may be willing to come to the school. (There also may be an attorney who is a parent of a child in the class and who would like to talk to a group of elementary school learners.) Attorneys are in a position to share information related to a range of legal topics and often are willing to assist teachers interested in creating mock trials or simulations. Some may even be willing to help debrief learners after they have experienced a simulation on a law-focused topic.

Judges are also frequently willing to serve as guest speakers. Their comments can help learners understand difficulties judges face as they grapple with complex issues. They can also help pupils understand that judges face certain constraints as they do their work.

A field trip to view a court in session is often an enlightening experience for learners. In planning for a court visit, it is important that the teacher understand that not all courtrooms are open at all times to the public and that there are some cases that are not appropriate for young learners. Usually, court visits should be arranged through the court clerk. This person is able to help the teacher work out details for a visit.

There may be branches of the Better Business Bureau and the American Civil Liberties Union in the local community. The Better Business Bureau has information that may help you develop lessons focusing on consumer law and consumer fraud. The American Civil Liberties Union is particularly interested in civil rights cases.

Finally, the local newspaper should not be overlooked as a source. Newspapers provide material that can be used in constructing episodes, in using story line, or in creating case studies and mock trials.

WEB CHECK

Note: Electronic addresses of sites on the World Wide Web change frequently. If the listed URL fails to work, use a standard search engine to locate the new address of the site.

- Mock Trials for Students

  URL—**http://dev.abanet.org/publiced/mock.html**

  This site, maintained by the American Bar Association, includes descriptions and ordering information for a number of mock trials. These have been organized in terms of their suitability for learners in different age groups. For younger children, there are some excellent mock trial lessons built around traditional fairy tales.

- *National Standards for Civics and Government*

  URL—**http://www.civiced.org/stds.html**

  Users of the Web can view and download the complete *National Standards for Civics and Government* document at this site. It provides detailed curriculum standards that are organized in sections focusing respectively on grades K–4, 5–8 and 9–12.

- *Civitas: A Framework for Civic Education*

  URL—**http://www.civiced.org/civitasexec.html**

  This site provides an executive summary of *Civitas: A Framework for Civic Education.* This is a curriculum framework developed for the purpose of revitalizing civic education in the schools.

- Center for Civic Education

  URL—**http://www.civiced.org/index.html**

  This site is the home page for the Center for Civic Education, an organization devoted to the improvement of instruction related to democratic government practices. There are links here to curricular materials, articles, and other Internet resources on civics and government.

- National Institute for Citizens Education in the Law.

  URL—**http://www.indiana.edu/≈ssdc/nicel.html**

  Material at this site relates to the work of the National Institute for Citizen Education in the Law. This group provides a number of school-based programs, including mock trials.

- National Endowment for Democracy
  URL—**http://www.ned.org/**

  This is the home page of the National Endowment for Democracy. This group seeks to strengthen democratic institutions throughout the world.

KEY IDEAS IN SUMMARY

1. Political science content has long formed part of the elementary social studies curriculum. Current emphases of lessons on political science include material related to such concepts as power, authority, freedom, justice, and alternative political systems.

2. Lesson content related to *micropolitical* organization focuses on the role of the individual in the political system. Lesson content concerned with *macropolitical* organization considers how the political systems act to accommodate conflicting demands of different groups.

3. In recent years, much work has been done to identify content standards for school programs that draw content from political science. One of the organizations leading this effort has been the Center for Civic Education.

4. Law-focused programs seek to help pupils (1) identify the basic functions of law, (2) think critically about issues related to laws and our legal system, (3) develop problem-solving skills related to solving legal issues, (4) identify values that guide the development of laws and legal processes, (5) accept the rights and responsibility of citizenship, and (6) develop realistic and honest views of our legal system, including both its strengths and its weaknesses.

5. Case studies are an excellent instructional vehicle for teaching law-focused content. Many cases are available from commercial sources. Teachers also write cases of their own. Case studies sometimes are devised from important cases that have already been heard and decided by the courts. At other times, case studies are built around controversial issues about which formal court decisions have yet to be rendered. Cases selected for classroom study should focus on issues of enduring value. For elementary school learners, cases should not be excessively long. Sometimes a few paragraphs of information will suffice. Case studies typically introduce learners to important facts related to the case and to relevant legal issues. Following the enactment of the case, the teacher leads a debriefing discussion to clear up misunderstandings and to reinforce learning.

6. The mock trial is another instructional approach that teachers often find useful. Mock trials are simulations that feature enactments of trials. Mock trials involve preparation, enactment, and debriefing phases. A sequence is followed that to some degree parallels the flow of activity in an actual trial. Mock trials are time-intensive activities. Often a full week of instructional time is required. For this reason, many teachers find it practical to use mock trials only once or twice during a given school year.

CHAPTER REFLECTIONS

Directions: Now that you have read this chapter, reread the case study at the beginning. Then, answer these questions.

1. How would you now respond to the comments of the school administrator?
2. What is the role of political science in the development of citizenship?
3. Is it possible both to promote loyalty to our government and society and, at the same time, to focus on controversial topics about which there is little public agreement?
4. What do you think can be done to prevent problems from groups who may not want certain topics discussed?
5. Do you agree that pupils in the elementary grades are too immature to understand and deal with controversial topics?

EXTENDING UNDERSTANDING AND SKILL

1. Write a short paper (three to five pages) on *good citizenship.* How do you define *good citizenship*? How do individuals learn citizenship? What does this imply for what you will teach and how you will teach it?
2. Review several social studies textbooks written for a grade level that interests you. Identify topics in the book from which you could include content drawing heavily on the discipline of political science. Briefly state your ideas about what you might include.
3. Select four or five key political science concepts that were introduced in this chapter. Begin to build a resource file of pictures, cartoons, newspaper articles, case studies, artifacts, and charts that would be useful in teaching these concepts to elementary pupils.
4. The chapter identified a number of children's books that could be used to teach the social studies. Identify other books that could be used. Briefly give a summary of each book, identifying the social science concepts that could be taught using it.
5. Interview two or three elementary teachers who teach at a grade level that interests you. Ask them to comment on the extent of their use of law-focused lessons. Also, ask them about their views regarding the relative importance of such studies in the classroom.
6. Develop a case study related to criminal, consumer, or family law that could be used for teaching law-focused content to a group of pupils. Prepare a lesson plan that outlines how the case study will be taught.

7. Develop a plan for using a mock trial in the classroom. Identify the case to be discussed, the role profiles that will be needed, and the format that will be used in presenting and debriefing the mock trial. Share your mock trial ideas with others in the class. Keep ideas provided by others in a "mock trial teaching ideas" notebook.

REFERENCES

BARR, I., & MCGUIRE, M. (1993). Social studies and effective stories. *Social Studies and the Young Learner, 5* (3), 6–8.

CENTER FOR CIVIC EDUCATION (1997, October). *Call for international participation in developing education for democratic citizenship: A framework.* Calabasa, CA: Center for Civic Education. [**http://www.civiced.org/framework_intro.html**]

CENTER FOR CIVIC EDUCATION (1994). *National standards for civics and government.* Calabasa, CA: Center for Civic Education.

HICKEY, M. (1990). Mock trials for children. *Social Education, 54* (1), 43–44.

PATRICK, J., & HOGE, J. (1991). Teaching government, civics, and law. In J. Shaver (Ed.), *Handbook of research on social studies teaching and learning* (pp. 427–436). Englewood Cliffs, NJ: Merrill/Prentice Hall.

SORAUF, F. (1965). *Political science: An informal review.* Englewood Cliffs, NJ: Merrill/Prentice Hall.

WASSON, D. R. (1994). Real-life scenarios for teaching the Bill of Rights. *Social Education, 54* (3), 169–170.

chapter 4

Content Sources: Economics, Sociology, Anthropology, and Psychology

This chapter will help you to:

◆ identify the role of economics, sociology, anthropology, and psychology in the elementary social studies program.

◆ describe the unique perspectives of economics, sociology, anthropology, and psychology.

◆ describe recent grade-level content-standard recommendations of the National Council on Economic Education.

◆ identify selected concepts and generalizations from economics, sociology, anthropology, and psychology in the elementary social studies program, and

◆ develop social studies lessons that focus on content from economics, sociology, anthropology, and psychology.

**Human Behavior Studied
From the Perspective of . . .**

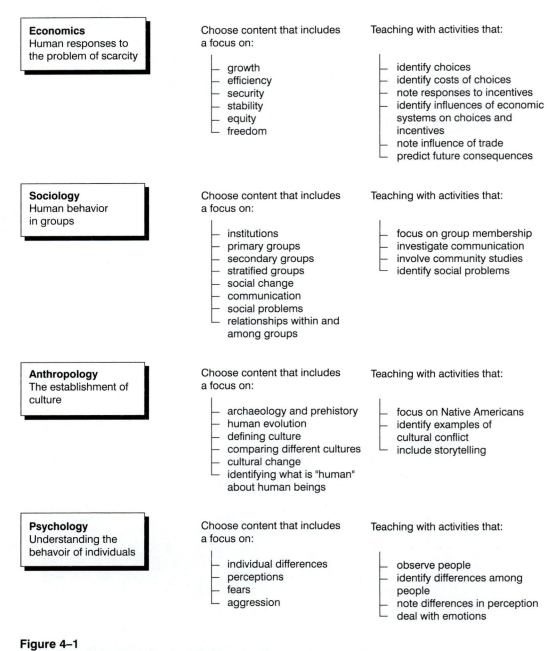

Economics
Human responses to
the problem of scarcity

Choose content that includes
a focus on:

- growth
- efficiency
- security
- stability
- equity
- freedom

Teaching with activities that:

- identify choices
- identify costs of choices
- note responses to incentives
- identify influences of economic
  systems on choices and
  incentives
- note influence of trade
- predict future consequences

Sociology
Human behavior
in groups

Choose content that includes
a focus on:

- institutions
- primary groups
- secondary groups
- stratified groups
- social change
- communication
- social problems
- relationships within and
  among groups

Teaching with activities that:

- focus on group membership
- investigate communication
- involve community studies
- identify social problems

Anthropology
The establishment of
culture

Choose content that includes
a focus on:

- archaeology and prehistory
- human evolution
- defining culture
- comparing different cultures
- cultural change
- identifying what is "human"
  about human beings

Teaching with activities that:

- focus on Native Americans
- identify examples of
  cultural conflict
- include storytelling

Psychology
Understanding the
behavoir of individuals

Choose content that includes
a focus on:

- individual differences
- perceptions
- fears
- aggression

Teaching with activities that:

- observe people
- identify differences among
  people
- note differences in perception
- deal with emotions

**Figure 4–1
Content from economics, sociology, anthropology, and psychology.**

Case Study

WHAT IS SOCIAL STUDIES?

Tamara Barnes was excited because she had been asked to be a member of a district committee that was going to make recommendations regarding the district social studies program. She felt that the current program lacked excitement and relevance, and she was looking forward to making a contribution.

At the first meeting Tamara noted that the committee included teachers, administrators, and parents. After some brief comments by the superintendent, the curriculum director took charge of the meeting. The first task on the agenda was to gather the perspectives of the committee regarding the social studies curriculum for the district. One of the parents was the first to make a statement.

"I am a concerned parent. I believe that social studies programs have been a dismal failure. Several surveys indicate that many of the students don't even know some of the important historical events or historical figures in our nation. I think the culprit is that we have had a watered down social studies curriculum. We have allowed too many soft, liberal topics to take time away from foundation subjects. It is time we reaffirmed that the social studies means history and geography. The elementary social studies is no place for concepts drawn from such subjects as sociology or psychology. Those subjects are weak academic subjects to begin with and include subversive topics such as how to 'get along' with each other and how to work in groups. They include foolish content on 'enhancing the self-concept.' These are topics that are contrary to the well known American virtues of individualism and self-sufficiency. I am going to fight to make sure that we have a 'back to basics' history and geography program starting in the primary grades. Those subjects will teach the values and provide the understanding that a good citizen must possess."

Tamara felt her enthusiasm begin to drain. Maybe this wasn't going to be as fun as she had imagined.

What Is Your Response?

Think about the comments of this parent. Then briefly respond to these questions.

1. To what extent do you agree or disagree with the statements of this parent?
2. Do you agree with the assumptions made about the nature of sociology and psychology and role of history in the social studies.
3. Do you agree that topics such as those mentioned should not be introduced in the elementary curriculum?
4. What are some topics from subjects such as sociology, psychology, and economics that should be included?
5. What statement would you make when it is your turn to speak?

INTRODUCTION

There are a number of social science disciplines that make important contributions to the social studies. Economics is one that has received considerable attention. It was identified in the Goals 2000: Educate America Act of 1994 as one of nine key subjects. As a result considerable resources are available to help teachers teach basic economic ideas and concepts at a variety of grade levels.

The other disciplines have received considerably less attention in recent years. However, they do offer some important perspectives and concepts. Although the content might not be labeled as *sociology, anthropology,* or *psychology,* a review of the curriculum and of social studies textbooks reveals that important aspects of these disciplines do form important segments of the social studies program.

ECONOMICS

Scarcity is the fundamental concern of economics. People's wants often exceed the resources needed to satisfy them. Hence, decisions must be made regarding how limited resources are to be allocated and which wants are to be satisfied. *Economics* is the study of approaches used in making decisions in response to the universal scarcity problem. As economic systems attempt to respond to the central issue of scarcity, they try to accommodate the important social goals of (1) economic growth, (2) economic efficiency, (3) security, (4) stability, (5) equity, and (6) freedom. Economics lessons help pupils understand that different economic systems have established different priorities. For example, some societies place more emphasis on the goal of economic security than on the goal of economic freedom.

Traditionally, many elementary economics lessons focused on consumer and personal economics. Consumer economics lessons focused on teaching pupils how to be alert, careful buyers. Personal economics focused on skills such as personal budgeting, management of savings accounts, and (for older learners) balancing checkbooks.

Today's more comprehensive economics programs go beyond consumer and personal economics. Increasingly, economics-oriented instruction attempts to provide pupils with a basic understanding of how the entire American economic system operates and how economic decisions affect everyday life.

Some economics content often can be included in lessons that draw most of their information from other subjects. For example, economic motivations of immigrants can be brought into history lessons focusing on movement of people from other lands to the United States. Lessons that describe decisions of particular kinds of businesses to locate in given places draw content from both geography and economics. Problems governments face in making laws that limit people's choices and that allocate tax revenues in certain ways are issues with relevance for both economics and political science. (See Table 4–1.)

Table 4–1
Recommended introductions of economics concepts by grade level.*

Economic Concepts	Kinder-garten	First	Second	Third	Fourth	Fifth	Sixth	Seventh	Eighth
Scarcity	new	review	review	review	review	review	review	review	review
Choice	new	review	review	review	review	review	review	review	review
Goods	new	review	review	review	review	review	review	review	review
Services	new	review	review	review	review	review	review	review	review
Opportunity cost	-	new	review	review	review	review	review	review	review
Resources	-	new	review	review	review	review	review	review	review
Natural resources	-	new	review	review	review	review	review	review	review
Human resources	-	new	review	review	review	review	review	review	review
Capital resources	-	new	review	review	review	review	review	review	review
Barter	-	new	review	review	review	review	review	review	review
Interdependence	-	-	new	review	review	review	review	review	review
Money	-	-	new	review	review	review	review	review	review
Producers and production	-	-	new	review	review	review	review	review	review
Consumers	-	-	new	review	review	review	review	review	review
Specialization	-	-	new	review	review	review	review	review	review
Division of labor	-	-	-	new	review	review	review	review	review
Productivity	-	-	-	new	review	review	review	review	review
Markets	-	-	-	new	review	review	review	review	review
Prices	-	-	-	new	review	review	review	review	review
Public goods	-	-	-	new	review	review	review	review	review
Economic systems	-	-	-	-	new	review	review	review	review
Market economy	-	-	-	-	new	review	review	review	review

(continued)

Table 4–1
Continued

Economic Concepts	Kinder-garten	First	Second	Third	Fourth	Fifth	Sixth	Seventh	Eighth
Circular flow	-	-	-	-	new	review	review	review	review
Trade/exchange	-	-	-	-	new	review	review	review	review
Factors of production	-	-	-	-	-	new	review	review	review
Investment in capital resources	-	-	-	-	-	new	review	review	review
Investment in human resources	-	-	-	-	-	new	review	review	review
Trade-offs	-	-	-	-	-	new	review	review	review
Demand	-	-	-	-	-	new	review	review	review
Supply	-	-	-	-	-	new	review	review	review
Equilibrium price	-	-	-	-	-	new	review	review	review
Competition	-	-	-	-	-	-	new	review	review
Cost of production	-	-	-	-	-	-	new	review	review
Profit	-	-	-	-	-	-	new	review	review
Entrepreneurs	-	-	-	-	-	-	new	review	review
Incentives	-	-	-	-	-	-	new	review	review
Taxes	-	-	-	-	-	-	new	review	review
Income tax	-	-	-	-	-	-	new	review	review
Property tax	-	-	-	-	-	-	new	review	review
Sales tax	-	-	-	-	-	-	new	review	review
Unemployment	-	-	-	-	-	-	new	review	review
Shortages	-	-	-	-	-	-	new	review	review
Surpluses	-	-	-	-	-	-	new	review	review

*Created by the Center for Economic Education, University of Nebraska at Omaha, on-line: <**http://ecedweb.unomaha. edu/eleconpt.htm**>. Based on guidelines from the National Council for Economic Education. Reprinted with permission.

The impact of innovation on the production of goods and services is one of the major emphases in economics.

Interest in promoting economic understanding among schoolchildren has intensified in recent years. The National Council on Economic Education, founded in 1949, today includes a national network of state councils and more than 260 university-based economics-education centers. This network, called *EconomicsAmerica,* provides services including teacher training, development of curriculum materials for schools, and assessment information for educators interested in economics. Suggestions for organizing elementary-level programs are included in many of its publications. We particularly like *Economics: What and When—Scope and Sequence Guidelines, K–12* (Guilliard et al., 1988) and *Voluntary National Content Standards in Economics* (EconomicsAmerica, 1997). For information, write to the National Council on Economic Education, 1140 Avenue of the Americas, New York, NY 10036. (See Figure 4–2.)

Economics-Related Classroom Activities

Some people see economics as an abstract subject of interest only to those who can generate enthusiasm for working with complex graphs and mathematical formulas. This is not true. Perspectives of economics have great practical value. Further, basic content can be taught in ways that interest pupils. Doubters should take a look at Wentworth and Schug's (1994) excellent article in *Social Education* article, "How to Use an Economic Mystery in Your History Course." In this article, the two authors introduce a *Handy*

Students will understand that:
Competition among sellers lowers costs and prices, and encourages producers to produce more of what consumers are willing and able to buy. Competition among buyers increases prices and allocates goods and services to those people who are willing and able to pay the most for them.

Students will be able to use this knowledge to:
Explain how changes in the level of competition in different markets can affect price and output levels.

BENCHMARKS

*At the completion of **Grade 4,** students will know that:*

1. Competition takes place when there are many buyers and sellers of similar products.
2. Competition among sellers results in lower costs and prices, higher product quality, and better customer service.

   *At the completion of **Grade 4,** students will use this knowledge to:*

   1. Identify competitors in their community, using the yellow pages of the telephone book.
   2. Explain how the opening of a second pizza shop in a small community affects prices, profits, service, and quality.

*At the completion of **Grade 8,** students will know the Grade 4 benchmarks for this standard and also that:*

1. Sellers compete on the basis of price, product quality, customer service, product design and variety, and advertising.
2. Competition among buyers of a product results in higher product prices.
3. The level of competition in a market is influenced by the number of buyers and sellers.

   *At the completion of **Grade 8,** students will use this knowledge to:*

   1. Give examples of price and nonprice competition in the athletic shoe market.
   2. Play several rounds of a market game in which the number of buyers is changed dramatically in each round, and explain the impact of these changes on price.
   3. Estimate the number of producers and consumers of cereals, guided missiles, agricultural products, and electricity, and generalize about the relationship between the number of producers and consumers and the level of competition.

Note: From *Voluntary National Content Standards in Economics* (pp. 17–19), by EconomicsAmerica, 1997, New York: National Council on Economic Education. Copyright © 1997 by the National Council on Economic Education. Reprinted with permission.

Figure 4–2
An example of an economics content standard.

Dandy Guide you can use to help pupils think and reason from an economics perspective. Content is based on an assumption that guides the work of professional economists, namely, "Human behavior results from choices people make based on expected costs and expected benefits." This assumption led Wentworth and Schug (1994) to develop six important related corollary statements:

- People choose.
- People's choices involve costs.
- People respond to incentives in predictable ways.
- People create economic systems that influence individual choices and incentives.
- People gain when they trade voluntarily.
- People's choices have consequences that lie in the future.

People Choose

This statement is based on the assumption that actions of individuals are rational. People make choices by considering alternatives and deciding how to use their scarce resources. The better people understand the alternatives open to them, the better their choices will be. This idea can easily be incorporated into elementary social studies lessons. For example, you may give pupils some imaginary money to spend, then have them decide how to spend it. They must think about their options. Their choices are likely to be better as they learn more about each option and as the number of options they know about increases. From this, it is a short step to discussing the idea that many things are scarce other than money. For example, recess time is a scarce resource: Only a limited amount of time is available. Children must think about how they will spend it. A discussion of this issue with a group of young children can provide them with important insights into the human need to choose and allocate scarce resources wisely. Older learners may apply their understanding of positives and negatives associated with individual decisions to content from other kinds of lessons. For example, you might discuss the choices that were available to people who, in the end, decided to move to a new community, a new country, or a new continent.

People's Choices Involve Costs

Choices involve costs. People choose things that appear likely to provide them with more benefits than would the alternatives. This idea can be incorporated into many kinds of elementary social studies lessons. For example, you might ask pupils to reflect on the costs borne by people in the United States during the previous two centuries who decided to move west. In addition to monetary costs, these people paid other prices. They gave up opportunities to visit old friends and relatives. They lost the comfortable familiarity of the terrain they had known for much of their lives. They gave up the relative safety of a well-developed society for the dangers of a rough-and-ready frontier. Why did they accept these costs? A discussion of this issue with learners might lead to several conclusions, including the possibility of riches from new lands, new opportunities for their children, and the ability to participate in setting up new governments in the new western lands.

People Respond to Incentives in Predictable Ways

Incentives encourage people to make a particular choice when they are confronted with alternatives. For example, in elementary schools the incentive of more recess time may encourage pupils to finish assigned tasks rather than talk to their neighbors. Changes in incentives often cause individuals to change the choices they make. If new incentives are attached to a particular option, it is more likely to be selected. Similarly, when incentives associated with an alternative diminish, the likelihood decreases that that option will be chosen.

Pupils can be introduced to the idea of incentives through role-playing activities that require them to make choices. For example, youngsters might act out roles in a situation the teacher explains in the following way:

> All right, I want two people to play roles. This is going to be a situation involving two friends. One person wants to play a game that requires the other person as a player. The other person would rather watch a TV program. The student who wants to play the game must try to make the friend want to play the game and give up the idea of watching television. Let's try to make this as real as we can. Do I have two volunteers?

After pupils have finished role playing this situation, the teacher can engage the class in a discussion on the incentives offered to encourage the person who wanted to watch television to play the game. Learners probably will suggest some incentives that didn't occur to the pupil who was the friend who wanted to play. The discussion might focus on *disincentives,* things designed to discourage the person from wanting to watch the television program. For example, the person who wanted to play the game might have suggested that the program was going to be a rerun that the other child had already seen. As part of the discussion, the teacher might point out the variety of incentives that are used to get people to do things. Coupons printed in newspapers are designed as incentives to encourage people to shop at certain stores. Advertisements regularly try to encourage a belief that their products will give more satisfaction or pleasure than those of competitors. To the extent individuals believe these claims, advertisements provide incentives for consumers to buy.

People Create Economic Systems That Influence Individual Choices and Incentives

This statement speaks to the relationship between the issue of economic freedom and the role of government. To help pupils begin to grasp the complex nature of the relationship between the twin ideas of economic freedom and economic justice, prompt questions such as these might be used to spark a discussion:

- Do you believe people should be completely free to make any choices they want to?
- What if someone exercises his or her freedom and makes a choice that hurts you? Is this right?
- What should be done about the problem of some people making choices that might hurt others?

These questions can lead pupils to an appreciation that even in market economies that place a high priority on giving economic decision-making authority to individuals, there is a need to place limitations on economic freedom in the name of fairness and justice. Much governmental policy is directed toward this end. The idea is that the government allows the maximum possible amount of economic freedom while making sure that individual rights and freedoms are protected. For example, regulations place restrictions on where industries can dump certain waste materials. These rules are designed to prevent pollution and protect the health of the general population. Even elementary pupils need to begin to understand that there is controversy regarding how much economic freedom is needed and how much government control is required. They will be thinking about and debating this general issue all their lives.

Lesson Idea 4–1

MAKING CHOICES

Grade Level:	Primary
Objectives:	Learners can (1) identify choices they have to make, and (2) explain how choosing one thing eliminates another that could have been chosen.
Overview:	Scarcity requires people everywhere to make many choices. The choices that people make in their everyday life reflect expected benefits and costs. One of the costs is that when one makes a choice, the possibility of having something else is eliminated. By focusing on the choices that they make in everyday life, young pupils can begin to appreciate this economic idea.
Procedure:	***Learning Set*** Ask pupils what they like about events such as Christmas or their birthday. After discussing several things they like, focus on receiving gifts. Tell them that deciding what gifts to request involves making choices because people can't buy everything we might want.
	Presentation Tell the class, "I would like you to pretend that I am going to get you a gift for one of those special occasions. I would like you to draw me a picture of five things you want." Collect the pictures when they are finished drawing.
	Select one student's picture. Tell the class that the items in the picture are all good things; however, you don't have enough money to buy them all. The price of each item is $2 and you only have $4. Ask the pupil who drew the picture to tell you which two things you should choose. Ask the student why he or she chose those items. Make sure to discuss what the pupil is choosing to give up by not making the other choices. Help the class see that the student is making choices based on expected benefits assumed to be more important than what is being given up.

Repeat the process with a couple of other pupils. Then discuss the following questions:

- Why couldn't we get everything?
- How do you decide what things you really want?
- How do you feel when you have to choose?
- Do you think people are able to get all the things they want? (This can lead to a discussion of how human wants expand more rapidly than the resources needed to satisfy them.)

Closure: Conclude the lesson by asking, "What did we learn about people's wants? Because people have many desires, what do they have to do? What do you need to think about when making choices?"

Pupils relate easily to the need for rules limiting choices. When they play games, they learn to follow rules that place restrictions on what they can do. Discussions of simple rules, such as "three strikes and you're out" in baseball, can lead students to consider governmental actions to limit choices for the purpose of promoting fairness. Role-playing exercises often work well to expand pupils' understanding of this issue. For example, you might try this idea. Set up a situation where you make every rule without allowing learners to express their wishes or make decisions, such as the oldest or all the boys or all the girls being allowed to make decisions for the entire class.

People Gain When They Trade Voluntarily
Because people are not self-sufficient, they need to trade. We do not make all of our clothes or grow all of our own food. People who are allowed to trade things they have in surplus for things they lack increase their ability to satisfy their needs. Many pupils have an intuitive grasp of this idea. They frequently trade things such as lunch items and baseball cards.

Simple activities can be used even in the primary grades to reinforce the idea that trade provides benefits to people. For example, two pupils might be asked to come to front of the class. One can be given bread, and one can be given lunchmeat. As everyone in the class will see, without trade one has only bread to eat and the other has only meat. However, if they trade, both can make sandwiches. Older pupils can investigate how communities, states, and regions trade things they have for things they want and need. All of this leads logically to such ideas as the interdependence of people and regions, the importance of transportation, and the function of money.

People's Choices Have Consequences That Lie in the Future
The choices people make do not have perfectly predictable consequences. People try to make decisions in ways that will provide them with benefits that outweigh the costs. Sometimes they are right; sometimes they are wrong. It is always possible that, even when people choose carefully, unforeseen circumstances may lead to unanticipated consequences. Elementary school children need to learn that they cannot simply go to a book

Understanding what is produced in different parts of the world leads to an understanding of the need for trade.

to find out how they should make a difficult choice. However, they also need to understand that good thinking about choices can help reduce the probability of making an unwise decision.

To help pupils think about what goes into making smart decisions, you can initiate a discussion on examples in learners' lives when their decisions have not worked out as expected. For example, they may have chosen to play outside only to find that rain cut their games short. Or, they may have purchased a new game and found some pieces were missing when they arrived home and opened the package. These personal examples provide a link to the more general understanding that unanticipated events are a constant of life. Many examples from the social studies illustrate this point. For example, founders of new communities in thousands of locations across the American West were convinced that their towns would blossom into huge metropolises. Despite these high hopes, few of these places became thriving cities; many disappeared entirely after a few years.

You will have many opportunities to introduce content from economics into social studies lessons. Because issues associated with economics are so intimately associated with decisions people must make throughout their lives, it is important to give pupils opportunities to experience economic reasoning in the elementary social studies program. (See Figure 4–3.)

The following are examples of central questions, concepts, and generalizations that are important when studying economics.

CENTRAL QUESTIONS (A SELECTION)

- How have different societies coped with the problem of scarcity?
- How do innovation and change influence the wants and needs of people?
- How can resources be allocated responsibly and fairly?
- What is the proper role of government in limiting the economic choices of people?
- Does the economic system provide for an equality of opportunity?
- Is the economic system stable over time, or is it characterized by periods of uneven growth?
- What are the possible consequences of alternative economic choices?
- What is the overall quality of life provided by the economic system?

CONCEPTS (A SELECTION)

Scarcity, resources, costs, benefits, opportunity costs, private property, public property, land, labor capital, specialization, division of labor, trade, supply, demand, producer, consumer, price, competition, incentives, goods, market, traditional economy, command economy, market economy, money

GENERALIZATIONS (A SELECTION)

- The wants of people are unlimited whereas the resources to meet those wants are scarce; hence, individuals and societies must make decisions as to which wants will be satisfied.
- Scarce resources are allocated to meet needs according to the values of those making the decisions.
- When individuals choose to allocate scarce resources to meet one need, they give up the opportunity to meet other needs.
- Unequal distribution of resources and population makes trade a necessary ingredient of economic well-being.
- Specialization and division of labor promote the efficiency of an economic system.
- The economic development of a nation is related to the availability of resources and capital, and to the quality of the labor force.
- The government plays an important role in the economic development of every society, but that role varies from place to place.

Figure 4–3
Central questions, concepts, and generalizations associated with economics.

Lesson Idea 4–2

ECONOMIC INCENTIVES

Grade Level:	3–4
Objectives:	The learners can (1) identify example of incentives used to influence people's behavior and (2) apply the idea of incentives to understanding the behavior of people in the past.
Overview:	Incentives are those things that are used to influence human behavior. Understanding the role of incentives in making choices

helps individuals understand the choices people made in the past. Incentives are commonly used in everyday life. Beginning with examples that pupils meet every day and then applying this lesson to historical events facilitates students' understanding of the past.

Procedure:

Learning Set   Begin by asking pupils if they would be willing to perform an undesirable task. Then ask them if they would perform the task if they received something they desired. Tell them that this is an example of an incentive, and that incentives are frequently used to get people to make choices they might not otherwise make.

Presentation   Divide the class into small groups and give each group a newspaper. Tell them you want them to go through the paper (especially the advertisements) and see how many examples of incentives they can find. Have them cut out the examples and paste them on a chart labeled *Incentives.* Each group can then share its chart with the class.

Tell pupils that incentives can be anything that a person thinks will be beneficial. For example, the people who settled our community or our state had some incentives that led them to think their life would be better if they settled here rather than at other places. Ask pupils what the incentives might have been for people to settle in our community or state. List these on the board and then tell them that in the next few days the class will do some research to see if their ideas about incentives are correct.

Closure:

Ask class members to define incentives. See if someone can provide an example of an incentive. Have some pupils state how they are going to use their knowledge of incentives in their study of the local community or state.

SOCIOLOGY

Sociology is a social science that has received scant attention in the elementary social studies curriculum. This is regrettable. Adults must confront pressures of all kinds that result from actions taken by formal and informal groups. Content from sociology provides pupils with insights into very important group processes. Citizens today are also confronted with a daunting array of social problems. How should we respond to youth gangs? What is to be done about the crime problem? What are the implications of the changing structure of the American family? Individuals familiar with important concepts and generalizations from sociology have special tools that can help them analyze and make rational choices among action alternatives related to these questions.

People everywhere live in groups. Further, each person belongs to several different groups beginning with the family and including social organizations, ethnic groups, political parties, and religious affiliations. Sociologists study groups; why they are formed, how they are organized, how they influence the behavior and the values of their group members, and why they fall apart. They investigate the formation of norms and values, how these are passed on from one generation to the next, and how they change over time. Sociologists have helped us understand that social behavior is complex. Their research has taught us that there are multiple causes and effects of social behavior. Changes in one area, such as the role of women in the workplace, have widespread effects because all institutions in a society are interrelated, and a change in one will result in changes in others.

An important concept in sociology is *socialization,* or how individuals learn what is right and wrong. Closely related to the concept of socialization is that of *role,* or how individuals learn their place in society and what is expected of them. A current issue related to the concept of role is that of gender bias and how males and females are influenced to accept a role based solely on gender.

We have numerous opportunities to incorporate perspectives from sociology into our elementary social studies lessons; some content has long been included. For example, primary-grade youngsters typically spend a great deal of time studying families. They may investigate roles and relationships between family members and examine family structures in other cultures. The study of groups is extended in subsequent elementary grades when pupils begin investigating their local community and how its residents live and work together. In the upper grades, pupils can deal with more sophisticated issues, including how group membership influences public opinion and why it is easier to have influence through groups than through individual action.

Figure 4–4 presents questions, concepts, and generalizations associated with sociology. These are useful when preparing lessons that draw content from this social science discipline.

Sociology-Related Classroom Activities

Sociology deals with our society and with many current issues. Hence, content from sociology has high potential as an information source for lessons pupils will find interesting and relevant. The following are ideas for including sociological content in the curriculum.

Group Membership

Pupils are members of a number of different groups. Understanding group membership and the impact of the group on the individual can be the focus of lessons, beginning in the primary grades. Class members can list the various groups to which they belong. This might include the family, religious groups, sports teams, classroom groups, and neighborhood play groups. A discussion of why people belong to different groups can follow.

In later grades pupils can begin to distinguish between primary and secondary groups by classifying the groups to which they belong as either one or the other. They should also begin investigating what they learn from different groups. Of special importance here would be discussing groups such as gangs that might teach unacceptable or antisocial behaviors and attitudes. The problems that arise when groups teach competing values, for example, the differences in values between a gang and the school or family, make an interesting focus for lessons. Pupils can also discuss the consequences of membership in a group that advocates unacceptable behavior.

The following are examples of central questions, concepts, and generalizations that are important in studying sociology.

CENTRAL QUESTIONS (A SELECTION)

- What are the influential social institutions in society?
- What happens when groups disagree with each other?
- How do societies teach individuals what is appropriate and inappropriate?
- How is disapproval for inappropriate behavior given?
- How are family relationships different today than in the past?
- How are family relationships similar or different in other cultures?
- How do the mass media influence public opinion?
- What forces facilitate societal change, and what forces hinder it?
- What are the various status, class, and power levels in society?
- What indications are there of prejudice and discrimination in society?

CONCEPTS (A SELECTION)

Socialization, roles, norms, values, sanctions, conflict, prejudice, racism, discrimination, customs, traditions, beliefs, social institutions, social stratification, social class, status, primary group, secondary group, ethnic group, cooperation, assimilation, immigration, competition, collective behavior

GENERALIZATIONS (A SELECTION)

- The family is the basic social unit in most societies and the source of most fundamental learning.
- Social classes have existed in every society, although the basis of class distinction has varied.
- Every society develops a system of roles, norms, values, and sanctions that guides the behavior of its members.
- The roles that a given individual plays often clash; this leads to role conflict.
- Societies must develop ways of solving conflict without violence or they may disintegrate.
- People behave differently in groups than they do individually.
- Primary groups play an important role in socializing individuals by communicating values and expectations.
- Status and prestige are related to the values held by primary social groups; behavior that is rewarded in one group may be discouraged in another.

Figure 4–4
Central questions, concepts, and generalizations associated with sociology.

The study of religious groups has received increased attention in recent years. Some individuals are calling for more attention in the social studies curriculum to the role of religion. Religion has been an important element in all societies, and any study of humans would be incomplete without addressing the religious dimension. Students can investigate the different types of religions in the local community and identify the part they play

The values, beliefs, and religious convictions of different people are a part of learning sociology.

in influencing attitudes and behaviors of people. In many communities, religious organizations spend considerable time and resources volunteering and addressing social problems. These topics are important additions to the social studies curriculum.

Investigating Communication

The impact of communication on the values and beliefs of people is an important dimension of learning. Citizenship education requires that individuals have what might be called "media literacy." Individuals must learn how to identify and analyze the messages sent by television, newspapers, movies, and radio just as they learn how to read and analyze messages in literature. The impact of mass communication on the attitudes and actions of people is especially important.

For example, recent media attention created the impression of an out-of-control crime wave in the United States, whereas statistics revealed that the crime rate actually decreased. The result of the impression caused by the media was to make people suspicious of one another and afraid to leave their homes or to participate in civic functions. These behaviors resulted because of perceptions (e.g., the impressions received from the inaccurate media accounts) rather than the reality (the actual statistics on the incidence of reported crime). We need to help pupils understand that communication can influence their behavior and that they need to know how to check the accuracy of what they hear.

The newspaper is an excellent source for lessons on issues associated with accuracy of communication (and for many other sociology-oriented topics, as well). Many newspapers have a program for schools that delivers newspapers to the classroom for a specified time. Pupils can review the paper, looking for articles that focus on the behavior of people in groups, what is acceptable and unacceptable behavior, social problems, and conflict between groups on the local as well as the international scene. Pupils enjoy using the newspaper as a text because the material is current, and they recognize the newspaper as something that is a part of the real world.

Another interesting unit can be developed on the impact of television or movies. Television viewing guides can be developed to help pupils look for specific items as they watch programs. You might have pupils focus on how conflicts arise, the types of conflicts portrayed, and how they are resolved. Older pupils can identify the messages being sent and how these are likely to affect viewers. Another appropriate focus might be advertisement and the logic used to influence behavior. In preparation for these experiences, you can introduce pupils to different forms of persuasion and propaganda. They can look for examples as they view television programs and commercials, and report their findings back to the whole class.

A useful technique for studying communication is *content analysis.* To teach this technique, begin by asking members of the class to identify an idea or an attitude they are interested in researching. Then assign them to count the number of instances that certain words, ideas, or attitudes are used in the media. For example, if pupils are interested in gender roles, they might count the number of times women are portrayed as professionals in television programs. Another example might be to simply count the number of stories included in the local newspaper about various topics such as crime, education, poverty, or politics. Comparing these numbers can lead to a discussion of the image one might get of the local community by reading the newspaper.

Community Studies

Community studies have long been an interest of sociologists. Because much of the primary-grade social studies curriculum emphasizes the local community, this forms a natural bridge for including sociological concepts. On the basis of personal experiences, young children can begin to study their local community by identifying different groups in the community. These might be ethnic groups, religious groups, business organizations, recreational groups, and social groups. Ask your pupils, "Why do you think people join groups?" They can discuss how it feels when a person goes to a new place and does not belong to any groups. They can then discuss the need for different groups in the community to learn to work together and accept the differences that exist among them. In the upper grades, pupils can investigate the groups found in a community and the ways group members try to resolve conflicts between groups. They can investigate this issue as they study the past or as they look at communities in other parts of the world. The newspaper can be useful for identifying different groups in the community. Many newspapers produce a local "calendar of events" that mention activities of a large number of community groups and organizations.

Identifying Social Problems

Social problems are a typical course of study in the social studies curriculum. Problems that might serve as the focus of study are crime and delinquency, racism and prejudice, poverty, homelessness, war, drug and alcohol abuse, and divorce. These are issues that intrude on the life of a large number of pupils. While some of these issues, such as drug and alcohol abuse, might be discussed in the health curriculum, the social dimensions of these issues are at least as important as the health dimension.

Lesson Idea 4–3

LEARNING ROLES

Grade Level:	1–3
Objectives:	Pupils can (1) list the similarities and differences in the roles of men and women, and (2) state where people learn their roles.
Overview:	All individuals in society learn roles. Youngsters sometimes think that the roles they have learned are the natural or right roles. When they encounter individuals who have a different understanding of roles, conflict can occur. This is an important concept to understand in current society as gender roles are being challenged. In addition, many youngsters from other cultures have a different understanding of the roles of men and women. This activity can provide the teacher with insight as well as serve as a useful lesson for pupils.
Procedure:	Provide the pupils with the following homework assignment the night before you are going to do the activity in class: Tell them you would like them to get their parents' permission to look through magazines at home and cut out pictures of men and women performing different tasks.

Learning Set   Allow a few pupils to share some of the pictures they gathered. Then collect all the pictures. Tell them that the class is going to put the pictures together in groups.

Presentation   Separate the pictures of men and women. Place pictures into different groups. These will be groups of men performing tasks and groups of women performing tasks. Ask the class what pictures of women could be grouped together and why. Then repeat for men. Allow the class to identify their own criteria for grouping the pictures. On the chalkboard, have a section labeled *women* and one labeled *men.* When all the pictures of women performing tasks have been grouped, ask the class for a label for each group, and write these labels on the chalkboard. Repeat the procedure for men. When the lists are complete, compare the two lists. What are the similarities and differences between the two lists? Why do you think there are differences? Where do people learn about what is appropriate for men and women to do? How are these ideas changing?

Closure: Use the following questions to review with the class: "What did we do today? What did you learn about how to group things? What did you learn about the kinds of tasks men and women do? As a final task, for each group, paste the pictures that go together on a large piece of butcher paper and write the label of the group at the top.

Homelessness is a relatively new concern and has not been addressed by most schools. Pupils in many communities see homeless individuals daily. They have questions about these people: "Who are they? Why are they homeless? Should I be afraid of them?" Homeless pupils are present in many classrooms. These pupils often feel different, excluded, and embarrassed because they do not have a home. Discussions on the many causes of homelessness, the problems that homeless people face, and possible solutions can lead to interesting lessons because homelessness is a current topic of concern for many pupils.

When you include current issues and social problems in the classroom, emphasize social action. Taking action based on personally held beliefs is one of the most important outcomes of social studies programs. Through social action pupils learn that their involvement can make a difference and that social studies is an important and relevant subject. In addition, pupils become highly motivated and get much personal gratification from seeing that their efforts make a difference.

In summary, although there has not been much attention on the sociological dimension of social studies, there are many natural bridges between the elementary social studies curriculum and sociological concepts. Social studies lessons should take advantage of the experiences and interests of pupils. Sociological content, perhaps more than that drawn from other disciplines, is well suited to do this. Lessons focusing on sociology allow us to address current issues that are interesting to pupils and have potential to help young people better understand the nature of their membership in the total human community.

Lesson Idea 4–4

IDENTIFYING ISSUES IN THE NEWSPAPER

Grade Level: 3–5

Objectives: Pupils can identify instances of group conflict and conflict resolution.

Overview: It is important for pupils to learn that group conflict needs to be resolved without resorting to violence. They can begin by identifying examples in the newspaper of group conflict and various forms of conflict resolution . They can then apply their understanding to the resolution of conflicts they experience.

Procedure: *Learning Set* Ask the pupils to describe examples of conflict between groups at school. These might be conflicts over the use of playground equipment or participation in activities in the classroom. State to the class that solving disagreements between groups is something they will have to deal with all of their lives. State that for the next few days the class is going to look for examples of conflict using the newspaper.

Presentation   Divide the class into groups. Provide each group with a large chart divided in the following manner:

Examples of Conflicts	How Conflicts Were Handled	Consequences

Each group is to look through the paper and find articles describing a conflict between groups. These might include disagreements between groups in the community that go to the city council as well as international disagreements between countries or groups. They are to cut out each article and paste it in the first column. They should then briefly identify how the conflict was handled. In some cases it may involve a compromise or a vote; others could involve fighting or even war.

Pupils can then identify or speculate on the consequences of the attempt to resolve the conflict. When all groups have finished, post the charts in front of the room. Each group presents its chart. When this is completed, lead a discussion on the different types of conflict resolution that were discovered and the consequences of each type. Ask each group, "How can we use this information to help us decide how to solve problems between groups?"

Closure:

Ask class members to share at least one thing they learned from the lesson. They can then be asked to watch television that night and identify at least one other example of a conflict and how it was resolved, using either a news broadcast or one of their favorite programs. When reviewing, ask the class, "What does television seem to be saying about how we resolve conflict?"

Lesson Idea 4–5

BENEFITS OF COOPERATION

Grade Level:

4–6

Objective:

Pupils can state at least one benefit from working cooperatively on a problem.

Overview:

Cooperative learning has become an important approach to learning. Cooperation is essential in working in groups to solve problems. This exercise is designed to get pupils thinking about the benefits of cooperation. The basic design is for the teacher to identify two relatively similar problems. The pupils attempt to identify possible solutions to one problem individually and to the second problem in groups. They then compare the outcomes and feelings associated with each approach. There are usually more solutions generated, more comprehensive solutions, and more satisfaction associated with the cooperative approach.

Procedure:

Learning Set   Tell the class of a time when you faced a problem all alone and had trouble coming up with a solution. Ask the pupils to share similar incidents. Tell them you are going to do an experiment on solving problems.

Step 1   Pose the following problem to the class: You are a member of an army in the days of knights in armor. You and your fellow knights have ridden far ahead of the other troops. You discover another group of knights preparing to attack, so you must get a message back to your troops. You are selected to deliver the message and you ride off. After hours of riding, you find the headquarters of your army. However, there is a big problem. The army has made its camp on the other side of a river that is too wide and too deep for your horse to swim across. It is too noisy for anyone to hear you if you shout. How are you going to get your message across the river? Tell the class, "I'm going to give you five minutes to write down every idea that you have. Write as quickly as possible until you hear me say 'Stop!' "

Step 2   After five minutes, share everyone's solutions. Tally the number of different solutions identified by the members of the class. Ask pupils how they felt while trying to solve the problem.

Step 3   Pose a second problem to the class: You are all on a field trip together on a school bus. You are on a mountain road. Coming around a corner, the bus skids into a ditch and is stuck. You need to get a tow truck. Some children discover that through a break in the trees they can see a service station with a tow truck way off at the bottom of the mountain. It is too steep and too far to climb down the mountain to get help. How will you get a message to the people at the station? This time, have everyone share ideas, thinking as a group. Take five minutes to find solutions. Listen carefully to the ideas of others and then tell them what you think. After five minutes, stop the discussion.

Step 4   Compare the solutions for the first and second problems. Ask, "Which problem generated more solutions? Which generated better solutions? How did you feel working alone and working with the whole class? What do you think this experiment

Closure:

shows? Can you think of other, similar experiments we could do that involve the actions of people in groups?"

Review with the class what was done. Ask, "What was one thing we learned today? How might we use what we learned?"

ANTHROPOLOGY

Anthropology is the study of the history of human culture. It examines the various ways in which people interpret and assign meaning to their social and physical world. Lessons in anthropology help pupils understand that the members of each culture tend to be *ethnocentric*. That is, they tend to believe that their own culture and interpretation of the world around them are the most natural and logical ones.

Anthropology shares many concepts with sociology but tends to focus more on the comparison of different cultures. Some anthropological studies focus on exotic and different cultures and therefore lead individuals to erroneously conclude that anthropology is the study of "funny people and strange lands."

As is the case with sociology, little emphasis has been placed on anthropology content in the social studies curriculum. This does not mean, however, that no content related to anthropology is being taught. Some topics associated with this discipline have long been a part of the elementary social studies curriculum. Units with such titles as "Native Americans," "people of other lands," and "early civilizations" all have roots in anthropology. Current interest in ethnic studies and multicultural education provides opportunities to include even more anthropological content.

The various ways people have sought meaning and interpreted their physical world are included in anthropology.

The following are examples of central questions, concepts, and generalizations that are important when studying anthropology.

CENTRAL QUESTIONS (A SELECTION)

- What is uniquely *human* about humans that sets them off from other species?
- How did humans get these qualities?
- What elements do different cultures seem to have in common?
- How do changes in one part of a culture influence the other parts?
- What are the values and beliefs of this culture, and how are they interconnected?
- What does the language tell us about the culture?
- How do individuals achieve adult status in the culture?
- How does the culture adapt to change?
- How are wealth, status, and power determined in the culture?
- How are the values, beliefs, and traditions passed from one generation to the next?

CONCEPTS (A SELECTION)

Culture, cultural change, cultural borrowing, cultural lag, adaptation, diffusion, cultural disintegration, ritual, religion, tradition, race, ethnocentrism, nuclear family, extended family, innate behavior, learned behavior, technology, invention

GENERALIZATIONS (A SELECTION)

- Every society has a set of interconnected beliefs, values, and knowledge called *culture* that influences its life.
- People around the world have responded to common needs and concerns in unique ways, thus creating different cultural systems.
- Individual groups of people believe their cultural system is the most natural and logical way to view the world and their relationship to it.
- Increased contact between cultures results in cultural change.
- The art, music, architecture, food, clothing, and customs of people produce a cultural identity and reveal the values of the culture.

Figure 4–5
Central questions, concepts, and generalizations associated with anthropology.

When taught from an anthropological prospective, these and similar topics provide pupils with significant insight about what it means to be human. Lessons based on anthropology help them to develop an appreciation for the rich diversity of cultures and people. Figure 4–5 presents central questions, concepts, and generalizations around which you may build lessons on anthropology.

Anthropology-Related Classroom Activities

In developing activities for use in the classroom, it is important to foster respect for other cultures. We should not exaggerate unfamiliar customs; pupils should not feel that they are studying funny people. When possible, the interrelationship between cultural elements should be presented so that pupils do not get a distorted view of a culture. Care needs to be taken to make sure that lessons get beyond stereotypes of people or groups. A goal should be to begin to break down destructive ethnocentrism. This does not mean that pupils are encouraged to give up their own culture. Rather, it means that they develop a respect for other cultures and realize that they may learn something from each other. The following are ideas for accomplishing these purposes.

Native Americans

Studies of Native Americans are common throughout the elementary social studies program. Studies may be included in the third grade as pupils study about the local area, in the fourth grade as they study about the state, and in the fifth grade as they study about the history and geography of the United States. The current problem is that what is taught about Native Americans is often based on stereotypes and myth rather than fact. It is not uncommon to visit a classroom where the tepee is used to illustrate the type of housing used by Indians. The fact is that Native American dwellings have varied significantly, and the tepee is an artifact of only one cultural region, the Great Plains.

We need to remember that there was and is a rich diversity of Native American cultures. For example, some Native American groups had permanent homes and engaged in farming. It is estimated that true farming existed among the southeastern tribes about 6,000 years ago (Gallant, 1989). Great cultural variation exists from region to region, and what is taught to pupils needs to be based on accurate information. It is important that teachers challenge television and movie stereotypes and not teach about Native Americans as if they belonged only to the past (Harvey, Harjo, & Jackson, 1990).

There is an abundance of material available that can be used to teach about Native Americans, including numerous books and other instructional resources. Excellent selections of children's literature that can be used to teach the anthropological concepts of culture and cultural change include Paul Goble's retelling of myths and legends of the Great Plains, such as *The Gift of the Sacred Dog* [Bradbury, 1980], Tomie De Paola's *The Legend of the Bluebonnet: An Old Tale of Texas* [Putnam, 1983], Shonto Begay's Navajo story, *Ma'ii and Cousin Horned Toad* [Scholastic, 1992], Michael Lacapa's Apache folktale, *Antelope Woman* [Northland, 1992], and Ekkehart Malotki's Hopi folktale, *The Mouse Couple* [Northland, 1988]. Share these stories with pupils, comparing their themes and settings. They can provide pupils with insight into cultural beliefs as well as an understanding of how different Native American groups related to their environment in different ways.

Some excellent nonfiction books are also available. These include *Cherokee Summer*, by Diane Hoyt-Goldsmith [Holiday House, 1993], *Sequoyah's Gift*, by Janet Klausner [HarperCollins, 1993], *The Gift of Changing Woman*, by Tryntje Van Ness Seymour [Henry Holt, 1993], and *Proudly Red and Black*, by William Loren Katz and Paula Franklin [Atheneum-Macmillan, 1993]. (This latter book is about individuals of mixed Native American and African American heritage.) Roy Gallant's *Ancient Indians: The First Americans* [Enslow, 1989] is a useful book for helping older students understand the stories of prehistoric Native American cultures. In a similar vein, Byrd Baylor's *One Small Blue Bead* [Charles Scribner's Sons, 1992] captures the excitement and significance of finding artifacts.

One approach that can help pupils understand similarities and differences and form generalizations is to construct *data retrieval charts.* These charts organize information according to the concepts you wish to teach. For example, you may construct a chart showing how characters in different stories face the issue of change. The following sample chart is based on the book *Annie and the Old One,* by Miska Miles [Little, Brown, 1971], a story about Navajo culture and beliefs.

Book	Character	Feelings	Result
Annie and the Old One	Annie	Tried to stop change	Felt guilty
"	Grandmother	Accepted change	Taught Annie an important lesson

Other examples from other books could be added as you read them. Once the data retrieval chart has been completed, you may ask, "Why did Annie dislike change? What did Annie try to do to stop change? Was she successful? What was the lesson that the grandmother tried to teach her? Can we stop change? What is the lesson we should learn about facing change?"

From the story and discussion, pupils can learn about another culture as well as how to cope with change in their lives. While they discover that change is inevitable, you may help them realize that there is also continuity. They can begin to look for elements of change and continuity in their environment.

Cultural Conflict

Cultural conflict is present in all of our lives. As times change, accepted customs and beliefs are challenged. Some cultures are able to adapt to challenges and others are not. Studies of cultural change and adaptation can begin by examining those aspects of your pupils' environment that are facing the prospect of change. For example, many school districts have changed the school calendar from the traditional calendar with a summer break to year-round attendance. There are many who oppose this change simply because it changes a long-held custom. Pupils can discuss the possibility of changing to a year-round calendar and what that might mean. They can predict other changes that might result from this one change. Other examples of customs that have changed or that are being challenged can be discussed.

Related to the concept of change are the problems that occur when two cultures meet. The results can be very disturbing for members of both cultures. Books such as the *Lotus Seed,* by Sherry Garland [Harcourt Brace Jovanovich, 1993], *The Double Life of Pocahontas,* by Jean Fritz [Puffin, 1983], and *The Talking Earth,* by Jean Craighead George [Harper & Row Junior Books, 1983] all deal with the conflict that occurs when two cultures come in contact with each other.

Many communities have individuals who have immigrated from other countries. They can be invited to the class to share their customs and talk about the difficulties they experienced trying to change and adapt to a new culture. Most classrooms will have pupils who have moved from one school or community to another. There is a need to adapt to new customs and new ways of living even in this type of change. Pupils can be asked to share the problems they experienced when trying to fit into a new place.

Storytelling

Storytelling has been a common method for passing on the customs and beliefs from one generation to another. Gathering the stories of a people is of interest to anthropologists. Books such as *Why Mosquitoes Buzz in People's Ears,* by Verna Aardema [Dial Books, 1975], can be used to illustrate how the stories people tell communicate the values and beliefs of people. All children like to hear and tell stories. A beginning point for including storytelling would be to have them share stories they have been told, discussing what they think the stories mean and what they tell us about the culture that told them. Class members can have fun collaborating as they then try to develop new stories that they could tell to younger brothers and sisters to teach them something important. An interesting extension would be to have the pupils think about the stories that are told in popular music. Ask, "What do these songs tell us about ourselves?"

Lesson Idea 4–6

LEARNING FROM AN ARTIFACT

Grade Level:	4–6
Objectives:	Pupils can (1) make at least one statement about a culture based on an investigation of an artifact and (2) explain how wrong conclusions can be drawn.
Overview:	Learning how an anthropologist might work in trying to get an object to tell a story need not require exotic materials or costly preparation. Pupils can have fun learning how to extract the story from an artifact by beginning with common objects in their environment. This activity can be enjoyable as well as educationally useful.
Procedure:	*Learning Set* Begin by asking the class how they think textbook authors know what conditions were like long ago. Inform them that written records or descriptions of historical life and times are often destroyed or lost. The things people have left behind, like tools, pictures, and houses, are what we call *artifacts*. Scientists named *anthropologists* and *archaeologists* find these things and analyze them to see if they can put together the story of the people who made them. Tell pupils that today they are going to pretend to be these scientists and see if they can discover what life was like for a civilization that lived long ago.
	Presentation Tell students the following: "I want you to imagine that you live 3,000 years from now, in about the year

A.D. 5000. You now live on another planet, and you have made a trip with a group of scientists to a planet called *Earth.* On this planet are many ruins. You begin digging in these ruins. After much hard work someone finds a jar full of coins. You don't find anything else. It is your job to see what you can tell about the people who lived here by looking at these coins and seeing if they can tell their story. (Provide each pupil with a nickel.) What can we tell about these people by only looking at this coin?" You may need to provide some hints and a model to get the class going. The following ideas are among those that typically emerge:

- The people must have been fairly advanced. They knew how to refine ore into metal to make the coins.
- They might have been bilingual because the coins seem to have two languages printed on them.
- The people were religious and believed in a god.
- They might have been skillful architects. There is a building on the back that shows some good building design.
- The term *United States of America* might mean that a group of governments banded together.
- The figure has a pigtail. Perhaps all the people who lived in the 1970s and the 1980s had pigtails and long hair.
- The male figure might be a king, a hero, or maybe even a god.
- They may have had a calendar because there is a large number that might represent the year the coin was made.
- The term *five cents* seems to indicate some sort of unit designation. What might that indicate?

It is sometimes useful to introduce some other coins. You might state that someone in another location found these coins. Provide a few pennies, dimes, and quarters for them to compare. Other statements might emerge as they note that most of the figures seem to be men and that the coins picture different buildings and symbols.

Have pupils discuss how statements drawn from artifacts can sometimes lead to wrong conclusions about the life of people. We do not all dress like the people pictured or live in buildings like those on the coins. Anthropologists and archaeologists need to find other ways of making sure their conclusions are correct. What could students do to check conclusions to make sure they are correct? The class might mention that they could look for other evidence such as pictures, the ruins of buildings, or perhaps written records to validate the conclusions.

Closure:

Review with the class. Ask, "What did we do today? Why did we do this? What did you learn from this activity that might help you as you read about ancient times? How might you use this when you look at exhibits in a museum?"

Lesson Idea 4–7

INVENTIONS AND TOOLMAKING

Grade Level:

4–6

Objectives:

Pupils will (1) create a tool from limited resources, (2) identify the difficulties in inventing something new, (3) identify the importance of new inventions and, (4) predict the changes that might occur in a culture as the result of an invention.

Overview:

The making of new tools or new inventions can have a profound effect on a culture. Throughout the ages, inventions, such as moving from the creation of stone tools to using metals such as bronze, have characterized dramatic changes in civilization. Making new tools or inventions from items existing in the environment demands a high level of creativity. In this lesson, pupils will have fun trying to create something as well as develop a deep appreciation for inventors.

Procedure:

Learning Set   Ask the pupils to define the word *invention*. Ask them to identify some inventions that they think are important. Ask them how they think life was different before the invention (include positive as well as negative influences). Tell the class that today they are going to invent a new tool.

Presentation   Provide teams of three or four pupils with the following items: an ice cream stick, a piece of string, and a 3 × 5-in. card. Tell the class that they need to invent a new tool using only these three objects. They do not need to use all the objects. Allow ample time for them to discuss and experiment with different types of things they can create. They can get additional supplies of these three items as they experiment.

Have the groups share their inventions. Choose one of the inventions and predict what changes might occur if people were to use it. As an alternative activity, provide pupils with a hypothetical invention and have them predict the consequences. For example, what would happen if a car was invented that never needed to stop for gas?

For an extension activity, have the class map an invention. They might begin with a common object, such as a clock, and begin to map the prerequisites that led to the invention of a clock. To do this, write the word *clock* in the center of a large piece of paper. On the top, write a statement describing the need that led to the invention. Drawing lines outward from the clock, list the prerequisites as the class thinks of them. These might include things such as electricity, gears, wheels, numbers, wires, and so on. At the bottom of the page, identify some of the consequences of the invention.

Closure: Debrief by asking the class, "What have you learned from the lesson?" Emphasize the point that an invention, although small, might have some long-term consequences and can even change our way of life.

In summary, anthropology is a fascinating subject that can help us learn about and develop a respect for our own and others' cultures. The subject offers an opportunity to deal with significant issues such as ethnocentrism, racism, cultural change, and ethnic and cultural pride. There are numerous opportunities to include anthropology content in the elementary curriculum.

PSYCHOLOGY

Few topics spark more interest than the idea of *self*. We are interested in many questions about ourselves. Why do we think and feel the way we do? How are we like or different from others? Why do some people seem to be smarter than we are? How can we learn to be smarter? How can we be happier? How can we understand the forces that influence our behavior?

Psychology focuses on understanding ourselves and the behavior of those around us. This kind of content makes perfect sense for an elementary social studies program dedicated to helping pupils understand themselves and their social world.

As a discipline, psychology has far-ranging concerns. Most lessons that include content from psychology focus on pupils' self-concept and sense of self-acceptance. Many lessons with psychological orientation are now found in programs that focus on drug and alcohol abuse. It has been recognized that these types of programs must help individuals develop a positive self-image to help them cope with life's pressures and stress.

Although psychological content is necessary in programs aimed at preventing drug abuse, opportunities for including content drawn from psychology in other parts of the social studies program are often overlooked. We need to understand human behavior if we are to understand history and the social sciences. If we know our own hopes, fears, aspirations, and motivations, we then have a foundation for thinking about these elements in other people at other times and places. Understanding what motivates people to do different things can, for example, help pupils understand the risks explorers were willing to take by venturing into unknown lands or the willingness of soldiers to enter into a battle in which they could die.

Another advantage of including psychological perspectives in the social studies curriculum is that pupils already have experienced many feelings and have observed others in their social world. As a consequence, they have formed some hypotheses about why people behave the way they do. Teachers can use these understandings as springboards to study others. Figure 4–6 presents questions, concepts, and generalizations central to psychology that are useful for organizing lesson content.

The following are examples of central questions, concepts, and generalizations that are important in studying psychology.

CENTRAL QUESTIONS (A SELECTION)

- In what ways are people alike, and how are they different?
- What accounts for differences among people?
- Why do people who observe the same event have different explanations of the event?
- Why do people act as they do?
- How do we use different senses to learn?
- Why do people grow and develop at different rates?
- What are the consequences of different developmental rates on personality?
- What makes people afraid?
- How do people react differently when they are fearful?
- What makes some people more aggressive than others?
- What are the basic needs of people?
- How do different people go about meeting those basic needs?

CONCEPTS (A SELECTION)

Learning, self-concept, individual differences, personality, acceptance, security, normal, abnormal, achievement, aggression, fear, perception, habit, motivation, uniqueness, innate behavior, heredity

GENERALIZATIONS (A SELECTION)

- All individuals have common needs, yet each individual is different in significant ways.
- Heredity and environment play an important part in shaping the personality of individuals.
- Human behavior is influenced by learned patterns much more than is the behavior of other species.
- Fear is a natural emotion that can be helpful in certain situations, but that can be harmful if it is irrational or left unrecognized.
- Humans are social beings who seek to establish positive relationships with others.
- All individuals have the needs to achieve, belong, be accepted, and be free from fear.
- Aggression is a natural reaction; it can be used in productive and unproductive ways.
- Individuals who use aggression in socially unacceptable ways often feel guilty.

Figure 4–6
Central questions, concepts, and generalizations associated with psychology.

Psychology-Related Classroom Activities

Psychology deals with the uniqueness of each individual and how personality is developed. Because of this focus, it is of great interest to pupils. Lessons focusing on psychology should begin with the experiences of the pupil and then move to the study of the behavior of others. An important goal of lessons should be to help individuals develop an understanding and an acceptance of self. A word of caution is in order: We need to take care that our lessons in this area are not overly intrusive and that they do not invade the privacy of our pupils.

Anthroplogy helps us develop a respect for people and cultures from around the world.

Observing People

Observation of human behavior is a major research technique used by psychologists. This tool can be very profitably used in the classroom. Pupils enjoy assignments that actively involve them, and they enjoy watching other people. To use observation in the classroom, we need to begin by showing members of the class how to record their observations. They need to learn to describe only what they see rather than to make interpretations about the behavior. They can describe both the circumstances and the reactions of those they observe. Once they have learned the technique of observing, they may then be taught how to interpret what they have witnessed. Assign them to observe people in different situations. For example, they may begin by observing the reactions of young children to certain stimuli or situations. They can watch younger children as they play, interact with others, or handle frustration. Older pupils might observe individuals at different ages to begin to understand some basic principles of growth and development. Other observations might take place using common situations around the neighborhood. For example, what happens when people are crowded together on an elevator or a bus? How do they react when something unexpected happens? Why might these reactions have occurred?

The school, playground, and cafeteria are good places for observing behavior. Pupils might observe what individuals do when they do not want to participate in a game with others. Do some individuals go off by themselves rather than play? What do they do? Why might they behave that way? Pupils can observe what happens when different people win or lose a game or what they do when there is a disagreement. Lively discussions of these episodes can take place back in the classroom as pupils share their observations and try to explain why people behave the way they do.

Individual Differences

There are a great number of things that we can do to help pupils begin to understand that although all people have some things in common, they are also different from each other. Lessons emphasizing individual differences can begin with young children by getting them to observe the physical differences between pupils in the classroom. This can easily be integrated with mathematics by making charts showing the different colors of eyes and hair and different heights of pupils in the room. Other opportunities for identifying individual differences can focus on different interests and hobbies that pupils might have. Discussion should emphasize that differences are natural and that it is important for people be different to meet the diverse needs of society. We might ask members of our class to think about what it would be like if everyone were good in reading and no one liked or had skill in math or music.

Pupils in upper grades can begin to focus on trying to understand what causes individual differences. They can begin to understand that some differences are the result of heredity and others the result of environment.

Perception

Pupils are often surprised to discover that not everyone perceives things in exactly the same way. Helping them understand that perception is selective and influenced by age, gender, values, prior experience, and motivation can result in interesting lessons. These lessons can be organized around a series of experiments that focus on (1) comparing eye-witness accounts of pupils who all witness the same event, (2) comparing reactions to and interpretations of art prints, (3) discussing something that all students have read, or (4) comparing individual interpretations of athletic events.

For example, heated debates can take place when the fans of two different teams are brought together to discuss a game. Fans of one team will see some incidents and tend to not notice other incidents that are noticed and then interpreted differently by other fans. Discussing what happened and why it happened can lead to an understanding of some of the basic principles of selective perception. A number of simple experiments in perception, described in most basic psychology books, can be adapted for use in the classroom.

Lesson Idea 4–8

OBSERVING HUMAN BEHAVIOR

Grade Level: 4–6

Objectives: Pupils will (1) collect data through systematic observation and (2) identify patterns and form conclusions from data.

Overview: Psychologists observe individuals and study their reactions to different situations. Elementary social studies lessons can

	help sharpen pupils' observation and help them begin to develop insight into the reasons for people's behavior.
Procedure:	***Learning Set*** Ask the class if they know what a psychologist does. Tell them that a psychologist is a scientist who studies and tries to understand human behavior. One of the ways the psychologist does this is by observing how people react to different situations. Tell the class that they are going to get to practice observing as psychologists.
	Presentation Introduce the Observation Record Form shown here. Tell the pupils that it is important to record only what they see, and not interpretations of what they think is happening. Present them with an example of how to make a systematic recording.
Observation Record Form:	Divide the class into teams to collect data by observing people in different settings. For example, assign one team the task of observing younger children on the playground and another team the task of observing older children. Those who do not play games could be observed by a third group. Make other group assignments as appropriate for the situation.
	After the observations have been completed, have the members of each team see if they can identify patterns in the data. They might try to answer questions such as the following:

- How was the behavior of people in groups different from that of people who were alone?
- How did they respond to disagreements and problems?
- Were there differences in the way younger and older children play?
- What special features of the place might have contributed to what the people did there?

	Have the groups share their findings and any patterns they noticed. Conduct a whole-class discussion of what the pupils think might account for the different patterns of behaviors that they observed.
Closure:	Ask the class to review what they did. Ask, "Why is it important to record only what we see, not what we think? What did we learn about making observations? What did we learn about human behavior?"

Emotions

Emotions are ever-present in our lives, ranging from happy to sad, loving to hating, peaceful to angry, and confident to fearful and insecure. All of us experience the whole range of emotions. Young children often have questions about them and may not understand what influences their emotions. They want to know, "Why do people fight? Should you ever be afraid? What causes people to like each other? Why do parents sometimes yell at you? Why do parents sometimes get mad at each other?" The important learning that can come out of a study of emotions is that all people have them and that it is okay to sometimes feel sad or angry.

Perhaps the best approach to studying emotions is to help pupils learn to be sensitive to their own emotions and to those of people around them. Emotions as a topic should be openly discussed in the classroom rather than ignored. We can set the tone by acknowledging when pupils are experiencing emotions through a simple response such as, "You are feeling sad." A nonthreatening way to introduce and include this topic is through role playing. Pupils can be placed in a role that has the potential for evoking an emotional response. They can then discuss how they felt and what caused that feeling. Different individuals might have different reactions to the same situation, and the reasons for this may be profitably explored.

Classroom meetings where pupils are gathered in a circle and encouraged to participate in a discussion of a topic, such as, "What makes you feel happy?" or "Why do people fight?" can result in valuable lessons. Hearing about the feelings of others is often eye opening to pupils as they begin to see that individuals have different reactions to common events.

A topic that has generated interest in recent years has been death education. Teachers and parents are realizing that death is a common occurrence in the life of many pupils. Pupils experience the loss of grandparents, friends, and pets. The traditional reaction of ignoring the loss can lead to unhealthy reactions. Although the immediate grief reactions of young children tend to be shorter and milder than those of adolescents, the long-term consequences in terms of psychiatric disturbances are greater (Grismer, 1994). Omission of discussion about death sends the message to pupils that this subject is not to be discussed, and therefore communication that might help the youngster cope with loss is hindered (Wass, 1982). Several studies do indicate that death education components in the curriculum do reduce pupil anxiety and help children develop better coping abilities (Grismer, 1994). A basic theme in effective programs is that death is a natural part of life and that grief is a natural and healthy response.

Lesson Idea 4–9

UNDERSTANDING PERCEPTION

Grade Level: K–3

Objectives: Pupils will state one reason why people might see a thing differently than others do.

Overview: Individuals' values and previous experience influence how they perceive reality. The following exercise combines art and social studies into a lesson to help pupils appreciate individual perception.

Procedure: ***Learning Set***   Tell the class that today they are going to see if people always see the same thing when they look at a picture.

      Presentation   Give pupils pieces of construction paper folded down the middle. Ask them to unfold the paper. Place a drop of paint right on or near the fold line. The paper is then refolded and pressed together. This produces a symmetrical image as the paint spreads on both sides of the fold line.

Allow the paint to dry for a few minutes and choose several of the prints to post in front of the room. Ask individuals to describe what they see in each of the paintings (encourage them to express different answers). Ask why they think that different people see different things in the paintings.

- How might things that are of interest to you have influenced what you saw?
- Did something you are familiar with help you see things in the painting?
- How do you think the descriptions might be different for people who live in other places?

Closure: Review with the class. Ask, "What did we find out today? How might this information be helpful when we listen to people tell us about something they saw?"

Although there is a shortage of material on death education, one place to begin is with children's literature. *The Fall of Freddie the Leaf,* by Leo Buscaglia [Charles B. Slack, 1982] and *Lifetimes,* by Bryan Mellonie and Robert Ingpen [Bantam, 1983] deal with the life cycle and can be used with primary-level pupils. *Goodbye Max,* by Holly Keller [Greenwillow, 1987], *The Tenth Good Thing About Barney,* by Judith Viorst [Alladin, 1984], and *When a Pet Dies,* by Fred Rogers [Putnam's, 1988] discuss the loss of pets. The loss of relatives is dealt with in *The Two of Them,* by Aliki [Greenwillow, 1979] and *Everett Anderson's Goodbye,* by Lucille Clifton [Henry Holt, 1983]. The Clifton book is also useful as it takes the reader in poetic form through the five stages of the grief process. *Bridge to Terabithia,* by Katherine Paterson [Harper & Row, 1977], and *Annie and the Old One,* by Miska Miles [Little, Brown, 1971], are well-written books that deal with different responses to loss and grief. They are appropriate for older children and are likely to elicit good discussions of life, death, fear, grief, and guilt.

WEB CHECK

Note: Electronic addresses of sites on the World Wide Web change frequently. If the listed URL fails to work, use a standard search engine to locate the new address of the site.

- National Council on Economic Education.

  URL—**http://www.nationalcouncil.org/ea.html**

  This site, maintained by the largest professional group with interests in promoting economic education in the schools, includes information about *Economics-America* (a comprehensive program featuring teacher training, curriculum materials, and assessment of K–12 economics programs). Many economics education–related materials can be ordered at this site.

- EcEdWeb.

  URL—**http://ecedweb.unomaha.edu/ec-cncps.htm**

  This site is maintained by an excellent economics education center at the University of Nebraska at Omaha. Curriculum guidelines, information about programs, and other materials of interest to elementary social studies teachers are available here.

- Psychology, Sociology, Education: Usenet Groups.

  URL—**http://world.std.com/~fic/news.html**

  This site includes information about Usenet Groups with a focus on psychology, sociology, and education.

- Teaching and Academic Resources.

  URL—**http://www/asanet.org/teaching.htm**

  This site, maintained by the American Sociological Association, has information related to sociology-related teaching approaches and curriculum. Much of the material is directed at college and university faculties. However, there are some items directed toward public school people.

- American Sociological Association.

  URL—**http://www.asanet.org/default.htm**

  The American Sociological Association is the leading professional organization for sociologists. This site includes wide-ranging information related to the general subject of sociology.

- American Anthropological Association.

  URL—**http://www.ameranthassn.org/**

  The American Anthropological Association is the leading professional organization for anthropologists. This site includes wide-ranging information related to the general subject of anthropology.

- Anthropological Resources on the Internet.

  URL—**http://www.ameranthassn.org/resinet.htm**

  This site contains a huge number of references to other Web sites with information related to the subject of anthropology. It's well worth a visit.

- American Psychological Association.

  URL—**http://www.apa.org/**

  The American Psychological Association is the world's largest organization of professional psychologists. This site includes wide-ranging information related to the general subject of psychology.

- PsychNET.

  URL—**http://www.apa.org/psy/psychnet/**

  This site includes a great deal of information related to psychology including links to a number of other psychology-related Web addresses.

KEY IDEAS IN SUMMARY

1. Economics lessons focus on scarcity and how people respond to this universal human problem. Two experts in economic education, Donald Wentworth & Mark Schug (1994), have suggested six key ideas that should be introduced to help pupils develop their economic thinking skills: (1) people choose; (2) people's choices involve costs; (3) people respond to incentives in predictable ways; (4) people create economic systems that influence individual choices and incentives; (5) people gain when they trade voluntarily; and, (6) people's choices have consequences that lie in the future.

2. Lessons based on economics help learners understand that individual economic systems establish different priorities as they respond to the central issue of scarcity and weigh the relative importance of six key social goals: (1) economic growth, (2) economic efficiency, (3) security, (4) stability, (5) equity, and (6) freedom.

3. Sociology is concerned with the behavior of individuals in groups. Lessons dealing with sociological content should help pupils learn about the influence of groups on their behavior, about group processes, and about why some groups change and adapt and others disappear.

4. Anthropology focuses on the central concept of culture and on how different cultural groups view the world. Lessons drawn on anthropological content can help pupils learn about different cultures and how these cultures respond to basic human concerns.

5. Psychology is often overlooked as a source of content for the elementary grades. However, it is a topic that has the potential for high pupil interest. Many pupils come to school already having observed human behavior and with ideas and theories about that behavior. Lessons focused on the content from psychology can greatly help pupils learn how to understand self and cope with situations they may face.

CHAPTER REFLECTIONS

Directions: Now that you have read this chapter, reread the case study at the beginning. Then answer these questions.

1. What specific points could Tamara make to justify the inclusion of content in subjects other than history or geography?

2. What would you tell a parent of a fourth grader about the relevance of content drawn from economics, sociology, anthropology, and psychology?

3. What sorts of pressures do you imagine might be brought to bear in support of teaching certain kinds of economics lessons? How would you respond to them?

4. There are a number of lesson ideas introduced in this chapter. Which of them particularly appeal to you? What elements of your favorite lesson ideas do you think would be especially good at motivating pupils?

5. What do you think you need to learn about economics, sociology, anthropology, and psychology in order to develop good lessons based on these subjects?

6. Have your ideas about what should be taught in elementary social studies classrooms changed as a result of reading this chapter? If so, in what ways?

EXTENDING UNDERSTANDING AND SKILL

1. Prepare a position statement in which you defend economics, sociology, anthropology, and psychology as important components of an elementary social studies program.

2. Review several social studies textbooks written for a grade level that interests you. Identify topics in the book where you could include economic, anthropological, sociological, and psychological content. Briefly state your ideas about what you might include.

3. Select four or five key concepts from the disciplines covered in this chapter. Begin to build a resource file of pictures, cartoons, newspaper articles, case studies, artifacts, and charts that would be useful in teaching these concepts to elementary pupils.

4. The chapter identified a number of children's books that could be used to teach the social studies. Identify other books that could be used. Briefly give a summary of each book, and identify the social science concepts that could be taught using the book.

5. Interview several teachers of a grade level of interest to you. Ask them about how social problems such as gangs, drug abuse, homelessness, and prejudice influence their classrooms. Identify example lessons that might help address these problems.

REFERENCES

EconomicsAmerica (1997). *Voluntary national content standards in economics.* New York: National Council on Economic Education.

Gallant, R. (1989). *Ancient Indians: The first Americans.* Hillside, NJ: Enslow.

Grismer, R. (1994). *Death education in the primary classroom.* Unpublished master's project, California State University, Fullerton, Fullerton, CA.

Guilliard, J. V., Caldwell, J., Dalgaard, B. R., Highsmith, R. J., Reinke, R., & Watts, M. (1988). *Economics: What and when—Scope and sequence guidelines, K–12.* New York: Joint Council on Economic Education.

Harvey, K., Harjo, L., & Jackson, J. (1990). *Teaching about Native Americans,* Bulletin No. 84. Washington, DC: National Council for the Social Studies.

Nelson, M. R., & Stahl, R. J. (1991). Teaching anthropology, sociology, and psychology. In J. Shaver (Ed.), *Handbook of research on social studies teaching and learning.* (pp. 420–426). Englewood Cliffs, NJ: Merrill/Prentice Hall.

Risinger, C. F. (1992). *Current directions in social studies.* Boston: Houghton Mifflin.

SAVAGE, M. K., & SAVAGE, T. V. (1993). Children's literature in middle school social studies. *The Social Studies, 84* (1), 32–37.

WASS, H. (1982). *Resources for helping young children deal with death.* (Report No. CG0116831). Gainesville, FL: University of Florida. (ERIC Document Reproduction Service No. ED 233 254.)

WENTWORTH, D. R., & SCHUG, M. C. (1994). How to use an economic mystery in your history course. *Social Education, 58* (1), 10–12.

chapter 5

Multicultural and Gender Issues

This chapter will help you to:

- recognize the diverse character of American society,
- describe issues teachers often consider when they plan lessons focused on multicultural and gender issues,
- point out basic goals of instruction focused on multiculturalism and gender,
- explain differences between single-group studies and multiple-perspective studies,
- cite examples of classroom activities that can help sensitize pupils to multicultural and gender issues, and
- identify sources of information available for use in lessons focusing on multicultural and gender issues.

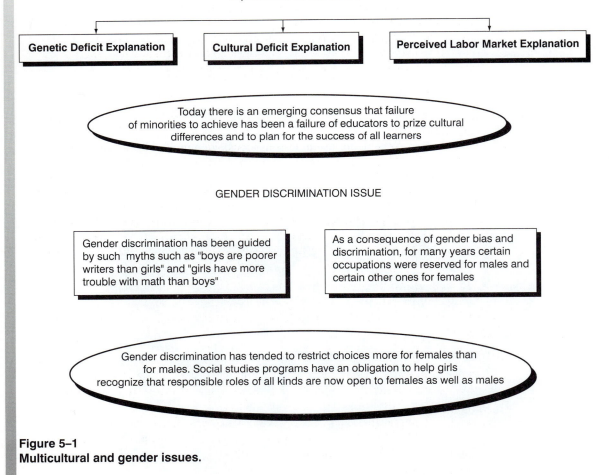

Lessons Focusing on Multicultural and Gender Issues Help Pupils to:

Understand our increasingly diverse society and appreciate the contributions people from many cultures make to our national life

Recognize that gender should not be an automatic barrier to any occupational role for which a person is otherwise qualified

MULTICULTURAL ISSUE

Traditionally, pupils from minority cultures have not done well in school. Among now-discredited explanations for this are the:

Genetic Deficit Explanation   **Cultural Deficit Explanation**   **Perceived Labor Market Explanation**

Today there is an emerging consensus that failure of minorities to achieve has been a failure of educators to prize cultural differences and to plan for the success of all learners

GENDER DISCRIMINATION ISSUE

Gender discrimination has been guided by such myths such as "boys are poorer writers than girls" and "girls have more trouble with math than boys"

As a consequence of gender bias and discrimination, for many years certain occupations were reserved for males and certain other ones for females

Gender discrimination has tended to restrict choices more for females than for males. Social studies programs have an obligation to help girls recognize that responsible roles of all kinds are now open to females as well as males

Figure 5–1
Multicultural and gender issues.

Case Study

ARE EMPHASES ON MULTICULTURALISM AND GENDER ISSUES INCONSISTENT WITH CORE AMERICAN VALUES?

The following comments were prepared by writers of two different newspaper opinion columns:

Writer "A's" Comments

The population of America's schools is more diverse than it has ever been. Providing learning programs that connect to the psychological worlds of young people from many different cultural traditions is a national imperative. Lessons that reflect a multicultural perspective signal to learners that we prize diversity.

Our nation cannot afford school programs that fail to ignite sparks of intellectual interest in *all* pupils. We must signal to young people of all cultural and ethnic back-grounds that they are individuals of consequence for whom our society imposes no artificial upper limits. Sound school programs that respond to multicultural and gender concerns are vital to our nation's future. They deserve our support.

Writer "B's" Comments

Fragmentation that pits group against group is one of the most vexing problems we face today. Cosseting of interest groups, especially those cultural and ethnic minorities whose self-appointed, politically ambitious leaders use inflammatory language to win special treatment, denies the common "Americanness" we share as citizens of this country.

School programs that emphasize multiculturalism and gender issues deny the importance of the social glue that binds us together as a people. Emphases on the importance of the "common good" and our "shared American perspective" are shunted aside in an irresponsible attempt to highlight those things that divide us. Lessons focusing on widely accepted American values are desperately needed in the schools today. We urge a renewed commitment to the idea of the "melting pot"—an image around which all of our citizens should be able to rally.

What Is Your Response?

Read the comments of each columnist. Think about the points each makes. Then, respond briefly to these questions.

1. Writer "A" comments on the changing ethnic and cultural makeup of schools and suggests that today's diverse group of pupils requires different kinds of programs than have traditionally been provided. Do you agree? If so, what changes would you recommend?
2. Writer "A" implies that many present school programs fail to encourage some learners, particularly those from ethnic and cultural minorities and those who are female, to develop their capacities to the fullest. Is this a real problem? Can you cite examples?

3. Writer "B" argues that school programs that seek to respond to special perspectives of individuals from different ethnic and gender groups are divisive. It this true? Can you cite examples to support your view?
4. Writer "B" suggests that school programs ought to emphasize a common set of core American values rather than perspectives of diverse groups. What strengths and weaknesses do you see in this argument?
5. If you were asked to take a position on the issues raised by writer "A" and writer "B," what would you say?

INTRODUCTION

Olivia Escobar, a first-year teacher, works in a largely white, affluent community. Her interactions with learners have convinced her that most of her pupils have little understanding of cultural groups other than their own. Many of their comments suggest that they believe people who are different from themselves, especially minorities, are less deserving and less intelligent. These young people have little appreciation for the diversity that characterizes American society today.

Steve Stepanovic, also a beginning teacher, is employed in a community very different from Olivia's. Most pupils in his class come from a cultural background not at all like his own. Many seem not to understand the importance of arriving at school on time and are often not prompt in turning in assigned work. Others in his class appear to have little respect for his own personal property. These attitudes contrast sharply with those shared by people in the small town where he grew up. The attitudes of his fifth graders make Steve uncomfortable, and he is not sure what he should do.

Challenges such as those facing Olivia Escobar and Steve Stepanovic confront many teachers in today's schools. The diversity of American society ensures that many learners come from cultural backgrounds different from those of their teachers. Responding to this difference requires more than simply learning something about perspectives of individual ethnic groups. Behavior patterns of individuals are shaped by many influences other than ethnicity. For example, a given child may at the same time be a member of a black culture, an urban culture, a youth culture, and a poverty culture. Many influences contribute to the diversity of today's elementary school population.

Schools must serve *all* children who attend. An important obligation of social studies is to help pupils understand the diversity of our society. One way we can do this is by preparing lessons that focus on multicultural and gender issues. The future stability of our country depends on citizens committed to the idea that perspectives of others are important and that the specific cultural groups to which they belong are parts of a larger, more diverse whole.

The issue of equity is a central theme in school social studies instruction. The concept extends beyond the perspectives of individual ethnic groups to embrace gender as well. Historically, women have not had as many personal and career options as men. Though there have been great changes in this situation in recent years, much work still remains.

One of the important goals of multicultural education is to help students develop respect for the rich diversity of human experience.

Multicultural and gender issues form a natural partnership, linked by the social goals of equality and fairness. The elementary social studies program seeks to produce young people who, as they begin assuming their responsibilities as citizens, will work to overcome injustice and inequality wherever they find them.

MULTICULTURAL EDUCATION'S MANY FACES

Educators have long recognized a trend toward increasing diversity among the nation's learners. Recent statistics reveal that of the nearly 50 million learners in the schools, around 40% are members of cultural and ethnic minority groups (Geddes, 1997; McDowell, 1998).

Traditionally, many children from minority cultures have not done well in school. This situation has resulted in underrepresentation of minorities in professional roles demanding college and university preparation. For example, African Americans make up slightly over 12% of the total U.S. population, yet they represent only 2% of all employed scientists and engineers (Strutchens, 1994).

Earlier in this century, some argued that minority learners failed to do well in school because they suffered from a genetic deficit. According to this view, learners from minority ethnic groups and cultures lacked the basic intellectual equipment to profit from instruction. Not surprisingly, individuals who subscribed to this position were reluctant to commit resources to serve the needs of ethnic and cultural minorities.

By the 1960s, scholarship had polished off the genetic deficit view as a serious explanation for academic problems experienced by minority group learners (although individuals occasionally still try to make a case for the theory). In its place, some people emphasized cultural deficit as an explanation. Proponents of this view suggested that many learners from minority groups did not do well because they did not have a "cognitively stimulating environment" at home (Erickson, 1987, p. 335). Erickson, who studied changing attitudes toward minority learners in school, pointed out that the cultural deficit view allowed educators to avoid responsibility for minority learners' failure to profit from instruction. Their failure to achieve was the fault of the home, not the school.

Over time, many educators came to see the cultural deficit view as a prescription for inaction and as a convenient escape from responsibility. Among more recent explanatory theories for academic difficulties of cultural and ethnic minorities have been the "communication process" and the "perceived labor market" views. According to the former, language patterns of minority students differ so dramatically from those of their teachers that these students fail to understand much of what occurs in the classroom. The "communication process" explanation has been criticized because it fails to suggest why some students from ethnic and cultural minorities do extremely well in school.

The "perceived labor market" explanation suggests that minority learners believe the employment market is rigged against them. Hence, they see no point in taking schooling seriously because they do not think that academic success will result in a good job. Critics have attacked this view. They point out that some minority students who do not do well in school do *not* reject the existence of an important connection between academic success and a good job.

In general, present-day critics have little use for explanations for minorities' poor academic performance that have attempted to place blame somewhere other than on schools and school programs. They argue that the real culprit has been our failure as educators to plan seriously for the success of *all* pupils in our classes, not just pupils from "traditional" white families. Instructional practices are needed that will develop levels of self-confidence among all young people in our classes.

Diversity is one of our strengths. As social studies teachers, we have an obligation to ensure that our learners appreciate the many cultural and ethnic threads that go together to make up our national tapestry. In recent years, many excellent models have evolved for creating lessons that illuminate perspectives of individual ethnic groups and cultures. One approach suggests developing instructional experiences with the following kinds of emphases:

- Lessons and programs directed specifically at culturally different children for the purpose of equalizing educational opportunities for them
- Lessons and programs designed to promote an appreciation for cultural differences among all learners
- Lessons and programs designed to preserve and maintain perspectives of individual cultures and ethnic groups
- Lessons and programs that seek to help children function in multicultural contexts

These approaches place important obligations on us as teachers. We must plan experiences that support an acceptance of multiple perspectives. This requires us to be on the lookout for examples of contributions made to our society by people who are members of many different cultural and ethnic groups.

The diversity of cultures represented in today's classrooms underscores the importance of teachers' need to learn about the background of their learners. Teachers who seriously consider cultural diversity are much more likely to succeed with youngsters from minority cultures than teachers who fail to take important cultural differences into account. To illustrate how children's cultural backgrounds can influence their expectations about what education and schooling are about, let's think about pupils recently arrived from Southeast Asia.

Many cultures in this part of the world expect young people to acquire new information through rote learning, and their schools emphasize this kind of instruction. If newcomers from Southeast Asia come into a classroom of a teacher who uses different instructional approaches, they may well be confused. As teachers, we need to be alert to these kinds of situations. With young new pupils from Southeast Asia, we might take time to teach them about how other teaching techniques work and, especially, about how we expect them to participate. These young people need assistance as they come to understand that rote memorization, while a worthy way of learning some content, is not the only reasonable approach.

GENDER ISSUES: SOME BASICS

For many years, certain occupations were widely believed to be the "property" of one sex. Many more roles were open to males than to females. Today, employers have begun to remove gender-based employment barriers and now are more inclined than before to focus solely on each applicant's qualifications (see Figure 5–2).

Despite considerable progress toward gender equity in all areas of our national life, residual attitudes persist. Such myths as "Females are not good in mathematics" and "Males tend to be poor writers" still have their adherents. Some people also continue to feel that males should not do such work as teaching kindergarten, nursing, and so forth, and that females, in turn, should not attempt firefighting, carpentry, surgery, and so on. An important purpose of social studies is to confront these gender-based biases openly. Pupils need to understand that many occupational roles will be open to them as adults. This kind of perspective has not always been reflected in the schools. Even today there is evidence that some teachers have different expectations for boys and girls.

Gender discrimination has tended to restrict choices more for females than for males. Social studies programs, therefore, have an obligation to provide pupils with examples of females who occupy a variety of responsible roles. Girls must recognize that increasing numbers of females play leadership roles in government, engineering, the physical sciences, and medicine.

The standard of living of citizens of the United States is being challenged by economic successes of other nations. There is a pressing need for us to develop *all* of our nation's intellectual resources. To this end, young people must be unconstrained by gender-related barriers as they pursue their personal and vocational objectives.

A speaker at a recent parent-teacher organization meeting made these comments:

We hear much these days about the importance of encouraging girls to think about many kinds of employment options. I'm not sure this makes good sense. Too many women today are working hard to build careers as professionals. Their work takes them out of the home and away from their children. The result is that thousands of children are being left to "raise themselves." It would be better for everybody if more bright women stayed home and gave their children the kind of nurturing needed for them to grow into responsible adults.

THINK ABOUT THIS

1. What are the strengths of this argument?
2. What are the weaknesses?
3. How would you respond to this person?

Figure 5–2
Are new roles for women undermining families?

GOALS OF LESSONS FOCUSING ON MULTICULTURAL AND GENDER ISSUES

The following are among the most important social studies goals addressed by lessons that focus on multicultural and gender issues.

- *The social studies program should help pupils develop a respect for cultures other than their own.* To accomplish this, you need to take action before instruction begins to find out how your learners feel about other groups and cultures. This kind of diagnostic information provides insights regarding pupils' initial levels of sensitivity toward others. You can use this baseline information to prepare lessons to challenge stereotypes and extend pupils' appreciation of diversity.
- *Pupils should be provided opportunities to work directly with members of different ethnic and racial groups.* Direct contact with members of other groups helps young people to value new friends. These relationships help pupils to appreciate the ethnic and cultural groups to which their new friends belong.
- *Pupils need to recognize the validity of different cultural perspectives.* This goal seeks to expand pupils' conception of what it means to be human. Lessons directed toward this end celebrate the rich diversity of the human experience. If successful, these lessons help pupils understand that different people have developed many acceptable responses to common human problems. The goal here is to attack the ethnocentric view that the experiences of any single cultural group represent the right or natural way to live.
- *The social studies program should help pupils develop pride in their cultural heritage.* This goal seeks to help pupils recognize that there is no one "American way." Though as a nation we commit to such core values as toleration of minority opin-

This procedure can be used with all but the very youngest pupils. Children in the primary grades should be asked to respond orally. Middle- and upper-grade pupils can write their responses.

To prepare for the exercise, gather together 8 to 12 photographs of members of different racial and ethnic groups. Ask pupils to look at each photograph and assign it one of the following descriptive words that they believe might "go with" the person depicted:

a. helpful	k. energetic
b. troublesome	l. hard-working
c. doctor	m. poor
d. teacher	n. wealthy
e. janitor	o. dirty
f. delivery person	p. kind
g. friendly	q. ignorant
h. hot-tempered	r. wise
i. lazy	s. sad
j. generous	t. helpless

Terms *a, c, d, g, j, k, l, n, p,* and *r* are associated with people who are viewed positively or who are perceived as having higher status. Terms *b, e, f, h, i, m, o, q, s,* and *t* are associated with people viewed negatively or as having lower status.

THINK ABOUT THIS

If large numbers of pupils assign negative/low-status terms to photographs of non-white American men and women, this suggests that a negative stereotyping problem exists. Lessons can then be planned to break down these narrow, unrealistic views.

Perform this exercise before and after a series of lessons designed to eradicate stereotyping. Compare the results to indicate whether pupils have developed more appreciation for members of groups that they initially negatively stereotyped.

Figure 5–3
Diagnosing stereotypes.

ion, the right to choose one's occupation, and so forth, the fabric of our society is enriched by many cultural threads. Hence, it is quite proper for pupils to take pride in their own cultural roots. Lessons associated with this goal seek to help pupils develop a positive self-image. When this occurs, pupils grow in their sense of self-worth, feel less threatened by people who are different, commit more strongly to the school program, and often get better grades. (See Figure 5–3.)

- *The social studies needs to emphasize conflicts between and among groups involving values that are often at the root of these conflicts.* Many issues that are in dispute in our society are not the result of disagreements about facts. People argue about them because their different values cause them to interpret the facts in different ways. Values orientations often are at the root of disputes among members

Understanding the music and celebrations of a group helps us gain insight into their beliefs and values.

of different cultural groups. As social studies teachers, we have an obligation to help pupils recognize that not all groups share the same values and priorities. (For an example of a general instructional approach to highlighting differences of values, refer to the discussion of decision making in Chapter 8, "Inquiry and Thinking Skills.")

MONITORING TEACHING PROCEDURES

Concerns about multicultural and gender issues require teachers to think carefully about procedures we use in implementing instruction. What you do as you teach can affect how individual pupils feel about themselves. Attention to the following guidelines can contribute to the development of a classroom atmosphere that supports successful lessons dealing with multicultural and gender issues.

- *Teachers should include learners of different ethnic, cultural, and social backgrounds when they organize pupils into groups.* There is evidence that this kind of mixing is not as common as one might hope. Sometimes race, socioeconomic status, and sex have been considered when teachers have made decisions about which

Some people tend to assign certain allegedly fixed characteristics to whole groups of individuals. Often these characteristics are negative stereotypes. The term *pigeonholing* refers to evaluating people on the basis of characteristics thought to be associated with their ethnic group or gender.

Think back on your own experiences in school. Did you ever feel certain people had prior conceptions about what you could or could not do even before they had an opportunity to assess your real abilities? Did you ever see pigeonholing happening to others?

THINK ABOUT THIS

1. If you ever felt yourself to be pigeonholed, describe your feelings. If you saw it happening to others, how did they feel and react?
2. In your opinion, what might cause a teacher to pigeonhole a pupil?
3. As a beginning teacher, what are some things you might do to minimize the possibility of assigning certain expectations to a given pupil based on nothing more than ethnic group membership or gender?

Figure 5–4
The problem of "pigeonholing."

pupils should be included in a given group. Grouping based on such variables can inhibit academic development and lead to low self-images.

- *As a teacher, you need to be aware of your own cultural perspective and to recognize how it may vary from that of some of your pupils.* Individuals differ in their learning styles. Learners' cultural backgrounds often affect preference for a given style. In a classroom that includes learners from different ethnic and cultural groups, several style preferences will be represented. Some pupils will need to manipulate objects, others will learn better by reading about new content, still others may respond well to graphic representations of information. Lessons that accommodate different learning styles are more likely to help pupils learn than are those in which content presentation assumes all youngsters learn in the same way.

- *Evaluation procedures should be as free from cultural and social bias as possible* (see Figure 5–4). Improper testing and evaluation procedures present serious obstacles even to highly motivated pupils from minority cultures. Standardized tests pose particularly difficult problems. The vocabulary used and assumptions made about prior life experiences of those who take standardized tests often are unrelated to the backgrounds of pupils from certain ethnic and cultural groups. Some tests even reflect a regional bias. For example, a test developed in Texas that asked pupils to identify an armadillo might well bewilder a pupil in New England, where armadillos are not as common a roadside sight.

One way to avoid bias in standardized tests is by developing assessments of your own, taking into account particular characteristics of members of the class. These kinds of assessments often do a much better job of providing accurate evaluation information than procedures developed by others who lack insight about the special characteristics of the pupils.

- *You need to monitor what you do in the classroom to ensure that you are not favoring any single group of learners.* Researchers have found that teachers' attitudes toward and expectations for individual learners influence their achievement (Good & Brophy, 1997). These expectations often are communicated to learners through teachers' actions. For example, you may ask certain pupils more challenging questions, provide them more feedback, and spend more time with them. It does not take others in the class long to figure this out. When pupils see what is going on, those who see that they are not in the favored group often develop less positive attitudes toward the teacher and the class, and their level of academic performance often declines.

If you truly want all of the people in your class to learn, you must behave in ways that signal that you believe each person has the potential to succeed. If you somehow signal to pupils that "it is natural for girls to have trouble doing math" or that "pupils from low-income homes can't be expected to read well," you are asking for trouble. These kinds of assumptions quickly reveal themselves to pupils. Further, these biases affect what the teacher does. For example, if a teacher believes that certain pupils are not going to read as well as others, there is a tendency for the teacher to put less effort into the instruction directed toward those pupils for whom the teacher has low expectations. This becomes a vicious circle in which the teacher's unfortunate a priori assumptions lead to halfhearted instruction which, not surprisingly, leads to poor performance on the part of those pupils.

CLASSROOM APPROACHES TO MULTICULTURAL AND GENDER ISSUES

Approaches used in developing these lessons feature either a single-group or a multiple-perspectives focus. The single-group approach, as its name implies, looks at a single group or culture in depth. For example, one instructional sequence might center on women's roles during a specific historical period. Another might examine experiences of immigrants from Southeast Asia.

Typically, the multiple-perspectives approach takes a given problem and explains how it is seen by two or more groups. These lessons help pupils step into the shoes of others and become more sensitive to their views. For example, to accomplish this purpose, we might select settlement of the United States as a theme and introduce the topic by emphasizing how this phenomenon was viewed by men and women who were English, French, Spanish, or Native American.

Single-group Studies: General Characteristics

Single-group studies must be free from damaging stereotypes and distortions. In preparing lessons of this kind, we have to become well informed about the group to be studied. Single-group studies are designed to help pupils learn more about special perspectives of the group they are studying. Optimally, they will complete their study with a good idea

The Taos Pueblo is a living example of the rich multicultural heritage of the United States.

of how group members interpret reality. To accomplish this, lessons have to go beyond superficial introduction of the group's clothing, food, and religious preference. There has to be careful attention to the group's values, ethics, and special cultural traditions.

Single-group studies should provide information about the group's history. This content helps pupils identify with struggles and experiences that, over time, have helped to shape members' attitudes. Additionally, historical content highlights relationships between the group and the larger society of which it is a part. Changes in this relationship over time often reveal much about present perspectives of group members. For examples, individuals who are suspicious of the motives of others may be members of groups that have been systematically and officially repressed in the past by representatives of a larger, majority culture.

Contributions of the focus group in such areas as art, music, literature, science, mathematics, and government often are included in these lessons. The study of cultural adaptation provides opportunities for pupils to understand that some groups have made innovative responses to trying conditions. For example, studies of certain Inuit groups (native peoples living in the far north, from Alaska across Canada to Greenland) often emphasize their adjustment to an extremely cold climate. Many of their practices were adopted by early European explorers of the far north. Without the contributions of the Inuit, successful exploration of the world's polar regions by people of European descent would have been impossible.

Single-group studies also focus on issues that reveal values of the group. Positions taken on key issues help define the group's priorities and help pupils recognize that individual groups have their own agendas. This insight contributes to pupils' grasp of the idea that healthy conflict is a hallmark of our democratic society.

Single-group Studies: Examples of Classroom Approaches

A group's music reveals much about how its members view the world. In the example provided in Lesson Idea 5–1, the national anthem of Mexico serves as the beginning point for learning about Mexican values and culture.

Lesson Idea 5–1

WHAT DOES A NATIONAL ANTHEM TELL US ABOUT PEOPLE?

Grade Level: 4–6

Objectives: Pupils will (1) develop one or more hypotheses about the history of Mexico, (2) identify two or more values or basic beliefs of the Mexican people, and (3) identify two or more sources that they can consult to validate and clarify their hypotheses.

Suggested Procedure: Ask class members if they know what is meant by the term *national anthem.* Discuss "The Star Spangled Banner" with the class. Ask pupils why the song is important. Go over the words. Ask members of the class to try to identify what the song tells us about the history and values of people of the United States.

Provide learners with copies of the English translation of the words of "Himno National," the national anthem of Mexico. (If available, play a recording of the anthem to familiarize pupils with the music as well as the words.) Review some of the unfamiliar words and symbols. Answer any questions. Ask pupils to state several hypotheses about what the anthem reveals about the history of Mexico. Write their ideas on an overhead transparency and project them for all to see or, alternatively, write them on the chalkboard.

Himno National

Mexicans when the trumpet is calling,

Grasp your sword and your harness assemble.

Let the guns with their thunder appalling

Make the Earth's deep foundations to tremble.

May the angel divine, O Dear Homeland,

Crown thy brow with the olive branch of peace;

For thy destiny, traced by God's own hand

In the heavens, shall ever increase.

But shall ever the proud foe assail thee,

And with insolent foot profane thy ground,

Know, dear country, thy sons shall not fail thee,

Ev'ry one thy soldier shall be found, thy soldier ev'ry one shall be found

Blessed Homeland, thy children have vowed them

If the bugle to battle should call,

They will fight with the last breath allowed them

Till on thy loved altars they fall.

Let the garland of life thine be;

Unto them be deathless fame;

Let the laurel of victory be assigned thee,

Enough for the tomb's honored name.

Lyrics by Francisco Gonzales Bocanegra,
music by Jaime Nuño

Ask members of the class, from what the anthem suggests, what they think is important to the Mexican people. Write their ideas on another transparency or on the chalkboard.

Ask pupils where they think they might get information about Mexico that they could use to test the accuracy of their ideas. Encourage them to think about such resources as books, films, interviews with people who have traveled to Mexico, and guest speakers of Mexican descent.

Divide the class into cooperative learning groups. Ask each group to work with one or more of the hypotheses generated by the class. Have each group find information relating to their hypotheses and make a report of their findings to the whole class.

Challenge group members to present their information in interesting and creative ways. Encourage pupils to use pictures, murals, or charts. Some groups may wish to use role playing as a way of making their reports to the class. After each group reports, ask the class to decide whether the hypotheses should be retained, modified, or rejected. This portion of the activity may generate new hypotheses, which you may then also discuss.

As a follow-up, some pupils might enjoy learning the Spanish words of the anthem.

Another rich source of material for lessons focusing on single groups is children's literature. Good literature for young people has a great deal of appeal for many of our pupils. The growing trend of using children's literature to teach reading ought to have a counterpart in the social studies. Outstanding children's literature provides a useful vehicle for teaching the perspectives of particular cultural groups. The example introduced in Lesson Idea 5–2 focuses on Native Americans. It draws on two well-known, popular books for young people, *The Legend of the Bluebonnet* by Tomie DePaola and *The Girl Who Loved Wild Horses* by Paul Goble.

Lesson Idea 5–2

HOW DO LEGENDS HELP US UNDERSTAND PEOPLE?

Grade Level:	1–3
Objectives:	Pupils will (1) identify two or three specific aspects of Native American culture as reflected in their legends, (2) cite one or more examples that illustrate how Native Americans view their relationship with nature, and (3) point out one or more aspects of Native American culture that might conflict with aspects of the dominant western culture.
Materials Needed:	*The Legend of the Bluebonnet* by Tomie DePaola (New York: G. P. Putnam's Sons, 1983) and *The Girl Who Loved Wild Horses* by Paul Goble (New York: Bradbury Press, 1978).
Suggested Procedures:	1. Begin by asking the class whether anyone has had experience riding or taking care of horses. Encourage pupils to share their experiences. Ask them to tell how they feel about horses. Introduce them to *The Girl Who Loved Wild Horses* by Paul Goble. Tell the class that you are going to read them a Native American legend about a girl who loved horses.
	2. Read the story. Stop as needed to clarify meanings of words, respond to questions, and share illustrations with the class.
	3. Ask questions such as, "What do you think this story means? What does it tell us about how Native Americans feel about their world? What things are important to them?" Read aloud the two songs at the end of the book. Then, ask questions such as, "What do these songs tell us? Do they reveal feelings that are different from those most of us have? What are the differences?"
	4. Read aloud *The Legend of the Bluebonnet* by Tomie DePaola. Ask questions similar to those you asked about *The Girl Who Loved Wild Horses*. Ask pupils what they think these people might have felt if others arrived and began hunting the wild horses and plowing under the bluebonnets to make room for houses and factories.
	5. Conclude the study by helping pupils find other books dealing with lives of Native Americans. Ask them to think

about traditional Native American customs as they read these materials. Particularly, urge pupils to consider how these customs might conflict with dominant western cultural practices.

Using language appropriate for learners, explain that when two different cultures come together, changes occur. Sometimes these changes bring harm to members of certain cultural groups. Often this happens because people in the larger or dominant cultural group fail to understand aspects of the other culture. As a class, consider what might be done to minimize this kind of damage to members of minority cultural groups.

To help pupils understand that females have many occupational roles open to them, we might develop a single-group lesson focusing on stereotyped views of what jobs are "proper" for women. Pupils need to understand that today's situation differs from past times when relatively few employment roles were thought "suitable" for females. Lesson Idea 5–3 illustrates an instructional approach designed to help pupils grasp this point.

Lesson Idea 5–3

WHAT JOBS CAN A WOMAN HAVE?

Grade Level: 4–6

Objectives: Pupils will (1) recognize that all jobs are open to women who qualify for them and that their gender is no longer a critical factor, (2) describe differences in kinds of jobs open to women today and those open to them 30 or more years ago, and (3) suggest two or more reasons why women enjoy more employment choices today than they did earlier in the century.

Suggested Procedures: 1. Ask class members to think about kinds of jobs women can have today. Write ideas on the chalkboard under the heading, *Jobs Women Can Hold.* Then, ask if there are any jobs women cannot hold. Write any pupil responses on the chalkboard under the heading, *Jobs Women Cannot Hold.* Save this information.

2. Divide class members into groups of about five pupils each. Provide each group with one or two copies of magazines that are at least 30 years old. (These can frequently be found at rummage or garage sales. Often they are available at modest cost from used bookstores and from resale shops such as Goodwill Industries.) Ask learners in each group to look for pictures of women at work. For each woman pictured, ask pupils to write down the nature

of the occupation shown (teacher, nurse, steelworker, and so forth).

3. Ask a spokesperson from each group to report the group's findings. Write this information on the chalkboard next to the information generated in step 1. Lead a discussion that requires pupils to examine both the original lists and the list developed after their work with the magazines. Ask them to point out differences and similarities between the lists.

4. Have students re-form into groups. Give each group several copies of current magazines. Again, ask pupils to look for illustrations of women at work and to note the occupational roles.

5. Ask a representative from each group to share the group's findings. Write the information on the chalkboard. Repeat the discussion outlined in step 3. Pupils should find more job roles represented in the current magazines than they did in either step 1 or step 3.

6. Next, ask pupils to compare the kinds of jobs for women found in magazines 30 or more years old with those found in current magazines. Ask them if they can explain any differences. Ask each pupil to write a short paragraph beginning: "As I think about jobs available to women 30 years ago and today, I conclude that . . ."

7. As a follow-up activity, some pupils may enjoy preparing a bulletin board featuring women in a wide variety of occupational roles.

Multiple-Perspectives Approach: General Characteristics

The multiple-perspectives approach focuses on a single issue, presented from the perspective of several groups. The approach is easily integrated into the elementary social studies program. For example, as we introduce a given event, such as the early European settlement of the Atlantic Coast of what is now the United States, we might examine this event from the perspectives of both the settlers and the indigenous Native Americans.

Multiple-perspectives lessons help pupils realize that common events often are interpreted in varied ways by different people. Their interpretations often are tied to the values of the groups to which they belong. Solutions that make sense to people in one group, because they are consistent with this group's values, may not seem good at all to members of other groups whose values are different.

Multiple-Perspectives Approach: A Classroom Example

Many films and books romanticize the westward movement of settlers across lands that today make up the continental United States. Accounts of this settlement often fail to give serious attention to the impact of the arrival of new people on individuals who were

Multicultural studies help us understand how different cultures have developed alternative ways of meeting basic needs such as shopping for food.

already occupying these lands. Lesson Idea 5–4 illustrates an instructional experience designed to help pupils understand that a common event often affects some people differently than others.

Other multiple-perspectives lessons can introduce pupils to conflicting accounts of historical events by using letters to the editor or editorials from different newspapers that present conflicting views of contemporary issues and by exposing learners to opposing viewpoints by scheduling class speakers from groups with different views on controversial issues.

Lesson Idea 5–4

MOVING WESTWARD

Grade Level:	3–6
Objectives:	Pupils will (1) identify two or more groups of people who were living in the western United States prior to the arrival of pioneers from the eastern United States, (2) identify several customs and ways of living of these people, and (3) state at least two influences on the ways of life of these people that were a direct result of the pioneers' arrival.

Suggested Procedures:

1. Have the class view a film or read a romanticized account of the westward movement or of the Old West. Ask pupils to think about what they saw or read. Ask them whether they would like to have lived at this time. Follow up with a question about the extent to which their opinions are based on what they have just seen or read. Introduce pupils to the idea that there were people already living in the western United States before the arrival of the pioneers.

2. Divide the class into several groups. Ask each group to find locations of people inhabiting the Old West in the early 1800s. One group might be assigned to identify places where different groups of Native Americans were living. Another might focus on locations occupied by settlers who originally entered the area from Mexico. Others might examine European groups such as the British, French, and Russians. Each group should be given a small outline map of North America. A spokesperson from each group should plot the location of the assigned population on the group's map.

3. After the small-group work has been completed, reconvene the class as a single large group. Ask spokespersons from each group to plot the location of the group's assigned population on a large map. If possible, make copies of this map and distribute them to everyone in the class.

4. Next, reconstitute the small groups. Ask each group to find additional information about its assigned population. In particular, have pupils find out the following:
   - When members of the assigned population first began to occupy the area they settled
   - What their motives for coming were
   - How they made a living
   - Interesting customs and lifestyles of these people

5. Bring the pupils back together as a single large group. Pose the possibility that pioneers from the eastern United States are about to move into the lands occupied by the people each group has studied. Challenge pupils to think about the probable reactions to this situation of the people who were already occupying these lands.

6. Ask pupils to go back into their small groups. Tell people in each group to develop a response to the movement of the pioneers into the area their assigned population occupies. Ask them to prepare this response from the perspective of members of the assigned population. Give pupils options. For example, some groups may wish to write a simulated editorial as a way of sharing

their views. Other groups may elect to have one or two pupils deliver reactions orally.

7. To follow up on the presentations of the individual groups, add the perspective of yet another group of people who were involved in the westward movement: the women. Read the following account to the class. It comes from the diary of a young woman who moved west with her husband:

> Only women who went west in 1859 understand what a woman had to endure. There was no road, no stores, and, many times, no wood for a fire. I had a new baby, and it was teething and suffering from fever. The child took nearly all my strength. I became weak. My weight fell and fell. In the end, I was all the way down to ninety pounds.
>
> After reaching Denver, we heard that gold had been discovered in the mountains. On the nineteenth of February, 1860, I was taken from my sick bed and placed in a wagon, and we started for the new mines. No woman had yet been there. After several days' travel we came late at night to Salt Creek. We tried the water and found it was no good. We tied the oxen to the wagon so they couldn't drink. Then we went to bed with nothing to eat. That night it got very cold.
>
> The next day we moved to Trout Creek and found the water good. Several men had left Denver a few days ahead of us. We wanted to join up with them but had seen no sign of them. Our men decided to mount a search. They shouldered rifles and headed out looking for footprints. Each went in a different direction. The men had not returned by dark, and I felt very alone. I allowed the small donkey to come into the tent with me. I put my head on him and cried in the loneliness of the soul. (Adapted from W. M. Thayer, Marvels of the New West, Norwich, CT: Henry Bill Publishing, 1888, pp. 246–253)

8. After pupils have finished making their group reports and have read and thought about the diary excerpt, ask them to make general statements about the impact of the westward movement on different groups of people. As a culminating activity, involve learners in developing a play, drawing a wall mural, or writing a personal history of the westward movement.

SOURCES OF INFORMATION

Multicultural Lessons

There are many sources of ideas for both single-group and multiple-perspectives approaches to multicultural learning. The *Education Index* includes many listings of articles in professional education journals that provide guidelines for such lessons. Specific examples frequently appear in journals such as *Social Education, Social Studies and the Young Learner, Journal of Geography,* and *The Social Studies.* Books are also available that include ideas for multicultural lessons. One that is particularly good is Carl A. Grant and Christine E. Sleeter's *Making Choices for Multicultural Education: Five Approaches to Race, Class, and Gender* [Prentice Hall, 1997].

A particularly useful classroom supplement for multicultural lessons is the Ethnic Cultures of America Calendar. This calendar is published annually and is available from Educational Extension Systems, P. O. Box 259, Clarks Summit, PA 18411. The calendar features information for each day of the year about celebrations and events that are meaningful to different ethnic groups in the United States. In addition, it contains several pages of information about the ethnic cultures of America, about various calendars in use throughout the world, and about holidays of many world religious groups.

An organization that devotes its attention exclusively to promotion of multicultural perspectives in schools is the National Association for Multicultural Education. This group publishes a quarterly magazine called *NAME* that features extensive lists of resources for teachers as well as practical ideas for incorporating multicultural lessons into school programs. For information, write to the national headquarters: 1511 K Street, NW, Suite 430, Washington, DC 20005.

The following information sources also may be useful in planning multicultural lessons:

- Balch Institute for Ethnic Studies, 18 South 7th Street, Philadelphia, PA 19106
- Center for Migration Studies, 209 Flagg Place, Staten Island, NY 10304
- Center for the Study of Ethnic Publications, Kent State University, Kent, OH 44242
- Immigration History Research Center, University of Minnesota, 826 Berry Street, St. Paul, MN 55114
- Institute of Texan Cultures, University of Texas, San Antonio, TX 78294

Lessons Focusing on Gender Issues

Many sources of information are available to help you plan lessons focusing on gender issues. A brief description of several good resources and their addresses follow.

The American Association of University Women Educational Foundation has been particularly active in encouraging school programs that make a difference in girls' lives. This group systematically gathers information about approaches that support efforts of females to excel.

The Women's Educational Equity Act Resource Center distributes gender-free materials developed by programs funded by the federal Women's Educational Equity Act and by other organizations concerned about gender issues. Many materials available from this group are of interest to teachers.

A good source of visual materials is the Organization for Equal Education of the Sexes, Inc. This group makes available more than 100 posters. Many of them feature women from history and contemporary women in nontraditional occupations. The collection is multicultural and includes women with disabilities. Each poster features a brief biography of the woman or women depicted. The materials are inexpensive. Write for details.

The Upper Midwest Women's History Center for Teachers makes available a long list. Write for details to the address given below. The Population Reference Bureau publishes a large wall chart, The World's Women: A Profile, containing information about women throughout the world. Write for ordering information.

Following are addresses of those groups previously mentioned, and others, producing materials of interest to teachers who wish to plan lessons that focus on gender issues:

- American Association of University Women Educational Foundation, P.O. Box 96974, Washington, DC 20077-7022
- ISIS—Women's International Information and Communication Service, P.O. Box 25711, Philadelphia, PA 19144
- Women's Educational Equity Act Resource Center, 55 Chapel Street, Newton, MA 02158-1060
- National Women's History Project, P.O. Box 3716, Santa Rosa, CA 95402
- Organization for Equal Education of the Sexes, Inc., P.O. Box 438, Blue Hill, ME 04614
- Population Reference Bureau, Inc., 2213 M Street, N.W., Washington, DC 20037
- Upper Midwest Women's History Center, Hamline University, 749 Simpson Street, St. Paul, MN 55104.

WEB CHECK

Note: Electronic addresses of sites on the World Wide Web change frequently. If the listed URL fails to work, use a standard search engine to locate the new address of the site.

- Balch Institute for Ethnic Studies

  URL—**http://www.avalon.net/~librarian/BalchWeb/balch.html**

  This site is the home page for the Balch Institute for Ethnic Studies. It includes extensive lists of materials related to multicultural issues. Many can be downloaded. Some unusual items are included here. For example, there are illustrations of how covers of sheet music, in times gone by, have provided stereotyped images of certain ethnic and cultural groups. Highly recommended.

- National Association for Multicultural Education

  URL—**http://www.inform.umd.edu/NAME/.index/natoffice.html**

  Information at this site is provided by the National Association for Multicultural Education, a group dedicated to promoting multicultural perspectives in the schools. Content references promising classroom practices, cites examples of reviews of multicultural materials, and describes sources of materials that might be incorporated into lessons.

- Multicultural Education Resources

  URL—**http://gilligan.esu7.k12.ne.us/~esu7web/resources/multi.html**

  Material at this site has been assembled by Educational Service 7 in the state of Nebraska. It includes an outstanding compilation of links to sites that have information related to such topics as culture, diversity, immigration, languages, multicultural education, and multicultural organizations. There are also useful listings of sites with content related to individual ethnic groups. Highly recommended.

- Center for Migration Studies

  URL—**http://cmsny.org/**

  The Center for Migration Studies is a long-established center for the study of all kinds of topics organized around the central issue of migration. There are links here to information about available publications and documents. Additional links tie to other organizations and government agencies with interests in migration and immigration.

- Internet Resources for Students of Afro-American History

  URL-**http://www.libraries.rutgers.edu/rulib/socsci/hist/afrores.htm**

  As the name suggests, information at this site organizes resources related to the history of African Americans. There are numerous links to individual documents as well as to entire collections of texts and other key resources.

- Educational Extension Systems

  URL—**http://www.simcoe.igs.net/homathtutor/ess.htm**

  This site displays information and interesting calendars published by Educational Extension Systems. These are The World Calendar, The Ethnic Cultures of America Calendar, and The Cultural and Festival Days of the World Posters. Each of these items might well be incorporated into an elementary social studies program.

- Institute of Texan Cultures

  URL—**http://www.texancultures.utsa.edu/**

  Information at this site relates to the several dozen ethnic groups that settled in the state of Texas. There are links here of interest to teachers.

- American Association of University Women Resources

  URL—**http://www.aauw.org/4000/resources.html**

Information at this site includes resources of various kinds assembled by the American Association of University Women. One of these links is to a related site titled, "Gender Equity Resources for K–12 Teachers." This is an outstanding source of information about issues related to gender-related topics, particularly as they pertain to females in public schools. Highly recommended.

- Upper Midwest Women's History Center

  URL—**http://www.hamline.edu/~umwhc/**

  The focus here is on women's history with a particular emphasis on ways to incorporate this information into school curricula.

- Women's Studies

  URL—**http://www.library.upenn.edu/resources/interdiscipline/gender/women/women.html**

  There are a number of useful links at this site to women's issues that have been organized under a variety of headings (African American Studies, history, music, religion, and so forth). In addition there are links to other Web addresses that provide additional relevant resources for individuals interested in women's studies.

- Women's Studies—Primarily US

  URL—**http://www.hist.unt.edu/09w-amm6.htm**

  There is an enormous collection of sites referenced at this address that relate to the general topic of women's studies. Extensive listings are provided for resources, guides, and programs, organizations, Hispanic women, UN 4th World Conference on Women, history, great women, women in the professions, health and abortion, and foreign women. There are also references to a number of Usenet newsgroups pertaining to women's studies.

- Equity Online

  URL—**http://www.edc.org/WomensEquity/**

  This site is maintained by the Women's Educational Equity Act Equity Resource Center. It includes information about ways to deal with certain school subjects that avoid gender bias and about many other issues connected to the issue of gender equity.

KEY IDEAS IN SUMMARY

1. Schools should serve *all* enrolled pupils. In our increasingly diverse society, this means that instruction must take into consideration learners who bring with them many different cultural and ethnic perspectives.

2. At various times, the academic performance of minority-group children has been viewed in different ways. The *genetic deficit* explanation, the *cultural deficit* explanation, the *communication process* explanation, and the *perceived labor market*

explanation have all been offered as reasons many children from minority cultures have not done well at school. Today, these explanations have been dismissed as weak excuses for the system's failure to serve the needs of minorities.

3. Lessons that focus on multicultural and gender issues seek to (1) help pupils develop a respect for cultures different from their own, (2) provide learners with opportunities to work with people from different groups, (3) help pupils recognize the validity of different cultural perspectives, (4) assist learners as they develop pride in their own cultural heritage, and (5) help pupils appreciate that different values often lead to conflicts between and among groups.

4. Teachers can use the following guidelines to help pupils become sensitive to diversity: (1) Learners of different backgrounds should be included in each group when the class is divided into smaller units for special projects. (2) As teachers, we need to be aware of how our own cultural perspectives may differ from those of some of our pupils. (3) Teaching methods need to be modified to accommodate a variety of learning styles. (4) Evaluation procedures must be free from cultural and social biases. (5) We need to monitor our teaching behavior to make sure that we are not unconsciously favoring any one group of pupils.

5. Classroom approaches to multicultural and gender issues include the single-group approach and the multiple-perspectives approach. The single-group approach seeks to help pupils become so familiar with one group that they can appreciate how its members interpret reality. The multiple-perspectives approach focuses on a single issue, introduced in a way that highlights views of several different groups.

6. Many sources of information are available for teachers who wish to develop lessons focusing on multicultural and gender issues. These include examples of lessons, background materials for pupils, instructional support items, and background information for teachers.

CHAPTER REFLECTIONS

Directions: Now that you have read this chapter, reread the case study at the beginning. Then, answer these questions:

1. What do you see as major purposes of lessons focusing on topics related to multiculturalism and gender? What are some strengths and weaknesses of arguments supporting and opposing increased emphases on these topics?

2. What are the implications of explaining low academic achievement of some minority learners as being caused by one of the following factors?
   - Genetic deficit
   - Cultural deficit
   - Communications problem
   - Perceived labor market problem

3. What are the arguments of and social remedies proposed by individuals who identify with each of the perspectives listed in question 2?

4. Have you personally experienced any problems as a result of either too little or too much emphasis in schools on lessons dealing with topics tied to multicultural or gender topics?

5. In what ways might your personal cultural heritage inhibit your ability to develop good multicultural lessons?

6. What are characteristics of multicultural programs that feature single-group studies? Multiple-perspectives approaches?

7. Is it possible for social studies programs to develop pupils' sensitivity to cultures other than their own and still develop an appreciation for their own culture? What problems might you face as a teacher in dealing with this potential difficulty, and what ideas do you have for responding to it?

8. When you were in school, were you or any of your friends directed to take certain courses because they were "better for boys" or "better for girls"? If your answer is "yes," how did you or your friends feel, and what are your thoughts about the long-term consequences of this kind of gender-based advice?

9. How would you defend lessons centering on gender in a community where many parents continue to believe that certain social roles and jobs should be reserved for males and others for females?

EXTENDING UNDERSTANDING AND SKILL

1. Observe an elementary social studies class. Note how the teacher interacts with male pupils, female pupils, and pupils from different cultural groups. Can you identify patterns that may cause difficulties for some learners?

2. Reflect on your own cultural background and your personal life experiences. What values are most important to you? What are your images of and expectations for members of different cultural groups? How might your perspectives affect your ability to teach people with different cultural perspectives?

3. Prepare a report on images of minority cultural groups and females in photographs in an elementary social studies text. Choose a text used at a grade level you would like to teach. Look for kinds of jobs being performed by minority group members and females. If time permits, do this with two books, one published recently and one published 20 or more years ago.

4. Prepare a plan for a single-group lesson for a cultural group different from your own. Include at least two suggested instructional approaches. Ask your instructor to critique your plan.

5. Organize a group of five or six people from your class. Identify two or three key episodes from American history (settlement of the West, initial legalization of slavery

in some states, the Homestead Act and its provision of free lands, the annexation of Texas, the Gadsden Purchase, the Boston Tea Party, and so forth). For each selected episode, brainstorm to identify as many approaches as you can to teach pupils how these events were viewed by members of different cultural groups. Prepare a copy of all ideas generated, and distribute this information to others in your class.

REFERENCES

ERICKSON, F. (1987). Transformation and school success: The politics and culture of educational achievement. *Anthropology and Education Quarterly, 18* (4) 335–356.

GEDDES, C. (project director). (1997). *Mini-digest of education 1997.* Washington, DC: National Center for Education Statistics.

GOOD, T. L., & BROPHY, J. E. (1997). *Looking in classrooms* (7th ed.). Boston: Addison-Wesley Publishing Company.

GRANT, C. A., & SLEETER, C. E. (1997). *Making choices for multicultural education: Five approaches to race, class, and gender* (2nd ed.). Englewood Cliffs, NJ: Prentice Hall.

MCDOWELL, L. M. (1998, February). *Public elementary and secondary education statistics.* Washington, DC: National Center for Education Statistics.

NATIONAL COMMISSION ON CHILDREN. (1991). *Beyond rhetoric: A new American agenda for children and families.* Washington, DC: United States Government Printing Office.

STRUTCHENS, M. (1994). Culture inclusive mathematics: Breaking down barriers. *Minority Teacher Recruitment, 3* (1) 1, 8–9.

chapter  6

Acquisition of Information and Individualizing Learning

This chapter will help you to:

◆ state uses of the structure of knowledge,

◆ define criteria for selecting instructional methods,

◆ explain the role of the social studies textbook,

◆ list elements of direct instruction,

◆ define variables that can be altered when individualizing instruction, and

◆ explain examples of approaches to individualized instruction.

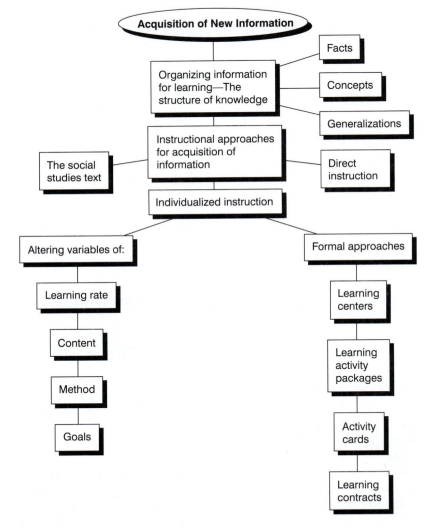

Figure 6–1
Acquisition of information and individualizing learning.

Case Study

I HAVE TO COVER THE CONTENT!

During a recent in-service workshop for teachers, the issue of pupil motivation for learning social studies material was addressed. The presenter emphasized that motivation increases when content is adapted to the topics and when issues are introduced that are of compelling interest to learners. More specifically, the speaker pointed out that "elementary children are interested in understanding people but may not be interested in people who lived long ago or far away. If we capitalize on the natural interest of young people to understand themselves and the world around them, motivational problems will diminish."

"That sounds fine," commented one of the teachers, "however, that's not realistic. I don't have the option to merely change the curriculum to fit the whims of my young people. The state has guidelines that identify what I am supposed to teach during the year. I am held accountable for covering that content, and standardized tests are used to measure whether or not I have done my job. Those tests are published in the local papers and if our children do not score high enough, we are subjected to criticism and pressure. In addition, the teachers that have my people in future years are going to assume that I have covered the curriculum. If I don't do that, people in my class will be at a disadvantage and poorly prepared to achieve success. I have no option but to cover the content of the textbook with no regard to whether the kids find it interesting."

What Is Your Response?

1. Do you think the suggestions of the presenter are unrealistic?
2. Do you think the points made by the teacher are valid?
3. What problems do you see with the points made by both individuals?
4. How can the need to motivate learners be reconciled with the requirement to address curriculum guidelines?
5. Should standardized test scores be the major tool for holding schools and teachers accountable? Why or why not?

INTRODUCTION

There is no one best way to teach social studies. There are a variety of appropriate instructional methods. The question is not, "What method is best?" Rather, we should ask, "What method is best for this group of learners, most likely to result in the accomplishment of important educational goals, and consistent with the nature of the content I am teaching?" Thus teaching is a deliberate decision-making process requiring consideration of several variables rather than a search for a limited number of foolproof ideas.

Unfortunately, surveys have found that social studies ranks close to the bottom of the list of subjects elementary pupils like (McGowan, Sutton, & Smith, 1990). This seems curious

Good social studies instruction involves gathering information from a variety of sources.

because the basic focus of social studies is people. Most of us find people intriguing and fascinating. We are interested in finding out about ourselves and those others who share this planet with us.

Consider how eager people are to share information about their own experiences. Daily newspapers feature dozens of human-interest stories. Racks at the supermarket checkout stand are filled with magazines that focus on the lives of people. Why then do pupils often see as boring and irrelevant the only subject of the curriculum that has people as a major focus? We suspect it has a lot to do with how the subject is taught and what is emphasized.

In order for us to move toward a more interesting and productive social studies we need to engage in self-reflection. Most of us get caught in the "tradition trap." We tend to teach the way we have been taught and assume this model is the appropriate one. If we spent a considerable amount of time when we were in school memorizing state capitals, the names of the presidents, and tedious lists of imports and exports, we assume that is what social studies teaching must be about. If we spent our days involved in social studies lessons requiring us to construct relief maps made of salt and flour and forts made of ice cream sticks, then these activities just naturally seem to find their way into our lesson plans. This is not to say that, under certain circumstances, these activities may not be worthwhile. What we do want to emphasize, though, is that tradition, alone, is an inadequate guide to selecting instructional experiences for our social studies lessons. To keep our social studies classes lively and relevant, we need to consider why we are selecting a particular instructional approach. What do we want our young people to learn? Why is this important? What is the most engaging way we can involve them in learning this information?

Lessons developed in light of this kind of reflection can make social studies one of the most engaging parts of the elementary curriculum. We look forward to your joining us in the effort to build involving lessons that help pupils understand their world and approaches to making it better.

ORGANIZING INFORMATION FOR LEARNING: THE STRUCTURE OF KNOWLEDGE

Answering the question What content should I teach? is a first step in planning a social studies lesson. This must involve more than simply deciding which facts should be taught. As mentioned in earlier chapters, social studies content can be drawn from a wide variety of sources. Any one subject is a source of more facts than can reasonably be included in a curriculum. Even if we could narrow down our list to a manageable number of facts, a lesson featuring nothing more than a long list of facts to be memorized has little potential to motivate learners.

Lessons featuring confusing jumbles of unrelated facts have given social studies a reputation for being boring and unrelated to the real world. One of the authors once overheard a parent responding as follows to his son's worries about his social studies grade: "That's okay, I could never figure out why it was important to learn all of those names and dates." If parents, pupils, and teachers are to view social studies as an important topic in the curriculum, they need to perceive that the content is important. This implies a need to include much more than arrays of isolated facts in our instructional planning.

One approach to this challenge features the use of the *structure of knowledge*. The structure of knowledge is based on the work of such important learning theorists as Jerome Bruner (1960) and Hilda Taba (1962). It provides a way to organize content according to the importance of its individual components. A given component of knowledge is viewed as becoming more important as it increases in explanatory power and in helping predict actions and events.

For example, any subject includes a huge number of specific bits of information called *facts*. However, a single subject has a more limited number of generalizations, principles, or main ideas. These big ideas can be used to organize facts and other more specific pieces of information. These major organizational patterns help scholars in individual fields interpret events and predict future events. A person who is considered to be an expert in a field, whether child growth and development or nuclear physics, is someone who has a firm grasp of these main ideas or generalizations.

The structure of knowledge identifies three levels or types of information. These levels move from the narrowest, most specific type to the broadest, most inclusive type. The three levels are defined as (1) facts, (2) concepts, and (3) generalizations (see Figure 6–2).

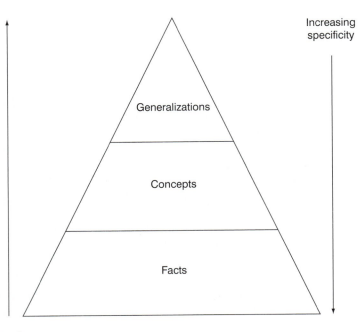

Increasing
transfer value

Figure 6–2
The structure of knowledge. Note the broad band of so-called facts at the bottom of the pyramid. There are fewer concepts and even fewer generalizations. Facts have limited transfer value. Concepts and generalizations, however, have wide transfer value that allows people who grasp them to understand and predict events. Facts, concepts, and generalizations are all important. Facts provide specific examples of concepts and generalizations. However, if they are not tied to important concepts and generalizations, they become bits of trivia with little utility. Facts chosen to be taught in social studies classes should be those that illuminate or help pupils learn important concepts and generalizations.

Facts

Facts are specific bits of information that relate to a specific event, time, place, or person. Here are some examples:

- Lincoln was born in 1809.
- Mountains cover between 10 and 15% of New Mexico's land surface.
- Wyoming has fewer residents than Colorado.
- Dover is the capital of Delaware.
- Mexico City has a larger population than New York City.

Because facts refer to specific circumstances, they have little explanatory and transfer power. For example, knowing that Thomas Jefferson was the third president of the United States, by itself, does not provide us with information that helps us explain or predict any other event. This does not mean that knowing Jefferson was the third president has no value. Certainly this information opens up the possibility of learning more about actions and events during his tenure in office that took place and still affect our lives. However, the fact that Jefferson was our third president offers a quite narrow and limited entrée to broader, more encompassing and sophisticated information.

Facts, however, are useful. They provide concrete and specific examples that serve as building blocks for the development of the next levels of the structure of knowledge. However, because there are so many facts about every subject, it is impossible to teach them all. We must choose those that are most important. Not to do so is to risk overwhelming learners with too many bits of information. For facts to be retained in the memory, they need to be organized around some common theme. This is where *concepts* become important. Concepts facilitate the organization of facts and provide important intellectual foundations for further learning.

Concepts

Concepts are wonderful intellectual tools that enable us to simplify our world and make sense out of large quantities of information. They are labels that we give to categories of information that have certain common attributes. For example, the concept *automobile* helps us organize a vast array of data regarding a mode of transportation that includes vehicles of different sizes, shapes, colors, and other special features. When we see a new model for the first time, we are able to quickly place it in the category *automobile*. Understanding that this new example fits into the category *automobile* also allows us to have certain expectations and provides us with some criteria for evaluating the example. How well, for example, does this new model fulfill the critical attributes of this mode of transportation?

In addition, the concept *automobile* links to other concepts such as transportation, mobility, change, production-line manufacturing, imports, exports, and so forth. Unlike facts that are tied to specific situations, concepts have broader applicability. The following are some examples of social studies concepts:

- Change
- Power   *Concepts*
- Government
- Latitude
- Culture
- Inflation

Concepts have assigned meanings or definitions. The defining characteristics of a concept are called *attributes*. For example, the concept *triangle* is defined by these attributes: (1) it is a two-dimensional figure and (2) it is enclosed by exactly three straight lines.

Concept learning helps pupils learn how to organize information into categories that are useful for storing and retrieving information.

In social studies, few concepts are as easily defined as *triangle*. Concepts such as *democracy, culture,* and *socialization* have many defining attributes. One of our challenges as social studies teachers is developing lessons that help pupils understand these complex concepts. This is something that needs to be done if we expect members of our class to master the even more sophisticated content embedded in generalizations.

Generalizations

Generalizations are statements of relationships among concepts. These statements of relationships often have an "if-then" characteristic. To follow our automobile example, a possible generalization could be, "As automobiles increase mobility, patterns of land use change." In this generalization, a relationship among the concepts *automobile, mobility,* and *change* is expressed.

This generalization also illustrates the explanatory and predictive power of generalizations and their transfer across time and space. For example, a lesson focusing on history could use this generalization to frame the study of transportation changes in American cities since the advent of the automobile. Lessons learned from this kind of study could provide the basis for transfer of learning related to pupil predictions, for instance, what might happen if personal transportation improved in parts of the world where few people presently own automobiles. Generalizations help us to understand and predict events. They concisely summarize huge volumes of information.

The "truth" of generalizations is determined by their reference to evidence. Some generalizations that we hold today may be changed in the future as more evidence is gathered. A good generalization is one that helps us arrive at useful explanations and predictions. If we find that existing generalizations are not useful in helping us explain events, we need to consider revising them. Instructionally, this means that we cannot be satisfied with just presenting a series of generalizations for pupils to learn. We need to encourage them to test the adequacy of existing generalizations by applying them to new situations. This process can provide the social studies classroom with excitement and energy.

Let us now apply the structure of knowledge to making decisions about what you will teach. The first step involves planning. As you review the curriculum for the grade you teach, you should identify generalizations you want the pupils to understand. Most curriculum guides are organized around main ideas or generalizations, although they may not be explicitly stated. If you do not find generalizations in the material you are using, review it and try to identify the main organizing ideas. (See Figure 6–3.) To see how this works, read the following passage and see if you can identify at least one generalization or main idea.

Comparing Prices

Mr. Jones lives in a small town about 50 miles from a large city. In his town are only a few stores. Mr. Jones likes to work in his garden, and there is one nursery in his small town. When he went to the nursery to buy a new rosebush for his garden, the price was $10.00.

A few days later, Mr. Jones made a trip to the large city. In that city there are several nurseries. He stopped at one of the nurseries and discovered that rosebushes were only $7.00. Why would the prices be less in the larger city?

One reason might be something called *competition.* In his small town there was only one choice of a nursery, and customers did not have any choice. The owner did not have to work as hard to get customers to come to the nursery because there was no other place for people to get what they wanted. However, in the large city, there were several nurseries and the owners had to compete with each other to get customers. They set their prices just high enough to make a profit but low enough to get customers to come to their nursery rather than one of the other nurseries.

Another reason why prices might be lower in the city is that there are more customers to buy the products. For example, the nursery owner in the large city might sell 50 rosebushes, and the nursery owner in the small town might sell 10 rosebushes. The owner selling 50 bushes can charge less for each bush and still make a profit. The owner selling only 10 bushes needs to charge more in order to make a profit and stay in business.

The generalization "competition leads to reduced prices" is not explicitly stated but is clearly implied. Identifying this generalization as the focus allows you some creativity and flexibility in your teaching. Perhaps your class has little interest in rosebushes, or you may have learners who are not skilled readers. You are not limited to using this short printed passage to teach this generalization. Once you have selected it as a focus for instruction, you are free to develop other approaches to convey the necessary information. For example, you might set up a simulation of some kind to help pupils grasp the relationahip between competition and reduced prices. The generalization provides a focus that can be used to help different pupils master the same content in different ways.

The following diagram illustrates how you can use the structure of knowledge for planning. Note that (1) the focus generalization is clearly stated, (2) the concepts that are embedded in the generalization are specified, and (3) specific content samples related to the concepts are identified.

Focus Generalization: _____

	Concept 1	**Concept 2**
Content Sample		
Content Sample		

A completed planning diagram might look something like this:

Focus Generalization: Different cultural groups use similar environments differently, on the basis of their cultural traditions, values, and levels of technology.

	Cultural Traditions	**Values**	**Technology**	**Use of Environment**
Content Sample Arctic Environment: Eskimo	(Facts relating to Eskimos)	(Facts relating to Eskimos)	(Facts relating to Eskimos)	Facts relating to Eskimos
Content Sample Arctic Environment: Laplander	(Facts relating to Laplanders	(Facts relating to Laplanders)	(Facts relating to Laplanders)	(Facts relating to Laplanders)

Figure 6–3
Using the structure of knowledge for planning.

Often it is necessary to adapt generalizations to the developmental level and needs of the pupils in a given classroom. They may need to be stated in relatively simple and concrete terms for primary grade pupils. For example, we could adapt the automobile generalization mentioned earlier to a first- or second-grade level by restating the generalization to read, "More cars bring many changes to our neighborhood." The focus of a plan built around this revised generalization could be the impact of transportation on a neighborhood and on the probable consequences of a decision to build new roads and highways in or near an existing neighborhood. For the fourth grade, the restatement might read, " Increased use of cars has brought many changes to our state." This restatement is more complex and abstract than the early-grades version, but it still focuses on the same basic idea of how changes in transportation lead to other changes.

Once focus generalizations are identified, the major concepts imbedded in them are identified. For example, the concepts *transportation, mobility,* and *change* would be central to understanding the generalization identified above. Once we have the concepts identified, we move on to consider what needs to be done to help learners understand them. Approaches that are appropriate for the age and background of the learners need to be identified. The concept of change, for example, needs to be taught using concrete, observable, and personal examples for the primary-grade pupil. Chapter 7 provides information on successful approaches to promoting concept learning.

After focus generalizations have been selected and key concepts identified, facts and other specific kinds of information can be identified. The decision about which facts and specific information to include is based on what is needed for pupils to understand the focus generalizations and concepts. Careful identification of the generalizations and concepts provides a useful screening tool for determining the relevance of individual facts and other pieces of highly specific information.

Using a structure-of-knowledge approach to planning helps us to respond to learner diversity and motivational concerns. We are free to choose many different kinds of content samples and illustrative facts as we plan lessons designed to help learners understand the guiding generalizations and concepts. This establishes a condition that allows us to incorporate material into our lessons that has high interest value for learners.

In summary, the structure of knowledge helps us to select and organize information for instruction by providing criteria we can use to select materials that will "connect" to our own group of learners. The approach allows us to maximize our creativity. It frees us from dependence on a specific text and allows us to ask, "What are alternative ways I can teach these concepts and generalizations?" The answer to this question can help us identify alternative content samples and learning activities that are particularly relevant to our own learners. The focus on main ideas, supported by teacher-selected materials that relate to the interests and developmental levels of individual pupils, stimulates learner interest and promotes learning that transfers to multiple situations.

INSTRUCTIONAL APPROACHES FOR ACQUISITION OF INFORMATION

Once the content has been organized to facilitate learning, the next step is determining how to teach it. There is no best way of teaching social studies. There is no method that is appropriate for meeting all of the social studies objectives, for all of the learners, in any setting. There are a variety of useful approaches. The skill is in knowing which approach to use in order to accomplish important outcomes for a given group of pupils. In making this decision there are several factors to consider.

First, we need to think about the proposed learning outcomes. There are multiple social studies learning outcomes. Among them are outcomes on basic information, skills, and values. In considering outcomes, we also need to think about how we would like pupils to apply what they have learned and about the relative sophistication of the thinking we are trying to promote.

A second factor to consider is the nature of the learners. What do we know about their prior knowledge, interests, and skills? Some of them will arrive in the classroom with a rich background in social studies, and others will have very little. Some will be interested in the social studies, while others may not hesitate to inform us that it is their least-liked subject. Some pupils will have good reading, research, and study skills; others will not. Children will arrive from a variety of cultural backgrounds, and some may not be proficient speakers of English. The wide range of their individual backgrounds ensures that no one instructional approach will succeed with all learners.

A third factor to consider is the availability of resources. All teaching methods require some support resources. If these resources are not present, instruction will not succeed. Consider, for example, the futility of planning Internet-related instruction for classrooms lacking computers with an Internet connection.

In summary, successful instruction results from appropriate consideration of the kinds of learning outcomes we are seeking, the nature of the learners with whom we are working, and the availability of specific kinds of support materials. Subsections that follow introduce some common instructional approaches. These include:

- Textbook-based instruction
- Direct instruction
- Individualized instruction

Textbook-based Instruction

The most common resource for teaching social studies is the textbook. Nearly all classrooms have textbooks. For some teachers, the text *is* the social studies curriculum. They feel compelled to cover the book in a page-by-page sequential manner. There are several potential problems with this approach. For example, no single textbook can adequately meet the interest and reading levels of all learners. Those who have difficulty reading may become frustrated and create discipline problems in the classroom.

Further, content in textbooks may be out of date. The process of writing, publishing, and adopting textbooks takes time. This means that some of the information they contain is several years old when they are published. The problem is compounded because school districts and states usually cannot afford to buy new books more often than once every five to seven years. Potentially, content a youngster reads in a textbook may be as much as a decade old—a significant problem in a subject such as social studies where information changes very rapidly.

Despite its limitations, the textbook can be a useful starting point for instructional planning. We can use a structure-of-knowledge approach as we review the text and identify the basic concepts and generalizations we want to use in our instruction. Once we identify these, we can think of ways to supplement the text content that will teach the identified concepts and generalizations in ways that work well with the characteristics of learners in our own classroom.

Suppose, for example, that we decided to look for additional material to teach this generalization: "The supply and demand for a good or service affect its price." This generalization can be easily adapted to meet the interests of learners of various ages and levels of sophistication. For example, even many younger children are aware that those toys in high demand have higher prices. Upper-grade pupils can investigate the same idea by considering tickets for sporting events or the cost of gasoline for cars as a function of demand. The point is that we can devise lessons that lead to an understanding of the generalization using materials, examples, and activities that are tailored to the nature of the specific youngsters we teach. These approaches may well feature *some* content from the textbook. But the textbook functions just as one of a number of sources of relevant information.

A difficulty many learners have in working with textbooks has to do with the style of writing. Social studies textbooks are not storybooks. They do not normally have a plot with familiar characters that pupils can follow. This makes it difficult for some learners to comprehend the material.

One of our tasks as teachers is to help people in our class cope with textbooks' sometimes-challenging prose style. To help learners' overcome their fear of drowning in the huge volume of content in the text, we can help them appreciate that they are not expected to recall every detail. Assignments that encourage learners to regard textbooks as simply one of a number of data sources they can use to seek answers to questions often work well. These assignments give them a well-defined purpose for reading. They allow learners to ignore irrelevant information as they seek out specific details needed to respond to questions. These kinds of assignments allow them to skip some material without feeling guilty and, in general, to feel much less intimidated when asked to extract information from their texts.

Another approach that is useful in helping learners obtain information from the text is to make clear to them how they will be expected to use what they will be reading. This is known as *informing them of the criterion task*. This simply means letting pupils know what they will have to demonstrate to the teacher to show that learning has occurred. Often we can convey this information by providing pupils with clear information about what they will be expected to learn from the assigned reading material. An example will clarify the importance of this step.

Suppose you are an elementary-school learner. Without providing you with any information about the purpose of this reading assignment, your teacher assigns you the following selection entitled "Mountains." Please read the passage now.

Mountains

In mountain regions the higher parts of the mountains are cooler than the lower parts. As air cools it is unable to hold as much moisture. When this happens the moisture in the air falls as rain or snow.

In North Africa the Atlas mountains stretch across the countries of Morocco, Algeria, and Tunisia. These mountains serve as a wall between the coastal areas and the Sahara Desert. During the winter, warm winds containing lots of moisture from the Atlantic and Mediterranean blow across these countries. As this warm air rises over the Atlas mountains, it cools and rain or snow falls on the mountains. As a result there is skiing in the Atlas mountains. This also means that most of the moisture is gone from the air, so the desert gets very little rainfall.

At the eastern end of the Mediterranean, winter winds blow from the Mediterranean across the hills and mountains in Israel, Lebanon, and Syria. As a result, the highest peaks of Lebanon are covered with snow for much of the year. These snow mountains are only about 25 miles from the coast where warm weather crops such as oranges can be grown.

There is a surprisingly large volume of information in this short passage. As a reader who has received no specific instruction from the teacher about what to look for, you might have focused your attention on one or more of a number of topics, including:

- Differences in air temperatures at different elevations
- The impact of air temperature on precipitation
- General locations of mountains in North Africa
- Specific countries in North Africa with mountains
- Mountains as a barrier separating the Sahara Desert and coastal areas
- Wind directions from the Atlantic and Mediterranean in the countries of Northern Africa during the winter months
- Reasons for winter rains in mountainous areas of Northern Africa during the winter months
- Explanation of why there is a desert on one side of the Atlas Mountains
- Wind patterns at the eastern end of the Mediterranean Sea
- Reasons snow is found in some areas of Lebanon that are only 25 miles distant from warmer coastal areas

Without teacher instructions about what to look for, individual learners who read this material may have quite different views regarding what the passage was about. If the teacher's view of what constitutes the important content in the passage differs from what some pupils focused on, these pupils may not perform well either during a follow-up discussion or on a comprehension check.

To avoid this situation, some simple directions to pupils before they read the passage would be helpful. Here are some examples of what might be done:

- "Read the passage to find out names of places in North Africa and the Middle East where it snows."
- "Read the passage and then make a diagram showing what happens to moisture-bearing winds when they are pushed upward by mountains."
- "Read to find an answer to this puzzle: Moist winds blow across the countries of Northern Africa; yet, parts of these countries include some of the driest land in the world, the Sahara Desert."
- "Read the passage and be prepared to explain how places that are only 25 miles apart can have very different climates."

Clear instructions of this kind communicate clearly to learners what they are to look for as they read and what they are to learn and/or do. They greatly reduce children's frustration levels and enhance the likelihood that they will focus on the appropriate information.

Another useful approach for using the textbook to acquire information is to construct and use graphic organizers so that learners can actually see the linkages and relationships among ideas presented in the text. Some examples for doing this are provided in Chapter 14, "Social Studies and the Integrated Curriculum."

Direct Instruction

Another common approach for helping learners acquire basic knowledge is *direct instruction*. This approach is also called *active teaching* (Woolfolk, 1998) or *explicit teaching* (Good & Brophy, 1997). This instructional model popularized by Hunter and widely used in many schools is an example of direct instruction. The approach features instruction that it is highly teacher-centered, includes presentation of information in small increments with much checking, and provides many opportunities for pupils to practice what they have learned. More specifically, direct instruction often has these characteristics:

- There is a strong and clear academic focus.
- Lesson objectives are clearly stated and communicated to the learners.
- Material is presented in a structured manner and in small increments.
- Pupils' work is monitored closely and understanding checked frequently.
- Teachers model what pupils are expected to do.
- Learners first practice responses under teacher guidance before engaging in independent practice.

The following sequence of events for applying direct instruction to the classroom is based on research in teaching fourth-grade mathematics (Good & Brophy, 1997).

1. *Daily Review (6-8 minutes).* Previously learned concepts and skills are reviewed or homework is checked.
2. *Lesson Development (About 20 minutes).* Teachers present new content through explanations, demonstrations, illustrations, and so forth. Teacher questions are used to check pupil comprehension and to promote discussion and meaningfulness.
3. *Seatwork (About 15 minutes).* Learners practice and apply what they have learned. There is active teacher monitoring and checking of work to hold the pupils accountable.
4. *Homework Assignment.* Learners are given regular homework assignments to practice independently what they have learned in class.
5. *Periodic Reviews.* Reviews are conducted at the beginning of each week to go over what was learned the previous week, and monthly reviews are conducted every fourth Monday.

Because this sequence was provided to guide instruction in fourth-grade mathematics, the time allocations and some of the specifics would need to be altered for social studies.

Direct instruction is effective for teaching basic information and basic skills. It works well for teaching the following:

- Clearly structured information.
- Skills that can be taught step by step.
- Content that is relatively unambiguous.
- Information that is frequently tested using standardized tests.

The approach works well for teaching (1) basic social studies facts and concepts and (2) basic skills such as map and globe and research skills. If this is the nature of what you are teaching, then direct instruction is an appropriate choice. However, much social studies content does not fall within these content categories. When other kinds of learning purposes are pursued, for example, lessons focusing on the development of higher-level thinking skills, other models discussed throughout the book need to be considered.

Lesson Idea 6–1 presents an example of a lesson organized around the direct instruction approach. Note how the lesson plan follows the model presented above.

Lesson Idea 6–1

LEARNING MAP SCALE

Grade Level:	3–6
Objective:	Pupils will be able to use the scale provided on a map to calculate the distance between two points.
Materials:	Two maps at different scales, at least two model cars of different sizes, an atlas for each two pupils, and a ruler for each two pupils.
Review:	What is a globe or a map? Why are globes and maps useful to us? Who can tell me what these symbols represent on a map?
Lesson Development:	

1. Display toy cars to the class. What are these? Are these the actual size of the cars? When you get toy cars, are they always the same size? How much bigger would the real car be? How can we tell? What do we call these? We call them models. Remember yesterday we said that a globe or a map is a model of the Earth or of some part of the Earth.
2. Display maps of the same area but at different scales. Notice that these are two maps that include a model or a picture of some of the same places. Suppose you wanted to go from place A to place B. (Display map with a large scale where the two places look close together.) Does it look as if these two places are near each other or far apart? (Display other map with smaller scale where the two places look much farther

apart.) As we look at this map, do they look close to-gether or far apart? Why do you think they look farther apart on the second map?

3. The reason that these places look closer together or farther apart is because these maps are drawn at different scales. Look at our toy cars. Some toy cars are bigger than other toy cars because they are made at different scales.

4. We always need to look for the map scale when we are trying to determine how far apart things are. Point out the scale on the classroom maps. We can use this to determine how far apart things are. What does it say on the map scale for map one? It indicates that 1 inch on the map is the same as _____ miles. Let me demonstrate how I can now determine how far apart things are. I take my ruler and I discover that these two places are 2 inches apart on the map. If 1 inch is the same as _____ miles, then I can add and find that these two places are _____ miles apart.

5. Lets' do the same thing with the other map. How many miles in 1 inch? How many inches apart are they? What do I need to do to find out how far apart they are?

Guided Practice: Open your atlas to page _____ . I want you to work in your pairs and I want you to find the distance between these places I have listed on the board. (Circulate around the classroom to monitor success and provide corrective feedback.)

Independent Practice: For your homework tonight I want you to find a map. It might be a city map or a highway map of our state. I want you to identify the scale of the map and figure out the distance between any four places on the map. Bring both the map and your work to class tomorrow.

Individualized Instruction

Another approach that can be used when the focus is on the acquisition of information is *individualized instruction*. Successful teachers understand that young people in their classrooms have a variety of interests and ability levels. Some may have a wealth of previous knowledge that will facilitate their rapid learning and growth. Others may lack necessary prerequisite knowledge and skill required for understanding. Individualized instruction helps us to respond to these diverse needs and interests.

The term *individualized instruction* means different things to different people. Some think of individualization as implying an independent study environment in which each pupil works alone. In our view, individualized instruction is not synonymous with isolated study and by no means requires that pupils always work by themselves. Indeed, working alone may be totally inappropriate for some pupils and for meeting certain kinds of needs.

Several variables are manipulated when teachers plan for individualized instruction:

* The rate of learning
* The content of learning
* The method used in learning
* The goal of learning

Altering the Rate of Learning

The rate of learning refers to the pace of instruction and learning. In a classroom where the entire class is taught as a single group, it is often assumed that all pupils learn at the same rate. In reality, some pupils grasp information rapidly; others require much more time. When there is no planning for these differences, pupils who finish quickly may become behavior problems, and those who do not master the material in the allotted time may come to see themselves as failures. Neither of these outcomes is desirable. Individualized instruction that alters the rate of learning makes provision for pupils who learn at different speeds. When this variable is manipulated, the goals, content, and methods of learning remain the same for all pupils. What is changed is the time allowed for individual pupils to complete the learning task.

Altering the rate of learning requires the teacher to break a learning task into several parts and develop a *criterion task* for each part. Pupils must successfully complete the criterion task for each part before moving on to the next one. Pupils who do not master the criterion task continue to work on instructional material related to the part of the lesson that has proved difficult for them. They are recycled back to more learning material related to this lesson part. After doing additional work, they are allowed to attempt the criterion task again. This general approach allows pupils to proceed as quickly or slowly as they need to master individual lessons. Self-paced materials in a programmed learning text or self-paced computer programs are approaches to individualization that alter the rate of learning.

Altering the Content of Learning

In individualized programs that alter the content of learning, different pupils in a class are allowed to study different content to reach a common objective. For example, when the program objective focuses on helping pupils master research and writing skills, individual pupils may be given wide latitude in selecting their personal research topics.

When individualization is attempted by altering the content of learning, pupils may choose the content they will study from among several provided alternatives. This allows them to choose options holding more interest for them than some of the choices they do not commit to. As a result, pupil motivational levels tend to go up. A learning activity package is one format that can alter content of learning. (A complete description of a learning activity package appears later in this chapter.) A typical learning activity package describes the learning goals and suggests several options learners might follow to achieve them.

In individualized programs that vary the content to be learned, some pupils may elect to work alone. Others may choose to work in groups. To succeed, individualized learning that depends on varying content must be supported by many different kinds of learning resources. Such lessons typically demand a considerable amount of teacher planning time.

Altering the Method of Learning

Individualized instruction that varies the method of learning seeks to respond to pupils' different learning styles. Some people prefer to learn new things by reading about them. Others must see them or touch them. Approaches to individualizing that alter learning methods often require all learners to master the same content and objectives, but allow individual members of the class to learn the material in different ways. Often pupils have permission to select from among several alternatives. For example, pupils learning about the role of law in our society may choose to read about this topic, view films or filmstrips, listen to audiotapes, see a videocassette, or participate in a simulation exercise. Pupils may also be allowed to provide evidence of their learning in different ways. Some may choose to participate in a role-play exercise. Others might paint pictures. Still others might write a formal report.

Altering the Goals of Learning

Instructional programs that respond to the need to individualize by altering the goals of learning are uncommon. This approach allows pupils to make major decisions about what they study and learn. In these days, when teachers feel the public is holding them accountable for teaching certain prescribed skills and knowledge to learners, the political environment does not favor widespread adoption of instructional programs that appear to give young learners too much control over what they study. Where such programs exist, the teacher functions primarily as a facilitator who tries to sort out and respond to pupils' personal interests. It is an approach that presumes individual learners to be the best judge of their own instructional needs.

Instructional programs that allow learners to control what is taught and learned are much more common in community education programs than in public schools. Community education course offerings are largely driven by learner demand. If enough people want to learn how to play the banjo, usually someone will be found to teach the course. If no one expresses this interest, the course will not be offered.

Figure 6–4 summarizes ways in which the four variables discussed can be manipulated to individualize instruction.

Examples of Formal Approaches for Individualizing Learning

Decisions about which variables to manipulate to individualize instruction reflect teachers' values and school and community expectations. The specific subject matter to be studied also plays a role. For example, it is reasonable to expect all pupils to learn basic arithmetic processes, such as adding and subtracting. It is unlikely that teachers would consider allowing pupils to alter the goals of learning to avoid dealing with this kind of content. On the other hand, altering methods and pace might make perfectly good sense.

Several formal instructional approaches have been developed as ways of packaging individualized instruction, including the following:

- Learning centers
- Learning activity packages
- Activity cards
- Learning contracts

Variable	Pupil Role	Teacher Role
Learning rate	Works at own pace; seeks assistance when needed	Makes assignments; monitors work; provides assistance; checks for mastery
Content	Chooses topics to be studied in achieving goal; finds resources; works alone or with others interested in the same topic; works at own pace	Sets learning goals; provides alternative topics for study; helps find resources; monitors work; evaluates final product
Methods	Decides how to study a topic; arranges the environment for study; works at own pace; may work with others interested in the same topic.	Establishes goals; identifies content to be learned; provides alternative approaches to learning; monitors work; evaluates final product
Goals	Chooses own goals to achieve; helps establish criteria for evaluation; submits final product for evaluation when satisfied.	Challenges pupils to consider what is important for them to learn; negotiates goals; evaluates and establishes time line with pupils; provides assistance when needed; monitors progress; evaluates the final product using criteria established in cooperation with pupil.

Figure 6–4
Altering variables to individualize instruction.

Learning Centers

Learning centers frequently are used to individualize instruction in elementary social studies programs. They are designated areas of the classroom that contain materials for learning and directions telling pupils what they are to do. Often an attractive visual display at the center is provided to motivate interest in the focus topic. Centers often include a variety of learning resources such as books, pictures, tape recorders, computers and software, videocassette players and videotapes, assignment sheets, and study guides.

Fold-down learning centers with cardboard sides, which include general instructions and some needed information, are popular. These can be set up on tables and are easy to store once lessons requiring their use are over. Figure 6–5 illustrates a learning center that focuses on map and globe skills.

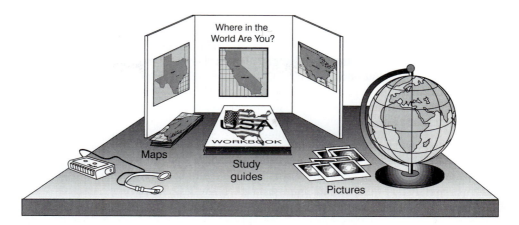

Figure 6–5
A learning center on map and globe skills.

In the learning center illustrated in Figure 6–5, a tape recorder with a cassette containing important information has been set up. The earphones allow individual pupils to listen to this information without disturbing others. Pupils may be instructed to use this center one or two at a time. Each pupil is free to go to the center when others are not using it. Often several centers are available for pupils to use. This makes it possible for several pupils to be working in centers at the same time.

The use of learning centers is an effective method for individualizing instruction.

Topic: Where in the World Are You?
Grade Level: 4–5
Objective: *Pupils can identify the type of map needed to solve a given problem.*
Intended Learning Outcomes: When you have completed this learning center, you should be able to identify different types of maps that can be used to solve different types of problems.

Sequence of Activities:

KWL

1. Take a minute to look at all of the material in the learning center. What do you already know about maps and globes? Make a chart with three headings: K = what I already *know*; W = what I *want* to know; L = what I have *learned*. Put what you already know in the K column. Put what you want to know in the W column. When you have completed work at the center you can fill in the L column with what you have learned.
2. Pick up the worksheet and listen to the tape. You may listen to the tape as many times as needed. When you have finished the worksheet and feel that all of your answers are correct, give it to the teacher. If you have a problem or do not understand something, ask the teacher for help.
3. Use the maps in the middle of the center to answer the following questions:
   • Which maps are best to use when you want to compare the populations of cities?
   • Which maps best help you to compare the elevations of different places?
   • Which maps are the best ones for helping you identify crops grown in different places?
   • Which maps are most useful when you want to know which places are in individual countries?
   • Which maps are most helpful when you want to find out climates of different places?
   • Which maps would be of most use to you in planning a trip from one place to another?
4. Application activity: Construct a map of our community. On your map, include something that is not usually found on a street map. (Examples: the types of stores, the location of stop signs and traffic lights, the location of fire hydrants, the location of apartment houses.)

Figure 6–6
Example of a learning center study guide.

Learning centers typically include study guides. A learning center's study guide includes questions pupils must answer and descriptions of activities they are to complete. Figure 6–6 displays a study guide designed for use in the center featured in Figure 6–5.

Learning centers allow teachers to manipulate several of the variables associated with individualized instruction. They can accommodate different rates of learning by allowing pupils to take as much time as they need to respond to questions and to complete activities.

Methods can be altered by providing pupils with alternative learning options. For example, directions at a learning center may allow pupils to choose ways of getting information from among the alternatives of listening to a cassette tape, reading a prose selection, or looking at a videotape.

When several learning centers are set up at the same time, the teacher may have to establish general time limits. For example, pupils may be told, "All learning center work must be finished by Friday." It is important that pupils be monitored when they are working at centers to ensure they are spending their time in a productive way. Pupils who complete their work before slower-working classmates need to be provided with enrichment activities. These will occupy them while others complete their learning center work. Sometimes teachers find it useful to allow talented early finishers to serve as tutors to help other learners.

Learning centers are a good option for teachers who have not had much prior experience in individualizing instruction. Their use does not represent a revolutionary break with familiar classroom routine. As a beginning, a teacher may wish to have only a single learning center. Others can be added as both teacher and pupils become more familiar with the approach.

Good learning centers require careful planning. Care must be taken to establish an appropriate content focus, to decide on appropriate learning activities for pupils, to gather needed learning materials, and to develop directions for users that are clear enough so that pupils will not need to ask for much clarification.

Learning Activity Packages

The *learning activity package* (LAP) provides a way of organizing individualized instruction. LAPS typically include these features:

- Pretest
- List of learning objectives
- Explanation of resources to be used
- Posttest or some other kind of evaluation procedure

To succeed when using LAPs, pupils must have the prerequisite skills and knowledge needed to accomplish the assigned tasks. Otherwise, they will become frustrated when doing work assigned with LAPs and will require a great deal of teacher help.

Not all of the material and information pupils need to complete work associated with a LAP needs to be included within the LAP itself. For example, the package may provide instructions directing pupils to information sources such as specific books, newspapers, and evening newscasts.

LAPs are basically instructional management tools. They allow teachers to organize instruction for pupils in convenient packages. They also allow teachers to create individualized packages for learners with specialized needs. For example, materials might be included in the LAP for hearing-impaired pupils allowing them to get information in print form that others might be asked to obtain by listening to audiotapes. A sample LAP is provided in Figure 6–7.

LAPs are useful vehicles for guiding pupils' work on research projects. They provide specific directions to learners regarding what they are to do. Pupils need to be monitored

Topic: Primary Sources
Grade Level: 5
Objective: *Pupils can identify primary sources and their importance when studying history*

I.   Pretest:

This learning activity package is about primary sources. If you know what a primary source is, answer the following questions and take your answers to the teacher. If you do not know, skip the questions and begin with the introduction.

1. What is a primary source?
2. Is our social studies book a primary source?
3. Is the newspaper a primary source?
4. Give one example of a primary source.

II.   Introduction

When you read our social studies textbook, do you ever wonder how the writers found out about the events they describe? They were not alive and were not participants in most of these events. Even if they were, they could observe only a few things that happened and could not know the whole story.

When you read an account of an event, you need to know how true or accurate it is. We all know that serious mistakes can be made when we believe something to be true that is not. Most people have to rely on the description of the event by others. Descriptions by people who were present when something happened are probably the most accurate. Information tends to get confused when it is passed from one person to another. People also forget things that happened to them a long time ago. You may recall how stories change when you have heard them from different people and some time after they happened. The same thing is true in history, and sometimes the stories or historical events we read about are quite different from what actually happened. By completing this LAP you will learn some ways of being a historical "detective" to check and see if the descriptions of events are accurate.

III.   Intended Learning Outcomes:

When you have completed this LAP you will be able to:

1. Define primary sources and secondary sources
2. Identify an example of a primary source
3. State how to use sources to check the accuracy of a description of an event

Figure 6–7
A learning activity package.

closely while they are doing work associated with LAPs. The teacher needs to help pupils keep busy at their assigned tasks and to counter a tendency many of them have to procrastinate. Careful monitoring also allows teachers to identify and respond to problems individual learners are experiencing.

LAPs allow teachers to alter the rate of learning, the method of learning, and even the content of learning. Pupils complete LAPs at their own pace. They may have opportuni-

IV. Activities

Definition: A primary source is a person or a record written by a person who was a participant or actual observer of an event. For example, individuals who attended a baseball game or who played in the game would be considered primary sources. An account of the game written by someone who was there, for example, the scorecard of the scorekeeper, would also be a primary source. Pictures of the game or stories told by people who were actually at the game, such as players, coaches, or spectators, would also be primary sources. A person who only read about the game in the newspaper and who then told a friend about the game would not be a primary source—he or she would be a secondary source. If you had a friend who went to the game and told you about it, he or she would be a primary source. If you then told someone else about the game, you would be a secondary source.

However, this does not mean that everything in the primary source will be accurate. Maybe your friend went to get a hot dog and missed some important action. It is always good to try and have more than one primary source.

1. Which of the following do you think would be primary sources in learning about the American War for Independence?
   • A diary of a soldier who was in the war
   • A movie about the war
   • Our social studies textbook
   • Letters from one general to another general
2. Read the story "The Shot Heard Around the World" in the social studies textbook. Next read the copy of the diary account of a British soldier. How are the stories different? Why do you think they are different? Also read the statements given by the men who were prisoners to their captors. Although they were present at the battle and can be considered primary sources, why might their accounts not be as accurate as we might like?
3. Why do you think it would be important to use primary sources when trying to understand what happened? What else might you need to think about when using primary sources?
4. If you wanted to write an account of how your school has changed in the last 10 years, what would be some primary sources that you could use?

V. Evaluation

Choose an event from the recent history of our community or nation. Identify some people or records that could be considered primary sources. If you identify some people, ask them to describe the event to you on a cassette tape. You may need to think of some questions you would like these people to answer on the tape. After listening to one or more tapes, write your history of the event. The teacher will help you with this. When you finish, turn in your account and the material you used, such as the tape, to the teacher.

Figure 6–7
Continued.

ties to select from among several alternative learning activities. Sometimes LAPs give pupils choices in kinds of content they may use to fulfill LAP assignment requirements.

Activity Cards
Activity cards describe choices pupils have as they decide how to go about learning assigned tasks. Each card focuses on one learning objective and suggests kinds of tasks

pupils might complete to master the material. Typically a set of activity cards focuses on the same general topic. Each card deals with a part of the topic.

Activity cards can be used in several ways. One approach is to assign certain cards to individual pupils on the basis of their special needs and interests. Another is to allow pupils to select cards focusing on a particular part of the general topic being studied. Teachers often begin work with activity cards by using them as extra-credit assignments for pupils who complete other work.

Activity cards are easy to organize and store; a large number can fit in a card file or shoebox. New cards can be added as they are developed. Cards can be kept from year to year and easily modified to accommodate changes in the overall grade-level social studies program. Particularly with older elementary pupils, teachers have found it useful to have learners develop activity cards of their own on topics of interest to them. Pupil-developed activity cards sometimes include marvelously imaginative activity suggestions. The process of participating in the development of their own learning tasks can give pupils a motivating sense of ownership in the instructional program.

Activity cards are useful vehicles for integrating content from many subject areas. For example, an activity card on the westward movement could well include activities drawing on mathematics, the arts, science, music, and other subjects. Figure 6–8 illustrates examples of three activity cards that were developed for use in an elementary social studies class.

Learning Contracts

A learning contract is an agreement between a teacher and an individual pupil. It states what the pupil agrees to do to satisfy certain learning requirements. The contract is signed by both the teacher and the pupil to indicate that both understand and agree to its terms. Learning contracts are of two types, open and closed.

Open learning contracts give the pupils a great deal of choice over such issues as the topic to be studied, the objectives, the learning activities, the assignments, and the criteria and procedures to be used for evaluation. They are most suitable for use with motivated, independent, mature learners. However, one of the authors had considerable success in using open learning contracts with some rebellious pupils who had refused to do any schoolwork. When they found they had some voice in what they would do and how they would do it, they could no longer fall back on many of the excuses they had used to justify doing nothing. Many of these pupils got busy and proved to themselves that they really could be successful learners.

Closed learning contracts are more common than open learning contracts. In contracts of this type, the teacher plays a more dominant role. The teacher, on the basis of his or her best professional judgment, identifies the objectives, describes learning activities and assignments, and lays out criteria and procedures for evaluating the learner's work.

A basic difference between a learning contract and many other schemes for packaging individualized instruction is that a given contract is designed specifically for a particular pupil. It is designed with a clear focus on this person's unique interests and aptitudes. Specific formatting of learning contracts varies, but large numbers of them include the following descriptions:

- What the pupil is to do
- What resources are to be used

Activity Card 1

Topic: Division of Labor
Grade level: Primary
Intended Learning Outcome: The pupils can provide examples of division of labor.

Activities:

1. Look through the magazines in the learning center.
2. Cut out five pictures of jobs that people are doing.
3. For each job write a sentence describing how this job helps others.
4. Draw a picture of a job you have at home.
5. Write a sentence telling how this job helps your family.

Activity Card 2

Topic: Goods and Services
Grade Level: Upper Elementary
Intended Learning Outcome: The pupil will identify businesses that provide goods and businesses that provide services.

Activities:

1. Look through the Yellow Pages of the phone book. Make a chart with three columns. In one column list at least 10 businesses you found that provide goods. In the second column list at least 10 businesses that provide services. In the third column identify at least 3 businesses that provide both goods and services.

Goods	Services	Both

2. Interview a relative or a friend. Find out whether his or her job provides a good or a service. Identify what he or she must know in order to do this job.

Activity Card 3

Topic: Local History
Grade Level: Middle Elementary
Intended Learning Outcome: The pupil will research an event in local history.

Activity: Are there any historical markers or historical sites in our community? If there is a marker, visit this site and write down what the marker says. Talk with other people in the community to find out what they know about the event described.

Once you have the information about the event, do one of the following:

- Prepare an oral report to give to the class.
- Draw a picture of the event.
- Write a play about the event and act it out for your class.

Figure 6–8
Activity card examples.

Learning Contract

Date: _____
Topic:

Activities:

I _____ agree to do the following social studies activities:

1.

2.

3.

4.

My work will be evaluated or graded using the following standards:

1.

2.

3.

I agree to have the work completed by _____.

_____   _____
Pupil Signature   Teacher Signature

Figure 6–9
Sample learning contract form.

- What kind of learning *product* the pupil is to produce
- What procedures will be used for evaluation.
- When all work is to be completed

    If you want to use learning contracts with learners who have never experienced this approach before, the best advice is to "think easy and think simple." It is important for pupils to understand exactly what they are to do to experience success. Success enhances self-esteem and increases motivation. A learner who succeeds with an initial learning contract will be much more interested in trying another one than a learner who fails. A sample learning contract is presented in Figure 6–9.

*   *   *

In summary, there are several variables that can be altered and there are several different approaches to individualized instruction. If you have the needed resources and learners who are able to work somewhat independently, then individualized instruction can be an effective strategy for helping pupils to learn information and skills.

As a teacher, you need to realize that your role changes when you use individualized techniques. You will still work hard, but you will work differently. For example, it takes tremendous amounts of time and energy to gather and organize materials. On the other hand, you may find that you commit less energy to tasks involving communication with the entire class. Some of the materials you prepare will take care of many of these essential communication chores. Individualized programs do not disengage you from the instructional role during class time. However, your role will change from that of a provider of information to a checker, monitor, and consultant. You will move about the classroom and work closely with individual pupils. A good deal of your time will be spent checking their work on one task and authorizing them to proceed to the next one. You will help people who are confused and work to get them back on the right track.

WEB CHECK

Note: Electronic addresses of sites on the World Wide Web change frequently. If the listed URL fails to work, use a standard search engine to locate the new address of the site.

- AskERIC Lesson Plans

  URL—**http://ericir.syr.edu/Virtual/Lessons/**

- Lesson Ideas

  URL—**http://www.teachnet.com/lesson.html**

  This site provides a gateway for information about lesson ideas for a variety of school subjects, including social studies. Social studies lessons are organized under the categories of geography, history, personal growth, and society.

- Social Studies

  URL—**http://www.npac.syr.edu/textbook/kidsweb/Mainsocial.html**

  This site provides access to a number of other sites that include examples of lesson plans and information about social studies content. Information is organized under the headings geography, government, and history.

- Personal Library Software

  URL—**http://ericir.syr.edu/plweb-cgi/fastweb?search**

  This site provides an excellent listing of social studies lesson plans. Many of them are designed for use in elementary school classrooms. This is a good place to look for specialized material. For example, one plan, designed for use with fifth- and sixth-grade pupils, focuses on steamboating in America. It includes a long list of supplementary readings to accompany the lesson.

- Geoworld's Social Studies Site Links

  URL—**http://home.istar.ca/~whamilto/sssites.shtml**

  This site features numerous links to outstanding sources of content for social studies lessons. Links are provided to the United Nations Home Page, the National Aeronautics and Space Administration Home Page, the Discovery Channel, and many other excellent sources of social studies content. Some links include examples of lesson plans. Highly recommended.

- Welcome to the Virtual Ellis Island Tour

  URL—**http://www.capital.net/~alta/index.htm**

  This site stands as an outstanding example of the kind of content available on the Internet that was not available to teachers and learners just a few years ago. Users, upon opening the site, are welcomed by a medley of patriotic songs. They are introduced to four immigrants who passed through Ellis Island on their way to the United States. Pupils select one and then follow this person through the trip from Europe to Ellis Island and the United States. There are wonderful examples of personal diaries and outstanding photographs. Highly recommended.

- Yahoo: Social Science

  URL—**http://www.capital.net/~alta/index.htm**

  This site includes a huge number of links to information sources that can provide good content for social studies lessons. Information is organized under more than 30 individual categories.

- Effective and Replicable Programs for Students Placed at Risk in Elementary and Middle Schools

  URL—**http://successforall.com/effect.html**

  This site features a long, well-written paper by two professors at Johns Hopkins University, Olatokunbo S. Fashol and Robert E. Slavin. They review a number of approaches for organizing content and delivering instruction. Information highlights characteristics shown to be effective in promoting learning among at-risk elementary and middle-school learners.

KEY IDEAS IN SUMMARY

1. Concepts are labels describing phenomena that share certain characteristics. Generalizations are statements of relationships among concepts. They are succinct statements that summarize what the best evidence indicates is true. Because of the explanatory and transfer value of concepts and generalizations, they should be important learning outcomes.

2. Textbooks are important tools to be used when teaching social studies. However, they should not determine the curriculum or be the only resource. Identifying generalizations that are being emphasized in a textbook can assist you in identifying

other examples that might be more appropriate to the learning needs and interests of the pupils.

3. Direct instruction is an effective approach for helping learners to acquire certain basic knowledge and skills. When these are the purposes of your lesson, then this is an appropriate helping instructional method.

4. Individualized instruction seeks to meet the diverse needs of pupils in the classroom. It does not mean, however, that all learners must work independently of each other. Some pupil needs are best met using individualized approaches.

5. Approaches to individualized instruction manipulate one or more of four sets of variables: (1) rate of learning, (2) content to be learned, (3) method of learning, and (4) goals of learning. The rate of learning is the variable that is most frequently altered. Individualized instruction that alters the goals of learning is the most rare.

6. Four common approaches to individualized instruction are learning centers, learning activity packages, activity cards, and learning contracts.

CHAPTER REFLECTIONS

Directions: Now that you have read this chapter, reread the case study at the beginning. Then, answer these questions.

1. Why do you think so many young people view social studies as one of their least favorite subjects?

2. How can the structure of knowledge help you address the problem of motivation and make social studies more relevant?

3. Reflect on your experiences in K–12 and higher education. Do you think the emphasis was on learning central concepts and generalizations? If these had received more emphasis, do you think you might have been more motivated?

4. How would you respond to this assertion? Standardized tests measure facts, so the emphasis in the classroom should be on the acquisition of facts.

5. There are some individuals who advocate the direct instruction approach for all lessons. What is your reaction to this assertion?

6. What do you see as advantages and disadvantages of using individualized instruction in the classroom?

EXTENDING UNDERSTANDING AND SKILL

1. Choose a social studies textbook for a grade level that interests you. Read one of the chapters in the book and identify one or more generalizations that the chapter

emphasizes. Then, identify concepts associated with this generalization. Brainstorm other approaches to teaching the same concepts and generalization.

2. Review the social studies curriculum content for a grade level that interests you. What are examples of content that you would teach using the direct instruction approach, and what might you teach through individualized instruction?

3. The term *social* in *social studies* implies groups. Indeed, one of the purposes of the social studies is to help learners understand how decisions are made in groups and to appreciate that people have varying perspectives on issues. If this is a priority, is it appropriate to use individualized instruction techniques in teaching social studies content? Write a position paper supporting or attacking this proposition: Individualized instruction has no place in the social studies program.

4. Select a social studies topic and learning objective. Prepare a set of learning activity cards for the topic. Include opportunities for the learners to make choices. Share your activity cards with others.

5. Work together with two or three others to prepare a learning activity package on a social studies topic.

REFERENCES

BRUNER, J. (1960). *The process of education.* Cambridge, MA: Harvard University Press.

GOOD, T., & BROPHY, J. (1997) *Looking in classrooms* (7th ed.). New York: Longman.

McGOWAN, T.M., SUTTON, A.M., & SMITH, P.G. (1990). Instructional elements influencing student attitudes toward social studies. *Theory and Research in Social Education, 18*(1) 37–52.

TABA, H. (1962). *Curriculum development: Theory and practice.* New York: Harcourt Brace and World.

WOOLFOLK, A.E. (1998). *Educational psychology* (7th ed.). Boston, MA: Allyn and Bacon.

chapter 7

Constructing Knowledge: Concepts and Generalizations

This chapter will help you to:

- identify characteristics of constructivist approaches and describe their relevance for elementary social studies instruction,
- point out approaches to developing pupils' metacognitive abilities,
- describe how questioning can be used to facilitate pupils' learning,
- distinguish between concepts and generalizations,
- explain *concept-attainment* and *concept-formation/diagnosis,* and
- describe steps in an *inducing-a-generalization* lesson.

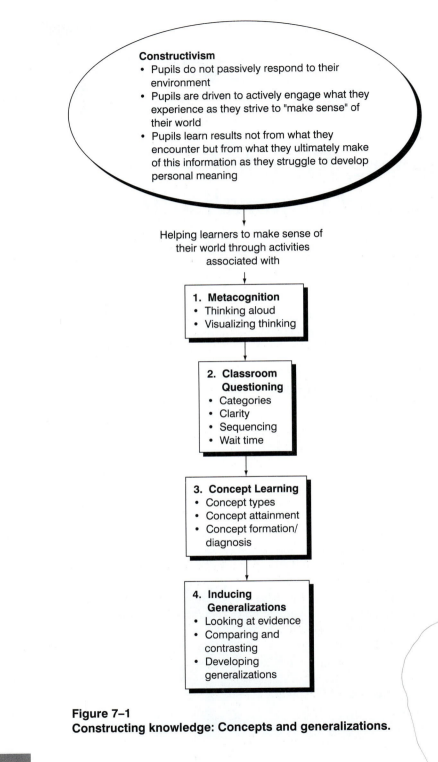

Constructivism
- Pupils do not passively respond to their environment
- Pupils are driven to actively engage what they experience as they strive to "make sense" of their world
- Pupils learn results not from what they encounter but from what they ultimately make of this information as they struggle to develop personal meaning

Helping learners to make sense of their world through activities associated with

1. Metacognition
- Thinking aloud
- Visualizing thinking

2. Classroom Questioning
- Categories
- Clarity
- Sequencing
- Wait time

3. Concept Learning
- Concept types
- Concept attainment
- Concept formation/ diagnosis

4. Inducing Generalizations
- Looking at evidence
- Comparing and contrasting
- Developing generalizations

Figure 7–1
Constructing knowledge: Concepts and generalizations.

Case Study

CAN PUPIL-DEVELOPED GENERALIZATIONS INCLUDE DANGEROUS BIASES?

The school district where Naomi Schwartz works as a fourth-grade teacher sponsored a workshop on teaching social studies. At the end of the session, Naomi raised this issue for the group to consider:

> I'm not sure I agree that it is always wise for us to present lessons that allow our kids to develop generalizations on their own. We have to remember that they are arriving at their conclusions on the basis of limited information. There may be a selection bias, however unintended, in the information we give them to work with. A result could be the develop-ment of some ideas that may reinforce stereotypes and result in conclusions about complex situations that are simplistic and irresponsible.
>
> Suppose I use an "inducing generalizations" technique with my fourth graders as we begin to study settlement of the Great Plains. What if, as a result of the information they study, some of them develop a generalization something like this:
>
> "Superior people, such as those who came into the Great Plains from the East, over time, defeat inferior people, such as the Native Americans who originally occupied the Great Plains."
>
> Now that extraordinarily biased statement may horrify those of us who are sitting here in this room, but isn't it possible that it's exactly the sort of thing some kids might come up with, given exposure to only a limited amount of information? I fear the answer is "yes," and I have to tell you I have great concerns about using an inducing-a-generalization approach with my young people.

What Is Your Response?

Think about Naomi's comments. Then, respond briefly to these questions:

1. Is it possible that elementary pupils might develop "explanatory" generalizations that are narrow, irresponsible, and biased?
2. Do you foresee any possible public-relations' challenges that might face teachers who use inducing-generalizations lessons?
3. Would it be possible to devise ways to help pupils avoid developing excessively narrow, stereotyped, and biased generalizations?
4. What might you do to select a range of content sufficiently broad that pupils would be unlikely to develop generalizations that fail to consider the broad range of perspectives that characterize the real world?
5. In summary, what do you see as strengths and weaknesses of the inducing-generalizations technique?

INTRODUCTION

Today, educators increasingly are committing to the idea that it is not enough for teachers to expose learners to content. For young people to acquire new information, they must be personally involved in constructing knowledge. This requires them to interact with the world around them in active ways. They must work with other learners as they look for patterns, resolve discrepancies, and "make sense" of the world in ways that are rooted in their past understanding and consistent with the cultural context within which they live. Instruction focuses on pupils' *interactions* with the content, not just on the *academic substance* of the content. This approach to instruction poses challenges for teachers.

For example, meaningful and active learner engagement with content takes time. As a result, fewer topics may be covered than in more traditional approaches. However, those that are investigated can be studied in greater depth. In a professional world where teachers are confronted with more and more standardized testing, there are legitimate concerns that a failure to cover certain content may result in lower scores on standardized tests.

Further, the emphasis on learners using their own intellectual powers to work through complex problems and issues and to develop answers based on their own thinking powers may result in some answers that, in the view of the teacher, are not right or correct. As Hein (1991) has noted, there is ". . . this tension between our desire as teachers to teach the truth, to present the world 'as it really is,' and our desire to let learners construct their own world. . . ." As professional teachers, we feel tugged both by (1) a predisposition to "get on with it" and tell our learners about the world as "it really is" (from our perspective) and (2) a recognition that some false starts and initially unsupportable conclusions are inevitable as learners begin to master more sophisticated thinking skills.

As pupils engage content and begin to discern useful explanatory patterns, they develop schemes to organize knowledge. Techniques that help pupils monitor their own thinking aid them in doing this. Good teacher questioning techniques help young people develop more sophisticated thinking skills as they work with new content. In addition, instructional approaches that focus on concepts and generalizations aid pupil learning. The explanatory power of concepts and generalizations helps pupils to transfer learning to new situations.

CONSTRUCTIVISM AND SOCIAL STUDIES LESSONS

Constructivism is an orientation committed to the view that learners do not passively respond to their environment. Rather, they are driven to engage what they experience as they strive to "make sense" of their world. What they learn occurs not from what they encounter but from what they ultimately make of this information as they struggle to develop personal meaning. For teachers, constructivism suggests that learners are involved in constructing their own knowledge and understanding rather than simply taking in isolated bits of information.

The constructivist view derives from multiple sources, particularly from the work of two prominent learning theorists, the Swiss Jean Piaget (Piaget & Inhelder, 1958), and the

Russian Lev Vygotsky (1962). Piaget emphasized that the construction of knowledge results from our personal interactions with the environment. Vygotsky suggested that the knowledge individuals construct is conditioned by their culture. That is, what we make of a situation is heavily influenced by our interactions with other people. The emphasis in constructivist learning on cooperative work with others draws heavily on Vygotsky's thinking.

Let us move now from this somewhat theoretical background to what constructivism suggests for teaching elementary social studies. First of all, it requires you to focus clearly on the learners you are teaching and how they are engaging the content. What they take away from your lessons depends much more on how they are personally involved with the new content than on the intrinsic nature of the content. If you expect learners to develop an emotional commitment to what you want them to learn, then it makes sense to develop lessons that focus on complete, complex, fully developed situations. This is in contrast to instruction that attempts to teach in isolation such things as map and globe skills, names of the states, products of countries, and so forth. This kind of basics-first instruction assumes that, at some future date, learners will put all this information together in ways that will help them understand real situations and problems. Constructivist teaching takes a different view. The assumption is that the so-called basics are best learned within the context of complete, complex situations that have the capacity for engaging pupils' interest.

Constructivist teaching requires teachers to help pupils develop thinking skills that will enable them to construct their own knowledge and understanding (Ringstaff & Yocam, 1994; Osberg, 1997). Further, there is a need to help class members control their own behavior and take responsibility for their own learning. Perhaps one of the most difficult aspects of teaching constructivist lessons is recognizing that when pupils are encouraged to think seriously about content and develop their own conclusions, there may be times when those conclusions differ from the teacher's. Finally, development of sophisticated thinking skills takes time. A trade-off that teachers committed to the constructivist approach have been willing to make is that the lack of superficial coverage of a large number of topics can be justified by helping learners develop sophisticated thinking skills that involve concentrated attention on a smaller number of topics.

Though individual teachers vary in what specific aspects of constructivist teaching they use in their classrooms, many feature some characteristics enumerated by Osberg (1997). These are:

- Instruction that focuses on depth rather than breadth
- Inquiry-oriented instruction designed to help learners transfer information to situations beyond the context in which it is learned
- Encouraging learners to change their perspectives as a result of considering new information
- Cooperative, collaborative learning rather than individual learning

METACOGNITION: TEACHING PUPILS TO MONITOR THEIR THINKING

Learning psychologists use the term *metacognition* to refer to conscious thought about how we think about a problem or dilemma. Pupils need to learn how to monitor their own thinking. This will help them select thinking approaches appropriate for various tasks they are trying to accomplish. Two approaches to helping pupils better monitor their thinking patterns are thinking aloud and visual thinking.

Thinking Aloud

The thinking-aloud approach is based on modeling, which research has shown to be a powerful instructional tool. As applied to thinking aloud, modeling requires the teacher to verbalize thought processes followed as he or she approaches a task. For example, suppose a teacher plans to have some fourth graders use maps to find distances (in miles) between selected pairs of U.S. cities. In preparation for this activity, the teacher might use a think-aloud approach similar to the example introduced in Lesson Idea 7–1.

Lesson Idea 7–1

FINDING DISTANCES

Grade Level: 4–6

Objectives: Pupils will be able to (1) locate selected cities on a map, and (2) use scale to calculate the distance between two points.

Procedure: Give pupils the following directions: "Today, your assignment will be to find the distances in miles between pairs of cities in the United States. To help you begin, let's pretend that someone gave me the same assignment I've given you. This is how I would go about it.

"I have to find distances between several pairs of cities. The first pair is Chicago and San Francisco. I begin by thinking about where these two cities are. If I don't know, I'll need to look in the back of the atlas, in the index. I need to find Chicago and San Francisco. For Chicago, I find a reference to B9. This tells me to go back to the map of the United States and find the letter B. (Do this.) There it is on the left side. Then I need to find the number 9 at the top. (Do this). Now, I'll simply move my finger even with the B until it is under the 9 at the top. Chicago should be near this spot. (Do this.) There it is! Now I know where Chicago is. I'll follow the same procedure to find San Francisco. The index tells me it is at C1. (Find San Francisco.)

"Now what I have to do is figure out the distance between Chicago and San Francisco. The first thing I am going to do is look at the scale at the bottom of the map. Remember we learned that the scale tells how many miles are represented by a given distance on the map. When I look at the scale, I learn that one inch on the map is equal to about 300 miles.

"The next thing I need to do is measure the distance on the map between San Francisco and Chicago. This is about six inches. Now, I know that one inch equals 300 miles. Six inches, then, has to be six times as far. So, I multiply six times

300 to find out about how far it is from San Francisco to Chicago. This turns out to be about 1,800 miles. (Briefly explain that this is a point-to-point air distance. Because of curves in highways, mountains, and other variables, the highway distance between San Francisco and Chicago is longer.)

"Now that I know how to compute the distance between one pair of cities, I can use the same procedure to compute distances between other city pairs."

Thinking aloud provides children with a model they can follow as they attempt a new task. Further, it points out to them the importance of thinking about how they are going to approach a learning activity before they actually begin working on it.

Visualizing Thinking

Visualizing thinking is another technique used to help pupils monitor their thinking processes. It helps them focus on the essential features of an assigned task. Teachers encourage pupils to prepare diagrams that indicate their understanding of the task and the kinds of information they will need. Pupils then use these diagrams to record notes about what they have read and learned. An example of this approach is illustrated in Lesson Idea 7–2.

Lesson Idea 7–2

THE UNHAPPY TALE OF THE MONGOOSE

Grade Level:	6
Objectives:	Pupils will (1) recall specific information from a reading selection, and (2) identify cause-and-effect relationships using a visual diagram.
Procedure:	Have all class members read this selection:

Pests have always bothered farmers. Crop damage from pests can be costly. At various times and places, landowners have tried to get rid of pests by introducing other animals that will eat them.

For example, in the 1800s, farmers in Argentina imported sparrows from England. These birds were brought in to eat moths. This did not work out as expected. The moths were eaten, all right, but the sparrows grew so numerous that they became a serious problem.

In the 1700s and 1800s, farmers in the West Indies tried several ideas to get rid of rats living in sugarcane fields. Some farmers imported weasels. Unfortunately, the weasels were attacked by a certain kind of fly, and they did not survive. Some farmers even brought in a species of ant that was famous as a "biter." They hoped that the ants would make life miserable for the rats. But the rats didn't suffer as much as the farmers had hoped, and rats continued to be a problem in the fields. One desperate group of farmers went so far as to import a number of giant toads that were reputed to be aggressive rat eaters. The toads, too, failed to get the job done.

In the early 1870s, West Indian farmers finally hit upon a solution that seemed to work. A small meat-eating animal called a mongoose was brought to these islands and released. The mongooses multiplied. Soon farmers noticed that the number of rats in their fields was decreasing. This good news was not to last, however.

After about 10 years, rats were becoming a problem again. The mongooses had discovered chickens. They preferred to eat chickens, and many flocks were lost. By 1900, the mongoose itself had come to be viewed as a dangerous pest. Governments in the West Indies paid hunters to kill them. The "solution" to the pest problem had turned into an even bigger problem for authorities.

To help pupils focus on key information as they read this selection, help them develop visual thinking by using diagrams to guide their reading and as a vehicle for taking notes. Abilities and interests of individual pupils in any class vary. Consequently, you may ask some learners to look for different things than others. One group might be given this assignment:

Learning Task One   Say to pupils, "Name some examples of animals that were released to control pests. What pests were they supposed to control?" In preparation for this learning task, students might develop a diagram such as the following:

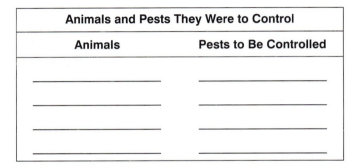

Animals and Pests They Were to Control	
Animals	**Pests to Be Controlled**
_____	_____
_____	_____
_____	_____
_____	_____

Learning Task Two   You might ask other pupils in the class to accomplish a task such as this: "What happened when the mongoose was first introduced? What happened that was expected? What happened that was not expected? How do you explain what people thought about the mongoose by 1900?"

A diagram such as this might help pupils accomplish this task:

Changing Attitudes Toward the Mongoose

What Happened When the Mongoose Was First Introduced?

_____

_____

_____

What Happened That Was Expected?	**What Happened That Was Unexpected?**
_____	_____
_____	_____
_____	_____

How Did People Feel About the Mongoose by 1900?

_____

_____

_____

Why Did They Feel This Way?

_____

_____

As pupils read the selection, they fill in the diagram. Teachers typically prepare visual-thinking diagrams for pupils who have not worked with them before. Once pupils gain experience with the technique, they make their own. The process of preparing diagrams helps pupils think visually and pay close attention to the specific requirements of the learning task. This helps them monitor and adjust their own thinking processes as they work on assignments. Improved understanding and enhanced self-confidence often result.

Using diagrams and outlines can help students see the connections between ideas.

CLASSROOM QUESTIONING

Good classroom questions act as prompts that help pupils develop meaning as they engage content presented in social studies lessons. Questioning is intimately associated with good teaching. This point has been recognized for years. Some authorities have gone so far as to define teachers as "professional question askers" (Aschner, Gallagher, Perry, & Asfar, 1961). In thinking about effective questioning, it makes sense to consider:

- Categories of questions
- Clarity of questions
- Sequencing of questions
- Wait time following questions

Categories Of Questions

Over the years, many schemes have been developed for categorizing questions. An extremely simple approach divides classroom questions into two broad categories: *low-level questions* and *high-level questions*. Low-level questions make modest intellectual demands of learners. Typically, they require pupils only to engage in knowledge-level and comprehension-level thinking. High-level questions demand more sophisticated thinking at the levels of application, analysis, synthesis, and evaluation.

Some organizational schemes further categorize questions according to their purpose or function. One such framework recognizes eight distinct categories of high-level questions (Marzano, 1992). These are:

- Comparison questions
- Classification questions
- Induction questions
- Deduction questions
- Error-analysis questions
- Constructing-support questions
- Abstracting questions
- Analyzing-perspectives questions

Comparison Questions

Questions in this category focus pupils' attention on similarities and differences. They include questions such as: "How are these two things similar? How are they different?"

Classification Questions

Classification questions ask pupils to group items according to characteristics they share. Examples are: "Which items should we put together? Why do you think so? If you wanted to tell a friend the 'rules' for putting something in each of these groups, what would you say?"

Induction Questions

Induction questions require pupils to arrive at conclusions based on their study of specific information. Questions of this kind help them seek relationships among specific items and develop explanatory principles or generalizations. Some examples include: "What similarities and differences did you observe, and how can you explain them? Is there a general rule that might explain what you've discovered?"

Deduction Questions

Questions in this category require a pattern of thinking that is the reverse of the pattern used in developing an answer to induction questions. In response to an induction question, the pupil considers pieces of information and then goes on to develop a general explanation. In a deduction question, learners begin with a general explanatory principle and then determine whether specific pieces of information are consistent with it. Here are some examples: "On the basis of the idea that each action has an equal and opposite reaction, what would you expect if we . . . ? What examples of free speech did you observe in the film?"

Error-Analysis Questions

Questions in this category force pupils to look for errors of logic or procedure. Such questions help pupils identify propaganda and other examples of data distortion. Here are some examples: "In what ways is the conclusion not right? What would be a better way to get the right answer? What information has been ignored by the person who decided this was true? What evidence would make you question this conclusion?"

Constructing-Support Questions

Questions in this category are designed to prompt pupils to look for information to support a position they have taken. Examples include: "What other information would support this conclusion? Under what conditions might this person's argument be true? What logical arguments support this conclusion?"

Abstracting Questions

Abstracting questions require pupils to identify patterns and relate them to new content. Often these questions include analogies and metaphors. Here are some examples: "What patterns did you notice in the short story we finished yesterday? How are these patterns similar to those in today's story? How is identifying a good idea like panning for gold? How might the saying 'Love is blind' apply here?"

Analyzing-Perspectives Questions

Questions in this category ask pupils to identify their personal positions and to consider the merit of other views. These questions seek to help them identify values that are important to others. Some examples are: "What are the assumptions behind your thinking? How would your conclusion differ if you held another set of assumptions? If you were a Native American living in the 19th century, how might you have viewed settlers coming into the West, and why?"

Clarity of Questions

Good questions are stated clearly. Unless a question is clear to pupils, it will confuse them because many answers may seem reasonable. Consider this question: "Who was the first president of the United States?" Because of the vague nature of the question, learners logically might answer, "a man," "a Virginian," "a general," "a farmer," or "George Washington."

These pupils would be able to answer the question with much more confidence if it were restated in a way that gave them a better idea of what the teacher really hoped they would say. For example, the teacher could have stated the question in this way: "What was the name of the first president of the United States?" This version is likely to prompt pupils to reply, "George Washington," which, in all probability, is the answer the teacher wants.

Setting the stage appropriately and setting the context for a question help pupils to understand what the teacher is looking for (Cazden, 1986). For example, a teacher might start a discussion with a low-level question to help pupils develop a general focus on a broad topic. ("Where is Chicago located on the map?") This could be followed by a higher-level question related to this general topic. ("Why do you think Chicago grew up at that particular geographic spot?")

Asking multiple questions before giving learners a chance to answer poses problems. When teachers do this, learners often become confused because they don't know which question they are supposed to answer. Discussions are much more productive when a teacher asks a single question and listens to and comments on pupil answers before asking more questions.

Sequencing of Questions

Many schemes for sequencing questions have been developed. We particularly like a simple approach that is useful for debriefing pupils. The focus can be a film, a story, part of a textbook chapter, or something else that has presented pupils with a situation where multiple perspectives are present. In approaching the task of discussing this kind of material, new teachers, in their eagerness to get pupils quickly into the complexities of the described situations, sometimes begin by asking questions that intimidate pupils. For example, they may start a discussion with a question that is heavily value-laden or with one that requires pupils to make a great leap beyond the literal information to which they have been introduced. This approach often leads to a classroom full of silent, fidgety youngsters.

A simple questioning sequence can avoid this problem. It involves just three major steps, and it begins with questions that are easy for pupils to answer and closely tied to the specific information they have just learned. Further, these questions don't require pupils to make value judgments. Nonthreatening opener questions give pupils confidence at the beginning of a discussion. They allow for a lot of information to be reviewed by the group and for the entire pool of new knowledge to be shared by the whole group. Once pupils are participating confidently in the discussion and once the basic facts have been brought out into the open, then the teacher begins to introduce more sophisticated questions. These will involve questions of value and of judgment that require pupils to go beyond simple recall of information. If an adequate *comfort level* has been established during the first phase of the discussion, pupils will be more inclined to take a chance and speak up during this second phase when they are asked to go public with somewhat risky value statements and personal interpretation.

The final stage of this three-step questioning process asks pupils to develop some broad conclusions or generalizations based on what they have learned or discussed. Such judgments require a great deal of personal interpretation and risk. However, with adequate base-building during phases one and two, pupils will be inclined to risk answers to these kinds of questions. Absent adequate preparation for this somewhat dangerous kind of responding to teachers' questions, pupils likely will remain silent.

The three phases in this questioning sequence are:

- Recalling specifics
- Comparing and analyzing views
- Concluding and generalizing

In stage 1, recalling specifics, the teacher asks simple questions designed to get all relevant information into the discussion. No interpretation is called for. ("What was the general sequence of events? What happened first, second, third, and so forth? Where did this story take place? What did these people eat for breakfast?")

In stage 2, comparing and analyzing views, the teacher begins asking questions designed to elicit the recall and explanation of different views and perspectives that were revealed in the focus material. There may be a focus on some contrasting values positions, and some questions will begin to ask pupils to go beyond the literal limits of the information they have encountered. ("What did the Native Americans think about the Puritans? What did the Puritans think about the Native Americans? Why do you think they had different views? What did the government in England think of the Puritans? What did the Puritans think of the government in England? How would you explain these differences?")

In stage 3, concluding and analyzing, the teacher asks questions designed to push pupils to formulate big explanatory ideas or generalizations. Questions often require pupils to stake out a values position. ("What makes people do the kinds of things some Puritans did to the Native Americans? Why did the Puritans and the Native Americans have such difficulty understanding one another? In general, why do people in different groups often fail to understand and appreciate one another?")

To see how this easy questioning sequence might work out in a classroom, let's look at an example. Suppose a teacher has asked the class to read about this situation:

> The small town of Noraville was shocked recently when a large dog attacked and severely injured a first grader who was waiting in the street in front of her house to catch a school bus. People in the town have been talking of little else.
>
> Some people point out that Noraville has no laws that require owners to keep dogs fenced in their own yards. They want the city council to pass a tough new leash law that would require owners to prevent their dogs from leaving their property.
>
> Dog owners have mixed reactions to this idea. Some think it would be a good solution. Others point out that the town has never had such a rule before and that there has never been a problem. Others wonder whether it makes sense for such a law to apply to all dogs. Some dogs, particularly tiny ones, represent no danger even to the smallest children, and owners of these animals feel they should not be penalized if one of their small pets briefly runs out of the yard. "How could my dog be a threat to anyone?" they ask.
>
> Parents of young children who aren't dog owners themselves have been the people who have been most interested in passing a new dog-control law. They argue that a law that prevents harm to even one child deserves to be enthusiastically supported.
>
> Members of the city council have been listening to arguments for and against the new law. They know they will have to make a decision, and they also know that some people in the town will be unhappy with any decision they make. Many members would be much happier if they didn't have to deal with this issue at all.

Recalling Specifics

TEACHER: All right, let's begin by just talking about what has happened. I want everyone who talks to tell me just one thing that is mentioned in what we just read. (Calls on pupils.)

Some examples of possible pupil comments:

- There was this dog that bit a girl.
- The girl was waiting for a bus.
- The dog didn't belong to the girl.
- People in the town are mad.
- Some people want a law to make people keep their dogs at home.
- Some people say all dogs aren't bad. Owners of little dogs don't think a law would be fair.
- Some parents are really upset. They want the city council to pass the law.
- People on the city council are afraid that some people will be angry if they pass a law and other people will be angry if they don't.

Comparing and Analyzing Views

TEACHER: In general, what do the parents seem to want, and why?

Some possible answers:

- Most of them seem to want a law.
- They're really worried about their kids.

TEACHER: What do the dog owners want, and why?

Some possible answers:

- It depends. Not all of them want the same thing.
- Some dog owners think a law would be OK.
- Other dog owners don't like the idea.
- Owners of small dogs don't think their dogs could ever hurt anybody. They don't want a law that requires them to keep their dogs in their own yards.

TEACHER: What concerns members of the city council, and why?

Some possible answers:

- They feel they are being pushed to take action, but they know that some people will be unhappy no matter what they do.
- They might be worried about doing something that would lose them votes.
- They probably are uncomfortable. They really wish they didn't have to deal with the issue.

Concluding and Generalizing

TEACHER: What does this information tell us about some of the people in Noraville?

Some possible answers:

- Depending on who they are, they have different opinions.
- Some people seem to think just passing a law will solve a problem once and for all.
- Some people don't like to deal with controversial issues.
- A new law that seems reasonable to some may seem unreasonable and unfair to others.

TEACHER: What does this story about Noraville tell us about people in general?

Some possible answers:

- People in communities tend to get really concerned and want to do something when children are threatened.

- An action that to some people seems to be a solution to other people seems to be nothing but another problem.
- Some people seem to worry more about their own inconvenience than about the well-being of other people.
- Community leaders, in making decisions, must balance views of many different people.

Wait Time Following Questions

What teachers do after they ask a question influences what pupils learn. *Wait time* refers to the period between the time the teacher asks a question and either (1) a pupil recognizes and responds, (2) the teacher goes on to another pupil who answers, or (3) the teacher restates the question or directs it to someone else. Research reveals that, on average, teachers' wait time lasts less than one second. There is merit in increasing this time to give pupils more time to think. Increasing wait time has been found to do the following (Rowe, 1986):

- Increase the probability that a pupil will answer the question
- Increase the length of learner responses
- Increase the likelihood that responses will involve speculative thinking
- Improve pupils' self-confidence
- Increase the number of learner-initiated questions
- Increase the total number of class members who participate in a discussion

LEARNING CONCEPTS

Concepts are labels applied to phenomena that share certain characteristics or attributes. For example, the concept *automobile* refers to something that has these attributes (among others):

- Functions as a personal vehicle, almost always with four wheels
- Powered by a gasoline or diesel engine (also, but rarely, by an electric motor)
- Direction of movement controlled by a circular steering wheel

Teaching pupils concepts such as *automobile* helps simplify their understanding of the world around them. Concepts provide a scheme that allows them to classify under a single label hundreds, even thousands, of individual examples that fit into the classification category. Once a young child grasps the basic requirements of what something must have to be called an automobile, he or she can quickly recognize examples that are associated with this concept or class regardless of differences in size, color, make, model, or age.

Recognition of a given concept also helps pupils distinguish between examples and nonexamples. For instance, mastery of the concept *automobile* makes it possible for learners to distinguish examples of this concept from trucks, buses, and motorcycles—

examples of related but somewhat different classes of objects. In short, concepts function as a kind of shorthand that allows people to group and recall information about a large number of things that share certain important characteristics.

Types of Concepts

There are three basic types of concepts:

- Conjunctive concepts
- Disjunctive concepts
- Relational concepts

Conjunctive Concepts

All defining attributes of a *conjunctive concept* must be present for something to be considered a proper example of this type. For example, the conjunctive concept *triangle* has these three attributes: (1) three sides, (2) a closed, two-dimensional figure, and (3) three interior angles. If any of these attributes is missing, it is not a triangle.

Disjunctive Concepts

In the case of *disjunctive concepts,* it is not necessary for *all* possible defining attributes to be present for something to be considered a proper example of the concept. The extra point in football is an example of a disjunctive concept (Fraenkel, 1980). There are three possible defining attributes (e.g., ways in which an extra point can be scored), but not all of them need to be present for an extra point to be awarded. The three defining attributes of the concept *extra point* are: (1) the ball can be run into the end zone following a touchdown; (2) the ball can be passed into the end zone and caught by an offensive player following a touchdown; or, (3) the ball can be kicked (not punted) through the uprights and over the crossbar following a touchdown. If any one of these three conditions (attributes) is present, an extra point is scored. Multiple attributes and the point that not all of them need to be present make disjunctive concepts somewhat more difficult for pupils to learn than conjunctive concepts.

Relational Concepts

Attributes of *relational concepts* bear a specific relationship to one another. Consider the concept *miles per hour.* There is a relationship between an attribute related to distance covered (miles) and an attribute concerned with time (hours). Mastery of relational concepts requires pupils to understand not only each attribute but also the nature of the relationship among attributes. As a result, relational concepts sometimes are difficult for pupils to learn.

* * *

In addition to problems associated with concept types, the number of defining attributes associated with a given concept affects the probable difficulty learners will have in mastering it. Concepts that have large numbers of associated attributes are particularly difficult. Abstract concepts that often are featured in social studies lessons, such as *democracy, citizenship, power,* and *socialization,* are examples of these kinds of complex, difficult-to-learn concepts. Because these concepts are important building blocks in many social studies lessons and are included in powerful explanatory generalizations, special attention needs to be devoted to teaching them to pupils in ways that are likely to promote real understanding.

Teaching Concepts

Concepts can be taught in various ways. Two formal approaches that are widely used are concept attainment and concept formation/diagnosis.

Concept Attainment

Concept attainment focuses on teaching concepts that the teacher has determined are important for pupils to know. The approach follows six basic steps:

- The teacher introduces the concept by name.
- The teacher presents examples of the new concept.
- The teacher presents nonexamples of the new concept.
- The teacher introduces a mixture of examples and nonexamples of the new concept; pupils attempt to distinguish between the examples and nonexamples.
- Pupils are asked to develop a definition of the concept of their own (e.g., explain what they see as its defining attributes).
- Pupils demonstrate their understanding of the concept by finding additional examples on their own.

The concept-attainment technique can be used to teach a variety of concepts. For example, a teacher who wishes to teach a relatively simple concept such as *desert* might begin by showing pupils pictures of a variety of desert regions. Next, he or she would introduce pictures of nondesert regions, and pupils would be told that these places were not deserts. During the next step, the teacher would show pupils a mixture of pictures: desert regions and nondesert regions. Pupils would be asked to identify those that were of desert regions. Then, the class would be asked to come up with a definition of *desert*. If pupils experienced difficulty, the teacher would provide some clues by asking them to look at the pictures of desert regions and nondesert regions and ask them to describe characteristics in the desert regions that were not present in the nondesert regions. (It is important that pictures of desert regions clearly reflect characteristics common to deserts.) Finally, pupils would be asked to identify other examples of deserts, possibly by looking through photographs in back issues of publications such as *National Geographic*.

More complex concepts, such as *justice* or *democracy*, can also be taught using this general approach. They will require more time because they have more defining attributes than a simple concept such as *desert*. Several class periods might be required. If the focus was on *justice*, a case study approach might be taken. After introducing the concept, presenting brief examples, and describing brief nonexamples, the teacher may present pupils with short "cases," some of which are examples of *justice* and some of which provide examples inconsistent with *justice*. Pupils could be asked to identify cases in which the described situation was consistent with their understanding of *justice*. Next, the teacher could ask them to define the concept in their own words. Finally, pupils might find and present to the class examples of *justice* they have witnessed in their own lives.

Concept Formation/Diagnosis

The concept-attainment technique focuses on teaching pupils concepts the teacher thinks pupils must know in order to understand important social studies content. It also is important for young people to learn how to develop concepts of their own. Learning how to categorize fragmented information into general categories helps us reduce the world's complexity. Concepts basically are category labels that provide convenient "containers" for vast quantities of related information. One procedure for helping pupils develop their own category labels is called *concept formation/diagnosis* (Taba, 1967).

Concept formation/diagnosis helps pupils to group and label isolated pieces of information. The teacher functions as a guide as pupils go through the process. Specifically, the teacher attempts to elicit a range of information from class members, encourages them to organize this information into groups sharing common characteristics, and concludes by asking them to generate labels descriptive of items in each group. These are the basic steps:

- The teacher asks an open-ended question designed to elicit as much data as possible from the class. As members of the class supply information, it is listed on the chalkboard, a chart, or an overhead projector transparency.
- When step one is complete and there is a great deal of unorganized information written where all class members can see it, the teacher asks pupils to organize information into groups. The teacher devises a symbol to place by items that go together. (Sometimes letters of the alphabet or numbers are used; sometimes the teacher develops other kinds of symbols.) Pupils need to be told that some items might go into more than one group.
- After items have been placed into groups, pupils are asked to develop concept labels. They are encouraged to come up with labels that define the general characteristics of items in each labeled group.

A key to the success of this technique is selection of a good open-ended question. This question should be one that prompts a large number of responses. It also is best if it is a question to which many members of the class will be able to contribute possible answers. (If larger numbers of pupils are involved in this early phase, the whole group will have a larger sense of "ownership" as the lesson unfolds.) Specific questions will vary depending on pupils' grade levels and interests, the content being studied, and the priorities of the teacher. Examples of opening questions appear in Figure 7–2.

After asking the open-ended question, the teacher should list *all* pupil responses. One of the purposes of this exercise is diagnostic. By listing all pupil responses without comment, the teacher is able to identify incorrect information that some members of the class believe to be true. This enables the teacher to correct misimpressions later, when there are opportunities to share new information with the class. One of the authors, when using the concept formation/diagnosis technique with a group of sixth graders, asked, "What would you expect if you were to visit Brazil?" Among the responses were dark-skinned

Questions used in the concept formation/diagnosis approach should relate to the content of the unit being studied. These are examples of the kinds of questions that might be developed:

- What jobs do people have?
- What kinds of things can you buy at the supermarket?
- Can we draw a picture of something we do at school?
- What do you think about when you hear the word *democracy*?
- If you were to tell another person about our state, what would you say?
- What do you think you would see on a visit to _____?
- What are the buildings like in our town?
- If you were a pioneer moving west, what would you take with you?
- Can we draw pictures of some things families buy with their money?
- What are some ways people can earn money?
- What did you see on our field trip?
- What do you think about when somebody says the word *summer*?

Figure 7–2
Opening questions for concept formation/diagnosis.

Africans, Spanish-speaking people, and primitive living conditions. Obviously, some class members did not know Brazil's location, were unaware that Portuguese rather than Spanish is spoken there, and had little idea that such cosmopolitan places as São Paulo, Rio de Janeiro, or Brasília existed.

The second step in a concept formation/diagnosis activity requires pupils to group the listed items. A prompting question often works well, such as this: "As you look at the items on our list, which ones go together, and why they go together?" This question helps pupils to think about criteria or attributes they are using as a basis for grouping. Sometimes pupils do not agree on where a given item should go. It is important to tell them that there is no one correct way to group information and that a single item can be assigned to more than one group.

The final phase of the lesson also begins with teacher questions. For example, the teacher might say, "What can we call each of the groups? We have used letters of the alphabet to designate them, but now let's give each group a real name. What names can we come up with that will tell us something about the kinds of things in each group?" Disagreements among pupils may arise. When pupils suggest several possibilities for labeling a given group, they should be asked to consider which one best describes items in the group.

In summary, the concept formation/diagnosis approach gives pupils practice in forming concepts. It gives them a process they can use to organize complex information into categories—a useful thinking skill for many areas of living. Teachers sometimes use the technique at the beginning of a new unit of study. The focus question and pupil responses center on the unit topic. The exercise promotes high levels of pupil involvement and establishes an initial context for what pupils will be studying. Sometimes, teachers keep information from the preunit concept formation/diagnosis exercise and involve learners in a similar lesson using the same focus question at the conclusion of the unit. Differences in pupil responses serve as an indicator of changes in learners' understanding as a result of their exposure to unit content.

INDUCING GENERALIZATIONS

Generalizations are statements of relationships among concepts. They are idea-dense condensations of what the best available scholarship has found to be true. They are useful for pupils learning social studies content because they provide efficient summaries of vast quantities of information. C. Warren McKinney and William D. Edgington (1997), who have made an extensive study of the use of generalizations in elementary social studies classrooms, note that "generalizations help students understand and explain the human condition. Through generalizations, isolated pieces of information can be organized, and as a result, students can make better sense of their world" (p. 78).

The *inducing-a-generalization* technique is commonly used to help pupils acquire important social studies generalizations. It helps pupils learn how to form generalizations through gathering evidence and applying their own thought processes. Before a teacher initiates an inducing-a-generalization lesson, it is important that he or she know that pupils understand the basic concepts associated with the focus generalization. Suppose a teacher wanted learners to master this generalization: "The global location of a nation or region contributes to its importance in international affairs." Pupils with no grasp of concepts such as *global location, nation, region,* and *international affairs* would have great difficulty in learning the generalization.

These steps are followed in an inducing-a-generalization activity (see Figure 7–3 for an example):

- Pupils look at evidence that the teacher has made available. They organize this information into appropriate categories.
- Pupils compare and contrast data in the categories and note relationships.
- Pupils develop statements (generalizations) that can explain the relationships and that they can apply to other similar situations.

In step one, the teacher introduces information related to the generalization. (Remember that pupils are not given the focus generalization. They receive only *information related to* the generalization. The purpose of this exercise is to encourage pupils to organize data, look for relationships, and develop explanatory generalizations of their own.) The next step involves organizing the information. Sometimes teachers may provide the class with information already organized into categories. More mature and sophisticated learners may themselves be required to do this.

During step two, pupils look at the information that has been gathered and organized. The teacher asks pupils questions related to the information. Examples of teacher questions are, "What do you notice about information in category A? In category B? What are the similarities? What are the differences?"

The following chart illustrates how data for an inducing-a-generalization lesson might be organized. Such a display helps pupils to discover relationships among categories and to develop statements explaining the relationship.

For this activity, the teacher decided to emphasize this generalization: *Types and varieties of services change as the size of the community changes.*

One axis of the chart identifies communities of different sizes. The other indicates the types of services and businesses. When information is displayed in this way, relationships between the two focus concepts (*community size* and *services*) can be easily displayed. Each cell of the chart is filled in as data are gathered. The teacher usually makes the empty version of the chart and asks pupils to fill in the information. Older learners may prepare blank charts without teacher assistance.

	Types of Services		
Community Size	**Government Services**	**Stores and Businesses**	**Industries**
Small rural community			
Moderate-sized city or community			
Large city			

After information has been added to each cell, the steps listed are followed. They are designed to help pupils develop generalizations relevant to the relationship between community size and types of services typically found.

1. What do you notice about the types of government services, stores and businesses, and industries in small communities? Moderate-sized communities? Large cities?
2. What are the similarities and differences you notice among these different communities?
3. Why do you think these differences exist? What statements can we make that help us predict or explain what we might find in other small, moderate-sized, and large communities we might study?

Figure 7–3
Organizing an inducing-a-generalization lesson.

Step three requires pupils to develop generalizations of their own. This step may frustrate pupils who are not accustomed to going beyond what they are given. The teacher needs to encourage pupils to take chances and make educated guesses based on their analysis of the data. Often teachers ask prompt questions, such as: "How do you account for these differences? What statements could we make that might apply to similar situations or places?"

A data retrieval chart helps students organize information so that relationships can be more easily identified.

As learners attempt to formulate generalizations, the teacher encourages them to justify their responses with reference to appropriate evidence. All pupil-developed generalizations are accepted. The adequacy of individual generalizations will be tested later when they are applied in unfamiliar contexts. As pupils apply their own generalizations to new situations, they will discover that some of them have a great deal of predictive power. Others will need to be revised as new evidence comes to light. A few may have to be abandoned altogether because there is simply too much contradictory evidence available. Lesson Idea 7–3 illustrates how an inducing-a-generalization activity might proceed.

Lesson Idea 7–3

COMPARING TWO COLONIES

Grade Level: 5–6

Objective: After reviewing the information presented on the chart, the pupils will make at least two generalizations that explain the differences between the two colonies.

Introduction: Say the following to the class: "How many of you have traveled to cities in other parts of the country? How are those places like where we live? How are they different from where we live? Every place in the world is different in some way from all other places. There are some things that explain why places grow to be very different. Once we understand these reasons, we can begin to understand places all over the world. Today I have some information on two colonies that were settled and established about the same time. Let's look at the information on the chart."

Procedure: Ask the following questions:

Step 1   "What do you notice about the nationality of settlers in Amstead and Martinville? What do you notice about the location of these two colonies? How would you describe Amstead 50 years after settlement? How would you describe Martinville 50 years after settlement?"

Name of Colony	Nationality of Settlers	Location of Colony	50 Years After Settlement
Amstead	Swedish	• Inland, away from the ocean • Rich farmland • Lots of water • Five-month growing season • Surrounded by high mountains • Lots of forests	• One political party in power • Most people go to the same church • Not very much industry • Most people live by farming • Change is very slow and most people continue to do the same thing for years • There are few new people moving in
Martinville	• English • French • German • Italian • Spanish	• Ocean location • Good harbor • Rocky, poor soil • Short growing season • Coal in nearby hills • Lots of water for power	• Several different political parties • Most people work in factories or businesses • People go to several different churches • Lots of disagreement about how things should be run • There is constant change in the community • Lots of new people are moving in.

Step 2 "Why do you think these two colonies grew so differently in those 50 years?"

Step 3 "What statements could we make that would explain the growth of these communities and that might be useful in understanding growth and change in other places?"

Write the statements that the pupils give on a chart or transparency to save for future reference.

Closure: Ask the class: "What did we do today? What did you learn? How might we use what we have learned?"

WEB CHECK

Note: Electronic addresses of sites on the World Wide Web change frequently. If the listed URL fails to work, use a standard search engine to locate the new address of the site.

- The Theory: Constructivism, The Challenge: Culture, The Medium: Information Processing Technology

  URL—**http://www.education.mcgill.ca/fedwww/wac/intedpsych/students/lgraha/paper.html**

  This site includes a general introduction to constructivism. A good bibliography is included for those who might wish to do more extensive reading on this topic.

- Constructivist Learning Theory

  URL—**http://netra/exploratorium.edu/isen/ten/constructivistlearning.html**

  Information in this article lays out a clear explanation of theoretical roots of constructivist teaching. The author does a particularly nice job of describing the dilemma faced by teachers who on the one hand want learners to engage content and derive meanings on their own and on the other hand want to be sure learners get the right or acceptable answer.

- Basic Education—A Critical Participation Opportunity

  URL—**http://pogo.edc.org/INT/HCD/chp4.html**

  Information at this site relates to a number of basic education issues. There is a brief description of research-based results of metacognitive teaching.

- What Is a Thinking Curriculum?

  URL—**http://www.ncrel.org/sdrs/areas/rpl_esys/thinking.html**

  This extensive article treats metacognitive teaching and other features of a curriculum designed to promote serious learner engagement with content.

- 1. Classroom Characteristics and Practices

  URL—**http://www.nwrel.org/scpd/esp/esp95_1.html**

  This material represents work of the Northwest Regional Educational Laboratory. It features a compilation of research related to effective schooling practices. One of the topics treated is research on classroom questioning.

- Social Studies Concepts

  URL—**http://www.osr.state.ga.us/bestprac/social/ss_toc.html**

  The State of Georgia Office of School Readiness has assembled material that is available at this site. It includes an outstanding list of concepts designed for use in social studies lessons intended for pre-kindergarten learners.

- Concepts

  URL—**http://mirrors.org.sg/tip/concept.html**

  This short document provides a brief overview of theories of concept learning. It includes excellent references for those who would like to know more about the topic.

- The Social Studies Curriculum: Conceptual Teaching

  URL—**http://www.sasked.gov.sk.ca/docs/midlsoc/g6currss.html**

  This material, organized and put on the Web by educational professionals in the Canadian Province of Saskatchewan, includes highly detailed information about such issues as grade-level placement of concepts and associated social studies skills. Highly recommended.

KEY IDEAS IN SUMMARY

1. Educators increasingly are committed to the idea that opportunities must be found for pupils to personally engage the new content they encounter in school programs. These approaches are founded on *constructivism,* an orientation to learning that holds that learners are driven to make sense of the world through a process of active involvement.

2. *Metacognition* refers to conscious thought about how, as individuals, we think about a problem or situation. Some patterns of thinking are thought to be more productive than others. School lessons focusing on metacognitive thought are designed to help pupils learn how to monitor their own thinking patterns. Two examples of such approaches are *thinking aloud* and *visualizing thinking.*

3. Good classroom questions help pupils develop meaning as they engage social studies content. The effectiveness of questions is influenced by such variables as their clarity, the sequence in which questions are asked, and the amount of time the teacher waits after a question is asked before (a) answering the question himself or herself, (b) calling on another pupil, or (c) asking another question.

4. Concepts are labels describing phenomena that share certain characteristics. Generalizations are statements about relationships among concepts. They are succinct statements that summarize what the best available evidence tells us is true. Because of the explanatory power of concepts and generalizations, specific techniques have been developed for teaching them to elementary pupils.

5. All of the defining attributes must be present for something to be considered a proper example of a conjunctive concept. A disjunctive concept may have several

defining attributes, but it is not necessary for all of them to be present at the same time for something to be considered a proper example of this concept category. Relational concepts have attributes that bear a specific kind of relationship to one another. Generally, disjunctive and relational concepts are more difficult for pupils to learn than conjunctive concepts. Concepts that have a large number of defining attributes are also difficult.

6. The concept-attainment technique focuses on teaching certain concepts that the teacher has selected for pupils to learn. The following steps are typically followed in a concept-attainment lesson: The teacher (1) introduces the concept by name, (2) presents examples of the concept, (3) presents nonexamples of the concept, (4) provides a mixture of examples and nonexamples of the concept, (5) asks pupils to define the concept, (6) provides opportunities for pupils to apply their understanding by finding additional examples of the concept.

7. The concept formation/diagnosis approach can be used to provide pupils with experience in forming concepts of their own. Lessons with this focus familiarize pupils with the process of forming concepts and, at the same time, provide the teacher with useful diagnostic information regarding misconceptions some pupils may have. The following steps are typical of concept formation/diagnosis lessons: (1) pupils respond to a stimulus, usually an open-ended question posed by the teacher, that is designed to elicit a large volume of pupil-generated information; (2) pupils are asked to organize the information they have generated into categories and to describe the basis for their grouping; (3) pupils develop a label for each category that clearly defines characteristics of the items grouped together under it.

8. The inducing-a-generalization technique helps pupils arrive at an explanatory generalization by applying their own logical thinking skills. The teacher begins by selecting a well-validated generalization and finding specific examples that support its truth. The learners are presented only with this evidence. They are challenged to develop an explanatory generalization that is consistent with the evidence. These steps typically are followed: (1) Pupils look at the evidence the teacher has gathered and organize it into categories; (2) pupils compare and contrast information and note relationships; and (3) pupils develop an explanatory generalization that explains noted relationships and that can be applied to other situations.

CHAPTER REFLECTIONS

Directions: Now that you have read this chapter, reread the case study at the beginning. Then, answer these questions:

1. The teacher in the case study worries about inappropriate learning as a result of pupils' exposure to a sampling of content that may not be an accurate reflection of reality. Is this a serious concern? What might you do to combat it?

2. The issue of breadth versus depth frequently comes up when social studies teachers discuss what they do in the classroom. What are some forces that encourage

coverage of a large number of topics and issues in social studies classes? What positives and negatives do you see associated with these forces?

3. Time is always a concern when teachers consider alternative elementary school social studies lessons. Techniques such as inducing generalizations take time to fully develop. Is such an expenditure of time justified? Why or why not?

4. Many generalizations have values embedded within them. Are pupils in elementary schools old enough to appreciate this point? Or are they likely to miss this point and conclude that generalizations they develop are value-free and not subject to challenge by others who may have different and/or conflicting values?

5. Much of the content of this chapter focused on techniques to help pupils engage content and generate personal understanding as a result of the generalizing process. Is it a good idea for pupils to do this? Does the teacher have a responsibility to be sure that they don't develop wrong or inappropriate knowledge? Explain your position.

6. Which of the teaching approaches discussed in the chapter would you feel most comfortable using? Why?

EXTENDING UNDERSTANDING AND SKILL

1. Much has been written about *constructivist* teaching and learning. Review several articles in professional journals such as *Social Education* and *The Social Studies* that deal with these topics. You may also find some useful information on the World Wide Web. Prepare a short talk based on your research for presentation to your class.

2. *Metacognitive* techniques are used to develop pupils' abilities to monitor their own thinking processes. Using examples provided in the chapter, develop a lesson focusing on content of your own choosing that features *visualizing thinking*.

3. Over the years, dozens of books and articles have been written about effective classroom questioning techniques. Prepare a resource file of six articles that suggest procedures for using questions effectively in the classroom. Share the material with your instructor, and be prepared to provide class members with a brief oral summary of your findings.

4. Much has been written about concept learning and concept teaching. Review articles in journals such as *Social Education* and *The Social Studies* that deal with these topics. Take notes on at least one specific technique for teaching a concept. (Select one not introduced in this chapter.) Share your information with others.

5. This chapter introduced an instructional procedure called *inducing generalizations* that involves pupils in a series of tasks leading them to develop generalizations of their own. Sometimes, too, generalizations are selected by teachers to provide a focus for their lesson planning. Do some reading about generalizations and prepare a short paper in which you describe some roles they can play in an elementary social studies program.

REFERENCES

ASCHNER, M. J., GALLAGHER, J., PERRY J., & ASFAR, S. (1961). *A system for classifying thought processes in the conduct of classroom verbal interaction.* Urbana: The University of Illinois.

CAZDEN, C. (1986). Classroom discourse. In M. Wittrock (Ed.), *Handbook of research on teaching.* New York: Macmillan.

FRAENKEL, J. R. (1980). *Helping students think and value* (2nd ed.). Englewood Cliffs, NJ: Prentice-Hall.

HEIN, G. E. (1991). *Constructivist learning theory: The museum and the needs of people.* Paper presented at the CECA (International Committee of Museum Educators) Conference, Jerusalem, Israel. Available Online— **http://netra.exploratorium.edu/isen/ten/constructivistlearning.html.**

MCKINNEY, C. W., & EDGINGTON, W. D. (1997). Issues related to teaching generalizations in elementary social studies. *The Social Studies, 88* (2), 78–82.

MARZANO, R. (1992). *A different kind of classroom: Teaching with dimensions of learning.* Alexandria, VA: Association for Supervision and Curriculum Development.

OSBERG, K. M. (1997). *Constructivism in practice: The case for meaning-making in the virtual world.* Unpublished doctoral dissertation. University of Washington, Seattle. Available Online—**http://www.hitl.washington.edu/publications/r-97-47/title.html.**

PIAGET, J., & INHELDER, B. (1958). *The growth of logical thinking from childhood to adolescence: An essay on the construction of formal operational structures* (A. Parsons & S. Milgram, Trans.). New York: Basic Books.

RINGSTAFF, C., & YOCAM, K. (1994). *Creating an alternative context for teacher development: The ACOT teacher development centers* (Apple Classroom of Tomorrow Research Report Number 18). Cupertino, CA: Apple Computer, Inc. Available On-Line— **http://www.research.apple.com/research/proj/acot/full/acotRpt18full.html.**

ROWE, M. B. (1986). Wait time: Slowing down may be a way of speeding up. *Journal of Teacher Education, 37* (1), 43–50.

TABA, H. (1967). *Handbook for elementary social studies.* Reading, MA: Addison-Wesley.

VYGOTSKY, L. (1962). *Thought and Language.* Cambridge, MA: MIT Press.

chapter 8

Inquiry and Thinking Skills

This chapter will help you to:

- cite general features of inquiry teaching,
- identify steps in a critical-thinking lesson,
- describe a sequence for a problem-solving activity, and
- point out features of creative-thinking lessons.

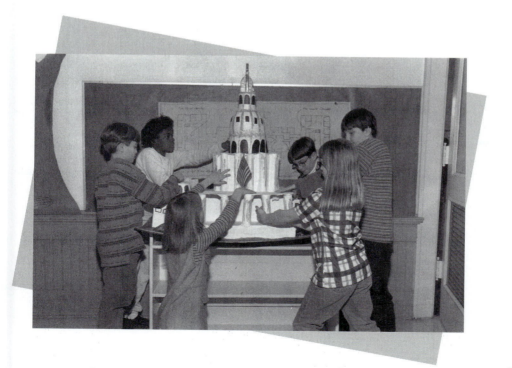

Developing Thinking by	Purposes	
Teaching pupils how to use inquiry approaches	Inquiry approaches encourage pupils to examine individual pieces of information for the purpose of developing explanatory principles and generalizations. They encourage development of the kinds of rational decision-making skills that pupils will need throughout their adult lives.	**Approaches** — Basic steps — Data charts — Delimiting and focusing

Varieties of Thinking	**Basic Characteristics**	**Implementing Procedures**
Creative thinking	Creative seeks novel solutions to perplexing problems. The product of creative thinking must be both *new* and *useful*.	Brainstorming — Focus problem presented — Pupils call out ideas — All ideas accepted — Ideas written down — Ideas discussed
Critical thinking	Critical thinking seeks to evaluate ideas. It always involves judgments based on evidence or highly informed opinion.	Analytic Brainstorming — Identify best solution to a problem — Discuss why best solution is not implemented — Identify ways to overcome obstacles — Name difficulties in implementing solutions — Identify logical first steps
Problem solving	Problem-solving thinking approaches are used when it appears likely that a given problem or situation has a correct, right, or most appropriate solution.	Basic Steps — Identify the problem — Consider possible approaches to its solution — Select and apply approaches — Reach a defensible solution
Decision making	Many questions people face have no clearly right or wrong answers. They must make responses by considering available options, weighing evidence, and considering personal values. This kind of thinking is called *decision making*.	Basic Steps — Identify the basic issue or problem — Point out alternative responses — Describe evidence supporting each alternative — Identify values implied in each alternative — Describe consequences that might follow implementation of each alternative — Make a choice from among alternatives — Describe evidence and value considerations used in making this choice

Figure 8–1
Developing thinking skills.

Case Study

THINKING SKILLS, STUDENT LEARNING, AND EVALUATING THE TEACHER

For many years, the elementary social studies specialist Felicia Littlebird has encouraged teachers to develop specific lessons designed to teach pupils how to engage in higher-level thinking. At the end of one of her recent presentations, a fifth-grade teacher made the following observations.

> Personally, I think these ideas are great. The research evidence about the importance of helping our young people engage in higher-level thinking is impressive. The findings also support what some critics of our schools have been telling us about how much better thinkers some foreign students are compared with our kids. To save time here, let me assure you that your recommendations make good sense to me. *But* . . . I do have a major concern.
>
> I'm a new teacher. I feel that everything I do is being watched by the principal and by parents. I don't have a track record yet. I have to watch my step to avoid getting a bad evaluation. Whether right or wrong, my sense is that I'm going to be evaluated mostly on how well my kids perform on tests.
>
> While I'm convinced that spending time teaching my pupils how to use higher-level thinking techniques can have a wonderful long-term payoff for them, I'm not at all sure that there will be anything in the short run that will show up in the form of improved test scores. In fact, test scores could go down. The time I take teaching them how to engage in higher-level thinking may come at the expense of lessons I could be teaching on content likely to appear on tests.

What Is Your Response?

Think about this teacher's concerns. Then, respond briefly to these questions:

1. Some critics of elementary school instruction claim that taking time to teach processes such as higher-level thinking skills steals time that could be devoted to teaching more important content. Do you agree or disagree?
2. This teacher suggests that people who support teaching pupils higher-level thinking skills have failed to convince administrators and parents of the worth of this activity. Is this a reasonable concern? Why or why not?
3. What ideas do you have regarding how a teacher's success in teaching pupils to use higher-level thinking skills might be measured and reported?
4. What kinds of conditions do you think would have to be present for this teacher to feel completely at ease with a decision to implement ideas introduced in Felicia Littlebird's workshop?
5. How would you advise this teacher if you were Felicia Littlebird?

INTRODUCTION

In the early years of our country, few people had high educational expectations for the general population. As the learning strategy specialist Karen Scheid (1993) points out, schools were considered to have succeeded when large numbers of people left able to write their own names. Today we want school graduates who read fluently and can go beyond the literal meaning of texts to make judgments and inferences. This suggests that schools need to help pupils become sophisticated thinkers.

The social studies specialist Walter Parker (1988) found that few teachers in elementary social studies lessons spend much time helping students develop their thinking skills. Many people believe thinking-skills instruction deserves more emphasis in elementary schools (Nickerson, Perkins, & Smith, 1985; French & Rhoder, 1992; Perkins, 1993–1994; Ruggiero, 1997). However, not everyone agrees.

Cheney, in *American Memory: A Report on the Humanities in the Nation's Public Schools* (1987), contends that teachers spend too much time teaching children learning processes and too little time teaching them important content. The argument Cheney and others (Ravitch, 1985; Hirsch, 1987) have made is that time devoted to teaching children skills, including thinking skills, steals time that could be better devoted to teaching important academic information. Perkins (1993–1994, p. 84) counters this position by noting, "You can often answer fact-based questions that you don't have answers for by extrapolating from what you know. If we can learn more facts by thinking about what we know, we can also know more facts by thinking about them as we learn them." In other words, good thinking-skills instruction helps rather than hinders pupils as they seek to master academic content.

The view that teachers should devote attention to teaching pupils *how* to think represents a majority opinion today. There is evidence that when pupils know how to use a thinking strategy and are aware of how it can help them master new content, they will use the strategy in new contexts (French & Rhoder, 1992). Pupils who leave school with highly developed thinking skills have powerful intellectual tools they can apply to problems they will confront throughout their lives.

Many approaches have been developed for helping elementary pupils improve their thinking skills. Among them are ideas for improving learners' abilities to do the following:

- Use inquiry approaches
- Engage in creative thinking
- Think critically
- Solve problems
- Make decisions

INQUIRY APPROACHES

Inquiry teaching introduces concepts to learners inductively. *Inductive learning*, which involves reasoning from the particular to the general, begins with the teacher introducing a number of specific examples. Pupils study the examples and try to pick out general patterns. They conclude by identifying a broad general principle drawn from the characteristics of the examples.

Suppose a teacher working with kindergartners wanted to teach the concept *bird*. The teacher might begin by showing these pupils pictures of different birds. A series of questions would prompt class members to identify common features in the pictures. To conclude the lesson, the teacher would help pupils develop their own definition of the concept *bird*, perhaps showing additional pictures of birds to help pupils determine the adequacy of their definition.

Inquiry learning might be thought of as an exercise in knowledge production. Learners are asked to develop conclusions based on their own consideration of evidence. The kinds of reasoning involved in inquiry learning parallels the rational thinking learners will be called upon to exercise throughout their lives.

Inquiry Teaching: Basic Steps

Inquiry teaching applies the scientific method to a variety of learning problems and is widely used in elementary social studies programs. The eminent American educational philosopher John Dewey suggested basic steps for sequencing inquiry instruction in his classic *How We Think*, originally published in 1910. The following steps used in implementing an inquiry lesson closely follow Dewey's recommendations:

- Describe the essential features of a problem or situation.
- Suggest possible solutions or explanations.
- Gather evidence that can be used to test the accuracy of these solutions or explanations.
- Evaluate the solutions or explanations in light of this evidence.
- Develop a conclusion that is supported by the best evidence.

Inquiry lessons can be used at all grade levels. A simple lesson might be used with pupils in the early primary grades who are beginning to learn how to work with maps and globes. An example of such a lesson is provided in Lesson Idea 8–1.

Lesson Idea 8–1

INQUIRY LESSON: MAPS AND GLOBES

Grade Level:	K–2
Objectives:	Pupils will (1) identify what selected map symbols represent and (2) state reasons for using different symbols on a map.
Suggested Procedures:	Guide pupils through the following steps:

Step 1

TEACHER: How many of you have ever been to a lake? To a river? Have any of you seen an ocean? How are all of these alike? (Pupils respond to each question. Probe until learners mention that all have water.) Did you know that there is more water in our world than land? People who make maps and globes have a problem. They have to have a way to help people recognize what areas are land and what areas are water.

Step 2

TEACHER: How do you think people who make globes have solved this problem? How do you think they might indicate where areas of water are located?

Sample pupil responses:

- Maybe they neatly print the word "water" at places where there is water.
- They may draw pictures of waves in areas where there is water.
- They may use a special color to show where the water is.

Step 3

TEACHER: Now we're going to act like scientists as we see which of our ideas are best. Let's look at this globe. (Hold up globe.) Can anyone give me the name of an ocean? (If nobody can, help the class.) All right, let's look at the Atlantic Ocean. Here it is on the map. How is it shown? (Pupils respond, "It's blue.") Let's look at the Pacific Ocean. Here it is on the map. How is it shown? (Pupils respond, "It's the same color—blue.")

(Put down the globe and point to a large U.S. wall map at the front of the room.) Here is the Atlantic Ocean and over here we have the Pacific. What do they look like? (Pupils respond, "They're blue.") These are what we call the Great Lakes. What do they look like? (Pupils respond, "They're blue.") This long thin part of the map represents our longest river. How is it shown? (Pupils respond, "It's blue, too.")

Step 4

Ask learners to reflect on evidence they have seen. Encourage them to consider the possible explanations they have suggested in light of this evidence.

TEACHER: On the basis of what we have seen, what do you think most map and globe makers do when they want to show water? (Pupils respond, "They color it blue.")

Do you have any ideas about why they have chosen this solution to the problem? I mean, why wouldn't they write *water* at various places or draw waves? (Pupils respond. Possible answers might include: "If they had to write *water*, they would have to write the word over and over again. Because some areas of water are small, it might be hard to squeeze the word *water* in the space. It would be hard to have enough room to write the word *water* on rivers. Drawing little waves might be all right for an ocean, but it would be hard to see on rivers. Drawings of little waves might make it hard to print other information.")

Step 5

This step concludes the lesson. It is designed to result in a general explanation or principle that can be applied in different situations.

TEACHER: From what we have learned, what can you say about how areas of water are indicated on maps and globes? (Pupils respond: "They are shown in blue.")

Let's work with this idea a little more. We'll spend a few minutes looking at some other maps and globes to see if this idea works. (Look with pupils at other maps and globes.) Conclude by praising learners' work and telling them that they have discovered a principle they can remember: "On most maps and globes, the color blue is used to show water."

Using Data Charts to Compare, Contrast, and Generalize

An important purpose of inquiry is helping pupils to learn how to compare, contrast, and generalize. *Data charts* are useful organizers of information that pupils can use as they engage in these thinking processes. A sample lesson featuring use of a data chart is provided in Lesson Idea 8–2.

Lesson Idea 8–2

NATIONS OF LATIN AMERICA

Grade Level: 6

Objective: Pupils will develop a generalization that explains the relationship among literacy, income level, and life expectancy by comparing data presented on a chart.

Suggested Procedures: Suppose you were about to introduce a unit focusing on nations of Latin America. A data chart constructed for this lesson would include information pupils would use to develop some generalizations. Later in the unit, pupils would spend time testing the accuracy of their generalizations. The data chart might look something like the one that follows:

Selected Characteristics of Four Countries in Latin America and of the United States

Country	Languages	Percentage of People Who Can Read and Write	Average Annual Income (Dollars)	Life Expectancy (Years)
Bolivia	Spanish and various Native American languages	83	1,100	60
Costa Rica	Spanish	95	2,900	76
Ecuador	Spanish and various Native American languages	90	1,675	71
Honduras	Spanish	73	806	69
United States	English and other languages, including Spanish	97	19,241	76

Distribute copies of this chart to each pupil. Alternatively, a large version can be drawn on the chalkboard or projected from an overhead transparency. Begin by asking pupils to look carefully at the chart and to respond to the following sequence of questions:

1. What are some similarities you notice among these countries? Possible student responses:
   - The label at the top refers to all of them as Latin American countries and the United States. So they're all in the same part of the world.
   - Spanish seems to be spoken by some people in each of these countries.
2. What differences do you note? Possible student responses:
   - More people are able to read and write in some of these countries than in others. Honduras has the lowest percentage of people who can read and write.
   - Life expectancies are different. In Bolivia, the age is only 60.
   - Average income is very different. In Bolivia, it's only $1,100 a year. In the United States, it's over $19,000 a year.

3. You have identified several important differences. Can you suggest some causes of these differences? Possible student responses:

- It seems people tend to live longer where income levels are higher.
- People also seem to live longer in places where higher percentages of the people can read and write.
- It seems to me that incomes go up when more people in a country can read and write.

(These are only examples. Members of a real class may develop different generalizations from the chart.)

TEACHER: These are all good ideas. Let me write them on the board. We are going to be studying Latin America for the next several weeks. As we do, let's try to find evidence to test the accuracy of our statements. I want each of you to take notes on these ideas. When you find new information, think about whether it supports or does not support these generalizations. When we finish the unit, we'll look again at these ideas to see whether we need to revise any of them.

The data chart helps pupils develop insights of their own. They become directly involved in the creation of new information. This information, in turn, provides a point of departure for further study. The opportunity to test their own generalizations often results in pupils' becoming more enthusiastic as they pursue additional study of a topic.

Delimiting and Focusing Pupils' Thinking

The volume of information presented in social studies lessons sometimes overwhelms pupils. This is a particular problem when they first encounter inquiry lessons. These lessons typically begin with an introduction of a large quantity of information that, at least in the minds of pupils, may seem fragmented and disjointed.

Suchman (1962) developed an approach designed to help pupils focus on relevant information and to dismiss irrelevant details as they begin to solve a problem. Suchman's idea builds on learners' natural curiosity. It begins by presenting learners with a puzzling or perplexing situation that Suchman calls a *discrepant event*. This is something that does not quite fit pupils' understanding of reality. After they are introduced to the puzzling situation, pupils ask the teacher questions about it. The major rule is that all questions must be capable of being answered "yes" or "no." Suchman's lessons have a gamelike feel that pupils enjoy. The basic steps follow.

- Pupils are presented with a discrepant event.
- They are encouraged to explain it by asking the teacher questions that can be answered either "yes" or "no."

- The exercise ends with a general discussion of explanations that pupils have suggested and processes they used to arrive at them.

To illustrate how you might use Suchman's approach, suppose you were interested in helping pupils understand that many of the foods we consume change form before we eat or drink them. You might build a lesson around cocoa. Cocoa, as a drink, probably will be familiar to most pupils; however, few may know that it comes from seeds or beans that grow in a pod on a tropical tree. Fewer still will understand that a roasting process must intervene before cocoa can be consumed.

An interesting thing about cocoa beans is that they are white. This makes an ideal discrepant event for the exercise. Few children will associate the color white with cocoa. If you wanted to use this lesson, you would have to locate a color photograph of a cacao pod that had been cut open to reveal the seeds. The lesson would begin by a reminder of the rules. You would then show the children the photograph and ask a simple focus question, such as, "What are these things, and what do we use them for?"

After they have experienced several of Suchman's lessons, pupils become adept at asking good questions. Good questions are ones whose answers eliminate great quantities of irrelevant information. This helps members of the class focus quickly on issues that are central to the solution of the focus problem.

CREATIVE THINKING

Creative thinking features novel approaches to perplexing problems. Many inventors are creative thinkers. The inventor of the forklift truck was inspired to build it after watching mechanical fingers remove doughnuts from a hot oven (Ruggiero, 1988). The usefulness of the forklift makes an important point about the object of creative thinking. It is not thinking devoted to the creation of something bizarre for which there is no immediate or potential use. To be a legitimate "creative product" something must be both *new* and *useful* (Slabbert, 1994).

Creative thinking helps us adapt to change. Experts believe that the pace of change is accelerating. Hence, helping pupils develop creative-thinking strategies that will allow them to accommodate conditions we cannot imagine today will be useful to them throughout their lives. Slabbert (1994) and others argue that it is just as important to teach young people creative-thinking skills, which will have lifelong relevance, as to teach them traditional subject matter content, which may soon become outdated. There is disagreement about what lasting effects can be expected from lessons focusing on developing pupils' creative-thinking skills. Some recent studies have suggested that the "cognitive abilities underlying creative performance differ from task to task" (Baer, 1993–1994, p. 80). This seems to suggest that no single creative-thinking lesson can be expected to generate abilities in pupils that will help them to develop creative solutions to all kinds of problems. The lesson for teachers seems to be that they must prepare creative-thinking lessons that focus on many different kinds of problems and tasks. By exposing pupils to a variety of creative-thinking experiences, we increase the probability that they will have developed thinking responses with practical value for the different kinds of problems they will encounter as adults.

Involving students in creative production motivates them and helps stimulate their imagination.

There is evidence that relatively little attention is being paid in elementary classrooms to the development of pupils' creative-thinking abilities (or, indeed, to the systematic development of any other thinking skills) (French & Rhoder, 1992). A number of creative-thinking techniques have been developed. One that is widely used is called *brainstorming*.

Brainstorming developed first in the world of business. It is designed to help people develop original solutions to problems. It places an initial premium on generating a huge volume of possible answers. When it is used in the classroom, pupils are encouraged to develop as many responses as possible to a focus problem. The rules for brainstorming are as follows:

- Pupils are given a focus problem. ("Suppose, because trees release huge amounts of oxygen into the air, that all nations in the world decided to ban all further cutting of trees for lumber. What might result from this decision?")
- Pupils are asked to call out ideas as rapidly as possible. A person is free to speak whenever someone else stops speaking. The idea is to generate a rapid outpouring of ideas. Pupils are encouraged to say whatever comes to their minds, as long as it is relevant.
- Participants are cautioned not to comment positively or negatively on ideas suggested by others. All ideas are accepted. This rule helps break down pupils' fears about saying something stupid.
- The teacher or a designated record keeper writes down every idea, often on the chalkboard. Whoever is chosen to do this should be a person who can write quickly. Responses from pupils often come fast and furiously.
- The teacher stops the idea-generation phase when the rate of presentation of new ideas noticeably slows.

- A general discussion of the ideas concludes the exercise. This discussion may prompt ideas for additional study. (For example, given the focus question used to illustrate these procedures, there might be follow-up research on topics such as alternative fuels, substitute materials for furniture, new construction materials for houses, and so forth.)

CRITICAL THINKING

The purpose of critical thinking is to *evaluate* ideas. It always involves judgments based on informed opinion. Properly, these judgments should be supported by defensible criteria (Lipman, 1988).

Critical thinking encourages generation of new ideas. Critical-thinking instruction sometimes is linked to creative thinking. When this is done, the creative-thinking part of the lesson occurs first. During this phase, pupils generate new ideas. During the second part of the lesson, they use critical-thinking skills to make judgments about these ideas.

Dunn and Dunn (1972) developed an adaptation of the basic brainstorming technique that encourages learners to think critically. An analytic brainstorming activity that requires use of critical-thinking skills includes the following steps. Pupils brainstorm responses to questions posed at each step. The teacher writes pupil responses so that everyone can see them.

- As an initial focus, the teacher encourages pupils to consider what the best solution to a problem might be. A fifth-grade teacher might use this question to begin the activity: "What would be the best thing we could do to make sure first graders don't get hurt on the playground?"
- Next, the teacher asks why these ideas have not already been implemented. ("What things are preventing us from doing any of these things to help solve this problem?")
- After pupils have responded to this question, the teacher asks another, designed to help pupils begin thinking about what might be done to overcome any obstacles. ("How could we overcome some of these difficulties?")
- At this point, the teacher asks pupils to consider problems they might encounter in implementing responses to the previous question. ("What might keep us from overcoming any difficulties we may face in trying to keep first graders from getting hurt on the playground?")
- Finally, pupils are asked to decide what should be the first step toward a realistic solution of the problem. ("Let's think about everything we have considered. What action should we take first to solve this problem? Be prepared to explain your choices.") Class members respond and defend their choices by referring to appropriate criteria.

PROBLEM SOLVING

Some problems have a "best," "correct," "right," or "appropriate" solution, given the evidence that is available. In working with these situations, teachers encourage pupils to follow a problem-solving approach. A typical problem-solving lesson includes the following steps:

- Identify the problem.
- Consider possible approaches to its solution.
- Select and apply approaches.
- Reach a defensible solution.

An example of how problem solving can be used in a social studies lesson is illustrated in Lesson Idea 8–3.

Lesson Idea 8–3

WEATHER PATTERNS

Grade Level: 5

Objective: Pupils will identify procedures that explain differences in climate in two different places.

Suggested Procedure: If you are interested in having learners understand weather patterns in different parts of the United States, you might engage pupils in the following dialogue:

YOU: I am going to write some information about temperatures in Boston and Seattle on the board. (Write the following information on the board.):

City	Average January low
Boston	23° (F)
Seattle	34° (F)

Does everybody remember where Boston and Seattle are? (Point out the locations of the two cities on a large wall map of the United States.) Now let's be detectives. I want you to explain these differences. Why is Seattle warmer than Boston in the winter?

Let's start by reviewing what we already know about what influences a place's climate. Who'll tell me one that is important?

JOSH: Well, places farther north sometimes are colder than places to the south.

YOU: Yes, that's true. What term did we learn to describe how far north or south a place is from the equator?

LASHANDRA: Latitude.

YOU: Latitude. Good. So one thing we might want to look at is latitude—that is, how far north of the equator Boston and Seattle are. All right, what else might we want to know?

SAMUEL: It makes a difference how high these places are. I mean, a place way up on a mountain is going to be colder than a place lower down.

YOU: That's a good idea. Remember, we use the term *altitude* to talk about how high a place is. Remember, too, we always compare its elevation with sea level. So, we may want to find out how high both Seattle and Boston are above sea level. Good. Now, what other things might we want to know?

RHEA: We might want to know if there is a lot of water close by and the direction the winds blow. That could make a difference.

YOU: That's a good idea, Rhea. For your information, class, winds that blow over a place mostly from the same direction are called *prevailing winds.* Now let's think about our ideas. There are three of them. First of all, we will want to know how far each city is north of the equator. Second, we will need to find out how far each city is above sea level. Finally, we'll need to look for information about nearby bodies of water and prevailing winds.

I want people at each table to find out information to answer these three questions:

1. How far north of the equator are Seattle and Boston? You can use the back part of the atlas to find out.
2. How far above sea level is each city? Look at page XXX in the almanac on your table to find out.
3. Are there large bodies of water near each city, and what are the prevailing wind patterns? Use your atlas, and see pages XX to XX in your text to find this information. (Monitor pupils as they work.)

All right, let's see what we learned. Who will tell me how far north each city is?

ANDREA: Boston is 42° 21′ north of the equator, and Seattle is 47° 36′ north of the equator.

YOU: Thank you, Andrea. Now, does this information explain differences in minimum January temperatures?

SUSAN: No, it doesn't make sense. I mean, Seattle's farther north. It should be colder, but it's not.

YOU: Yes, it's a bit puzzling, isn't it? Let's go on to another possible explanation. How about altitude? What did you find?

GRACIELLA: Seattle's about 10 feet above sea level, and Boston's about 21 feet.

YOU: Does this explain differences in winter temperature?

ROLAND: I don't think so. There isn't all that much difference. I mean, 11 feet doesn't seem like much to me.

YOU: I think you're right, Roland. The ceiling of this room is about 12 feet higher than the floor. If we keep the air circulating in the room, there probably is not going to be much difference in air temperature anywhere in our room. What else might explain differences between winter temperatures in Seattle and Boston?

DEJUAN: Well, both cities are on water. The winds generally blow over both cities from the same direction—out of the West. I'm not sure that this means anything. I mean, why should this make winter temperatures different?

YOU: That's a good question, DeJuan. Let me give you a hint. In the wintertime, areas of water are warmer than areas of land. Where does the winter wind come from that blows over Seattle and Boston?

RENEE: Out of the West.

YOU: Keep working with that idea, Renee. What is west of Seattle? What is west of Boston?

RENEE: Well, it's mostly Pacific Ocean west of Seattle. It's just land, other states and stuff, west of Boston.

YOU: And why might that be important? What effect might the location of these two cities have on their winter weather?

STEWART: Well, water stays warmer than land in the winter. In Seattle, the wind blows over water. Maybe the wind warms up before it gets to Seattle.

YOU: Stewart, you're on the right track. Now what about Boston's situation?

STEWART: Well, in the wintertime, the winds out of the West blow over cold land before they get to Boston. Maybe that's why its colder in the winter in Boston than in Seattle.

YOU: I think we've solved our problem.

Problem solving and decision making in groups help students identify alternatives and weigh evidence.

DECISION MAKING

Many questions we face have no right answers. Various responses might be appropriate. Issues of this kind force us to choose from among alternatives. We do this by thinking about available options, weighing evidence, and considering personal values. Thinking of this kind is known as *decision making* (Beyer, 1988).

The following steps are included in many decision-making lessons:

- Identify the basic issue or problem.
- Point out alternative responses.
- Describe evidence supporting each alternative.
- Identify values implied in each alternative.
- Describe possible consequences that might follow selection of each alternative.
- Make a choice from among various alternatives.
- Describe evidence and values considered in making this choice.

There are many possibilities for using decision-making lessons. For example, as part of their effort to help develop pupils' citizenship skills, many schools have a student council. Suppose a group of fifth and sixth graders decided that upper-grade members (from grades five and six) ought to be pupils who have been attending the school for at least three years. Their idea is that newcomers are unfamiliar with the school's traditions and won't be able to represent its true interests well. Present school policy allows any student in grade five or six to run for membership on the student council.

A teacher who was presented with this idea might capitalize on the situation and engage pupils in a decision-making lesson. An example of how such a lesson might develop is given in Lesson Idea 8–4.

Lesson Idea 8–4

DECISION MAKING: ELECTING SCHOOL OFFICERS

Grade Level: 5–6

Objective: Pupils will apply steps of the decision-making process to a problem.

Suggested Procedure: Guide pupils through these steps:

Step 1   Frame the issue as a proposition worded in this (or a similar) way: "No fifth grader should be allowed to run for membership on the student council unless he or she has been in this school for at least three years."

Step 2   In this case, there are only two basic alternatives. Alternative one is to support this policy. Alternative two is to maintain the present policy, which allows any fifth or sixth grader to seek election to the student council.

Step 3   Some of the following evidence might be used to *support* the idea that only fifth and sixth graders who have been in the school three years should be allowed to run for the student council.

- This is a special school that is different from all others. Pupils who have been here for at least three years appreciate its special qualities.
- Learners who have been in the school for at least three years tend to know more people than those who are relative newcomers. They will be better able to represent the interests of all people in the school.
- Some issues, such as deciding how to keep first graders from getting hurt on the playground, have been considered before. Fifth and sixth graders who have been in the school for at least three years will know what has been tried before and what has and has not worked.

Some of the following evidence might be used to *oppose* the idea that fifth and sixth graders on the student council should have been in the school at least three years.

- Bright people who are new to the school learn quickly about its special qualities. It makes more sense to have a fifth- or sixth-grade student council member who really wants to work on the council than another person who may have been in school longer but who isn't especially interested in being a member.

- New people may bring new ideas that can be used to solve problems that others have been unable to resolve.

Step 4 The following values might be among those expressed by people who *support* the new proposal.

- Traditions are important; they are likely to be better appreciated by people who have years of familiarity with them.
- People with more experience make more responsible decisions than people with less experience.

The following might be values cited by people who *oppose* the new proposal.

- Maintaining broad interest in student government is more important than ensuring that individual members meet strict qualifications for office.
- Years in the school do not necessarily translate to a commitment to the school and its traditions.

Step 5 The following consequences might be noted by a *supporter* of the three-year requirement.

- Pupils who have been in the school at least three years are likely to help the student council adopt decisions that will please more people in the school than council members who have spent less time enrolled in the school.
- If pupils have been in the school three or more years, they will help the council make better and more efficient decisions. This will happen because they will be very familiar with procedures and ideas that have been tried before.

The following consequences might be cited by an *opponent* of the three-year rule.

- Many in the school will become apathetic about the student council. They will not have any sense of ownership in the organization and will be little inclined to support its decisions.
- A decision to require people to have been in the school at least three years before allowing them to run for student council will create two classes of pupils. One category, the politically powerful *upper class,* will include fifth and sixth graders who have been in the school three or more years. The second class, or *lower class,* will include all other fifth and sixth graders.

Step 6 At this point, pupils make a decision to either support or oppose the idea of requiring fifth and sixth graders to have been members of the school for at least three years before allowing them to run for student council membership.

Step 7 A person *supporting* this decision might describe evidence and values related to this issue in this way:

"I like the idea that people who have been in school here for at least three years know what the school is really like. I think the school is pretty good just as it is. I think people who have been here for a few years feel more like I do than someone new would. These people are also likely to know a lot of people in other grades. I think that's important, too."

A person *opposing* the idea might describe values she or he thought relevant to the issue in this way:

"I think we need to have the smartest people in the fifth and sixth grades on the student council. Some of them may not have been in our school all that long. I want to be sure we don't have a rule that keeps them from running. Also, if I ever had to go to another school, I wouldn't like being shut out of things because I hadn't gone there as long as somebody else."

In summary, the decision-making sequence allows pupils to think through alternative solutions to problems. Teachers, as they encourage class members to think about these alternatives as well as evidence and values related to each, involve children in the kinds of thinking challenges that adults face daily. As a link to the adult world, decision-making lessons have a definite place in the elementary social studies program.

FINDING MORE INFORMATION

Interest in helping pupils develop their thinking capacities has spawned an enormous amount of writing on this topic. You may wish to look over some information sources that we have found to be particularly useful:

- BEYER, B. K. (1988). *Developing a thinking skills program* Boston: Allyn & Bacon.
- BRUBACHER, J. W., CASE, C. W., & REAGAN, T. G. (1994). *Becoming a reflective educator: How to build a culture of inquiry in the schools.* Thousand Oaks, CA: Corwin Press.
- COSTA, A. L. (Ed.). (1991a). *Developing minds: A resource book for teaching thinking* (Vol. 1). Alexandria, VA: Association for Supervision and Curriculum Development.
- COSTA, A. L. (Ed.). (1991b). *Developing minds: Programs for teaching thinking* (Vol. 2). Alexandria, VA: Association for Supervision and Curriculum Development.
- CRAWFORD, K. M. (Ed.). (1997). *Learning together through inquiry.* York, ME: Stenhouse Publishing.
- GARNER, R., & ALEXANDER, P. A. (1989, Spring). Metacognition: Answered and unanswered questions. *Educational Psychologist, 24* (2), 143–158.

- JOYCE B., & CALHOUN, E. (1997). *Learning to teach inductively.* Boston: Allyn & Bacon.
- MELTZER, M., & PALAU, S. M. (1996). *Acquiring critical thinking skills.* Philadelphia: W. B. Saunders.
- NAGEL, N. G. (1996). *Learning through real-world problem solving: The power of integrative teaching.* Thousand Oaks, CA: Corwin Press.
- ROSS, E. W. (1994). *Reflective practice in social studies,* Bulletin No. 88. Washington, DC: National Council for the Social Studies.
- SCHEID, K. (1993). *Helping students become strategic learners.* Cambridge, MA: Brookline Books.

WEB CHECK

Note: Electronic addresses of sites on the World Wide Web change frequently. If the listed URL fails to work, use a standard search engine to locate the new address of the site.

- Creative and Critical Thinking

  URL—**http://curry.edschool.virginia.edu/curr...r_Guite/Time_Line/ creativethinking.html**

  This site features examples of eight separate categories of activities that can be used as parts of lessons designed to promote creative and critical thinking.

- A Model for Case Analysis and Problem Solving

  URL—**http://www.cba.neu.edu/~ewertheim/introd/cases.html**

  Stimuli for lessons designed to improve pupils' problem-solving abilities take many forms. This site suggests how a problem-solving approach can be used to respond to issues introduced in case studies. A six-step approach for problem analysis is introduced.

- Teaching Thinking Skills

  URL—**http://www.nwrel.org/scpd/sirs/6/cu11.html**

  This site summarizes information developed for the School Improvement Research Series of the federally supported Northwest Regional Educational Laboratory. It includes a rich array of terms and definitions related to thinking skills. In addition, there are succinct summaries of research findings related to the impact of various thinking-skills approaches on learners. The material concludes with an extensive bibliography.

- Thought and Language

  URL—**http://www.mindspring.com/~frudoph/lectures/Thought/thought.html**

  Material at this site focuses on academic work by scholars who have observed what people do when they are thinking and who have taken particular care to note their errors.

KEY IDEAS IN SUMMARY

1. Should teachers spend time teaching thinking skills directly? Today, many people think so. Some critics, however, argue that time spent teaching thinking skills diverts time from instruction that could better be spent on more purely academic subject matter. In response, some authorities claim that pupils learn academic subject content better when they also receive instruction focusing specifically on thinking-skills development.

2. Inquiry approaches utilize inductive learning processes. They begin by introducing pupils to isolated pieces of information. Pupils proceed through a series of steps that culminate in their development of an explanatory generalization. General steps in an inquiry lesson are: (1) describing essential features of a problem or situation, (2) suggesting possible solutions or explanations, (3) gathering evidence to test these solutions or explanations, (4) evaluating solutions or explanations in light of this evidence, and (5) developing a conclusion based on the best evidence.

3. Data charts can be used to develop pupils' abilities to compare, contrast, and generalize. They typically feature information displayed in a matrix. Pupils use individual cells as they look for patterns, identify similarities and differences, and draw general conclusions.

4. Suchman (1962) developed an inquiry approach that can help pupils reduce the volume of information they must consider when confronted with a problem. It features a focus issue introduced by the teacher and interrogation of pupils by the teacher , with questions that can be answered either "yes" or "no." Through this procedure, pupils learn to reject broad categories of irrelevant information and to focus on information that will help them solve the problem.

5. Creative thinking requires learners to consider perplexing problems in novel ways. The product of good creative thinking must be both new and useful. Brainstorming is one technique teachers use to develop pupils' creative-thinking skills. This procedure encourages them to generate responses in a lively, uninhibited way.

6. Critical thinking requires that judgments be made in light of defensible criteria. Dunn and Dunn (1972) developed an analytic adaptation of brainstorming that is useful for developing pupils' critical-thinking abilities.

7. Problem-solving techniques are used when issues have correct, right, or most appropriate answers. A typical problem-solving lesson includes four steps: (1) identify the problem, (2) consider possible approaches to its solution, (3) select and apply approaches, and (4) reach a defensible solution.

8. Some problems have several possible solutions. The specific decision a person reaches results from considering evidence and weighing personal values. Decision-making lessons can be used in a variety of circumstances in elementary social studies programs.

CHAPTER REFLECTIONS

Directions: Now that you have read this chapter, reread the case study at the beginning. Then, answer these questions:

1. Should tests be designed that focus on pupils' abilities to use specific higher-level thinking techniques, or should the success of these techniques be measured indirectly by looking at pupil scores on more traditional content tests?

2. Are there really differences among what we call *inquiry approaches, critical thinking, problem solving,* and *creative thinking,* or are these just fancy labels used to describe processes that are more alike than different?

3. Monitoring one's own thinking takes time. Can a logical case be made for teaching pupils to monitor their own thinking when time spent doing so substitutes for lessons focusing on more traditional academic content? Why or why not?

4. Interest in developing higher-level thinking skills has been a priority of many educational leaders for decades. If this is true, why do you suppose social studies specialists have found so little classroom instructional time dedicated to this kind of teaching?

EXTENDING UNDERSTANDING AND SKILL

1. Think about a social studies topic you might teach at a particular grade level. Find a passage in an elementary text that deals with this issue. Identify at least two learning tasks you might develop for pupils of different ability levels. For each, prepare a visual-thinking diagram.

2. Articles on inquiry teaching frequently are featured in journals such as *The Social Studies* and *Social Education.* Copy two or three articles that describe the use of inquiry techniques at the elementary level. Share them with others in your class. Use material from one of the articles to develop a lesson plan that features inquiry learning.

3. Review chapter material on Dunn and Dunn's analytic brainstorming technique. Identify a social studies topic suitable for presentation using this procedure. Develop a plan outlining what you would do at each phase of the lesson.

4. Review material in this chapter on data charts. Prepare a data chart for making comparisons and contrasts among creative thinking, critical thinking, and problem solving. Share the chart with others in your class. Class members may wish to keep copies as review material for a quiz.

5. Suppose you are asked to address your school's parent-teacher organization on this topic: "Approaches to Improving Thinking Skills." Prepare a draft of your remarks. Ask your instructor to critique your work.

REFERENCES

BAER, J. (1993–1994). Why you shouldn't trust creativity tests. *Educational Leadership, 51* (4) 80–83.

BEYER, B. K. (1988). *Developing a thinking skills program.* Boston: Allyn & Bacon.

BRUBACHER, J. W., CASE, C. W., & REAGAN, T. G. (1994). *Becoming a reflective educator: How to build a culture of inquiry in the schools.* Thousand Oaks, CA: Corwin Press.

CHENEY, L. V. (1987) *American memory: A report on the humanities in the nation's public schools.* Washington, DC: National Endowment for the Humanities.

DEWEY, J. (1910). *How we think.* Boston: D. C. Heath.

COSTA, A. L. (Ed.) (1991a). *Developing minds: A resource book for teaching thinking* (Vol. 1). Alexandria, VA: Association for Supervision and Curriculum Development.

COSTA, A. L. (Ed.) (1991b). *Developing minds: Programs for teaching thinking* (Vol. 2). Alexandria, VA: Association for Supervision and Curriculum Development, 1991.

CRAWFORD, K. M. (Ed.) (1997). *Learning together through inquiry.* York, ME: Stenhouse Publishing.

DUNN, R., & DUNN, K. (1972). *Practical approaches to individualizing instruction.* New York: Parker.

FRENCH, J. N., & RHODER, C. (1992). *Teaching thinking skills.* New York: Garland.

GARNER, R., & ALEXANDER, P. A. (1989, Spring). Metacognition: Answered and unanswered questions. *Educational Psychologist, 24* (2), 143–158.

HIRSCH, E. D., JR. (1987). *Cultural literacy: What every American needs to know.* Boston: Houghton Mifflin.

JOYCE B., & CALHOUN, E. (1997). *Learning to teach inductively.* Boston: Allyn & Bacon.

LIPMAN, M. (1988). "Critical thinking—What can it be?" *Educational Leadership, 46* (1), 38–39.

MELTZER, M., & PALAU, S. M. (1996). *Acquiring critical thinking skills.* Philadelphia: W. B. Saunders.

NAGEL, N. G. (1996). *Learning through real-world problem solving: The power of integrative teaching.* Thousand Oaks, CA: Corwin Press.

NICKERSON, R. S., PERKINS, D. N., & SMITH, E. E. (1985). *The teaching of thinking.* Hillsdale, NJ: Lawrence Erlbaum Associates.

PARKER, W. C. (1988). Restoring history to social studies—Had it ever left? *Educational Leadership, 45* (7), 86.

PERKINS, D. (1981). *The mind's best work.* Cambridge, MA: Harvard University Press.

PERKINS, D. (1993–1994). Thinking-centered learning. *Educational Leadership, 51* (4), 84–85.

RAVITCH, D. (1985). *The schools we deserve.* New York: Basic Books.

ROSS, E. W. (1994). *Reflective practice in social studies,* Bulletin No. 88. Washington, DC: National Council for the Social Studies.

RUGGIERO, V. R. (1997). *The art of thinking: A guide to critical and creative thought* (5th Ed.). New York: Longman Publishing Group.

RUGGIERO, V. R. (1988). *Thinking across the curriculum.* New York: Harper & Row.

SCHEID, K. (1993). *Helping students become strategic learners.* Cambridge, MA: Brookline Books.

SLABBERT, J. A. (1994). Creativity revisited in education: Reflection in aid of progression. *Journal of Creative Behavior, 28* (1), 60–69.

SUCHMAN, J. R. (1962). *The elementary school training program in scientific inquiry* (Report to the U.S. Office of Education, Title VII, Project 216). Urbana, IL: University of Illinois Press.

chapter 9

Group Learning

This chapter will help you to:

- recognize the importance of group learning experiences in the social studies program,
- describe the procedures that can be used to prepare learners for group learning experiences,
- state what a teacher must do to plan and implement classroom debates, role-playing lessons, and simulations, and
- identify the characteristics of several different cooperative learning techniques.

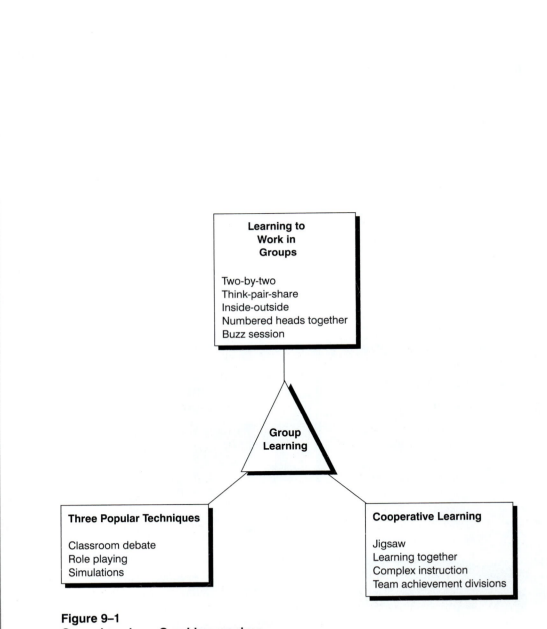

Figure 9–1
Group learning—Graphic organizer.

Case Study

DOES GROUP WORK INHIBIT INDIVIDUAL DEVELOPMENT?

Third-grade teacher Ping Yee attended a workshop this summer focusing on group learning in elementary social studies. She came back to her school eager to implement some of the procedures she had learned. Ms. Yee's principal, Gretchen Stein, thought third graders might benefit from some of the techniques introduced in the workshop. To familiarize parents with these approaches, she asked Ping to address the parents at a meeting of the school's parent-teachers organization. Ping agreed to do so.

On the night of the meeting, most parents seemed supportive. A few were noncommittal. But two or three argued against using more group learning techniques. Their arguments included these points:

- Small-group activities allow individuals to hide. It is easy for a child to become lazy and let other group members do the real work.
- Small groups put bright pupils at a disadvantage. They end up doing the work for less able learners. This isn't fair. It inhibits the development of less able pupils because, in small groups, they are not held individually accountable for their own work.
- History shows that groups can put severe psychological pressures on individuals who do not see things the way most in the group see them. This can be dangerous. Group pressures can force sensitive young people to publicly express views they don't hold. At best, this promotes lying. It may even do psychological damage to youngsters who do not understand why their views are always seen as "wrong."
- In the real world, people are held accountable for their actions as individuals and not for the actions of their groups.

What Is Your Response?

Think about these parents' concerns. Then, respond briefly to these questions:

1. Does group learning allow some pupils to escape responsibility for their own actions? If there is a possibility this might happen, what action might a teacher take to remedy it?
2. How do you feel about the claim that bright pupils are required to carry an unfairly heavy load when group-learning instruction is used? What evidence from your own experience supports or argues against this point of view?
3. Do members of small instructional groups in school have the power to exert too much pressure on individual group members? Why or why not?
4. In the real world, are individuals treated as they are because of what they do as individuals or because of their membership in certain groups? What evidence could be presented in support of each position? How do you personally feel about this issue?
5. Most opposition to increasing the amount of group-learning work in third-grade social studies classes is directed against small-group instruction in general. Are some kinds of group learning more likely to cause difficulties than others, or do these concerns apply equally to all group-learning techniques? Explain your answer.

INTRODUCTION

Most school instruction features a teacher working with all students in a classroom at the same time. This familiar scene is an example of *large-group instruction*. We will use the term *group learning* in this chapter to refer to smaller instructional groups. These groups range in size from about 2 to 15 learners.

In recent years there has been a trend toward more use of group learning. One reason for this is we now know more about the learning process than we used to. Many learning theorists now believe that more learning occurs when pupils are actively engaged in organizing new information and connecting it to what they already know (Winitzky, 1991). Ways of organizing learners that maximize their opportunities to engage new material and identify connections with prior knowledge are desirable. Well-organized group-learning lessons allow for this kind of active pupil exploration.

Another advantage of group work is that it allows individuals to work closely with others who may have different learning styles (Jarolimek & Foster, 1993). Exposure to alternative learning styles broadens pupils' receptivity to information delivered in different ways and helps them to develop more comprehensive and sophisticated problem-solving approaches.

The popularity of group learning has also been promoted by a number of specific instructional approaches that emphasize it, and that include well-defined roles for both teachers and learners. The sophistication of these techniques gives direction to us as we plan to use group approaches and helps us deal with the complaint of some skeptics that group work is merely "sharing ignorance."

Group learning is especially important in social studies lessons. Studies indicate that group learning is used more frequently in this part of the school curriculum than in other subjects. There are several reasons for this. The term *social studies* implies human interaction. Further, some of the intended outcomes of group learning are congruent with the goals of social studies (Winitzky, 1991). These include acquiring the skills necessary for participation in a democratic society, developing an appreciation for racial and ethnic differences, working productively with others, respecting the opinions of others, understanding individual differences, contributing to the welfare of the group, developing a positive self-concept, and accepting a variety of viewpoints.

Group-learning approaches vary in how many learners are assigned to each group. Numbers differ depending on the purposes of the group activity and the prior experiences of the pupils. Some group activities can accommodate fairly large groups of learners. Others work best when only two or three pupils are working together. Pupils who have little or no previous experience working with groups may need to start by first working with only one or two other pupils, moving into larger groupings only when they acquire the necessary skills. Many classroom groups function well with four to six pupil members. This number seems to work well when the expectation is that group members will discuss content (Cohen, 1986).

Group learning has several advantages for the elementary social studies classroom. Instruction that organizes learners to facilitate idea exchange and high participation levels helps to refine learners' abilities to work well with others. Group learning makes sense for the teacher in other ways. New teachers are often amazed at the range of individual

Working in groups facilitates the exchange of ideas and can promote higher levels of student involvement.

differences within a given classroom. Lessons directed at an entire class often fail to meet the needs of some class members. Organizing pupils into smaller groups allows you to respond more directly to particular needs of individual learners and use the range of skills and abilities in a positive manner.

There is evidence that group learning helps to develop warmer relationships between teachers and learners (Olmstead, 1974). This occurs for several reasons. First of all, breaking the class into small groups allows teachers and pupils an opportunity to work together on a more personal basis. This allows pupils to hear better and to feel they are more important as individuals. Additionally, the teacher is better able to appreciate how pupils are reacting to lesson content. By correctly interpreting pupil reactions, the teacher can respond quickly when learners signal confusion or lack of interest. This kind of rapid adjustment of instruction in response to pupil reactions often results in enhanced levels of learner success and motivation.

Levels of active pupil involvement increase in small-group work. In part, this occurs because it is difficult to avoid participating when relatively few people are involved. Second, participation is less intimidating. Many learners who hesitate to speak before the entire class willingly participate as members of a small group. Thus small-group learning is especially appropriate for pupils who need to learn oral language skills—for example, pupils with limited English proficiency.

An important side effect of enhanced levels of learner participation is an increase in individual learners' commitment to decisions made by their group. This occurs because the group experience fosters a sense of "ownership" in decisions. In large-group instructional settings, pupils are less likely to develop such an allegiance to conclusions emerging from discussions of issues.

Certainly there are difficulties associated with group learning approaches. For example, we have to engage in careful planning for these approaches to be successful. Pupils need to understand exactly what they are to do and what the expected learning outcome is. They may not know how to work productively with others or how to develop and share ideas in the context of a group. All this means that the teacher needs to provide students with specific instruction on how to work in groups. The teacher also has to be careful how he or she assigns specific individuals to groups. For example, little is gained by organizing a group to *discuss* a controversial issue if, at the outset, each group member holds the same opinion.

In addition, there are always some pupils who are not enthusiastic about working in groups. This may be true of individuals who have been successful in a competitive classroom environment. They tend to think they can do the task better by themselves. They may be reluctant to share their success with others or to compromise their ideas. Sometimes they will simply take over the work and do it by themselves. The teacher has to convince them of the value of working and sharing with others.

This chapter suggests procedures for introducing learners to group work; discusses ways to implement classroom debates, role-playing exercises, and simulations; and points out several cooperative learning approaches.

PREPARING PUPILS TO WORK IN GROUPS

Successful group work does not just happen. There are some skills and perspectives that students need in order to derive maximum benefit from group experiences. The prior experiences of learners in different classrooms vary. Some may not have had much experience with working in groups. When this is the case, attempts to use group work may be unsuccessful. To enhance the likelihood that small-group assignments will be successful, we have found it useful to put learners through experiences designed to orient them to group work and help them achieve success and satisfaction from the experience.

When first introducing group work, we need to give members of our class a good reason for doing it. They need to understand why they are engaged in this activity. You might point out that this kind of activity will help them learn skills of working together that will be valuable to them in life. You need to help them appreciate the importance of sharing information and participating in democratic decision making. It is important that the initial group activities have very clear, concrete outcomes. Pupils need to have success so that they can gain satisfaction from the experience and begin to see the value of group activity. Group work leading to a clear, tangible result provides a *product* that gives pupils evidence that something worthwhile has occurred.

The first tasks chosen should be those that rather naturally incorporate a variety of skills and abilities. They should invite collaboration and make it desirable. This gives pupils an incentive to work together. Early on, it is best to have short group activities that are worked regularly into the lessons rather than a long-term group project. These short-term activities allow pupils the opportunity to begin building group process skills and to experiment with different approaches.

It is extremely important that consistent routines and procedures for group work be established and taught to the class. Pupils need to know how to move to groups, how to get materials, what their particular role involves, what to do if there is a question or a problem, and what to do when the activity is completed. Teaching these routines and constantly reinforcing them will help ensure that the group work is efficient and productive. In addition, it helps prevent teacher stress!

Initial approaches that can be used to acquaint pupils with group activities and allow them to learn how to work productively together include:

- Two-by-two
- Think-pair-share
- Inside-outside
- Numbered heads together
- Buzz session

Two-by-Two

This approach is especially useful in helping break the ice when you are forming a new classroom group. To initiate the activity, ask each pupil to find out a specific bit of information about one other person. Once this has been done, pairs of pupils are joined to form groups of 4. Members of the groups share and try to remember the information about all 4 individuals. The groups of 4 are then joined to form groups of 8, the groups of 8 joined to form groups of 16, and the groups of 16 to form one large group. At each stage, pupils are to try to remember information about each person. The multiplication of group size can be conducted up to the size you feel appropriate, given the age and maturity of people in the class, and the class size.

Lesson Idea 9–1

WORKING IN GROUPS: TWO-BY-TWO

Grade Level:	3–6 (earlier grades with clear instructions and careful monitoring)
Objectives:	Pupils will (1) gain information about their classmates, (2) learn how to work together, and (3) develop a sense of cohesion and friendship in the classroom.
Overview:	This exercise is particularly useful as an "ice breaker" at the beginning of the school year when learners in a class may not know each other well. The example is designed for a class of 32; group size must be adjusted for smaller or larger classes.

Procedure:

Learning Set: Relate to the class the importance of making friends. Remind them that this class of individuals will be spending a lot of time together over the new year and in order for it to be a fun classroom, making friends is important. Inform them that the beginning of making friends is learning about other people. Today, they are going to learn something about others in the class.

Presentation: Give the following instructions for the seven steps of the exercise.

Step 1:   Listen carefully. Do not do anything until I say, "Ready . . . go." I want each of you to stand up. Then, walk over and find somebody you don't know well. You will have half a minute to do this. Any questions? (Respond to questions, if any.) Ready . . . go! (Each pupil finds a partner.)

Step 2:   I want you to find out three things about your partner. First, find out your partner's name. Second, find out your partner's birthday. Third, ask what your partner would do if someone gave him or her $300 that had to be spent this Saturday. You will have two minutes to do this. (Pupils follow instructions in this and each subsequent step. Monitor activities and call "time" when the limit is reached for each step.)

Step 3:   You have done very well. Now let's make things more interesting. I want you and your partner to get together with another pair of partners. This will make a group of four. When you have formed your groups of four, I want each of you to tell the three other members of the group the things you learned about your partner. Remember these are (1) your partner's name, (2) your partner's birthday, and (3) what your partner would do with $300 that must be spent this Saturday. I want everybody in the group to try to remember the answers for each group member. You will have four minutes to do this. Are there questions? Ready . . . go!

Step 4:   Now you are really going to be challenged. I want each group of four to get together with another group of four. This will create a group of eight. Do the same thing in the group of eight as you did in your groups of four. That is, take turns providing information about your partner. I want all of you to try and remember information about everybody in your group. Are there questions? You will have six minutes to do this. Ready . . . go!

Step 5:   Now let's find out who our memory champions are. I want each group of eight to get together with another group of eight to make a group of sixteen. Follow the same procedure as before. You'll have eight minutes this time. Ready . . . go!

Step 6:   Now it's time to really stretch our memories. Let's all get together in a giant circle. Then, I want you to use the same process as before. Let's do this for about eight minutes. Are there any questions? Ready . . . go!

Step 7: Now, is there anybody who can provide all three items of information about everybody in the group? Who wants to start? (If there are learners willing to try, call on them. Provide supporting comments. If no one wants to try this, ask if anyone can provide one or two items about each person in the class.) Are there others who would like to try? (Process continues until as many pupils as wish to volunteer have had a chance to participate.)

Closure: Ask the class, "What did we learn today? What did you learn about listening to other people? What did you learn about re-membering information? How might we use what we have learned in other situations?"

Teachers who have never used two-by-two before are often astonished at the large number of learners who will be able to provide information about everybody in the class at the end of the activity. The exercise makes learners more comfortable with one another and builds a sense of cohesiveness. Learners who know something about one another tend to settle into academically oriented group work better than those who are assigned to work with comparative strangers.

Think-Pair-Share

This introduces the idea of small-group learning by getting the pupils together in groups of two. In this technique, begin by giving the class a question or a problem. In the first phase, each student is to think individually about the question or problem. After a short time, give a signal, and pupils then begin to work in pairs to share their responses. When the pairs have had ample opportunity to discuss, each pair shares its responses with the rest of the class (McTighe & Lyman, 1988).

An advantage of the think-pair-share approach is that it helps pupils learn how to discuss and share their ideas with others. It can help them learn that "two heads are often better than one." The technique also helps pupils to understand the importance of integrating ideas and of compromising.

Inside-Outside

This approach is useful in helping pupils begin to learn effective group work skills. In this method, members of one group, the "outsides," observe the working of another group, the "insides." Each member of the outside group is assigned to watch one person and is told to look for some specific things. It is sometimes best for the "outsides" to take notes on their observations. The inside group is given a task to complete or a problem to discuss. When the inside group has completed the task or has had ample time to discuss the issue, the groups change places. Members of the new outside group are reminded of their assignments. When the new inside group has completed its task or has had ample time for discussion, the whole class then is pulled together, and individuals share the types of things that contributed to the success of the group. Pupils who have had an opportunity to participate in this type of activity tend to work more productively when they are assigned to participate in group learning than those who have not. Sometimes we (the authors) use inside-outside with our classes several times during the year to reinforce good group work skills.

Lesson Idea 9–2

WORKING TOGETHER: INSIDE-OUTSIDE

Grade Level: 4–6

Objectives: Pupils will participate in a class discussion and identify behaviors that contribute to a productive discussion.

Overview: Group learning requires learning special collaborative skills. Many pupils are unaware of the behaviors that contribute to successful group work. This procedure helps them begin to learn group work skills by having them observe others and identify those behaviors that contribute to productive work. Learners who go through an exercise of this type tend to work more productively when they are assigned to participate in group learning activities than are those who have not. Sometimes teachers use inside-outside several times during the school year to reinforce good group participation skills. Pupils tend to like the activity.

Procedures: *Learning Set*   Ask the class, "How many have watched team sports such as basketball or football? What happens if one person on the team tries to do everything and doesn't work with the other players on the team? The team usually doesn't succeed unless everyone on the team does his or her part. That is the same way it is when we work together in the class. It is important for everyone to work with the others so that the whole group can be successful. Today we are going to see if we can identify those things in group work that help a group be successful."

Presentation: To begin, divide the class into two large, even groups. For example, if there are 24 pupils in the class, have 12 learners in each group. Arrange enough chairs in a circle to seat all the members of one of the groups, who are asked to sit in the chairs. The seated group is called the *inside group*. Members of the other group arrange themselves behind the circle of chairs. This is the *outside group*. Each member of the outside group is assigned to observe what one member of the inside group does during a discussion and to take notes on this person's behavior. After giving these instructions, provide the inside group with a controversial topic (this should be a matter of genuine interest to learners). For example, a group of fourth graders might be asked to discuss this idea:

> *It should be the law that every fourth grader is in bed no later than 9:00 p.m. on school nights.*

Before the discussion begins, provide additional information to members of the outside group regarding kinds of observations to note. Ask pupils to observe the extent to which their assigned person does each of the following:

- Takes an active part in the discussion
- Makes comments that logically follow what the previous speaker says
- Summarizes something said earlier in the discussion
- Makes comments that keep the group from arriving at a premature conclusion
- Supports comments made by someone else in the group
- Refers to evidence to support a point

At this point, begin the discussion. Allow it to go on for 8 to 10 minutes. At this point, members of the inside group and the outside group change places. Remind members of the new outside group what they are to do. The new inside group begins discussing the topic. This second discussion also continues for 8 to 10 minutes.

To conclude the activity, lead a debriefing discussion with the whole class. Introduce information gathered by the note-takers. Point out the kinds of verbal behavior that help keep discussions going in a productive way (supportive comments, willingness to listen, careful attention to points made by previous speakers, and so forth).

Closure: Ask the class, "Why did we do this activity today? What did you learn that will help you when you work with others?"

Numbered Heads Together

This approach introduces pupils to the idea of group scoring and individual accountability. Begin by organizing pupils into groups of four or five, and give each pupil a number. Then present a question or problem to the entire class. Each group must discuss the question or problem. Tell pupils that they must make sure that every member of the group knows the answer. After an allocated period of time, call a number, and the pupils in each group with that number raise their hands. If they are able to give the correct response, their team gets a point (Kagan, 1989).

The advantage of this approach is that all the group members must share and must listen if they want their group to do well. This group-learning arrangement helps a large number of pupils review and discuss important questions in a minimum amount of time.

Buzz Session

The buzz session is a very simple procedure that can be used to introduce pupils to doing group work in social studies. Often the buzz session is tied directly to academic content when a new unit of study is about to begin. It does not need to take a great deal of time; 10 minutes is usually sufficient. Begin by organizing the class into groups of four or five pupils each. If possible, members of each group should arrange chairs in a circle so that they all face one another. Each group is asked to select a recorder, who will write down group responses.

Then provide a topic. Group members are to quickly identify a question or an item of information about the topic. The recorder records all responses. One effective technique when using this at the beginning of a unit is to have each group make two columns. In one column, members state what they think they already know about the topic. In the second column, they write questions about what they want to learn about the topic. At the end of the activity, collect these lists. You can then record this information on chart paper or on an overhead transparency and share it with the class.

Lesson Idea 9–3

BUZZ SESSION: MOVING TO AMERICA

Grade Level: 5

Objective: Learners can list questions they have about the settlement of America.

Overview: This activity is especially useful for beginning a unit of study. In addition, it helps pupils learn the group work skills needed to make group learning successful.

Procedures: ***Learning Set***   Ask how many members of the class have moved from one community to another. Ask what kinds of things they had to think about as they prepared for the move. Explain that today the pupils are going to pretend that they are settlers moving from England to America. They are going to work together in groups.

Presentation: Say to the class, "We are going to be learning about the lives of some of the early permanent settlers to come to North America from England (point out location of England on a large globe or world map). They landed and established settlements here (point out location of New England).

"I want you to suppose that you were living in England in the early 1600s. You are thinking about coming to America, but you know very little about what America might be like. Knowing which questions to ask could be very important in deciding whether to go and what you might need to take in order to survive. Why do you think knowing the right kinds of questions to ask is so important? (Get a few responses from the class.) Today you are going to work together in groups. Each group is to try and identify as many questions as possible that these people might have had about moving to North America. Make sure that one member of your group records the questions on a piece of paper. Do not spend time today trying to answer the questions. Just try to identify as many questions as possible.

"Don't start until I give you the signal. This is going to go fast. I will give you 10 minutes. I would like every member of each group to think of at least one question. Now, before we start, do you have any questions? (Respond to questions, as necessary.) All right, let's begin." (Learners begin to talk or "buzz" in their respective groups. Call "time" after 10 minutes.)

After the buzz period has concluded, pick up the questions from each group and share these with all learners. You may wish to write some of the questions on the board or on an overhead transparency. The class in the example above might develop questions such as these:

- How will I get to America?
- How long will the trip take?
- What kinds of animals will I find?
- What will I eat?
- Where will I get my clothes if there are no stores?
- What will happen if I get sick?
- What will the weather be like?

These and other questions can provide a focus for the study of the new unit. Since pupils have developed the questions themselves, they frequently are eager to find some answers. The buzz session often motivates students to learn new material. The interest it generates helps them master content and, at the same time, may increase their interest in doing additional work in groups.

Closure: Ask the class, "What did we do today? What are the advantages of working in a group for this type of activity? What do we need to do next?"

This technique provides useful diagnostic information about what pupils already know and about possible misconceptions they may have. This information is valuable as you ponder content to be included in your lessons. For pupils, the approach provides an initial focus on a topic they will be studying and also contributes to the development of productive group behaviors.

THREE POPULAR GROUP TECHNIQUES: CLASSROOM DEBATE, ROLE PLAYING, AND SIMULATIONS

The following are three popular approaches to group learning. Each of the techniques is a well-defined, systematic approach to instruction. Each of the approaches can be used at varying levels of sophistication depending on the abilities of the pupils in the classroom.

Classroom Debate

People whose only exposure to debates has been formal debate tournaments in high schools and universities may wonder how debate might be regarded as a useful group activity. The classroom debate is organized differently from the format used in tournament debates. It features teams of pupils who prepare positions on each side of an issue. Members of the two teams participate actively during the debate itself.

There are many ways to organize classroom debates. One version features teams of seven pupils each. Assignments are made as follows:

- Three learners take the *pro* position.
- Three learners take the *con* position.
- One learner plays the role of *critic*.

The teacher explains that members of the pro team will gather as much information as they can that supports a controversial proposal. Each member will be expected to play an active role in arguing the pro team's case. Similarly, members of the con team will gather information that can be used to attack the same controversial proposal. Each member will play an active role in arguing the con team's case. The critic will learn as much as he or she can about the positions of the pro team and the con team. This critic's function will be to ask probing questions toward the end of the debate that will highlight weaknesses of both positions.

To get the activity started, select a controversial issue that will serve as a focus. Make sure that adequate background materials are available for team members. Time must be provided for team members to prepare their case. (Monitor pupils during this time to render assistance and to ensure they are staying on task.)

The controversial issue is usually described in terms of a proposal that implies a change. The following are examples:

- "Resolved that all people in this school should be required to wear uniforms to school."
- "Resolved that the environment of Antarctica should be protected by forbidding tourists to visit that continent."
- "Resolved that schools should be in session at least eleven months of the year."
- "Resolved that families should be required to pay children for taking out the garbage."
- "Resolved that classroom rules should be made by teachers, not members of the class."

The classroom debate follows a general sequence. The following example reflects what might be done in an upper-grades class during a 50-minute period:

1. Each member of each team speaks for two minutes. Individual pro and con speakers alternate. Approximate time: 12 minutes.
2. Members of the pro team cross-examine members of the con team for a team total of six minutes. Then, members of the con team cross-examine members of the pro team for a team total of six minutes. Approximate time: 12 minutes.

3. Members of each team make final statements. All team members are encouraged to speak. Total time allotted to each team is three minutes. Approximate time: six minutes.
4. The critic is invited to ask probing questions of both pro team and con team members. The critic, at his or her discretion, may choose to direct a question at either some or all members of each team. The function of the critic is to point out weak spots in arguments made by members of both teams. Approximate time: eight minutes.
5. At this time, the class as a whole votes to determine a winner. Approximate time: two minutes.
6. The teacher debriefs the class. It is important that comments be as supportive as possible. Learners need to understand that speaking up is not going to elicit negative teacher reactions. During the debriefing phase, the teacher might use focus questions such as these:
   - What were the best arguments you heard?
   - What impressed you about those arguments?
   - What other points would you have brought up if you had been on the pro team? The con team?
   - Should the critic have asked some other questions? If so, what should the critic have asked?

Classroom debate is a technique that can generate high levels of interest. It provides an opportunity for large numbers of pupils to get actively involved in the learning process.

Role Playing

Role playing serves several purposes that are consistent with objectives of the elementary social studies program. The technique can help learners do the following:

- Develop their interpersonal relations skills
- Recognize perspectives of others
- Appreciate perspectives of others
- Recognize the impact of one person's decision on others
- Master academic content by replicating roles of people who participated in real events

Role playing is adaptable for use with learners at all elementary grade levels. It begins with a problem. We often find it useful to introduce pupils to the technique by presenting them with a situation they or members of their family might have faced.

Once a situation has been developed and presented to learners, participants need to be selected. Sometimes we ask for volunteers; sometimes we appoint pupils to play each part. Learners should have the option to refuse to play a role. The role-playing exercise does not work well when they feel they are being required to do something they would prefer not to do. Most often, more pupils want to participate than these are roles available.

Lesson Idea 9–4

ROLE PLAYING: HOW CAN NEEDS BE MET?

Grade Level: 4–6

Objectives: Pupils will identify perspectives of different characters and state the impact of one person's actions on others.

Overview: Role-playing activities can help accomplish several purposes. They can help pupils develop an understanding of different perspectives by assuming different roles. In addition, they help pupils learn to discuss and share with others in a group setting. This activity is designed to provide the pupils with a realistic setting, one they may experience in their own homes. Thus, the outcome may help them understand everyday problems. It is best if the entire class is involved in the role playing. Those who are not assigned roles should be observing during the enactment. It is also useful to have two or three enactments so that a variety of perspectives can be presented and the actions of the characters compared.

Procedures: *Learning Set:*   Begin with the following question: "Do you ever have times in your family when everyone seems to want to do something different and people get upset?" Tell the class that today they are going to talk about those types of situations.

Presentation: Say to the class: "Today we are going to act out a situation similar to what might happen in our families. Here is the situation:

"Mr. Jones is a single parent. He has four children. These are Jill, a 14-year-old high school freshman; the twins, Tom and Sid, 8-year-old third graders; and 7-year-old Jessica, a second grader.

"It is 5:00 p.m. on a Thursday evening. Mr. Jones has had a difficult day at work. He had many interruptions, and he wants to get back to the office no later than 6:30 p.m. to catch up on some paperwork.

"Jill is panicky about an algebra test she must take on Friday morning. She wants Mr. Jones to go over the material with her. She needs help right after dinner. At 7:00 p.m. she will have to stop studying algebra and watch a special public television production of *The Merchant of Venice* for her English class.

"The twins, Tom and Sid, have a Cub Scout meeting that begins at 6:30 p.m., where they are both receiving awards. They are hopeful that their father will be there to see them receive the awards.

"Jessica's church group will be having a short meeting from 6:30 to 7:30 p.m. The meeting is at the church, about four miles from the house. She will need to be taken to the meeting and picked up after it is over.

"The problem is, how can the needs of each person be met? I am going to choose a few people to play the roles of Mr. Jones, Jill, Tom, Sid, and Jessica. I want you to pretend you are that person and see if your team can act out a way of solving this problem. For those of you not acting, I want you to see if you can identify things that contribute to the solution and things that get in the way. Also, try to identify why you think each character acts the way he or she does, and see if you have some better solutions."

When the enactment is complete, take a couple of minutes to ask the participants how they felt when certain things happened. Then choose another group to see if they can act out the situation in a different way.

Closure: Ask the class, "What do you think are the important things you learned as a result of our lesson today? How do you feel about doing lessons like this? What do we all need to do to make lessons like this successful?"

Once players are selected, provide them with background information about their parts, and give them time to think about how the individuals they are playing would react to the basic problem.

A good role-playing lesson involves the entire class, not just the pupils playing parts. Pupils who are not playing roles should be assigned to look for specific things as the enactment proceeds. ("How realistic were Mr. Jones's responses to Jill?" "What other arguments could the twins have made to make a stronger case?") Pupils should be told to be ready to comment during the discussion following the role-playing enactment.

Sometimes, we find it useful to have two or three enactments of the same basic situation. When this is done, numerous learners can be actively involved as role players. Knowing they may be called upon to play roles in a subsequent reenactment, pupils pay closer attention during the initial enactment.

The following steps have been found useful in implementing role playing (adapted from Joyce & Weil, 1996):

1. *Enactment.* Role players act out responses. They are encouraged to be as realistic as possible. The teacher may intervene occasionally to remind learners of their roles, of the basic problem, and of issues relevant to the situation.
2. *Discussion and evaluation.* The teacher leads a discussion. Pupils who were to look for specific things are asked to speak. The teacher highlights motives and priorities of individual characters. Courses of action different from those that came out during the enactment are sometimes discussed.
3. *Reenactment.* When feasible, reenact the situation to give additional pupils opportunities to play roles. Such reenactments also allow more responses to the problem to be considered.
4. *Final discussion and debriefing.* If there have been reenactments, this phase begins with a discussion and evaluation similar to the one that followed the initial

Figure 9–2
Preparing a role-playing
exercise.

Identify an issue you might teach as part of your elementary social studies program that could be taught with a role-playing exercise. Describe the problem as clearly as possible. Then, indicate specific roles to be played by the participants. Be sure to indicate participants' unique perspectives on the problem. If circumstances permit, you might ask students in your social studies methods class to assume roles and go through the exercise as part of a class activity. You might play the teacher and take others in the class through the entire role-playing sequence (enactment, discussion and evaluation, reenactment, final discussion, and debriefing.)

enactment. This phase concludes with the teacher summarizing major points players made during the enactment. Learners' ideas are actively solicited at this time. Some teachers use this final phase to ask learners about other issues they would like to study using the role-playing technique. (See Figure 9–2.)

Simulations

The terms *games* and *simulations* are often used interchangeably. However, they have somewhat different meanings. Games usually involve a situation where individuals or groups compete with one another within a set of rules where there is a means of determining winners and losers. Simulations are designed to place participants in situations that closely parallel those found in the real world. Simulations simplify reality to highlight certain key ideas. For example, a simulation designed to focus on the legislative process may emphasize negotiation and deemphasize other features of legislative decision making. Simulations may not have winners and losers. The participants in the simulation may all achieve their goals. The object is for each participant in the simulation to make decisions and to experience the consequences of the decision. Simulations are basically more elaborate role-playing activities. Activities that incorporate the elements of reality as well as elements of games—such as winning and losing—are usually called *simulation games.*

Learners are intensely involved during simulations. Often they have opportunities to talk and to move to different parts of the room. Many pupils find simulations to be highly motivating. They have the potential to add an important real-world dimension to elementary social studies instruction.

Simulations vary enormously in their complexity. Some are simple board activities derived from popular commercial simulation games such as Monopoly®. Others are elaborate schemes that may require computers to manage and take many days to play. An example of a computer simulation appropriate for elementary pupils is the popular "Oregon Trail," available in most computer software stores. The popularity of personal computers and the potential for use of computer simulations as a means of instruction for decision making has increased interest in simulations.

Often simulations involve dividing participants into several groups. For example, there might be a simulation of an international conference on the control of terrorism. Individual groups may be assigned to play the roles of diplomats from individual countries or groups of countries.

Most simulations that are suitable for use in elementary social studies classrooms are not excessively complex. They typically can be played in one or two class sessions, though a few require more time. Many are available from commercial sources. Simulations suitable for use in elementary schools are included in the annual *Grades K–6 Social Studies Catalog,* available on request and free of charge from Social Studies School Service, 10200 Jefferson Boulevard, P. O. Box 802, Culver City, CA 90232-0802.

Simulations require learners to assume roles, make decisions, and face the consequences of their actions. They tend to be more complex in their organization than role playing. Hence, more time typically is required to prepare pupils to participate in them, and more support material may be required. A complete simulation activity moves through these four phases:

- Overview
- Training
- Activity
- Debriefing

Overview

During this phase, we introduce pupils to the simulation. Parts to be played by individual learners are described, and assignments to these parts are made. General rules of the simulation are introduced at this time.

Training

This amounts to a "walk-through" of processes to be followed once the simulation begins. Select several learners, assign them parts, and use them to illustrate how class members will be involved once the simulation begins. Invite learners to ask questions as you explain how the simulation will operate.

Following this introductory information, pupils should be allowed to review their roles. If the simulation features several groups, group members should be allowed to meet to discuss their roles and to plot preliminary strategy.

Activity

This is when the actual simulation activity takes place. During this time, you play the roles of discussant, coach, and referee. At times, pupils may not grasp the point of the simulation. You may find it necessary to stop the action for a moment to help pupils think about their decisions and to explain the purpose of the activity.

Some pupils may not know how to respond to certain developments. You can coach them as they consider their options, and ideas can help inexperienced simulation participants gain in confidence. As pupils' expertise grows, gradually disengage from the coaching role.

It is common for disputes to arise during simulation activities. Often there are situations for which the rules fail to provide a specific action guideline. When this happens, you need to intervene and make a ruling that will allow the simulation to continue.

Debriefing

This is a critically important part of any simulation activity. During debriefing, lead a discussion highlighting various events that occurred during the activity. The discussion helps pupils recall things that might have escaped their notice during the fast pace of the activity itself.

Debriefing discussions sometimes focus on specific decisions made and their desirability relative to alternatives. Sometimes debriefing concerns the design of the simulation. What issues were forced to the front because of the rules of the simulation? What did the designers of the simulation omit? Often, individuals will want to critique their own performances and suggest ways they might act differently were they to do the exercise another time.

Teachers with no prior experience with simulations tend to allow insufficient time for debriefing. This severely limits the effectiveness of the simulation as a productive learning activity. It is during the debriefing that the important concepts and procedures are discussed and the learning is reinforced.

COOPERATIVE LEARNING TECHNIQUES

Cooperative learning is an approach that emphasizes working together. This approach to teaching is particularly appropriate for use in social studies lessons, as it replicates the kind of cooperative activity that characterizes much of adult social, economic, and political life. Those advocating cooperative learning point out that it is especially suited for coping with individual differences within the classroom. Individuals with a variety of skills and ability levels learn to work together in heterogeneous groups.

Cooperative learning approaches feature positive interdependence, face-to-face interaction among learners, individual accountability, and student instruction in appropriate interpersonal and small-group skills (Good & Brophy, 1997). *Positive interdependence* refers to situations where pupils realize that they are interdependent and everyone in the group must contribute to achieve success. Positive interdependence can be fostered through a division of labor, giving each group member a specific task, or through the use of group incentives or a group grade. For example, some approaches use total group scores or the improvement scores of group members to determine group rewards. Positive interdependence appears to be a key characteristic of cooperative learning approaches that result in increased achievement.

Face-to-face interaction refers to group tasks that require pupils to interact with each other, as opposed to tasks where each pupil works independently and the material is then just compiled into a final product.

Individual accountability is another key area where many attempts at cooperative learning flounder. Most people are familiar with the situation where one or more group members fail to do their job and depend on others in the group to do all the work. Individual accountability makes each pupil accountable for making a contribution to the group. This can be accomplished by giving individual grades or reinforcements in addition to group grades. However, in cooperative learning approaches these grades are based on the effort and the contributions of the individual in achieving the group goal, not just on individual achievement.

There are several ways this can be done. Individuals within the group can rate the contribution of team members, individuals can perform a self-evaluation, or the teacher can review the contributions of each member by reviewing a portfolio from each pupil that contains material he or she gathered and used during the group project.

As already indicated, group learning techniques will not be successful unless pupils are taught the necessary skills. Just being told to cooperate is not enough. Individuals will need to be taught not only the necessary interpersonal skills, but the specific roles they will need to fill in the particular cooperative learning approach being used.

Researchers have found that cooperative learning approaches result in higher levels of mastery and better retention of concepts than situations in which pupils compete against one another as individuals. In addition, peer acceptance and peer encouragement are improved. This is possible because of the powerful influence of the peer group and the increased opportunity for becoming involved in discussions involving higher levels of reasoning (Good & Brophy, 1997).

A number of cooperative learning approaches have been developed. Four popular approaches are introduced here:

- Jigsaw
- Learning together
- Complex instruction
- Teams achievement divisions

Jigsaw

The jigsaw method is a group learning technique that requires each person in a group to accomplish part of a larger assignment. The entire assignment cannot be finished until all parts of the jigsaw are fitted together. There are many possible applications of the jigsaw method in elementary social studies classrooms. One adaptation to the approach is what might be termed *jigsaw twins.* In this approach, two pupils are teamed together to become the experts on a topic. This is especially useful when pupils may have limited proficiency in English or may have learning difficulties that might hinder their ability to master the material and communicate it to the home team.

Teachers sometimes provide a blank data chart that learners can use to record information. Such a chart for the example presented in Lesson Idea 9–5 would have the names of the five countries listed across the top. The terms *religions, languages, major income sources, major terrain features,* and *educational system* would be written vertically down the left side. Pupils are invited to write notes in the appropriate cells of this matrix.

When pupils in a given group have completed their work, they let the teacher know they are ready for their evaluation. The teacher then assesses their work and provides reactions to members of the group.

In an adaptation of this approach, often called *jigsaw II,* each group receives points based on the scores of the pupils during an evaluation (Borich, 1996). This addition heightens interest by making it important for each person in the group to learn his or her expert role and for all members to listen and learn from each other.

Lesson Idea 9–5

JIGSAW: SOUTH AMERICA

Grade Level: 6

Objectives: Each pupil will (1) learn and chart information about one South American country, (2) become an "expert" about one aspect of a country and teach it to others in the group, and (3) work cooperatively in a group.

Overview: The jigsaw approach is useful in social studies, especially when a topic has several parts to develop and research. If some of the pupils have limited English proficiency or a learning difficulty, team them with another to become an "expert pair" on that particular aspect of the country. In this example, the class is learning about South America. For each of the countries, you want the class to learn something about the history of the relationships with other countries, the ethnic and language backgrounds of the people, the major resources and industries in the country, the terrain and the major regions, the religious beliefs, and the form of government. Rather than try to cover all countries, choose several because they offer some interesting contrasts, such as Brazil, Argentina, Columbia, Paraguay, and Peru.

Procedure: *Learning Set*   Say to the class, "Today we are going to begin learning about South America. But we are going to do it a little differently. When you work in a company, you usually have different people who are experts on different things. For example, a manufacturer might have an expert on running the machines, an expert on designing the products, an expert on advertising, and an expert on selling. For the company to be successful, each expert must learn as much as possible about the job and must help others in the company understand what needs to be done. For the next several days, each of you is going to become an expert on some aspect of a South American country and will teach others in your group about that part of the country."

Presentation   Divide the class into "home" groups. Present to them the aspect of the country they will study. You can then assign each member of each home group the task of becoming an expert on one aspect. Tell the experts that they will be responsible for learning as much as possible about that aspect and when they return to their home group, they will have to teach the others what they have learned.

   Divide the class into expert groups by having the experts from each group gather together in different parts of the room. For example, all of the experts on government will gather together, all of the experts on culture and language, and so on.

Tell the class that the first country they will be studying will be Brazil. Present each group with a packet of material on the aspect of Brazil about which they are to become experts. Each group then begins working together, organizing the material and discussing it.

Each expert group may need to work together for more than one day. Part of their assignment will be to develop an outline, maps, diagrams, or pictures that they will use to present their information to their home group.

Closure: This activity will probably take several days. At the end of each day, bring the day to a close by reviewing how the groups are working together, and make suggestions on what they need to do to next.

In summary, the jigsaw method promotes the development of productive group behavior. Pupils learn to listen attentively to others. This is encouraged because contributions of all group members are needed to complete the assigned task. The procedure also helps develop cooperative, mutually supportive attitudes among class members.

Learning Together

The learning-together method features a less formal organizational structure than the jigsaw method (Johnson & Johnson, 1985; Johnson, Johnson, Holubec, & Roy, 1984). In learning together, organize pupils into groups whose members reflect a variety of interests and abilities.

Once the groups are formed, give every group an assignment that requires the attention and involvement of each person. The technique works best when many talents and interests are represented in each group. This allows individual pupils to work on parts of the overall project that are compatible with their own enthusiasm. The assignment usually requires pupils to develop a "product" of some kind. This might be a set of written responses to questions, a research report, a play to be presented to the class, or a group oral report. Members of a group receive grades based on the quality of this final product.

Roles of individual pupils within each group can be quite varied. Typical roles that might be found in a group would be those of group manager, recorder, researcher, illustrator, editor, and materials organizer. However, the roles vary according to the task. For example, if you wanted a group of fifth graders to write a short play about life in colonial New England, you could assign your pupils roles as head writer, general manuscript editor, set designer, and sound effects chairperson. All could assist in preparing the actual content of the play.

In learning-together lessons, each pupil receives the same grade. This feature of the technique encourages individuals to pool their talents. There is an incentive for each pupil to do his or her best to ensure that all members of the group receive a good final evaluation. Johnson and Johnson (1985) report that learners who have had experience in working together tend to support the idea that it is fair to award the same grade to each group member.

In some cooperative learning approaches, each student has a specific responsibility and the success of the groups depends on the participatioin of all students.

During a learning-together lesson, monitor each group carefully. Pupils may have problems that have to be resolved. Try to be available to clear up misunderstandings and to help group members complete the required learning product.

Complex Instruction

Complex instruction has some similarities to the learning-together approach. Pupils in groups are assigned roles. These are specific procedural roles such as facilitator, materials manager, timer, and resource person, and they will vary according to the needs of the task.

A key element of complex instruction is that the learning tasks need to be tasks that are open-ended and that require high-order thinking, multiple abilities, and multiple resources. Good tasks are open-ended in two ways. First, the process that pupils can use to arrive at a solution is left up to the group. Second, the task is one for which there is no single correct answer or solution. To ensure that tasks will be available that allow for these kinds of open-ended decisions, units used as foci for complex instruction activities are organized around the central concepts and generalizations or "big ideas" of an academic discipline.

An identified generalization or big idea is used as the theme of different learning centers that allow groups to explore the related ideas and concepts in different contexts (Cohen, Lotan, Whitcomb, Balderrama, Cossey, and Swanson, 1994). For example, a political science generalization stating, "When the people believe that the government no longer represents their interests, a revolution usually occurs," might be the focus of a complex instruction unit for a fifth-grade class studying the Revolutionary War. Several learning centers could be organized around specific examples of incidents that led colonists to believe the government was unresponsive. In each of these centers pupils would explore the evidence by examining primary sources, reading different accounts, examining artifacts, looking at pictures, consulting textbooks, or listening to music or to speeches. Other centers could include examples of other times and places where people faced this same issue. These could include a variety of contexts such as local organizations, tribal conflicts, and in other parts of the world.

Each group is provided with an activity card that describes the specific activities pupils will engage in while working at a given center. Groups rotate through the centers, with each group working at a different center each day. In addition to a number of questions that the group needs to consider, the activity card also contains a specific group application task. This task might be for pupils to build something, role-play, or create something. At the end of each day, each group shares its product with the rest of the class. Pupils are then encouraged to improve on or create new products when they have the opportunity to work in the center.

In addition to the group product, each member of the class must write an individual report on his or her understanding and participation in the group. This provides for individual accountability in addition to a group product.

Complex instruction is organized around research findings indicating that individual participation is a strong predictor of learning gains (Cohen, Lotan, Whitcomb, Balderrama, Cossey, and Swanson 1994). Therefore, a primary task of the teacher is to increase participation of all students in the groups. This is especially critical for low-status students. Low-status students rarely participate in groups, are often ignored by other learners, and frequently are not given the opportunity to fully participate. Thus, for these young people, often group work proves to be not particularly beneficial. To overcome this problem, complex instruction provides two solutions.

One approach is what is termed *multiple abilities treatment*. This is accomplished prior to the beginning of group work as the teacher names the different skills and abilities that will be needed to successfully complete a task. The purpose is to help the pupils see that this is different from normal school tasks and that cooperation will be necessary in order to be successful.

A second approach calls on the teacher to *assign competence* to low-status students. The teacher accomplishes this by being alert for opportunities to make supportive public statements concerning the contributions and the perspectives of low-status students.

Complex instruction emphasizes the development of cooperative norms. These are the behaviors required for successful group work. The basic norms emphasized sometimes take the form of simple rules, such as:

1. You have the right to ask anyone in your group for help.
2. You have the duty to assist anyone in the group who asks for help.
3. You must justify your arguments with evidence.
4. If you want to assist somebody else, you must restrict yourself to explaining how something is to be done rather than actually doing another person's work yourself.

Teams Achievement Divisions

We begin *teams achievement divisions* by dividing the class into four- or five-member teams. Each team includes some high achievers, some low achievers, some boys, and some girls, ideally from different cultural and ethnic backgrounds (Slavin, 1994). After we introduce new content through traditional large-group instruction, each team is given a set of study worksheets. These worksheets describe tasks to be accomplished and problems to be solved. These tasks and problems relate to the content that has been introduced to the class as a whole.

At this point, each team begins to work. Team members may quiz each other, tutor each other, or take other action they feel is necessary to accomplish the assigned work. Once a group has finished its work, team members take a test on the material. They may not help one another on the test. Group members are scored separately.

There are several approaches to computing team scores. Teachers who have worked with their pupils for some time have a good idea of each pupil's expected test score. The teacher makes a list of these expected, or base, scores. When tests are scored, one point is awarded toward the team's score for every point a member of the team exceeds his or her base score. Usually there is a maximum number of points that any one pupil can contribute to the team total. (Often this is set at 10 points.) This would mean, for example, that a learner with a base score of 32 who scored 80 still would contribute only the 10-point maximum to the total team score. An example of a group score for an achievement team is given in Table 9–1.

Note in the table that Calvin, although he had the lowest actual test score, still contributed 10 points to the team total. This happened because his test score of 35 was much higher than his base score of 20. Also note that Dinah had a base score of 96 and got a score of 100. She also contributed 10 points to the team total because she got a perfect score. This provides an incentive for the higher-scoring students to do well.

Student teams achievement divisions encourage academically challenged pupils. They have an incentive to do as well as they can. Even though their individual scores may not be high, they have opportunities to make important contributions to the total scores of the teams to which they are assigned. This technique also encourages more able pupils to assist less able members of their group to master the content. This is true because all members of the group will profit when these youngsters' performances exceed the expectations reflected in their base scores. Indeed, in teams achievement divisions, each

Table 9–1
Calculating scores for an achievement team.

Student	Base Score	Quiz Score	Team Points
Alan	49	56	7
Bertha	50	48	0
Calvin	20	35	10
Dinah	96	100	10
Carlos	75	80	5
Team Score			32

member of a group has a stake in the learning of every other member. Hence, there is an incentive for all group members to help each other.

*   *   *

In summary, cooperative learning techniques require the following teacher decisions:

- Selecting a topic that lends itself to group work
- Making decisions about group size and composition
- Providing appropriate materials
- Identifying the parts of the lesson and sequencing the lesson
- Monitoring the work of pupils in groups and encouraging participation by all
- Intervening when necessary to solve problems
- Evaluating outcomes

Because of the social nature of many aspects of the subject, cooperative learning approaches are particularly suitable for use in elementary social studies programs. Many teachers find that these techniques enhance pupils' interest and improve general levels of achievement.

WEB CHECK

Note: Electronic addresses of sites on the World Wide Web change frequently. If the listed URL fails to work, use a standard search engine to locate the new address of the site.

- WWW Constructivist Project Design Guide

  URL—**http://www.ilt.columbia.edu/k12/livetext-nf/webcurr.html**

  This source can help you develop cooperative learning units. You will also find links here to other useful Web sites.

- Teachers Helping Teachers

  URL—**http://www.pacificnet.net/~mandel/**

  This site is a resource for getting teaching ideas and information about a variety of topics of interest to teachers. Teachers share their insights with each other.

- AskERIC

  URL—**http://ericir.syr.edu**

  This site contains thousands of free lesson plans and articles on a variety of topics. It provides an index that helps make your search easier.

- A Guide to Maximizing Learning in Small Groups

  URL— **http://www.cs.ukc.ac.uk/national/CSDN/html/EDUres/small-group-learning.html**

  Information available at this site provide excellent guidelines for pupils who are organized into small working groups.

- Teaching Strategies

  URL—**http://www.ca.sandia.gov/outreach/2020/2020TStrat.html**

  Information at this site includes some "how to's" related to jigsaw, cooperative learning, and a number of other useful instructional approaches.

- Cooperative Learning

  URL—**http://www.ca.sandia.gov/outreach/2020/2020TStrat.html**

  This excellent site contains a wealth of information related to the use of cooperative learning techniques. It is maintained by the Mid-Atlantic Association for Cooperation in Education. Highly recommended.

KEY IDEAS IN SUMMARY

1. *Group instruction* refers to instruction that is directed at classroom groups ranging in size from about half of the total class to as few as two pupils. Many group instruction techniques feature high levels of interaction. They have the potential to improve learners' abilities to work with others and at the same time promote learning of new content.

2. Successful group learning requires that teachers plan carefully. Pupils must understand exactly what they are to do, and they must know what they are expected to learn from the activity. Teachers must exercise care in assigning individuals to groups. Many group procedures work well when each group includes pupils with diverse academic abilities, interests, and points of view. Materials used in group learning activities must be prepared in advance and must be easily accessible to group members. Finally, teachers need to monitor groups carefully when they are working on assigned tasks.

3. Teachers who want to use group learning techniques with their learners sometimes find that their students have had little prior experience working together in small groups. To facilitate learner functioning in groups smaller than the class as a whole, teachers sometimes use several introductory techniques. Among these are two-by-two, think-pair-share, numbered heads together, inside-outside, and buzz sessions. Some of the techniques focus exclusively on developing learners' techniques for working productively in groups. Others help them learn how to focus on academic content in a group setting.

4. Many group learning techniques are suitable for use in elementary social studies classrooms. Three popular techniques are (1) classroom debate, (2) role playing, and (3) simulations. Classroom debate features teams of pupils who are assigned to prepare positions to either support or oppose a controversial proposition. Role playing allows learners to appreciate perspectives of others by responding to situations in a manner consistent with the views of a character they are assigned to play. Simulations help pupils learn by involving them in structured simplifications of reality that help them to grasp the complexities of important processes and issues.

5. Cooperative learning techniques seek to replicate in the classroom many of the kinds of cooperative activities that characterize adult social, economic, and political life. Numerous cooperative learning approaches have been developed. Four approaches that are very applicable in elementary social studies classes are (1) jigsaw, (2) learning together, (3) complex instruction, and (4) teams achievement divisions. Many cooperative learning methods seek to give each learner a personal stake in the learning of all members of his or her group.

CHAPTER REFLECTIONS

Directions: Now that you have read this chapter, reread the case study at the beginning. Then, answer these questions.

1. How would you respond to concerns about some of the pupils doing all the work for others when group learning approaches are used?

2. Some of the criticisms of group learning raised in the case study seem to assume that the concerns apply to all group learning approaches. Are there important differences among individual approaches that might make individual concerns more applicable to some techniques than others? Cite examples to support your answer.

3. What is your personal experience with group learning? Did you like or dislike instructional arrangements that group a small number of learners together? How do you explain your personal reactions to this approach to instruction?

4. Some teachers are uncomfortable with the group grading techniques used for some cooperative learning approaches. What is your personal reaction to group grades?

5. Two-by-two and inside-outside are used primarily to improve learners' skills at working in groups. Is it defensible to take time away from content-oriented teaching to focus on the development of such skills?

6. Many cooperative learning approaches emphasize cooperation and mutual support. At the same time, they downplay competition. Some people argue that much of life features competitive activity. If this is true, does it make sense for teachers to involve pupils in procedures that are not designed to encourage competitive behavior?

EXTENDING UNDERSTANDING AND SKILL

1. Prepare a list of the group learning techniques introduced in this chapter. Interview an elementary teacher. Ask whether he or she uses any of these procedures to teach social studies lessons. Also, ask whether the teacher uses other group approaches. Summarize what you learn in your interview in an oral report to your social studies methods class.

2. In recent years, there has been an explosion of interest in cooperative learning techniques. (You might want to begin by looking up *cooperative learning* in the *Education Index*, available in your library. Your instructor also may be able to direct you to specific sources of information.) Identify one or two cooperative learning techniques that were not introduced in this chapter. Be prepared to explain to your instructor how these techniques work. If time permits, you might involve other class members in a lesson featuring one or more of these approaches.

3. Identify content from this chapter that might be taught to social studies methods students using the jigsaw method. Plan a lesson involving class members in your suggested approach.

4. To familiarize yourself with two-by-two, use the technique as a way to break the ice when a large group of people get together. You might try it at a party, at a church function, at an orientation session for new university students, or in some other setting. Share your experiences in using the procedure with members of your social studies methods class.

5. Following procedures for a classroom debate, organize members of your methods class into teams to debate this issue: "Resolved that exposing learners to cooperative learning techniques in school will diminish their ability to succeed in a competitive society." Ask other members of the class to observe the debate and to critique the technique.

REFERENCES

BORICH, G. (1996). *Effective teaching methods* (3rd ed.). Englewood Cliffs, NJ: Merrill/Prentice Hall.

COHEN, E. G. (1986). *Designing group work: Strategies for the heterogeneous classroom.* New York: Teachers College Press.

COHEN, E. G., LOTAN, R. A., WHITCOMB, J. A., BALDERRAMA, M. V., COSSEY, R., & SWANSON, P. E. (1994). Complex instruction: Higher order thinking in heterogeneous classrooms. In S. Sharan (Ed.), *Handbook of cooperative learning methods.* Westport, CT: Greenwood Press.

GOOD, T., & BROPHY, J. (1997). *Looking in classrooms* (7th ed.). New York: HarperCollins.

JAROLIMEK, J., & FOSTER, C. (1993). *Teaching and learning in the elementary school* (5th ed.). Englewood Cliffs, NJ: Merrill/Prentice Hall.

JOHNSON, D. W., & JOHNSON, R. T. (1987). *Learning together and alone* (2nd ed.). Englewood Cliffs, NJ: Prentice Hall.

JOHNSON, D. W., JOHNSON, R. T., HOLUBEC, E., & ROY, P. (1984). *Circles of learning: Cooperation in the classroom.* Alexandria, VA: Association for Supervision and Curriculum Development.

JOHNSON, R. T., & JOHNSON, D. W. (1985, April). *Structuring conflict in science classrooms.* Paper presented at the annual meeting of the National Association of Research in Science Teaching, French Lick, IN.

JOYCE, B., & WEIL, M. (1996). *Models of teaching* (5th ed.). Englewood Cliffs, NJ: Prentice Hall.

KAGAN, S. (1989). The structural approach to cooperative learning. *Educational Leadership, 47* (4), 13.

McTIGHE, J., & LYMAN, F. T., JR. (1988). Cueing thinking in the classroom: The promise of theory-embedded tools. *Educational Leadership, 45* (7), 18–24.

OLMSTEAD, J. A. (1974). *Small-group instruction: Theory and practice.* Alexandria, VA: Human Resources Research Organization (HumRRO).

SLAVIN, R. E. (1994). *Educational psychology: Theory and practice* (4th ed.). Boston, MA: Allyn and Bacon.

WINITZKY, N. (1991). Classroom organization for social studies. In J. Shaver (Ed.), *Handbook of research on social studies teaching and learning* (pp. 530–539). Englewood Cliffs, NJ: Merrill/Prentice Hall.

chapter 10

Developing Prosocial Behavior

This chapter will help you to:

- describe the importance of prosocial behavior as an outcome of the social studies program,
- identify the relationship between (1) values and attitudes and (2) prosocial behavior,
- describe sensitive issues related to teaching values and morality,
- point out components of a four-level framework for organizing learning associated with values and morality,
- explain how a moral-dilemma approach can be used in helping develop pupils' moral reasoning abilities, and
- prepare role-playing experiences for use in the elementary classroom.

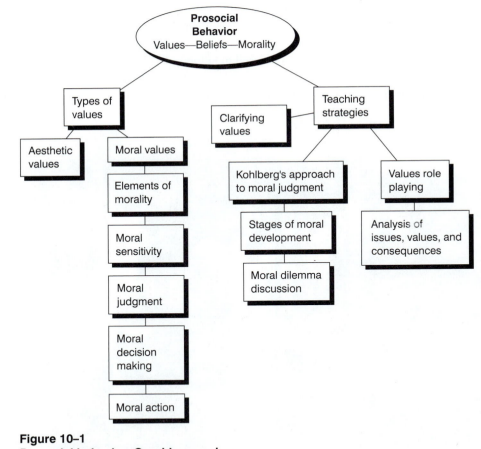

Figure 10–1
Prosocial behavior: Graphic organizer.

Case Study

DOES IT MAKE SENSE TO TEACH COMMON VALUES TO SUPPORT PROSOCIAL BEHAVIOR?

Joe Simpson and Marie Bellaby, both fifth-grade teachers, recently were designated by Manisha Ramy, the principal of Culver Elementary School, as members of a team charged with identifying certain values that all teachers in the school should be teaching to their pupils. Both have found this to be an extremely frustrating assignment. Joe recently shared his concerns with Ms. Ramy. This is what he said:

> *I want you to know that Marie is a great colleague. I respect her. But we just don't see things in the same way. I am "pro choice" all the way; Marie is just as committed to the "pro life" position. I am totally opposed to capital punishment; Marie supports it and thinks it's a real deterrent to crime. I think the government should provide some tax support to all schools, including those run by churches and private organizations; Marie is opposed to this idea, especially to using tax money to support parochial schools.*
>
> *I think there are important strength differences between men and women that make it legitimate for some occupations such as firefighting to be restricted to males; Marie thinks every occupation ought to be equally open to both genders. I think spanking children, assuming parental permission has been obtained, is a perfectly legitimate way for teachers to discipline members of their class; Marie is totally opposed to corporal punishment in the schools. I think the government has gone too far and has caused our country to lose jobs to overseas competitors by placing an excessive number of environmental regulations on industry; Marie thinks the health of future generations is seriously at risk from pollution and that more government regulation is needed.*
>
> *As you can see, our values simply differ. We just don't see a lot of issues in the same way. If the two of us can't agree on these things, how can we propose a set of values that should be taught to every pupil in school?*

What Is Your Response?

Read the information above. Think about Joe's concerns. Then, respond briefly to these questions:

1. Are the differences Joe describes so serious that any attempt to identify a set of values to be taught to all learners will fail? Why or why not?
2. Joe claims to have identified quite a few important differences in how he and Marie see key issues. Are these differences common, or is this a rather unusual situation? Why do you think so?
3. If the principal insists that Joe and Marie continue to try to identify common values to be taught to all pupils in the school, what do you think will happen?
4. If you were the principal, how would you respond to Joe's comments?
5. Does the school have a legitimate interest in passing on certain values to all pupils?

INTRODUCTION

Fans of the *Star Trek* series know that people from Vulcan make decisions in ways that strike Earthlings as strange. They look only at evidence and then apply their logical reasoning powers. We do more than that. Any time we make a choice, values and attitudes come into play. Since these predispositions influence adults as they go about the business of daily living, schools have an obligation to help young people understand issues associated with values and attitudes.

To be sure, teaching about values and morality is a controversial area. Because we live in a pluralistic society, individuals immediately start asking, "Whose values and whose morality?" In addition, the values domain is viewed as private and a matter of personal choice and therefore not a legitimate area of concern for public schools that serve all segments of society.

However, during the latter part of the 1990s a number of violent incidents involving schoolchildren shook the nation. Those involved students as young as 8 and 9 performing such heinous acts as killing classmates and teachers at several schools and murdering a young girl for her new bicycle. These acts caused a nationwide uproar as individuals sought answers for these crimes. Many individuals became convinced that these acts signaled a rising tide of violence based on an absence of values and morality in the young. Thus attention was directed toward programs that would address this issue. Many of these programs were labeled as *character education.*

The term *character education* is often used in order to avoid the possibility of controversy associated with term *values.* There is no standard definition of what is meant by *character education.* Advocates of character education emphasize a variety of different programs and outcomes ranging from school climate and environment to drills on lists of *virtues* (Lockwood, 1997).

In 1996 a Task Force on Character Education in the Social Studies formed by the National Council for the Social Studies released a report entitled *Fostering Civic Virtue: Character Education in the Social Studies* (1996). This report stated that citizens must have a commitment to fundamental values such as life, liberty, equality, truth, pursuit of happiness, and promotion of the common good. The report called for a renewed commitment on the part of social studies teachers to teach character and civic virtue. Though instruction tied to issues associated with values can be controversial, the task force urged teachers not to be "timid or hesitant" about working toward these goals.

Lickona (1993), one of the leading advocates for character education, states that we "share a basic morality, essential for our survival; that adults must promote morality by teaching the young, directly and indirectly, such values as respect, responsibility, trustworthiness, caring, and civic virtue" (p. 9). In another publication, Lickona (1997) adds honesty, fairness, integrity, compassion, self-control, and moral courage to the list of values. He contends that these are not merely subjective preferences but universal moral values that affirm human dignity and promote the good of the individual as well as the common good. (See Figure 10–2.)

In social studies the focus is on people. Any understanding of people would be incomplete and distorted unless we consider their values, beliefs, and views of morality. We cannot, for example, understand most historic or current events unless we understand

The following editorial appeared in a local newspaper:

We applaud efforts of local school authorities to put important new substance into the elementary social studies curriculum. The new curriculum provides the pupils with much needed training in making complex decisions.

The program works like this. Pupils are given unfinished stories. At the end of each story, a major character faces a difficult choice. There is no clear-cut right answer. Pupils are asked what they would do in the situation. They role-play responses and then discuss the values implicit in the decisions they made.

This kind of activity is really outstanding. It helps young people understand that life's issues are complex. They need to understand that there are no easy and simple answers to many of the dilemmas we face.

On the other hand, our society has determined that answers to some questions are *not* open to debate. For example, we do not countenance a discussion that murder might be right. That it is wrong is universally acknowledged.

We at the *Journal* would be pleased if the new curriculum would add a few lessons pointing out to pupils that there are some positions not open to debate. Not all truths are relative.

THINK ABOUT THIS

1. Do you agree that there are universal values that should be taught to pupils?
2. What do you think would be included as universal values?
3. What do you see as the potential problems with trying to teach universal values?

Figure 10–2
Should pupils be taught that some things are absolutely right or wrong?

the values and beliefs of the people involved. Social studies has an important role in focusing student attention to these important dimensions of human behavior.

There is nothing new about the expectation that public schools should be concerned about these issues. As an institution, "the school has always been seen as one of the means by which the culture transmits its values from one generation to the next" (Rogers & Freiberg, 1994, p. 277). There is disturbing evidence that we have not been succeeding as well as we would like in encouraging young people to embrace behaviors widely held to be moral. Some frightening statistics support this point. In one recent year, almost half of the hate crimes in this country were committed by people under 21 years of age. On another topic, a survey of middle school and high school students found that nearly one-third of the students claimed they would willingly participate in a hostile act against a member of another cultural group (Heller & Hawkins, 1994). Given the increasing ethnic diversity of our country, these views hint at significant social problems to come. Will there be warring factions in the United States similar to those that strain the social fabric in Northern Ireland, parts of Africa, and Bosnia? We like to think not, but present trends suggest a need for countervailing measures in the schools.

Social studies teachers have to perform a delicate balancing act. On the one hand, they foster the development of pupils as individuals. On the other, they seek to nurture a commitment to certain core moral perspectives that represent a kind of "social glue" that binds together everybody in the country. Collectively, the behaviors that are thought to contribute to the stability and betterment of our society are called *prosocial* behaviors.

Prosocial behavior has been recognized as an important part of character education since ancient times (Wynne & Ryan, 1997). We have chosen the label *prosocial behavior* to help focus attention on those attitudes, values, and actions that contribute to the stability and betterment of society as opposed to a focus on those personal and private values held dear by individuals. We have chosen this label for the chapter deliberately, in order to distinguish this approach from some approaches that view character education as indoctrinating young children with the right virtues.

As teachers, we do need to realize our ethical obligations to be cautious about imposing our personal moral perspectives on those that we teach. We believe that the focus on prosocial behavior does lead to personal reflection and the development of the moral and ethical perspectives that are usually labeled *character education.*

Researchers have found some interesting variables that influence how people feel about certain kinds of things. For example, we now know that individuals empathize more with people they believe to be similar to themselves and with people they are likely to meet personally than with people living in distant places (Hoffman, 1993). The "familiarity-similarity" bias and the "here and now" bias have important implications for us as social studies teachers. They suggest a need for lessons that emphasize similarities among people and that attempt to make "real" the people who live at some distance from us. We need to avoid the "strange lands and funny people" perspective that sometimes occurs when we study people who live far away in different cultures. Instruction must strive to inculcate a truly global perspective that helps pupils to break down the feeling that there is a "they" out there who are fundamentally different from "us" (Perry & McIntire, 1994).

Developing prosocial behavior requires more than providing information to pupils. It involves consideration of values and personal ethics. People take action only when evidence is supported by a strong sense of personal commitment and belief. Since this is true, the social studies program, as it seeks to promote the development of pupils' prosocial behavior, must permit them to consider individual values and morality and allow them opportunities to act on their beliefs. Acting on these views by becoming involved in activities that contribute to the betterment of society and the community, such as service projects, is viewed as an important aspect of prosocial behavior.

Lessons that deal with values and morality must be prepared and presented carefully. They should encourage learners to act in informed and intelligent ways as they seek to bring about change. This chapter offers suggestions about how the social studies program can contribute to the development of these behaviors.

VALUES, MORALITY, AND PROSOCIAL BEHAVIOR

Prosocial behaviors include those individual actions that contribute to the general well-being of humankind. They are directed toward the good of others as opposed to being exclusively concerned with the self.

Prosocial behavior rests on the values and sense of morality of the individual. Values are those bedrock beliefs that give direction to a person's life. They are convictions that are so deeply rooted that they guide people as they make decisions about how they spend their time, talents, and money. Types of values range from aesthetic values, concerned with issues relating to beauty and style, to moral values, concerned with broad questions of right and wrong.

Aesthetic Values

Aesthetic values reflect personal choice. They carry no connotations of right and wrong or of good and bad. For example, one person may prefer classical music; another may prefer country-western music. Neither preference is right or wrong. Each is a simple aesthetic preference of an individual. Aesthetic values add a stimulating variety to life.

Aesthetic values deserve attention in the social studies program. First of all, it is important for pupils to learn that others may have aesthetic preferences that differ from their own. Different cultures have different views of beauty that can be an important part of their culture. To understand these cultures we must also understand their aesthetic values. Comparative study of aesthetic values of different cultures and societies adds an important dimension to lessons in elementary social studies programs.

Similarly, individuals within our society have differing aesthetic values. These different values should not be used to label or stereotype them. Tolerance for diversity of aesthetic perspectives is an important outcome of social studies instruction.

Second, pupils need opportunities to clarify their own aesthetic values. Individuals who are clear about those things they prize and value need to be encouraged to develop commitments and to take action in support of these values. For example, a person who strongly values the beauty of nature can be encouraged to act on that aesthetic value by becoming involved in actions that preserve the environment.

Moral Values

Moral values do carry connotations of right and wrong. Moral values influence patterns of interpersonal relationships, and they help people define appropriate and inappropriate behavior. Among moral values that are of particular interest to the social studies teacher are those focusing on justice, equality, fairness, basic rights such as life and liberty, freedoms such as religion and speech, respect for human worth and dignity, and the rule of law. Some moral values are deeply held throughout the world. For example, all world cultures hold human life to be sacred. Murder is everywhere considered to be an immoral act. Such basic moral values ought to be emphasized in every social studies program. The actions and lives of others and the study of other cultures have little meaning unless they are related to these concepts of morality.

James Rest's Framework

James Rest (1983) provides a framework that can be helpful to teachers as they consider how to incorporate a consideration of moral values into the social studies curriculum. He developed a four-level framework to identify the elements included in lessons focusing on values and morality:

- Moral sensitivity
- Moral judgment
- Moral decision making
- Moral action

Moral Sensitivity

The *moral sensitivity* level focuses on developing sensitivity to the moral component of issues. Developing moral sensitivity is an important step in helping individuals develop prosocial behavior. Daily we read accounts of individuals who acted without being sensitive to the ethical and moral aspects of their behavior.

In the classroom, this level can be addressed as teachers prompt students to search for the values and ethics that are a part of nearly every situation. Moral sensitivity can arise in first-grade classrooms, as teachers discuss cooperation and sharing in a family, to sixth-grade classes discussing ecology and protection of the environment. Problem solving at this stage focuses on pupils looking at more than simple evidence when making a decision.

This level can easily be accommodated in nearly all social studies classrooms without posing much threat or controversy. As a teacher you are not asking students to make choices or take a personal stand. You are not intruding on personal values or asking students to take a stand that might be unpopular with parents but are simply helping students be sensitive to the moral and ethical components of issues.

Moral Judgment

The *moral judgment* level moves a step beyond moral sensitivity. At this level the emphasis is on an analysis of previous decisions that have implications of right and wrong embedded within them. The student is being asked to make a judgment. Do you think the action was right or wrong? They proceed to analyze the principles or values that led to these decisions. Pupils learn that people who have different basic values have different conceptions about what constitutes moral behavior. As a result, they learn that it is possible for people to defend, on moral grounds, very different decisions about a common issue. In addition this level prompts students to consider their own values as they judge the appropriateness of previous decisions they or others have made.

Although this level does provide for the possibility of more controversy, it is a level that can be dealt with quite appropriately in the social studies classroom. Most actions are not clearly right or wrong. There are multiple perspectives from which one can view previous actions. Those different perspectives will lead to different conclusions regarding right or wrong behavior. Was it right for the colonists to violate British law? Is it right to remove people and tear down their homes in order to build a highway, shopping center, or sports stadium? Discussions of decisions focusing on moral judgment can make for lively debates and can serve to enliven social studies classrooms.

A State Board of Education recently held a public hearing on a proposed new elementary social studies program. Members of the public were invited to speak. One person who spoke at the hearing made the following comments.

The proposed social studies program asks children to inquire into the personal values of some of the historical people they are studying. These children will be asked to comment about whether they personally approve of the values of these people.

It seems to me that this is going to lead children to ask their parents about their attitudes and values. I don't think this is appropriate for children this young. It may be fine when they are older and out on their own. Young children should accept their parents as they are. The social studies should concentrate on just teaching the facts.

THINK ABOUT THIS

1. Why do you think the designers of the program included lessons focusing on values?
2. Do you agree with this speaker's assertion that these lessons have the potential for undermining parental authority?
3. What points could be made to counter this testimony?
4. How does your reaction to this statement reflect some of your own values and beliefs?

Figure 10–3
Should young children learn about values?

Moral Decision Making

The *moral decision making* level requires people to move beyond judging previous actions as right or wrong. They are placed in the position of making a personal decision based on their views of morality and defending the position. This process typically has several different levels. At the first level, students are confronted with an unsolved problem. They are introduced to information related to the problem and are challenged to consider different value positions that might be taken in resolving it. They are asked to describe alternative decisions that would be consistent with different value positions. They can be asked to comment on the possible consequences of these alternatives. Finally, they are asked to make personal decisions about the problem and to defend their positions.

Applying moral decision making to the classroom requires considerable planning and sensitivity on the part of the teacher. You need to make sure that the environment is a safe one where students do not feel coerced to take a position. You need to walk the thin line between prompting the students to reflect on their values and make decisions consistent with them and making the students feel that their decision is not acceptable. This is not an easy task, and it requires a clear understanding of the role of the teacher as someone who helps students clarify their values rather than someone who inculcates a previously determined view of right and wrong. Moral decision making does have an important role in the classroom, but it will be used less frequently than moral sensitivity and judgment.

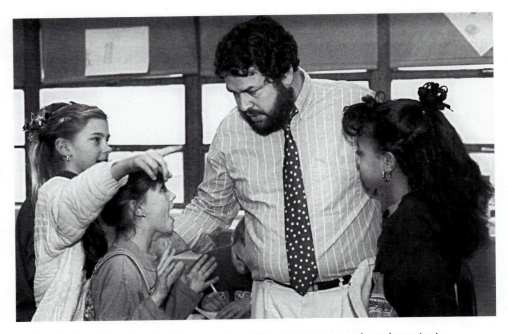

Understanding alternative solutions and possible consequences is an important component of learning values and prosocial behavior.

Moral Action

The *moral action* level is the highest level. The individual is required to go beyond talking to actually doing. The intent at this level is to get individuals to the point of taking actions consistent with the values they profess. For example, if we believe that a given situation violates our views of right and wrong, we need to be prompted to take action. This requires that individuals have a clear sense of their own values system and actions that are consistent with it. Again, this can be a difficult level for many of us because we may have a conflict between values that we hold. For example, an individual may have a value system that opposes abortion. But is bombing an abortion clinic an appropriate action? The dilemmas inherent in the moral action level have been the grist for many works of literature and for many movies. The level of moral action reflects a much stronger value commitment than the level of moral decision making.

The moral action level in the elementary social studies classroom is much more difficult to deal with than the first three levels. It is the level that is likely to create the most controversy. It requires considerable sophistication on the part of the students, and there are limits on what teachers can do to prompt moral action. You need to encourage students to act in ways that are consistent with their beliefs. However, care must be taken not to coerce or force them to take a given action. There are some places where moral action can be applied in the elementary grades. For example, if students take a position that littering is wrong, then they should be prompted to pick up trash on the school grounds. If they take a stand on prejudice, they need to consider their actions when choosing teams or working with others. By beginning with these actions, we hope that the learning will be transferred to more personal and complex issues.

DEALING WITH VALUES, MORALITY, AND PROSOCIAL BEHAVIOR IN THE CLASSROOM

Several instructional approaches have been developed for addressing values issues and morality issues in the classroom. The best of these call for active participation by pupils and demand high levels of personal involvement. Certain techniques are useful for developing moral sensitivity and moral judgment. Others are appropriate for encouraging decision making and moral action. In this section, we discuss aspects of clarifying personal and aesthetic values, and introduce a technique called *values-situation role-playing*. We then discuss Kohlberg's (1975, 1980) approach to developing moral judgment, and conclude with suggestions for teaching moral decision making, with special attention given to teaching relating to analysis of issues, values, and consequences.

Clarifying Personal and Aesthetic Values

Clarifying those things that are important in one's life is an essential step toward developing commitments and taking action. People often are confused about the values that influence their choices. Instructional techniques designed to heighten pupils' sensitivity to their own values do not focus on issues that have right or wrong answers. Neither do they force pupils to select any one position. Their purpose is to help learners think about what values are important to them and whether their behaviors are consistent with these values. Simon, Howe, and Kirschenbaum (1978) outline several procedures that are useful for this purpose, including rank ordering and unfinished sentences. Lesson Ideas 10–1 and 10–2 illustrate how you might choose to implement these approaches.

Lesson Idea 10–1

WHAT WOULD YOU DO WITH YOUR TIME?

Grade Level:	3–6
Objective:	Pupils will identify the influence of values on the choices people make.
Overview:	This is a "rank ordering" lesson. It begins with the teacher giving pupils several alternative actions, and asking learners to rank the alternatives according to their individual preferences. Pupils are given a minute or two to think. Then they are invited to share their rankings and their reasons for making their choices.
Procedures:	*Focus* Introduce this component by saying the following: "All of us have made decisions about what we do with our free time. Today, I would like you to pretend that it is Saturday morning. You have three things you can do. I would like you to think about these three things. Then, decide which one would be your first choice, which one would be your second choice, and which one would be your third choice. When we finish, if

you want to share your choices with others in the class, you may. But, you may also keep your ideas to yourself if you want to. Here are the three choices:

- You can watch your favorite program on television.
- You can play with your best friend at his or her house.
- You can spend the day with your family at the park.

Think for a minute about your choices. Would anyone like to share his or her ideas with us?"

Discussion   Initiate a class discussion of the alternatives (a sample beginning follows):

JOSÉ: I would want to go and play with my friend.

YOU: Why did you choose that first?

JOSÉ: Well, I don't get to see my friend much anymore, and I think playing with friends is more fun than the other things.

SHARON: I would want to go with my family because we always have fun when we do things together. I think a person's family is more important than friends or TV.

(Discussion continues until all who want to respond have had an opportunity to do so.)

Debriefing   Bring closure to the discussion by making generalizations, such as the following: "Today we have discussed how people might make different choices about what to do with their time. Some think that spending time with their families is important. Others think that spending time with friends is a good idea. Others feel it is a good idea sometimes to do something just by yourself. All three of these are reasonable ideas. When we make choices, we have to think about what is most important to us. We also need to think about the possible results of our choices. For example, will spending time with a friend hurt the feelings of a member of our own family? If so, we might need to rethink our choice."

Lesson Idea 10–2

UNFINISHED SENTENCES

Grade Level: 5–6

Objective: Pupils will state things they value by completing sentences.

Procedures: Unfinished sentences help pupils think about what they value. Begin by preparing some partial sentences, called *sentence stems,* that deal with ideas that interest pupils. Next, tell learners to complete the sentences. Younger pupils usually are asked to do this orally. Older pupils may write complete sentences that incorporate the given sentence stems.

Focus Begin by saying the following: "Today I am going to read you the first part of a sentence. I would like you to complete the sentence using your own words. Write your new sentences on your own paper. We will do several sentences. When we finish, I will ask any of you who want to share your sentences to read aloud what you have written. Here are the unfinished sentences I would like you to complete." Read stems one at a time, giving pupils time to add their own words to build complete sentence:

- If I could describe myself to someone else, I would say that I am . . .
- The person we have read about who I would most want to be like is . . .
- The thing I am best at is . . .
- I am happiest when . . .

Discussion Initiate discussion, as in the sample beginning that follows:

YOU: Who would like to share some sentences with us? Chou.

CHOU: I am happiest when I draw pictures.

YOU: Why does that make you happy?

CHOU: Well, people tell me I draw good pictures, and I like to hear them say that.

YOU: Are there other reasons why some people might like to draw?

BILLY: Some people can tell about what they feel better by drawing pictures than by talking. It makes them feel good to draw about their feelings.

YOU: Does anyone else wish to share a sentence? (Discussion continues as long as pupils are willing to share their sentences.)

Debriefing Provide closure by making generalizations, such as the following: "Today we have all had an opportunity to respond to some sentence stems that allowed us to think about ourselves. If we think about the kinds of people we want to be and the things we enjoy, then we need to think about what we can do to become those kinds of people. Some of you might want to spend more time thinking about and writing these sentences. You may do so during the rest of the day when you have finished other work. If some of you want to talk to me individually about your sentences, I will be glad to talk with you."

Values-Situation Role Playing

As pupils begin to develop a personal sense of morality, they become more sensitive to situations where moral principles need to be applied. Role-playing activities help them recognize these situations. They call on learners to make value judgments as they make decisions consistent with their understanding of the worldview of the person whose part they are playing.

Learners' moral sensitivity can also be enhanced by lessons calling on them to look for values and moral issues in history and in present political and economic conflicts. *Values-situation role playing* is a technique that helps learners become more sensitive to moral and values issues. It confronts them with a values and moral dilemma that calls on them to test alternatives and to explore possible consequences of various responses.

In a short debriefing session, the teacher and members of the class discuss each response. These are the typical steps:

- Introduce pupils to a situation.
- Select individuals to role-play their responses.
- Discuss each response with the class as a whole.
- Debrief at the end of the exercise. Draw attention to the pros and cons of each response, and call attention to other possible responses that pupils may not have considered.

There are several ways to introduce pupils to a focus problem for a values-situation role-playing activity. You might propose a simple situation, or pupils might respond to a question such as, "Can you think of a time when you had a hard time deciding the right thing to do?" Another approach is to provide class members with an unfinished short story. Typically, a character in the story is faced with making a difficult choice. Pupils role-play this character and make a choice that seems sensible to them. The short-story approach works well because when the stories are well written, they capture pupils' interest and generate enthusiasm for the role-playing activity. Values-situation role playing can focus on many kinds of issues. In the lower grades, teachers often focus on self-understanding and on understanding others. In the middle and upper grades, pupils are exposed to more content from history and social sciences. At these grade levels, values-situation role-playing lessons often are used to help learners better understand value dilemmas that people have faced in other times and places. Lesson Ideas 10–3 and 10–4 present samples of this approach.

Lesson Idea 10–3

VALUES-SITUATION ROLE PLAYING: SELF-UNDERSTANDING

Grade Level:	K–2
Objective:	Pupils will identify difficulties associated with solving personal problems and state alternative choices to a given problem situation.

Overview:

The purpose of values-situation role-playing lessons that focus on self-understanding is to help pupils think through some of their personal problems. Lessons might relate to such issues as self-doubt, worries about the future, concerns about grades, and fear of the dark. They are designed to help pupils realize that many personal problems are complex. They do not have absolutely right or wrong answers. Solutions depend on many factors, including personal values.

Procedures:

Focus Story   Begin by telling the class the following story:

> *Joel hates the dark. When his mother tucks him in at night and turns out the light, he waits quietly until she leaves the room. Then he leaps out of bed and silently runs to the light switch. When he hops back into bed, he feels good and goes right to sleep.*
>
> *Joel's mother has told him there is nothing scary about the dark. His uncle has offered to take Joel fishing this weekend if he can go a whole week without turning on the light in his room after his mother tucks him in and leaves. Joel really wants to go fishing. But he knows something terrible will happen to him and that he'll never get to sleep if he's alone all night in a dark room.*
>
> *On Monday night, Joel's mother puts him to bed, reminds him about the possible fishing trip, turns off the light, and leaves the room. Joel is nervous. What should he do?*

Role Playing and Discussion   Initiate role playing and encourage students as in the following sample:

YOU: John, you go first. Pretend that you're Joel. You're in the bedroom trying to decide what to do. Tell us your idea.

JOHN: I really want to go fishing, but there's no way I can go to sleep in the dark. I'm going to stuff a pillowcase along the bottom of the door and turn the light on. That way, my mom won't know I've turned it back on.

YOU: All right, class, we've heard John's idea. How do we feel about it?

ROSA: I don't think Joel will be able to sleep. He'll worry about whether his mother will look in to see whether the light's out.

JAMES: Maybe Joel won't feel good inside. I mean, he may fool his mom, but he'll know he's done something wrong.

(Other comments from pupils follow.)

> YOU: Sarah, why don't you play Joel this time?
>
> SARAH: I really want to go fishing, but I'm so scared of the dark that I just can't stand it. I'd tell my mom that I just can't go to sleep with the light off.
>
> YOU: How about some ideas about Sarah's approach to the problem?
>
> RODNEY: That idea is going to make Joel unhappy. He's not going to go fishing. It's also going to make his mother unhappy. Joel still won't be sleeping with the light off. I don't think it's much of an answer.
>
> JILL: Maybe Joel's mom should come up with a new plan. If Joel is this afraid of the dark, a whole week is going to be too hard. Maybe she should expect only one or two nights of sleeping in the dark at first.

(Other pupil comments follow.)

Debriefing   Bring closure by making generalizations, encouraging further discussion as appropriate.

> YOU: Let me list some of the ideas we've identified:
>
> - Joel should give up the fishing trip because he's too afraid of the dark.
> - Joel should pretend he's sleeping in the dark by putting a pillowcase at the bottom of the door so his mother won't know he's turned the light back on.
> - Joel's mother should be asked to set a more reasonable number of nights with no light. This will give Joel a better chance to succeed.
>
> PAULA: Maybe Joel's mother should talk to him about why he's so afraid of the dark.
>
> JOYCE: It might help if his mom said she used to be afraid of the dark, too. Maybe she could explain how she got over this problem.
>
> LUIS: I think Joel's mom should buy him one of those small night-lights. You know, the kind that uses a Christmas tree lightbulb. Maybe she'd let him keep this small light on when the big light was turned off.
>
> YOU: These are interesting ideas. Any others?

(Discussion continues.)

> YOU: Have any of you faced a situation similar to Joel's? What did you do? Why did you act in this way?

(Discussion continues.)

Lesson Idea 10–4

VALUES-SITUATION ROLE PLAYING: USING CONTENT FROM HISTORY

Grade Level: 5

Objectives: Pupils will (1) identify conflicting values when confronted with choices and (2) state possible consequences associated with alternative choices.

Overview: Values-situation role-playing lessons with a historical focus seek to help pupils appreciate value dilemmas people have faced in the past. They help them understand that value conflicts have always been a part of the human experience.

Procedures   *Focus Story*   Begin by telling the following story to the class:

> In 1862, Joseph Fender was 17 years old. He lived with his mother and father in central Kentucky. For months, talk had been of little other than the Civil War. Joseph looked forward to June, when he would become a soldier. But which side should he choose?
>
> Joseph's mother's family, the Gibsons, came from central Ohio. All of his Gibson cousins were fighting in the Union army. His father's family came from Tennessee. His uncles and cousins on his father's side were fighting in the gray uniforms of the South.
>
> "Joseph," his mother called, "here's a letter for you from Grandfather Fender." Grandfather Fender lived in Memphis, in western Tennessee.
>
> Joseph's grandfather wrote, "Your father writes that you will be going off to join the war in June. In my heart, I know you will remember your southern roots. All of the Fenders are fighting for the South. Your father's Kentucky tobacco lands are really part of the South. Your speech is like that of the rest of the family here in Tennessee. You belong in a gray uniform. May God give you the insight to make the right decision."
>
> Grandfather Fender's letter certainly didn't make matters easier. Just yesterday, Joseph had received a letter from Cousin Norman, his mother's nephew, who lived in Cincinnati. Joseph recalled the words of Cousin Norman's letter: "I am home on leave from the Union forces. Believe me, I'm proud to be in a blue uniform. With all of our factories here in the North, we have excellent equipment and supplies. There is little doubt we'll win. But even more important, we have 'right' on our side. All of the Gibson people have joined up. We expect to see you in a Union uniform soon. The Ohio River joins Ohio and Kentucky. Kentucky has more

shared interests with Ohio and the North than with the South. Remember, even our brave President, Abe Lincoln, was born in Kentucky."

Role Playing and Discussion   Initiate role playing and encourage students, as in the following example:

YOU: I am going to ask several of you to pretend that you are Joseph. I want you to tell us what you would have done and why. Who wants to be first?

(Several pupils play the role of Joseph. After each portrayal, lead a follow-up discussion.)

Debriefing   Bring closure by making generalizations, discussing all of the positions mentioned by the several role players. Steer the discussion to ensure that pupils emerge with a thorough understanding of the value conflicts inherent in the focus situation.

These role-playing exercises actively involve pupils in making choices involving conflicts of values. They help them to recognize that choices have consequences. Often, even the best choice has accompanying results that are not completely desirable. Lessons such as those illustrated in Lesson Ideas 10–3 and 10–4 help pupils think seriously about consequences tied to alternative courses of action. They help them realize, too, that difficult problems rarely have easy solutions.

One key to success in values-situation role playing is using good focus stories. Many teachers write these themselves. Several other sources are available. One that we particularly like is *Role Playing in the Curriculum,* by Fannie R. Shaftel and George Shaftel (1982).

Kohlberg's Approach to Developing Moral Judgment

When people make moral judgments, they make subjective decisions about right and wrong. In doing so, they apply certain criteria. Kohlberg (1975) identified six stages of moral development. People at each stage apply certain criteria and logic when they make moral judgments. Kohlberg contends that the stage of development is best identified by the reasoning given for taking an action, not by the specific action. Therefore, rather than identifying actions and labeling them as right or wrong, experiences need to be provided so that individuals identify the criteria they use in judging the morality of an action.

Stage 1: Punishment and Obedience Orientation
People at this stage make decisions based on their respect for raw power. Their decisions about whether something is right or wrong are based on the probability of being punished. Their obedience to rules and regulations is based on a fear of punishment. Therefore, if there is no punishment or one does not get caught violating a rule, the action was acceptable. For example, an elementary child at this stage might state, "I help take care of my younger brother because if I don't, my mother will punish me." The action is not based on concern for others or the values of cooperation; the concern is a self-centered one based on the avoidance of punishment.

Stage 2: Instrumental Relativism

People who are at this stage make judgments about whether things are right or wrong based on the potential advantage they might receive. Judgments of right or wrong are not based on what might be considered important values, such as compassion or respect for others. Rather, they are based on a selfish concern: "What is in it for me?" It is the logic of reciprocal back-scratching: "I'll be your friend if you will do my math." Once the need for someone to help in math is gone, the friendship is over.

Stage 3: Interpersonal Concordance

At this stage, individuals judge right or wrong on the basis of the feelings of a group with which they identify. This stage is often demonstrated when people justify their actions by stating, "Everybody is doing it." This is sometimes called the "good boy, good girl stage." Actions are based on how individuals think others will view them if they behave a certain way. In other words, values and the sense of morality are based on perceptions of what a peer group believes is right rather than on any self-chosen principles. For example, an elementary student might choose to return a lost item to the owner, not because of respect for personal property, but on the reasoning, "When people see what I have done, they will think I am a good person."

Stage 4: Law and Order Orientation

People at this stage decide issues on the basis of their respect for established rules, regulations, and traditional social practices. If something is against the law, it is seen as wrong; if it is not against the law, it is acceptable. This legalistic orientation leads to debate concerning what is legal rather than what is right or moral. This has been a common defense for individuals accused of war crimes. They state that the laws of the land required them to act as they did and therefore they should not be judged as doing anything wrong. Elementary students operating at this stage may respond to a reprimand with, "But there is no rule that says I can't do it."

Stage 5: Social Contract–Legalistic Orientation

Judgments of right and wrong in this stage are not based exclusively on laws. Rather, they involve consideration of the formal rules and guidelines of the entire society and of personal values and opinions. When no guidelines for a particular situation are available, people at this stage rely on personal insights. Individuals at this stage are also willing to challenge formal rules that they believe are unfair or unjust for society. For example, they may believe that following a formal rule, such as being required to report on friends and neighbors who do not conform to certain practices, is detrimental to the health of society, so they violate it. It is likely that only a few elementary students in the upper grades will reach this level and use this type of moral reasoning.

Stage 6: Universal Ethical Principles Orientation

At this stage, people make decisions based on individual conscience, taking into account such universal principles as respect for human life, love, and dignity. There is no necessary reliance on formal rules, traditions, or other guidelines. The universal principles guiding decisions are chosen by people who make the decisions; they do not need to be suggested by others. For example, people might take a stand on freedom of speech even for those with whom they disagree. Censorship might be opposed even though a person individually might not agree with a given book and the stand will be criticized by friends: "I know my stand will not be popular, but I want to take a stand in support of the idea of freedom of speech. In the long run, respect for this principle is more important than the short-term anger of my friends."

This highest stage is one that few people attain. Most of us spend most of our lives identifying those universal principles we hold and trying to act in ways that are consistent with them. In the elementary classroom we may see few examples of reasoning at this level. We can, however, present examples of individuals who have acted at this level.

Moving from Stage to Stage

People progress through these stages sequentially. No one can use the third-stage reasoning who has not previously passed through the first and second stages. Moral development stops at different stages for different people. Some never go beyond stage one. Only a very small number of people reach the highest stages of moral development (Kohlberg, 1980).

According to Kohlberg's theory, a person at a given stage is capable of making decisions based on the logic of this and all lower stages. People are not thought capable of making decisions based on the logic of stages they have not attained.

Movement upward from one moral stage to another is believed to be facilitated by exposure to a higher stage of moral reasoning. If, for example, individuals are never exposed to reasoning beyond the punishment-obedience stage, then their moral reasoning will stay at that stage. It is believed that individuals are capable of understanding the logic associated with the stage just above their own stage but are not likely to understand moral reasoning involving logic more than one stage above that level. The goal, then, is to find ways of exposing students to higher levels of moral reasoning. Kohlberg proposes discussions focused on moral dilemmas as one way of doing this. (See Figure 10–4.)

Discussions of Moral Dilemmas

The intent of this approach is to present moral dilemmas to the class. These dilemmas should not be ones that have clear-cut right or wrong answers. The intent is to get individuals to reflect on their reasoning when making a decision regarding the dilemma. As individuals share their reasoning, they are exposed to different levels of reasoning and growth is facilitated. As individuals attain higher levels of reasoning over time, they gradually move to the next higher level of moral development. The steps in the process are:

- Introduce the moral dilemma.
- Ask pupils to suggest tentative responses.
- Divide pupils into groups to discuss their reasoning.
- Discuss the reasoning and formulate a conclusion.

Introducing the Moral Dilemma   The dilemma selected should be an issue that has meaning for pupils. It should also have some of the complexity of the issues they will face as adults. The material introducing the dilemma should be short and tightly focused on the situation. A dilemma can be introduced in prose form, on film, on cassette tapes, or

Moral reasoning can be used to counsel individual pupils as well as to consider moral dilemmas in class. In listening to a pupil's explanation for misbehavior, the teacher can note the logic and try to identify the moral reasoning stage it represents. Then, the teacher tries to respond with logic that is a single stage higher than that represented by the pupil's explanation. Consider these examples:

EXAMPLE 1

TERESA: Yes, I did look at Anne's paper. I mean, I did it just a little.

TEACHER: Tell me exactly what happened.

TERESA: Anne's terrible in math, and I'm pretty good. I said I'd let her peek at a few of my math answers if I could see a few of her social studies quiz answers.

TEACHER: Teresa, I'm concerned about your reputation. Do you want all of your friends thinking you're a cheater?

EXAMPLE 2

TERESA: Yes, I did look at Anne's paper. I mean, I did it just a little.

TEACHER: Tell me exactly what happened.

TERESA: Anne's terrible in math, and I'm pretty good. I said I'd let her peek at a few of my math answers if I could see a few of her social studies quiz answers.

TEACHER: Teresa, I want to read you a section from our school handbook. It says that "any pupil who cheats may be subject to appropriate punishment as designated by the principal or by district policy." We simply must follow the rules.

THINK ABOUT THIS

1. What moral stage is suggested by Teresa's response?
2. What moral stages are reflected in the teacher's response in each episode?
3. Which teacher response is the more appropriate? Why do you think so?
4. What other different responses would you make if you were this teacher?

Figure 10–4
Moral reasoning and individual pupil counseling.

in some other suitable manner. The following is an example of a moral dilemma that might serve as a focus for a discussion:

Kim Kamatsu is in the sixth grade. She has an older brother in junior high school. Her twin sisters are in the third grade.

   Kim's father, Henry, used to make a good living as a steelworker. The plant where he was employed closed six months ago. He has taken odd jobs here and there, but has not found anything permanent. The family has had a difficult time financially. Savings are gone. Kim's mother, Katherine, works at a low-paying job. She worries about how she will feed and clothe her family.

Today, Kim is shopping with her mother in a large grocery store. As she walks down the aisle, she notices seventy-five dollars worth of food stamps that have fallen from a shopper's purse. She stoops to pick them up. Kim looks at the stamps and thinks about what they will buy. Should she keep them, or should she return them to the person who lost them?

Asking Pupils to Suggest Tentative Responses.   After the class has been introduced to the dilemma, each pupil is asked to write down what she or he would do, along with a brief explanation of the decision. It is important that students first think about their responses individually. They need to identify their reasoning without pressure from the group. Next, the teacher asks (for the above example) for a show of hands from those pupils who think Kim should keep the food stamps and those who think she should return them.

Dividing Pupils into Groups to Discuss Their Reasoning.   The teacher then divides the class into five or six groups, taking care to ensure that each group includes pupils who want Kim to keep the food stamps and those who want her to return them. The teacher instructs pupils to take turns in their groups explaining their choices, emphasizing that the discussion is to focus on *why* pupils made their decisions, not on what they chose. The teacher circulates from group to group to keep pupils on task.

There is a good chance that most groups will contain pupils at different moral reasoning levels. As a result, many pupils in a group may have an opportunity to be exposed to logic characteristic of a moral development level that is one stage higher than their own. This can help them move to a higher stage. These discussions should be kept brief. With fifth and sixth graders, for example, 5 or 10 minutes is plenty. The idea is to maintain intense interaction. When the teacher senses that the discussions have gone on long enough, she asks each group to select a spokesperson.

Discussing the Reasoning and Formulating a Conclusion.   During the concluding phase of the exercise, the teacher provides either a large chalkboard area or strips of butcher paper and marking pens. The spokespersons write their group's reasons supporting each viewpoint. The reasons are displayed so the whole class can see them.

The teacher leads a discussion covering all noted reasons, being careful to remain nonjudgmental and accepting of each pupil's idea. The teacher tries to elicit comments reflecting a mixture of moral reasoning states.

After this discussion, the teacher asks each learner to take a piece of paper and write down the three or four best reasons that support the position he or she does not support personally. This requires pupils to think carefully about logic other than their own. Learners then write down the three or four most compelling reasons supporting their position. The teacher does not collect these papers but may choose to elicit this information from learners during individual conferences.

* * *

In summary, moral reasoning discussions help learners think about their own logic as well as the logic of others. During the exercise, opportunities arise for them to be exposed to levels of reasoning different from their own. This exposure may help some pupils ad-

Group discussion of a moral dilemma facilitates growth to higher levels.

vance to higher moral reasoning levels. There is some concern, however, that some teachers implement moral reasoning discussions by posing issues that are overly complex for adults, let alone students. In addition, many of the moral dilemmas normally used are artificial situations that are not likely to be faced by students (Lockwood, 1997). It is best to try to include real-life situations that are consistent with the developmental level of the students.

When we use moral reasoning discussions in the classroom, we should not set our expectations too high. Many variables over which we have little personal control influence what goes on during a discussion. For example, in a given group, there may be little disagreement among members about the course of action to be taken in response to the given problem. It is possible, too, that only a few levels of moral reasoning will be represented among group members. Finally, some pupils may not be able to articulate their reasons for selecting a particular response.

Despite these limitations, moral reasoning discussions are a useful tool. They have the potential to sensitize some pupils to the perspectives of others. For these individuals, the technique may well promote growth toward higher stages of moral development.

Teaching for Moral Decision Making: Analysis of Issues, Values, and Consequences

Teaching for moral decision making is an approach designed to encourage pupils to make decisions that are consistent with their own values and their own understanding of morality.

Figure 10–5
A framework for analyzing issues, values, and consequences.

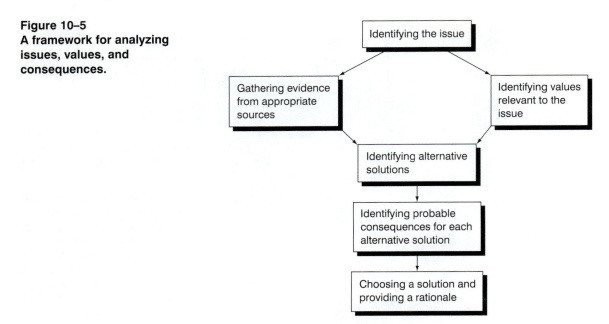

Lessons typically require learners to analyze several value positions related to a single issue. They are asked to suggest possible decisions consistent with each value position and to identify probable long-term consequences that might result from each choice. At the conclusion of these lessons, the teacher asks pupils to make and defend a personal decision about the focus issue.

Analysis of issues, values, and consequences helps pupils understand that the decisions individuals make reflect their values. The technique is applicable in a variety of situations. It can be used in lessons designed to promote learners' self-understanding and in those designed to foster an appreciation of decisions made by others. For this latter purpose, we often use subject matter from history or social science.

When the purpose is to work with content focusing on self-understanding, these steps are followed:

- Identifying the issue
- Gathering evidence from appropriate sources
- Considering the values that are relevant to the issue
- Identifying possible solutions
- Pointing out consequences of the possible solutions
- Making a decision and providing a rationale

Figure 10–5 illustrates these steps and indicates the general flow of this activity.

An example of how issues, values, and consequences might be analyzed to promote self-understanding is provided in Lesson Idea 10–5.

Lesson Idea 10–5

ISSUES, VALUES, AND CONSEQUENCES:
SELF-UNDERSTANDING—WORRY ABOUT THE FUTURE

Grade Level: 5–6

Objectives: Pupils can (1) state values relevant to a given issue, (2) identify possible actions and probable consequences tied to each, and (3) apply their values to a task requiring them to choose a course of action.

Procedures: ***Identifying the Issue***   Present the following information to the class. Evidence suggests that many young people in the upper elementary grades worry about the future. For example, they may wonder whether they will be able to "make it" when they get to high school. Older brothers, sisters, and friends often tell them how difficult high school work is. Some fifth and sixth graders even worry about their future social life. Will they develop a good personality? Will they be popular? Will they find a job? Many other concerns bother young people in this age group.

Some authorities suggest that these anxieties will resolve themselves as these people mature. They contend that worries will naturally disappear as these fifth and sixth graders grow older and become more confident about their ability to meet challenges of all kinds. Other experts believe that these worries do not always just go away as people grow older. Some young people may continue to be plagued by serious anxieties about the future well into senior high school. These authorities believe that fifth- and sixth-grade pupils should receive systematic help to relieve them of anxiety brought on by excessive worry. The issue is simply this: Should there be specific programs for fifth- and sixth-grade pupils to help them deal with their worries?

Gathering Evidence From Appropriate Sources   Introduce information directed to helping pupils understand both sides of the issue. In looking for information to present, we have found it useful to develop guiding questions that suggest kinds of information that might be needed, such as the following examples:

- What is worry? Is all worry bad?
- Do adults worry, too?
- What conditions bring on worry?
- What ways are there to deal with worry?

Considering the Values That Are Relevant to the Issue
Your questions at this point help pupils identify some values relevant to the discussion. Here are examples:

- If a person says people should not have worries, what does this tell us about what this person considers to be important in life?
- Some people say worries will go away in time. Others say they won't and that we need to help people with worries right now. What priorities would people in each of these groups assign to an effort to "do something" about the worries of young people in school?

Identifying Possible Solutions   A number of possibilities might arise in a discussion. You might receive the following suggestions from pupils after asking, "What should be done about the worries of fifth and sixth graders?"

- The school should have special "worry counselors."
- Parents should take these problems seriously and make time to listen to children as they talk about their worries.
- The school should introduce a course dealing with worries about the future.
- Nothing should be done. Worrying will go away in time.

Identifying the Consequences of Possible Solutions   At this point, ask pupils to think about the consequences of the possible solutions to the problem they have suggested. Possible questions and potential pupil responses follow: "What might happen if we established special 'worry counselors' in each school?"

- More people might have worries because now there is somebody to talk to about them.
- Worries would not bother people so much because the "worry counselors" could help.
- Maybe counselors couldn't do some of the things they do now because they would be so busy dealing with pupils' worries.
- People might worry just as much but not be so concerned about their worries. This would be true because they would know that the counselors could help.

"What might happen if we did nothing at all about this problem?"

- Some would continue to worry so much that it would interfere with their ability to do well in school. That's what happens now.
- When they get to high school, most people will have outgrown the worries they had in the fifth and sixth grade.
- Some people will always worry no matter what. So if we do nothing, it won't make much difference.

Making a Decision and Providing a Rationale   At this point, ask questions that encourage pupils to make a personal decision about the problem. Also, ask pupils to suggest their reasons for making this decision. During this phase of the lesson, you might ask questions such as the following:

- What should we do about the "worrying" issue?
- Why did you make this choice?
- What convinced you that this choice was the best one?
- What would your choice tell others about the things in life that you consider really important?

Closure: To conclude the lesson, refocus on its central points, asking questions such as the following:

- What have we learned about what people think about when they make decisions?
- How can decisions tell us about what the decision makers think is important?
- What has this lesson taught you about your own priorities?

Often, analysis of issues, values, and consequences is used to help pupils appreciate that decisions made by others reflect certain priorities. For example, decisions that leaders in the past made to shape historical events often required agonizing choices among competing values. An issue suitable for a lesson of this type is one for which at least two competing viewpoints can be identified. The steps followed are slightly more complex than for lessons focusing on personal or social understanding.

- Identify the general issue.
- Describe Faction A.
- Identify the information seen as relevant by Faction A.
- Describe the relevant alternatives open to Faction A.
- Point out possible consequences of each Faction A alternative.
- Describe Faction B.
- Identify the information seen as relevant by Faction B.
- Describe the relevant alternatives open to Faction B.
- Point out possible consequences of each Faction B alternative.
- Relate and compare the alternatives open to each faction; relate and compare the probable consequences of each alternative; make decisions.
- Apply to another setting.

Figure 10–6 provides a graphic of the flow of events in a lesson of this kind. Lesson Idea 10–6 features a lesson on analyzing issues, values, and consequences designed to help pupils appreciate values dimensions of issues faced by people in the past.

Figure 10–6
Developing pupils' sensitivity to decisions others have had to make: A framework for issues, values, and consequences analysis.

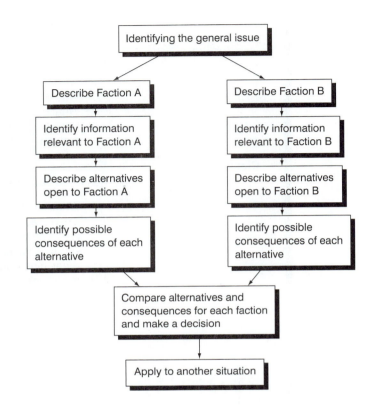

Lesson Idea 10–6

ISSUES, VALUES, AND CONSEQUENCES: APPRECIATING DECISIONS MADE BY OTHERS

Grade Level: 5

Objectives: Pupils will (1) state views, possible actions, and conflicts associated with two competing positions and (2) apply the steps of this analysis to a new problem.

Procedures: Provide the class with the following information, initiating discussion and asking questions as indicated.

Identifying the General Issue   In 1710, when today's United States was still a colony of Great Britain, John Peter Zenger came to New York from Germany. He started a newspaper called *The New York Weekly Journal.* All went well until 1732. In that year, a new governor, William Cosby, came to New York Colony from England. When he arrived, he found that the man who had been acting as temporary leader in New York had been drawing his salary. Cosby wanted the man to pay him the money, even though, in truth, the man had been doing Cosby's job. By using some shady tricks, Cosby succeeded in having a court decide in his favor, and there was a decision that Cosby should get the money.

After this happened, John Peter Zenger reported in his newspaper all of the questionable things Cosby had done. Cosby was furious. He accused Zenger of libel. *Libel* means damaging a person's reputation by publishing false, defamatory information about that person in a public forum such as a newspaper. Zenger denied that he was guilty of libel because the things he printed were true.

The issue is: Should John Peter Zenger have been found guilty of libel?

Describing Faction A (Cosby and His Judges):   Cosby was the governor of New York, the king's own representative. He had responsibility for the overall administration of the colony. He was concerned about letting the colonists develop the idea that they had any real powers of their own. He felt that any attack on him was also an attack on the king.

Identifying the Information Perceived as Relevant by Faction A   The judges selected by Cosby felt Zenger had committed libel. English law at this time did not allow a jury to make this decision. The judges, alone, decided whether a given act was libelous. The only job of the jury was to decide whether a person accused of writing a libelous article had actually written it.

Describing the Relevant Alternatives Open to Faction A   In response to your questions about these alternatives, pupils might generate answers such as the following:

- They could have done nothing. This might just be something that would have blown over in time.
- They could have brought Zenger to trial.
- They could have banished Zenger from the colony.

Pointing Out the Possible Consequences of Each Faction A Alternative   In response to prompting questions, the pupils might suggest the following:

- If they decided to do nothing, attacks on the governor might have gotten worse. This could have led to real problems.
- If they took Zenger to trial, some unexpected outcome might have resulted. However, in the past Cosby had good luck in getting judges to see things his way.
- If they sent Zenger out of the colony, he might have made trouble elsewhere in America. If he went to England, he might have made trouble for Cosby by planting vicious rumors among his enemies there.

Describing Faction B   John Peter Zenger was a journalist. He was eager to increase the circulation of his paper over that of the rival *New York Gazette.* He was interested in appealing to readers who were interested in extending the rights of the colonists.

Identifying the Information Perceived as Relevant by Faction B   Zenger and his attorneys believed that the old English idea that judges should decide whether something was libelous should be changed. Judges were too easy for the English to control. Juries, on the other hand, were something else. They tended to be made up of colonists. Zenger and his lawyers felt that juries, not judges, should decide whether the crime of libel had been committed.

Zenger's people also felt that someone should not be able to claim he had been libeled if the information printed in a newspaper could be shown to be true. Thus, they were interested in demonstrating the truth of what Zenger had written.

Describing the Relevant Alternatives Open to Faction B   In response to your questions, pupils might identify the following alternatives:

- Zenger could have retracted what he had originally printed, and he could have published an apology to the Governor in the hope that the libel suit would be dropped.
- Zenger could have agreed to stand trial in the hope that he would win his case.
- Zenger could have fled the colony.

Pointing Out the Possible Consequences of Each Faction B Alternative   Pupils might generate answers such as the following in response to prompting questions:

- If Zenger had retracted what he had said, he would have weakened the case the colonists were trying to make for extending their authority.
- If Zenger agreed to stand trial, he took a chance of being found guilty. On the other hand, a trial would provide an opportunity for him to share his views with a larger audience. Also, he might win his case.
- If Zenger fled, he would lose any immediate influence he might have in New York in support of increasing the authority of the colonists. On the other hand, he might be able to make life uncomfortable for Cosby if he could get to England and talk to some of Cosby's enemies.

Relating and Comparing the Alternatives and Consequences and Making a Decision   Ask questions to help pupils contrast the positions of the two factions. The following are some questions you might ask, and possible pupil responses:

"What similarities and differences do you see between the alternatives open to each side?"

- Both sides thought about the possibility that Zenger might choose to leave.
- Both sides considered pluses and minuses of taking the case to trial.

"What differences in viewpoint are represented by the two sides?"

- Cosby and his people felt that a libel had already been committed. The trial would be simply to see whether Zenger was responsible for writing the libelous article. Zenger and his people denied that libel had been committed. They claimed that there was no libel, since the material printed in the newspaper was true.
- Cosby and his people were afraid of extending the power of the colonists. Zenger and his supporters were eager to extend the power of the colonists.

"What was most important to each side?"

- Cosby saw preserving his authority as most important. He viewed Zenger as a threat to his authority and to that of the king.
- Zenger wanted to extend the rights of the colonies. He wanted to do this by establishing the idea that anything can be printed about a person so long as its truth could be proved. This would give great freedom of expression to the colonists.

"Did Zenger have a right to print articles critical of the governor?"

- I don't think so. The governor was the king's representative. Zenger was a threat to law and order.
- Yes. If he couldn't be critical, then very bad governors could have done all kinds of terrible things, and few people would ever have known about them.
- He might have had this right some place, but not in New York. If he wanted to print critical articles, he should have gone to England.

"What do you think really happened in this case?"

Lead a discussion focusing on this question. To conclude the discussion, tell the class what actually happened to Zenger and Governor Cosby.

The outcome of the Zenger case shocked Governor Cosby. First, the jury was convinced by the arguments of Zenger's attorney that judges should not decide whether something is libelous. This should be left to juries. Second, the jury decided that there was no libel in a case where the person writing the article could prove the truth of what he or she had written. John Peter Zenger, as a result, was found not guilty.

The Zenger case established the principle that juries, not judges, decide when a libel has occurred. Further, it established an important principle regarding freedom of the press: that there is no libel when material printed can be shown to be true.

Applying to Another Situation   The final phase of the lesson attempts to tie such an episode from another time or place to something more familiar to pupils' own experiences. At this point, you might ask questions such as the following:

- The Zenger case changed some rules that courts had followed for a long time. Can you think of any new rules that have changed how we live and do things? (If pupils have trouble, provide examples, such as 55 mph speed limit, racial integration, changes in local school rules, and so forth.)
- How do people react to change? Do all people like change? Why do you think some people may support a given change and other people oppose it?
- Are newspapers today free to criticize public officials? Is this right a result of the famous Zenger case?
- How do you feel personally about what can be printed in a newspaper? What does your answer tell us about some things in life that you believe to be really important?

WEB CHECK

Note: Electronic addresses of sites on the World Wide Web change frequently. If the listed URL fails to work, use a standard search engine to locate the new address of the site.

- Infomine K–12 Education & Instructional Resource Facilitator

  URL—**http://lib-www.ucr.edu/k12info.html**

  This site includes thousands of resources for teaching just about any topic included in K–12 education.

- ERIC Clearinghouse for Social Studies/Social Science Education ERIC/ChESS

  URL—**http://www.indiana.edu/~ssdc/eric-chess.html**

  This is a repository of current social studies materials including curriculum guides, journal articles, research reports, and lesson plans.

- Teachers Helping Teachers

  URL—**http://www.pacificnet.net/~mandel/**

  Teachers offer help to each other at this site, and it contains a special section on social studies.

KEY IDEAS IN SUMMARY

1. Prosocial behavior is behavior that contributes to the betterment of society. It rests on the morality of individuals. One purpose of social studies is to help young people develop a sense of concern that will lead them to take positive action to improve the community, state, and nation. It is particularly important that schools attend to this matter. Young people commit a high percentage of the total number of antisocial acts.

2. There is general agreement that schools have some obligation to promote the development of moral patterns of behavior among learners. However, some school programs that have attempted to do so have been criticized for allegedly encouraging patterns of behavior inconsistent with those espoused in some pupils' homes.

3. Aesthetic values reflect personal choices. They do not carry connotations of right or wrong. Moral values, on the other hand, do carry implications of right and wrong. They help people define what kinds of behavior are appropriate and what kinds of behavior are inappropriate.

4. James Rest (1983) developed a four-level framework for identifying components that can be included in lessons emphasizing values and morality. These levels are (1) moral sensitivity, (2) moral judgment, (3) moral decision making, and (4) moral action.

5. Many instructional techniques are available for helping learners clarify their personal and aesthetic beliefs. Simon, Howe, and Kirschenbaum (1978), for example, recommend procedures involving rank ordering and unfinished sentences.

6. A widely used approach to increasing pupils' moral sensitivity is values-situation role playing. This technique allows learners to become more sensitive to moral and values issues. It is applicable to issues ranging from those focusing on present personal problems of pupils to those drawn from historical contexts that center on moral dilemmas people have faced in the past.

7. Lawrence Kohlberg (1975, 1980) developed a six-stage framework for analyzing individuals' stages of moral development. People at each stage are thought to apply certain criteria to problems and to use certain logical patterns as they seek solutions. These stages are (1) punishment and obedience orientation, (2) instrumental relativism, (3) interpersonal concordance, (4) law and order orientation, (5) social contract–legalistic orientation, and (6) universal ethical principles orientation.

8. According to Kohlberg, people progress through the stages sequentially. Because those at higher levels are thought to have more concern for others than those at lower levels, followers of Kohlberg are interested in having individuals move to higher stages. One instructional approach that has been developed for this purpose is discussions of moral dilemmas. These discussions expose learners to moral reasoning at stages of moral development higher than their own. This exposure is thought to facilitate their movement toward higher stages of moral development.

9. Moral decision-making activities help pupils make decisions that are consistent with their own values and their own personal understanding of morality. Lessons with this focus involve learners in analyses of issues that feature a problem with a number of potential solutions. Each possible solution tends to reflect a somewhat different set of values priorities. Pupils are taught to recognize values underlying each alternative, make choices among the alternatives, and defend their choices. Analysis of issues, values, and consequences is a technique that can be applied to many kinds of issues.

CHAPTER REFLECTIONS

Directions: Now that you have read this chapter, reread the case study at the beginning. Think about other chapter content. Then, answer these questions:

1. What are the obligations of the schools regarding transmitting certain key values to all pupils?

2. What are some uses you might be able to make in your own classroom of James Rest's values and morality framework?

3. How do you feel about discussing moral dilemmas in elementary school classrooms? What problems might you have to overcome to use this technique successfully?

4. Why might a teacher wish to analyze issues, values, and consequences when teaching elementary social studies?

EXTENDING UNDERSTANDING AND SKILL

1. Interview a district-level social studies curriculum director. (If that cannot be arranged, find an elementary teacher involved in social studies program planning.) Ask about the amount of emphasis given to lessons focusing on attitudes and values. Seek details about the nature of instruction provided, any problems with parents and other school patrons, and teachers' reactions to working with this kind of content. Prepare a report and share it with your class.

2. Survey two or more elementary social studies textbooks. How many of the suggested activities focus on attitudes or values? Prepare a chart to display your findings.

3. Read 10 articles in professional journals that provide practical ideas for dealing with attitudes and values in the elementary social studies classroom. (You may wish to consult the *Education Index* to locate your articles.) Write a brief description of each suggested approach. Share what you have found with others in your class.

4. Prepare three role-playing situations, two moral reasoning dilemmas, and one situation to be used as a focus for a lesson on analyzing issues, values, and conse-

quences. Develop these for a grade level you would like to teach. Write a description of each approach. Ask your instructor to review your descriptions.

5. Start a newspaper clipping file featuring conflicts among people having different value priorities. Try to include at least 12 items. Discuss some of these items with others in your class. Point out how they might provide beginnings of elementary social studies lessons.

REFERENCES

HELLER, C., & HAWKINS, J. (1994). Teaching tolerance: Notes from the front line. *Teachers College Record, 95* (3), 337–368.

HOFFMAN, M. L. (1993). Empathy, social cognition, and moral education. In A. Garrod (Ed.), *Approaches to moral development* (pp. 157–179). New York: Teachers College Press.

KOHLBERG, L. (1975). The cognitive-developmental approach to moral education. *Phi Delta Kappan, 56* (10), 670–675.

KOHLBERG, L. (1980). Education for a just society: An updated and revised statement. In B. Munsey (Ed.), *Moral development, moral education, and Kohlberg* (pp. 455–470). Birmingham, AL: Religious Education Press.

LICKONA, T. (1993). The return of character education. *Educational Leadership, 51* (3), 6–11.

LICKONA, T. (1997). Combating violence with values: The character education solution. In Y. Tomoda (Ed.), *Patterns of Value Socialization in U.S. Primary Schools: A Comparative Study.* Osaka, Japan: Faculty of Human Services, Osaka University.

LOCKWOOD, A. T. (1997). *Character Education: Controversy and Consensus.* Thousand Oaks, CA.: Corwin Press Inc.

NATIONAL COUNCIL FOR THE SOCIAL STUDIES. (1996). *Fostering civic virtue: Character education in the social studies.* Washington, DC: National Council for the Social Studies.

PERRY, C. M., & McINTIRE, W. G. (1994). High school seniors' concern for others: Predictors and implications. *High School Journal, 77* (3), 199–205.

REST, J. (1983). Morality. In P. Husen (Ed.), *Handbook of child psychology* (Vol. 4). New York: Wiley.

ROGERS, C., & FREIBERG, H. G. (1994). *Freedom to learn* (3rd ed.). Englewood Cliffs, NJ: Merrill/Prentice Hall.

SHAFTEL, F. R., & SHAFTEL, G. (1982). *Role-playing in the curriculum.* Englewood Cliffs, NJ: Prentice-Hall.

SIMON, S. B., HOWE, L. W., & KIRSCHENBAUM, H. (1978). *Values clarification.* New York: A&W Visual Library.

WILLIAMS, M. W. (1993). Actions speak louder than words: What students think. *Educational Leadership, 51* (3), 22–23.

WYNNE, E., & RYAN, K. (1997). *Reclaiming our schools: Teaching character, academics, and discipline.* Columbus, OH: Merrill/Prentice Hall.

chapter 11

Social Studies Tools: Maps, Globes, and Graphs

This chapter will help you to:

- recognize problems often experienced by elementary pupils when they work with maps, globes, and graphs,
- identify key map, globe, and graphing skills,
- describe map, globe, and graphing skills appropriate for pupils in different grades,
- point out basic characteristics of maps and globes,
- suggest teaching approaches useful for helping pupils master map, globe, and graphing skills,
- identify basic concepts pupils must know before they can cope successfully with map and globe activities, and
- state how to teach pupils to encode data and interpret graphs and charts.

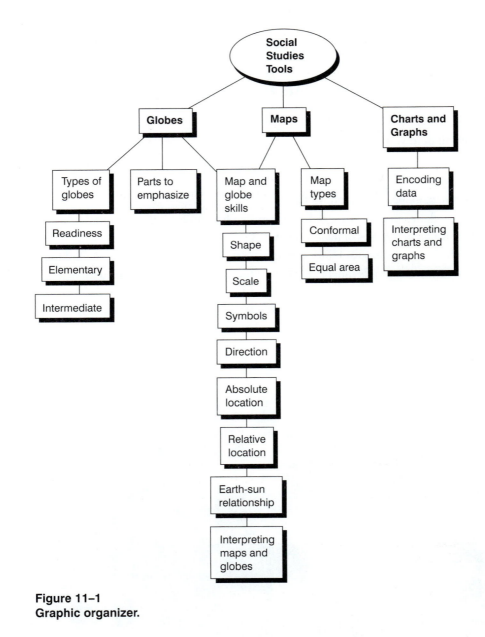

Figure 11–1
Graphic organizer.

Case Study

DOES IT MAKE SENSE TO SPEND SO MUCH
TIME ON MAP AND GLOBE SKILLS?

Recently, a committee was established at the State Department of Instruction to revise the social studies curriculum. The committee asked teachers from throughout the state to send in their written reactions and suggestions. Ingrid Stein, who has been teaching sixth graders for many years, provided these comments.

> I am concerned about the emphasis given to map and globe skills in the elementary grades. Sure, we can all use some basic map skills in order to use highway maps. But why spend so much time on skills that have limited usefulness? Is this really a "critical life skill"? Who really needs to know how to determine latitude and longitude? What difference does it make? Spending time on this content takes away valuable time that could be spent on more important content and ideas.
>
> As I have been thinking about all of the time we spend on this content, I have concluded that we teach it not because it's important, but because it is easy to assess on standardized tests. Related test items are easy to construct, and results give us a concrete score we can publish in the newspapers.
>
> I do not think ease of test construction is a good rationale for establishing our instructional priorities. For this reason, I recommend that the new standards reduce the emphasis on map and globe skills (such as those focusing on latitude and longitude) in favor of more "meaty" academic content.

What Is Your Response?

1. Do you agree that map and globe skills are of limited use to people? What is the purpose of map and globe skills?
2. What should be the criteria for deciding what to include in the curriculum? Should the content be selected according to its relevance to lives of adult citizens?
3. The writer suggests that the content was selected because of ease of testing. From your own experience, do you think certain topics were included in schools simply because it was easy to develop test items relating to them?
4. If you were asked to react to the position taken in this letter, what would you say?

INTRODUCTION

Several years ago one of us was working with a group of teachers on the topic of map and globe skills. One of the teachers was not convinced that this topic was of much importance. She stated, "I don't know how to read a map and I'm still alive." Certainly it is true that skill in what might be called *social studies tools* is not required for survival. However, it is equally true that people who do not possess these tools are limited in their ability to understand the world around them much as are people who lack good reading skills.

Maps, globes, and graphs are devices that can be used to represent specialized information. Understanding how this information is presented can help all of us look for relationships and patterns that might otherwise go unnoticed. In addition, individuals unsophisticated in the understanding of these tools are easy marks for those who use them for propaganda purposes. For example, you would not have to search very far to find graphs and charts that are used inappropriately in an attempt to persuade readers that a particular view is warranted.

We are living in an interdependent world where anyplace on the globe is only minutes away. What is happening in one part of the world will affect all of us. For example, air pollution in one part of the earth will influence other parts. Depletion of the rain forest will result in climatic changes elsewhere. Now more than ever our children need to understand the relationships between different phenomena across the face of the Earth. This understanding begins with the teaching of simple map, globe, and graphing skills in elementary social studies. Maps and globes are tools that can be used to plot information and discover relationships that might other go unnoticed. To test your own understanding of some of these relationships, take the following quiz.

Are the following statements true or false?

1. Reno, Nevada, is west of Los Angeles, California.
2. The west coast of South America is in the same time zone as New York City (Eastern Time).
3. If a person flew first from New York to San Francisco and then flew an equivalent distance west from San Francisco, he or she would be more than one-third of the way across the Pacific Ocean.
4. Because Juneau, Alaska, is much farther north, it has colder average January weather than Philadelphia, Pennsylvania.

Here are the answers: Numbers 1 and 2 are true, and numbers 3 and 4 are false. Do not feel bad if you made some mistakes. Many adults find such questions difficult. They are even more perplexing to elementary pupils who have little experience in working with map and globe skills. On the other hand, children and adults who are solidly grounded in these skills should have little difficulty in answering such questions correctly. Before going on, let us pause a moment to explain the answers.

The question about Los Angeles and Reno is confusing because most people look at flat maps of the United States rather than globes. Many of these maps distort the shape of the West Coast. They make it look like a relatively straight north-south line. Since Los Angeles is on the coast and Reno is inland, it is only natural for people to conclude that Los Angeles must be farther west. In reality, the southern part of the West Coast lies in a generally southeasterly direction from the northern part. This is why it is possible for Los Angeles to be east of Reno. The relationship is quite apparent on a globe. Perhaps because of the names of the two continents—North America and South America—many people assume that South America lies directly south of North America. It does lie south, but it is also considerably east of most of North America. This is why it is true that the west coast of South America lies in the same time zone as the eastern United States.

Children, and adults too, often greatly underestimate the size of the Pacific Ocean. The Pacific Ocean covers about one-third of the earth's surface. In very rough terms, it is about 10,000 miles (16,090 kilometers) from the West Coast of the United States to the western boundaries of the Pacific. This is more than three times the distance from New York to San Francisco. This relationship is often unnoticed because many of the maps used in classrooms in the United States are divided down the center of the Pacific Ocean. Therefore, individuals rarely see a map that covers the entire span of the Pacific. A colleague recounted an incident that illustrates this misconception. He was flying from the east to San Francisco. As the plane approached the airport the person seated next to him remarked, "Since I'm this far west I may as well hop on over to Japan."

Many middle-grade children have some understanding of the parts of the globe, such as the equator and the poles. They also recognize that, on the average, the winter temperatures in the northern areas of the Northern Hemisphere are colder than in the southern areas. Many of these pupils, though, have not grasped the point that other conditions, such as elevation, wind patterns, and proximity to warm water also influence temperature. They need to understand these relationships in order to answer the question about the January temperatures in Juneau and Philadelphia correctly.

Though it is much closer to the equator than Juneau, Philadelphia sits at the eastern edge of a large continental land mass. Because the prevailing winds here blow off the cold continental interior in the winter, the January weather can be very cold. Juneau, by way of contrast, sits on the coast and enjoys moderate winter temperatures because the prevailing west winds blow in off the warm Alaska current.

GLOBES

Globes deserve more attention than they receive in many social studies classrooms. Some of the misunderstandings learners have about the world might be eliminated if they were given more experience in working with globes and relatively less in working with maps. Globes provide the best representation of our spherical planet. Maps, dealing in only two dimensions, distort shapes and areas; this distortion can lead to serious misconceptions (see Figure 11–2).

For example, many flat world maps use a projection that makes Africa look smaller in area than North America. Surprisingly large numbers of middle-grade pupils believe that this is true. Such maps also make Greenland look as large as South America. In fact, South America is nine times larger. Globes avoid these distortions. The relative sizes of the world's landmasses appear on the globe as they actually exist.

Though the increased use of globes can help pupils gain a better appreciation of size relationships, globes pose problems as well. Globes are bulky. Ideally, there should be enough globes so that no more than 3 or 4 pupils at a time need to work with one. In a class of 25, this would mean six or more globes. Often, there is simply not sufficient space to accommodate such a large number.

Not long ago, some middle-grade pupils were surveyed to determine what they knew about selected topics in geography. The following are some of the mistaken "facts" about the world that were revealed in their responses.

1. On any map, the Atlantic always lies to the right.
2. It is not possible for a river to flow in a northerly direction.
3. In the Northern Hemisphere, every place north of Location A has colder winters than Location A itself.
4. Africa is a country.
5. More Spanish-speaking people live in Spain than in any other Spanish-speaking country.
6. The northern-most point of the 48 connected U.S. states is the northern tip of the state of Maine.
7. It is about the same distance from New York to London as from Seattle to Tokyo.

THINK ABOUT THIS

1. Which of the misstatements do you believe to be the most widespread? Why do you think so?
2. In general, what are the sources of this misinformation?
3. As a teacher, what might you do to help learners correct mistaken impressions such as these?

Figure 11–2
Examples of some children's misconceptions.

There are serious problems associated with using globes to teach certain kinds of content. Globes include the entire Earth's surface. Because of the scale of the globe, individual areas appear to be quite small. This scale means that many details must be omitted on the globe. If the purpose of the lesson is to learn some of the detail and the patterns of a given region, the globe as a tool would not be as good a choice as a map.

Suppose you wanted to teach something about Romania. Romania is about 425 miles (684 kilometers) across from east to west. On a standard 16-inch globe, Romania occupies less than 1 inch of space from east to west. Little detail can be included in such a small space. A larger globe would involve other difficulties. A globe large enough for Romania to be 36 inches across would be 48 feet in diameter. Such a globe would need to be installed in a special building.

Though they do have limitations when the purpose is to study small parts of the Earth's surface, globes are ideally suited to helping learners grasp other kinds of content. As noted previously, they are excellent vehicles for displaying the proper area and location arrangements. They can be used to help develop skills associated with location that involve the use of latitude and longitude. The concept of the great-circle route is much better taught with a globe than with a map. Earth-sun relationships—as they relate to issues such as day and night, the seasons of the year, the 24-hour day, and time zones—are best taught using globes.

Kinds of Globes

Three common globe types are found in elementary schools: (1) readiness globes, (2) elementary globes, and (3) intermediate globes.

Readiness Globes

Readiness globes are designed to introduce basic information about globes. They are used mostly in the primary grades. Bright colors are often used to depict the individual countries. The detail does not go much beyond labels for the major countries, the names of capital cities and other large population centers, the names of major oceans and seas, and the labels for the equator and, sometimes, for the tropic of Cancer and the tropic of Capricorn. Occasionally, a few additional details are found.

Even readiness globes sometimes contain a bewildering array of information for very young children. Some pupils in the early primary grades experience difficulty in distinguishing between the areas of land and water. One teacher reported having a readiness globe that used the color blue to depict certain political areas as well as water areas. One child in the class described Wyoming as a major lake!

Elementary Globes

Elementary globes are good for use with fourth, fifth, and sixth graders. They include more detail than readiness globes. This detail may overwhelm children in the primary grades. The additional information often includes the lines of latitude and longitude, the details regarding the scale of the globe, the indications of major world wind patterns, and the depictions of the directions of the major ocean currents. These globes often provide the locations of many more cities and towns than do readiness globes.

Intermediate Globes

Intermediate globes are best suited for use with older, intermediate-grade learners. They include even more detail than elementary globes. Many of them, for example, include notations of world time zones. Many, too, include an *analemma*. An analemma is the figure-eight-shaped figure that cuts through the equator (Figure 11–3). It indicates the locations where the sun is directly overhead at noon on each day of the year.

Some intermediate globes also have a horizon ring. A horizon ring is a circular band that surrounds the globe. It has the degrees marked off on its inner surface. The globe can be rotated at will within the ring. By using the degree markers, pupils can engage in relatively sophisticated calculations of degree differences and time differences between pairs of locations on the globe.

Parts of the Globe That Need to Be Emphasized

The information presented on globes is of no use until youngsters understand what it means. There are substantial differences in the types and amounts of information introduced on various kinds of globes. By the end of their elementary social studies experience, youngsters should recognize the functions of major features of the globe. These

Figure 11–3
The analemma. An *analemma* is used to indicate the latitudes at which the sun is directly overhead at noon on each day of the year. The northern limit of the analemma is the tropic of Cancer, where the sun is directly overhead on June 21–22. The southern limit is the tropic of Capricorn, where the sun is directly overhead on December 21–22. The sun is directly overhead at noon at the equator twice each year: once on March 21–22 and again on September 21–22. The apparent movement of the sun is a result of the earth's annual movement around the sun. Because the earth's axis always points to the North Star, at some times of the year the sun's rays strike most directly at points south of the equator, at the equator, or north of the equator. To receive a clearer picture of why this happens, see Figure 11–10. Some teachers find that pupils enjoy pointing out where the sun will be overhead at noon on their birthdays.

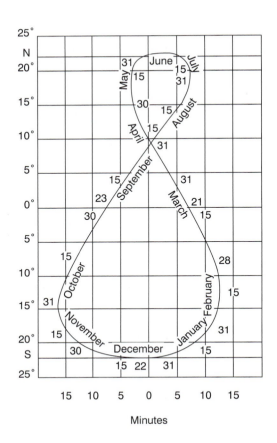

include the equator, the tropic of Cancer, the tropic of Capricorn, the North Pole, the South Pole, the international date line, the prime meridian, the horizon ring, the distance scale, the world time zones, and the analemma.

Pupils should be able to apply basic globe skills to solve problems such as finding locations using latitude and longitude, explaining the seasonal changes according to Earth-sun relationships, pointing out the function of the international date line, and explaining the time difference between selected pairs of world locations. Examples of how proficiency in these skills might be developed are introduced later in the chapter.

MAPS

Maps are used more frequently than globes in most elementary social studies classrooms. Properly used, maps can be very effective instructional resources. They can be designed to accomplish many purposes, they cost less than globes, and they do not consume much storage space.

The strengths of the map as a teaching devise need to be counterbalanced with an understanding that maps are an imperfect representation of the Earth. A three-dimensional surface cannot be transformed into a two-dimensional surface without distortion. To illustrate how this might happen when explaining maps to children, carefully remove half of the peel from an orange. By placing the peel on a flat surface and pushing down on the peel, it can be illustrated that something must "give" before the spherical surface can be converted to a flat plane.

Many maps illustrate only a portion of the Earth's surface. A survey of the wall maps permanently on display in elementary classrooms in this country would probably reveal more U.S. maps than maps of other parts of the world. Pupils' continuous exposure to such maps has the potential to lead to false conclusions. The widespread notion among middle-grade pupils that "north is always up" and "the Atlantic is always found on the right-hand side of a map" may be the result of years of seeing it so positioned on U.S. maps attached to classroom walls. They have failed to distinguish between north, south, east, west, and up, down, right, and left. This confusion leads to another misconception. We have heard individuals proclaim that no rivers in the world flow to the north. Naturally, water cannot flow up! However, because north is not up, many great rivers of the world do indeed flow to the north.

It is important to get maps down from the walls. Place them on the floor and orient them so that individuals can see that north and south are directions quite different from up and down. Use a variety of maps so that pupils also note that features such as the Atlantic Ocean may be in a position other than on the right side.

Constant exposure to a large wall map of the United States also has the potential to confuse pupils about the proper size relationships among places in the world. Elementary school children often tend to overestimate the physical size of the United States (this is also a problem with some adults). This results in a failure to appreciate the magnitude and importance of other places in the world.

Using a variety of maps of different scales and comparing them can help individuals begin to overcome this misconception. Transparencies of maps of different parts of the world that are the same scale can be placed on top of each other in order to make comparisons of size.

World maps are a common wall feature in elementary school classrooms. To some degree, individual maps reflect characteristics of one of these two basic types: conformal maps and equal area maps.

Conformal Maps

Conformal maps are prepared in such a way that the shapes of the land areas—for example, Australia—are the same on the map as on a globe. An important example of a conformal map is the Mercator projection map, named for a famous mapmaker who lived in the 16th century (see Figure 11–4).

To understand how a Mercator projection map is made, imagine a clear glass globe with land areas outlined in dark ink and a tiny light in the center. The globe is placed on a table so a line passing through the North Pole, the light in the center, and the South Pole is perpendicular to the tabletop. A cylinder of paper is slipped over the globe. The light source

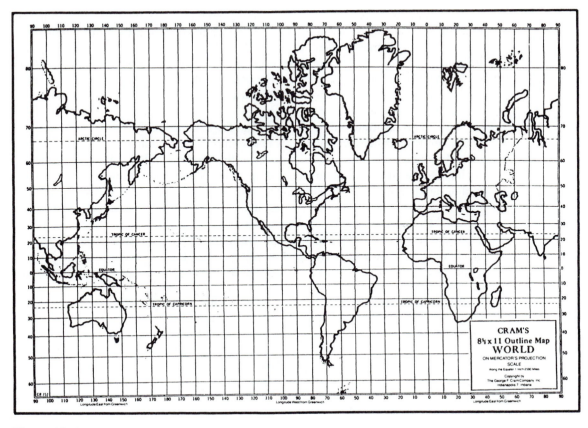

Figure 11–4
An example of a conformal world map: Mercator's projection.
Source: Copyright George F. Cram Co., Inc., Indianapolis, IN. Reprinted by permission.

causes shadows to be cast on the paper cylinder from the boundaries of the land areas. The mapmaker carefully traces these shadows. When the cylinder is unwrapped, the result is a Mercator projection map of the world. (In reality, the process is done mathematically. But the principles are as described here.)

The Mercator projection produces a world map that maintains accurate shapes of landmasses. However, relative sizes of places are not accurately portrayed; as the distance from the equator increases, the size distortion is greater. Places in extreme northern and southern locations are depicted as much larger than they appear on a globe.

The distortion in land areas on Mercator projection maps can lead to unfortunate misunderstandings. As noted, pupils who do not often work with globes and who see a Mercator map every day often mistakenly conclude that Greenland is as large as or even larger than South America. Greenland's apparent size on a Mercator projection map is a result of its great distance from the equator. South America, on the other hand, lies across the equator and hence is relatively undistorted.

Figure 11–5
An example of an equal area world map: Robinson's projection.
Source: Reprinted with permission from Edward B. Espenshade, Jr., ed., *Goode's World Atlas,* 18th ed., p. xi. Chicago: Rand McNally, 1990.

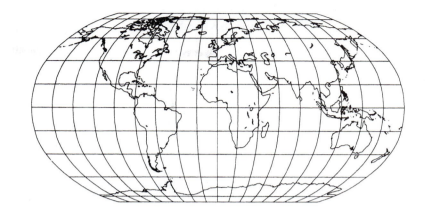

When conformal maps are the only world maps available, it is particularly important to give pupils opportunities to work with globes, and to explain to them why the sizes of landmasses in extreme northern and southern regions are distorted on Mercator maps. Pupils should be given opportunities to compare and contrast globes and world maps so they can appreciate that conformal maps distort sizes of some landmasses.

Modifications of the Mercator projection reduce some of these extreme area distortions. In general, though, these modifications give up the Mercator projection's total consistency, with the shape of landmasses as depicted on the globe, as a tradeoff for less distortion in area. Such maps are not truly conformal.

Equal Area Maps

Equal area maps of the world are drawn in such a way that the relative size of landmasses, as reflected on the globe, are preserved. As noted previously, Greenland is approximately one-ninth the size of South America. On an equal area map of the world, Greenland and South America are drawn to reflect this true size relationship. Compare the areas of Greenland and South America as they appear in the Mercator projection map in Figure 11–4 and in the Robinson's equal area projection map in Figure 11–5.

Preserving proper size relationships among land areas requires that some distortion occur in their shapes. It is not possible for an equal area map to be drawn so that all shapes are as they appear on the globe.

There are relatively few equal area world maps hanging in classrooms as compared with conformal world maps. Traditionally, educators (many with little formal training in issues associated with maps and globes) have opted for maps featuring landmasses shaped as they appear on globes.

Because of the enormous distortions of areas of some important world landmasses on conformal maps, equal area maps should be available in every elementary classroom. Ideally, each classroom should have one world map of each type. Exposure to both conformal and equal area maps and to globes provides children with a solid grounding in relative sizes and areas of landmasses. Such lessons, too, reinforce the idea that all renderings of a sphere onto a flat surface result in important distortions.

BASIC MAP AND GLOBE SKILLS

Eight basic map and globe skills are of interest to the elementary social studies teacher:

- Recognizing shapes
- Utilizing scale
- Recognizing symbols
- Utilizing direction
- Determining absolute location
- Pointing out relative location
- Describing Earth-sun relationships
- Interpreting information on maps and globes

In the subsections that follow, we introduce basic information about each basic skill. In addition, we provide ideas about sequencing instruction from the early grades through the middle grades and into the upper grades.

Recognizing Shapes

Recognizing shapes is one of the most fundamental map and globe skills. Though this skill may appear to be simple or even simplistic, many sophisticated analyses in geography require a grasp of the importance of physical shapes, particularly those of landmasses. For example, recognizing the shapes of the major landmasses of the world is an essential first step in locating places on Earth. In addition, recognizing the physical shape of features is fundamental to developing additional insight. Appreciating that a narrow peninsula may have a climate that varies dramatically from that of a central location at the heart of a continent requires that a person know what a peninsula is. The kinds of learning associated with recognizing shapes increase in complexity as children move through the elementary program.

Utilizing Scale

Scale is an abstract and difficult concept. Teachers often find that teaching pupils to understand and use this concept is one of their most challenging assignments (see Figure 11–6). Scale is difficult because it requires the concurrent understanding of two subordinate understandings. Each of these can frustrate pupils, especially those in the early elementary grades.

First, to appreciate scale, a person needs to know that geographical features (mountains, rivers, oceans, and so forth) can be visually depicted in a convenient way. For example, it is possible to represent a mountain by taking a photograph of the mountain. Learners need to grasp that the mountain is real; they need to know the photograph is real; and, most important, they need to understand that there is a connection between the mountain as depicted in the photograph and the mountain itself.

Scale can be a challenging concept for children in the early grades. However, it can be related to something they all understand. Most of them will have toys that are models of real objects. They can all understand that a model car looks like the real thing, only it is smaller so that they can play with it. The scale is the ratio between the size of the model and the actual object. They can also note that the same type of model car can be made in different sizes. Some models are larger than others, but all still look like the real object.

Maps follow the same rule. They are models of the real thing produced at different sizes or scales according to the needs of the person using the map. Another activity that can help pupils grasp the concept is to use a camera that produces instant prints. Familiar objects in the classroom can be photographed from different distances. Pupils can measure the real object and then the size of the object in the different pictures. They can then establish a scale for each of the pictures. They can also notice the differences that occur as they move further away from the object. Maps are much like these snapshots taken at different distances.

TRY THIS

1. Check to see if any children in the classroom (or their parents) are hobbyists involved with model trains or airplanes. If possible, have them bring a model and one of the boxes for the model. Such a box has the scale printed on its side. Older pupils can use this ratio or scale to calculate how large the actual object would be.
2. Provide pupils with graph paper. The class can then measure the classroom and draw it to scale on the graph paper. Each square on the graph paper can represent a set interval, such as 1 foot.

Figure 11–6
Helping children understand scale.

Second, a child looking at a photograph of a mountain needs to recognize that there is a knowable physical size relationship between the size of the mountain as it exists on the Earth's surface and the size as it is depicted in the photograph. A sound understanding of the principle of using small, convenient representations as reliable indicators of the size of large phenomena is fundamental to an appreciation of scale. Pupils who lack this basic knowledge have a difficult time grasping the idea that the scales on maps and globes can be used to make accurate statements about the actual sizes of the physical features of the Earth.

Recognizing Symbols

Both maps and globes feature many symbols. Symbols are the language of maps and globes. In order to gather data from maps and globes, individuals need to be able to decode the symbols. This makes reading maps a process something like reading a book.

Having students create their own map legend is a useful strategy in helping them learn map symbols.

However, the symbols on maps and globes are usually easier to decode than the combination of letters that make up a printed word. These symbols are a convenient shorthand representation for the kinds of phenomena that exist in the world. For people who understand them, they efficiently communicate a tremendous amount of information. But for individuals who do not know what they mean, they are confusing marks that can lead to serious misunderstandings. Because symbols are so basic to an understanding of maps and globes, recognizing symbols has long been recognized as one of the most important map and globe skills.

Lesson Idea 11–1

LEARNING ABOUT MAP SYMBOLS

Grade Level:	1–3
Objectives:	Pupils will create symbols to represent real objects.
Suggested Procedure:	Six ideas for helping beginning learners understand map symbols follow.

    1. Cut out well-known symbols for businesses and other organizations from newspapers and magazines. For example, you might select symbols representing the Olympics, the United Nations, McDonald's, Texaco,

and many other organizations, firms, and groups. Ask how many youngsters recognize each symbol. Explain why symbols are used (to save time, to provide for ready recognition, and so forth). Does the school have a mascot? Is there a symbol that represents a favorite sports team? Lead into the idea that map makers and globe makers use many symbols.

2. Let pupils decide on five new clubs that should be started in the school. Once they have identified these groups, set them to work developing a symbol for each club. Sometimes it works well to organize learners into teams for this activity. Follow up with a discussion about what goes into a good symbol. (It is easy to remember and quickly communicates a great deal of information about the group or thing for which it stands.)

3. To prepare children to work comfortably with the symbols that will appear on the maps or globe they will use, develop sets of flashcards. On one side will be the symbol. On the other side will be the thing for which the symbol stands. These cards can help youngsters grasp the meaning of symbols.

4. Another technique to help pupils learn the meanings of symbols used on maps involves the use of simple two-part puzzles. These can be made from construction paper. From sources such as *National Geographic,* find pictures of things that are depicted by symbols on maps. Paste a picture on the top half of a sheet of construction paper. On the bottom half, draw the symbol used for the thing depicted. Then cut the sheet into two parts. Give pupils a mixed group of top and bottom sheets. Ask them to try to fit the sheets together by using their knowledge of symbols. When the sheets fit properly, they know they have matched the symbol to the thing it depicts. (See Figure 11–7.)

5. Ask pupils to develop symbols for the school desks or tables, for the teacher's desk, for the doors, and for the chalkboards. Then give them a blank outline map of the classroom. Ask them to use their symbols to indicate the locations of these objects. Display the finished products, and ask several volunteers to explain their maps.

6. Have pupils create a simple map featuring a key that explains the symbols they choose to include. Ask them to explain what they might see if they took a trip along a specified route depicted on the map. Remind them to refer to the meanings of the symbols provided in the key. An example of such a map appears in Figure 11–8.

Figure 11–7
Example of a simple symbol for a church. Pupils put the two parts of this simple puzzle together in an exercise designed to help them see the connection between the symbol and the object for which it stands.

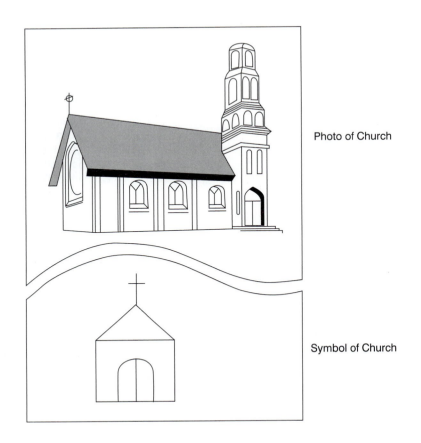

Photo of Church

Symbol of Church

Pupils must recognize that symbols represent real objects. A map or a globe in its entirety is a symbol; it represents the Earth's surface or part of the Earth's entire surface. Pupils need to understand that even the colors on maps and globes function as symbols. Younger pupils are sometimes confused about this. When they see Kansas depicted in orange, they may receive the impression that everything in Kansas literally is orange. You need to be careful to explain the symbolic nature of maps as a whole as well as the meaning of the more specific symbols indicating things such as airports, highways, boundary lines, and large cities.

Recognizing shapes, utilizing scale, and recognizing symbols all have different educational emphases at different grade levels. These emphases are summarized in Table 11–1.

Utilizing Direction

The proper use of globes and maps depends on an ability to become properly oriented to direction. A sound understanding of the major and intermediate compass directions is basic to pinpointing locations. It is particularly important that learners master and

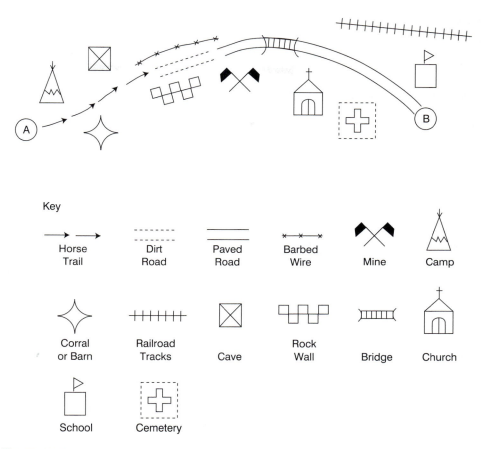

Key

→ →	- - - - -	═══════	×—×—×	(crossed flags)	(camp symbol)
Horse Trail	Dirt Road	Paved Road	Barbed Wire	Mine	Camp
(corral symbol)	+++++++	⊠	(rock wall)	(bridge)	(church)
Corral or Barn	Railroad Tracks	Cave	Rock Wall	Bridge	Church
(school symbol)	(cemetery symbol)				
School	Cemetery				

Figure 11–8
Example of a pupil-produced map using simple symbols. *Directions:* Describe a trip a person might make along this route starting at point A and finishing at point B. Use the key below each symbol to interpret the meaning of each symbol on the map.

use the concept of direction before working with wall maps. Otherwise, pupils will tend to use such terms as *up* and *down* when referring to *north* and *south,* and *right* and *left* when referring to *east* and *west.* These inappropriate terms can contribute to the development of inaccurate information (the Pacific Ocean always lies to the left).

Determining Absolute Location

Determining absolute location requires pupils to locate any point on the Earth's surface. To adequately perform this task, learners must be familiar with the lines of latitude and longitude. Specifically, they must understand how a longitude-latitude grid system can be used to identify the "address" of every location on Earth. Generally, teachers have

Table 11–1
Grade-level emphases for (1) recognizing shapes, (2) utilizing scale, and (3) recognizing symbols.

	K to Second Grade	Third to Fourth Grade	Fifth to Sixth Grade
Recognizing Shapes	Introduction to basic information about shape. Recognition that the Earth is basically round. Recognition of the basic shapes of continents and oceans.	Recognition of the shapes of smaller landmasses such as islands, peninsulas, and isthmuses. Recognition of smaller bodies of water such as lakes, bays, and sounds.	Recognition of certain types of map distortions. Identification of the patterns of flow of major rivers. Identification of the shapes of major physical regions.
Utilizing Scale	Introduction of basic concepts such as *larger* and *smaller.* Recognition of simple increments of measure (such as city blocks). Identification of objects of different size in pictures.	Utilization of the scale on simple maps. Solution of simple distance problems using scale. Recognition that scale may vary from map to map and globe to globe.	Utilization of the many kinds of scale. Recognition that the amount of detail on a map varies with its scale.
Recognizing Symbols	Recognition of the meanings of common signs (stop signs, etc.). Recognition that some colors on maps are regularly used to represent land and water. Understanding that symbols stand for real objects in the world.	Utilization of symbols for major landscape features on maps and globes. Identification of the traditional symbols for cities, highways, airports, etc.	Utilization of symbols on special-purpose maps. Recognition that the same symbol may mean different things on different maps and globes.

pupils work with very simple grids before they introduce the global system of latitude and longitude (Figure 11–9; see also Lesson Idea 11–2).

Lesson Idea 11–2

LEARNING ABOUT ABSOLUTE LOCATION

Grade level: 2–4

Objectives: Pupils will apply knowledge of the grid system to locate places on maps.

Figure 11–9
An example of a grid activity to help pupils learn how to find places when given the coordinates of longitude and latitude.
Directions: Find the secret word by placing an X in each of these squares: C2, C5, C8; D2, D5, D8; E2, E3, E4, E5, E8; F2, F5, F8; G2, G5, G8.

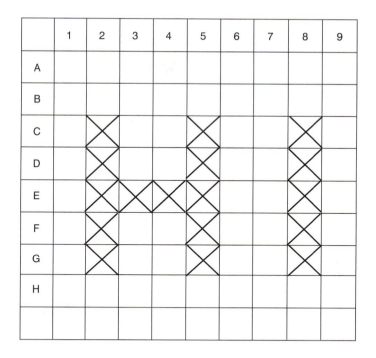

Overview:

Pupils can learn that everyplace on Earth has an "address." This address is determined by using a grid system. The following are five ideas that can help pupils learn how to identify the addresses of different places on the face of the Earth.

Procedures:

1. Prepare a simple grid system using chart paper. Number the row of squares across the top and designate the first column using letters. Choose a simple word and color in the squares to form the letters of the word. Provide the pupils with graph paper and have them fill in the numbers and letters in the first row and the first column. Call out shaded squares using the coordinates and have pupils fill in that space on their papers. Keep calling the coordinates until the "mystery" word is revealed.

2. Provide the pupils with a simple outline map of the world. The map should include latitude and longitude designations and a compass rose. Play a "Find the Continent" game with the members of the class. Give latitude and longitude and ask the pupils to name the nearest continent.

3. In a learning center, provide several short books about various countries of the world. Inside the cover of the

book neatly print the map coordinates of the country described in the book. Have the pupils find the country using the latitude and longitude and color it on an outline map.

4. In a learning center, provide several newspaper articles with datelines from a number of cities around the world. Attach each article to a sturdy piece of paper. Above each article, write the latitude and longitude of the dateline city. Have the pupils use a globe or an atlas to locate the city.

5. Write an itinerary about a journey to various cities of the world. Instead of naming the cities, identify them only by latitude and longitude coordinates. Give these to the pupils and ask them to name the cities and plot the route of the traveler on an outline map.

Here are some possibilities:

- Latitude 22° 53′ 43″ S, longitude 43° 13′ 22″ W (Rio de Janeiro)
- Latitude 62° 28′ 15″ N, longitude 114° 22′ 00″ W (Yellowknife, Northwest Territories, Canada)
- Latitude 48° 50′ 14″ N, longitude 2° 20′ 14″ E (Paris, France)

Pointing Out Relative Location

Relative location refers to the location of one place in terms of one or more other places. When Chicago is described as being north of Houston, east of Omaha, and west of New York, we are referring to Chicago's relative location.

Many elementary social studies programs begin building the skill of pointing out relative location by helping pupils to first recognize relative location with regard to familiar places. For example, we might help them understand the relative location of the school by pointing out its position according to nearby parks and homes. Often the local community is pinpointed by referring to its location relative to other places in the state. Later, we might go on to reference its location to places in the nation and the world.

Different aspects of utilizing direction and of determining absolute and relative location are emphasized when these concepts are taught at different grade levels. These emphases are summarized in Table 11–2.

Describing Earth-Sun Relationships

Proper understanding of Earth-sun relationships is an essential ingredient of knowledge regarding diverse topics such as global time, the seasons, and the changing annual wind patterns. Many elementary youngsters find content related to Earth-sun relationships difficult.

Table 11–2

The grade-level emphases for (1) utilizing direction, (2) determining absolute location, and (3) pointing out relative location.

	K to Second Grade	Third to Fourth Grade	Fifth to Sixth Grade
Utilizing Direction	Introduction to the four cardinal compass directions. Very basic introduction to latitude and longitude.	Description of the location of continents according to directional locations from one another. Location of the prime meridian. Utilization of a compass to orient a map and of the compass rose on a map. Introduction to the intermediate directions.	Recognition of the differences between true and magnetic north. Utilization of intermediate directions to provide precise information about locations and paths of travel.
Determining Absolute Location	Utilization of terms such as *right, left, up, down, front, back, near, far.* Location of places on a globe as being north of the equator or south of the equator.	Introduction to the use of grid systems. Location of the places on maps and globes using simple grid systems.	Location of places using the coordinates of latitude and longitude. Identification of the degree position of important lines latitude including the equator, the Arctic and Antarctic circles, and the tropics of Capricorn and Cancer.
Pointing Out Relative Location	Description of one place in a room in relation to other places in the room. Identification of the location of the school in relation to other parts of the community.	Description of the location of the state within the nation. Location of the local community in relation to its location in the state and the nation.	Location of the local community relative to any other place on the globe. Description of the relative location of any two points on the globe.

Part of the problem is our language. We speak of the sun *rising* and *setting*. This terminology is based on an illusion that makes sense. As residents of the Earth's surface, we are not physically aware that the globe is spinning on its axis. Hence, the rising and setting terminology does accurately describe what we see, but this language does not properly describe what is going on. Adults (most of them, at least) know that the sun does not move in this way, but rather that the Earth's spinning only makes it appear to do so. Younger elementary children lack this understanding. Many of them really believe that it is the sun that does the moving.

As they progress through the elementary program, learners are exposed to the concepts of the *seasons*. They are taught that the seasons change because the angle of the

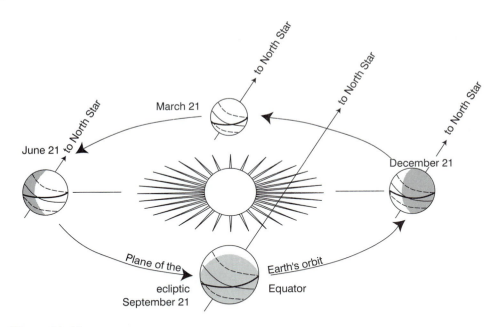

Figure 11–10
Earth-sun relationships. The figure depicts the location of the Earth in relation to the sun on key dates. Many elementary pupils have difficulty accepting the idea that the Earth does not swing back and forth or wobble on its axis. A figure such as this can help to explain what actually happens. The Earth's axis always points toward the North Star. Note that the sun strikes its surface directly at different points at different times of the year.

sun's rays strikes some parts of the Earth's surface more directly at certain times of the year than at others (Figure 11–10). Many children who grasp this basic idea have trouble understanding exactly how this happens. Some conclude erroneously that the Earth wobbles back and forth on its axis, thus causing a change in where the sun's rays strike most directly. Teachers find they must work very hard if pupils are to grasp exactly how the seasonal change can occur without *global wobble*.

Interpreting Information on Maps and Globes

The skill of interpreting information on maps and globes is the broadest of them all. It is perhaps the most important for elementary social studies programs because it establishes a purpose for many of the other map and globe skills. Unless programs involve pupils in using the other skills, pupils may see the instruction that focuses on these skills as boring and directed toward no useful end. But when these skills are used to produce new information, pupils tend to appreciate their importance. Table 11–3 summarizes the different grade-level emphases used when teaching pupils how to describe Earth-sun relationships and when teaching them how to interpret map and globe information.

Table 11–3
Grade-level emphases for (1) Earth-Sun relationships and (2) interpreting information on maps and globes.

	K to Second Grade	Third to Fourth Grade	Fifth to Sixth Grade
Describing Earth-Sun Relationships	Recognition of the terms *fall, winter, spring, summer, day,* and *night.* Identification of the direction of sunrise and sunset. Description of how the Earth's turning causes night and day.	Description of how the Earth moves around the sun. Description of the inclination of the Earth on its axis.	Description of the relationship of the sun to the equator, Tropic of Cancer, Tropic of Capricorn, Arctic circle, and Antarctic circle. Recognition that the globe is divided into 360°. Understanding that the Earth has 24 time zones that are 15° wide. Utilization of the analemma to determine where the sun's rays strike the Earth most directly on each day of the year.
Interpreting the Information on Maps and Globes	Interpretation of information from pictures and simple maps. Recognition that no one, not even a person in space, can see the whole Earth at one time. Construction and interpretation of simple local neighborhood and community maps.	Preparation of more complex local and community maps and the interpretation of information contained on these maps. Description of the population distributions and terrain features on maps. Explanation of the basic causes of climate by referring to the information on maps.	Prediction about the probable climate of a place by viewing maps to determine its elevation, proximity to ocean currents, latitude, and continental or coastal position. Explanation of the geographical constraints on historical or current events through reference to maps. Prediction of elevation change by examining river flow direction on maps.

TEACHING ALL OF THE SKILLS AT EACH GRADE LEVEL

Sometimes, new teachers assume that the more basic skills (such as, perhaps, symbol recognition) should be taught to younger children and that these learners should not be exposed to the more advanced skills. There are two difficulties with this approach. First, there is nothing inherently either easy or difficult about any of these skills. Each can be taught at varying levels of complexity. A teacher would not expect kindergarten children and sixth graders to engage in similar learning activities or to develop similar depths of understanding about a given skill. Yet each group should be exposed to appropriate learning experiences for each skill.

Second, when teachers of younger children decide to omit teaching a difficult skill, they often eliminate that of interpreting information. This is a serious mistake. This skill allows pupils to put to work the other skills they have learned as they try to solve problems.

Interpreting exercises help pupils see a purpose for lessons that require them to master map and globe skills. These activities extend their ability to make sense out of their world. If such activities are eliminated in the early grades, many pupils will see little use in learning the other basic map and globe skills. As a result, teachers may face serious motivational problems, which can inhibit learning.

USING CHARTS AND GRAPHS

The vast amount of information available to the average person can be overwhelming. We live in a data-rich society where data and statistics are commonly used to convince and persuade. Many times this information is presented in the form of charts, graphs, or tables. These specialized forms of presenting data simplify information and often present it visually in a way designed to help us identify relationships. However, graphic representation of information can also confuse the unsophisticated. To prevent this from happening, learners need to understand how to represent and interpret information in charts and graphs.

Encoding Data on Charts and Graphs

In order to understand the data presented in graphic form, individuals must first have knowledge of how information is encoded. This understanding can begin in kindergarten and first grade as pupils practice working with all sorts of concrete data. For example, the teacher might engage them in graphing the number of boys and girls in the class, the number of pupils who have birthdays in each month of the year, the number of rainy days in a month, the temperature for each day, or the number of individuals who ride the bus or walk to school. There are abundant opportunities for the creative teacher to use concrete data to teach pupils how to make charts and graphs.

It is useful for pupils to learn that there are three basic types of graphs: *bar graphs, pie graphs,* and *line graphs.* The choice of the type of graph to use relates to the type of data to be encoded and the possible uses of this information. For example, charting the number of boys and girls in a given classroom could be accomplished using either a pie chart or a bar graph. Both types could show the relationship. However, a pie graph usually requires an understanding of a sophisticated concept, *percentage.* A bar graph is more easily understood by pupils who are not yet familiar with percentages. Further, a bar graph is often easier to construct than a pie graph, and its format allows for a closer correspondence between real objects and information displayed on the graph.

In summary, during the early elementary years it is best to keep the data to be encoded simple and concrete. As pupils have numerous experiences with graphs and develop an understanding of them, they can then move to abstract and complex forms of graphic representations.

Interpreting Charts and Graphs

Once pupils have learned how to construct charts and graphs, they need to learn how to interpret the displayed information. They need to be asked to interpret the data and make inferences. The interpretation process can begin with simple observations. For example, when the birthdays of class members are presented by month in a bar graph, the class can be asked to make simple interpretations, such as which month has the most birthdays, which month has the least birthdays, and so forth.

As pupils grow older they can be challenged to make more sophisticated interpretations. For example, graphing the makes and models of cars in the school parking lot can lead to some interesting interpretations that might explain why some types of cars seem to be heavily represented and others are absent.

There is a wealth of information in graph form that can be used as a focus for inquiry. For example, graphs on the life expectancy of people by states show some intriguing variations among the states. An interesting lesson could be built around an activity calling on pupils to form hypotheses that might explain these differences.

As pupils develop more experience constructing and interpreting graphs, they need to learn how graphs and charts are sometimes used to distort data. For example, erroneous interpretations often are made when irresponsible producers of bar graphs fail to start at zero.

To see how this can happen, consider this situation. Suppose that two classrooms are having a contest to see who reads the most books. One class reads 110 books and the second reads 120 books. A graph starting at zero would lead to the conclusion that the two classes were fairly close. However, suppose that the chart actually started with a baseline of 100 books instead of 0 books. Such a chart would show only the number of books in excess of 100 read by each class. The resulting chart would imply that one class read twice as many books as the other. (This would happen because there would be a graph 10 books high for the class that read 110 books and 20 books high for the class that read 120 books.) This irresponsible graph would imply that there was a huge difference in the totals read by each class—a conclusion, of course, that is at odds with reality (110 books in one case and 120 in the other). See Figure 11–11 for an illustration of responsible and irresponsible bar charts that display the information about these two classes. Note that the irresponsible bar chart starts at 100 rather than at 0.

Similarly, a different impression can be created by bar graphs when the units of the grid system are changed. For example, rather than having squares represent each unit, rectangles can be used to create the impression that the slope is either steeper or flatter. For example, suppose a car salesperson wants to create the visual effect that another make of car is much more expensive. A line chart could be created using rectangles for each unit of analysis with small sides of the rectangle across the bottom and the long sides running toward the top. The image would be a steeply sloping line. To create the opposite image the long sides could be placed across the bottom of the graph: the slope now looks much flatter, creating the visual effect that there isn't much difference.

Figure 11–11
Examples of responsible and irresponsible bar charts. Note that the information is based on numbers of books read by children in two classrooms. Pupils in one classroom read 110 books. Pupils in the other read 120.

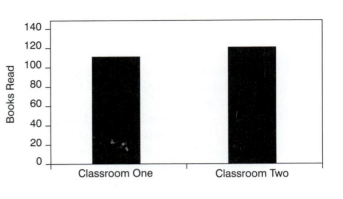

Responsibly drawn bar chart comparing numbers of books read by pupils in two classrooms

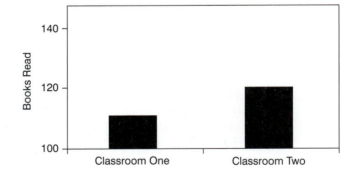

Irresponsibly drawn bar chart comparing numbers of books read by pupils in two classrooms

Understanding these tricks can be useful in helping students spot attempts to influence their interpretation. They can apply this skill by looking for examples of deliberate data distortions in advertisements and the media. Pupils often find this activity interesting and motivating. They understand that this is helping them make better decisions.

WEB CHECK

Note: Electronic addresses of sites on the World Wide Web change frequently. If the listed URL fails to work, use a standard search engine to locate the new address of the site.

- Map Machine

  URL—**http://www.nationalgeographic.com/resources/ngo/maps/**

  This National Geographic Society site provides maps, flags, and information about each country in the world.

- Mapmaker, Mapmaker, Make Me a Map

  URL—**http://loki.ur.utk.edu/ut2kids/maps/map.html**

  This University of Tennessee site provides a tutorial on mapmaking.

- Great Globe Gallery

  URL—**http://www.fpsol.com/gems/geography.html**

  This site offers links to a variety of maps and globes with views from satellites, weather maps, and medieval globes.

- U.S. Geological Survey

  URL—**http://www.usgs.gov/**

  This site contains an abundance of learning resources on working with maps.

- County Outline Maps

  URL—**http://www.lib.utexas.edu/Libs/PCL/Map_collection/county_outline.html**

  This is a complete collection of county maps for all fifty states.

- How Far Is It?

  URL—**http://www.indo.com/distance/**

  This site calculates the latitude and longitude of any two cities in the word and the distance between them. It allows you to generate maps of the two places.

- U.S. Bureau of the Census

  URL—**http://www.census.gov/**

  This site features a large number of sources of valuable statistical information. Data here can be used for a variety of social studies projects and lessons.

KEY IDEAS IN SUMMARY

1. Many adults have confused ideas about the locations of places on the globe. Elementary pupils are even more likely to have an inadequate grasp of the map and globe skills needed for the proper understanding of geographical location. Some misunderstandings result from a complete lack of information, others from inadequate information. For example, large wall maps sometimes distort sizes of landmasses.

2. Globes should receive more attention in elementary social studies classrooms. Only the globe shows places on Earth with a minimum of shape and size distortion and with accurate relative placement of water and land areas. To be useful as teaching tools, there should be at least one globe available for every three or four pupils.

3. Globes have disadvantages. They are bulky. They are rather expensive. They do not lend themselves well to teaching certain kinds of content. For example, if a teacher wanted to teach about a relatively small area, perhaps the state of South Carolina, the area of interest would be too small on a globe to be of any practical value. A globe large enough to display South Carolina at a size sufficient for learners to see easily might be too large to fit in the classroom.

4. Three common types of globes are found in elementary schools. These are (1) readiness globes (2) elementary globes, and (3) intermediate globes. Readiness globes include only basic information. Elementary globes include latitude, longitude, and other details not included on readiness globes. Intermediate globes include even more information.

5. Maps are useful for teaching certain kinds of content, such as the study of relatively small areas. Typically they are less expensive than globes and are much easier to store.

6. Because they attempt to represent a sphere on a flat surface, all maps include distortions. On conformal world maps, shapes of land areas are as they are on the globe, but the areas of landmasses distant from the equator are greatly distorted. On equal area world maps, areas of landmasses are consistent with areas as they appear on the globe, but shapes may be distorted. Teachers need to instruct pupils about the problem of distortion. Ideally, pupils should have opportunities to compare and contrast depictions of places in the world as they appear on the globe, on a conformal world map, and on an equal area world map.

7. There are eight basic map and globe skills. They are (1) recognizing shapes, (2) utilizing scale, (3) recognizing symbols, (4) utilizing direction, (5) determining absolute location, (6) pointing out relative location, (7) describing Earth-sun relationships, and (8) interpreting information on maps and globes.

8. It is desirable to introduce all eight map and globe skills at each level of the elementary school program. The skills are common to all grade levels, but the activities used to introduce and reinforce them change.

9. It is especially important that pupils have opportunities to use map and globe skills to solve problems. Such experiences help establish the importance of these skills. Additionally, they can extend learners' understanding of the world and, by so doing, build interest in other aspects of the social studies program.

10. Charts and graphs are other special ways that important information is presented. Today, much information is presented in graphic form. Consequently, pupils need to learn how to create and interpret data presented in this way.

CHAPTER REFLECTIONS

Directions: Now that you have read this chapter, reread the case study at the beginning. Then, answer these questions:

1. What factors contribute to misunderstandings many pupils have about the relative locations of places on the Earth's surface?

2. What are some advantages of using globes to provide learners with basic understanding about shapes and sizes of different lands?

3. What are the characteristics of readiness globes, elementary globes, and intermediate globes?

4. What are general characteristics of conformal world maps and equal area world maps?

5. What are the eight basic map skills?

6. Suppose you were challenged to defend the inclusion of map and globe skills in the elementary social studies program. How would you respond?

7. In the past, some people have said that the skill of interpreting information on maps and globes is too sophisticated for pupils in kindergarten to second grade. How do you feel about the suggestion that this skill be reserved for older learners? Why do you take this position?

8. Many pupils have a difficult time understanding that the Earth does not wobble back and forth on its axis. The axis always points to the North Star, regardless of the time of year. What might you do to help learners grasp this point?

9. Suppose you were assigned to teach map and globe skills to a group of third graders. What would you use maps for? What would you use globes for?

10. Children in the elementary grades often greatly underestimate the size of the continent of Africa. What might you do to help them understand the size of this continent relative to the size of North America? Relative to the size of the United States?

EXTENDING UNDERSTANDING AND SKILL

1. For each of the eight basic map and globe skills, prepare a lesson directed at the age group you would like to teach. Discuss your suggestions with others in your class and with your instructor.

2. Interview four or five pupils who are at a grade level you would like to teach. Ask questions to determine the accuracy of their information about subjects such as (1) the relative locations of major U.S. cities, (2) the directions of flow of major U.S. rivers, and (3) the relative sizes of the continents. Share your findings with others in your class.

3. Look at two elementary social studies textbooks. Do a content analysis of each to determine how much attention is paid to developing pupils' understanding of the eight basic map and globe skills. Prepare a short paper in which you describe the relative attention paid to each skill.

4. Earth-sun relationships are difficult for many pupils to understand. With one or two other pupils, gather needed materials and prepare a lesson that you would use to

teach Earth-sun relationships to a grade level of your choice. Deliver the lesson to your class and solicit suggestions for its improvement.

5. Begin developing a file of different charts and graphs. Cut out different types of graphs that are used to display data. Be alert for examples of graphs that deliberately distort data. Construct another form of the graph so that you can use it to show pupils how different interpretations might be made using the same data but two different representations.

chapter 12

Planning Instruction

This chapter will help you to:

- ◆ define aims, goals, and learning intentions,
- ◆ describe relationships among aims, goals, and learning intentions,
- ◆ develop instructional units, and
- ◆ write lesson plans.

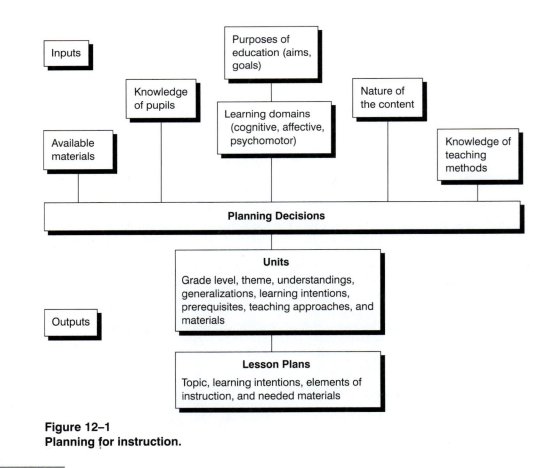

Figure 12–1
Planning for instruction.

Case Study

IT SEEMED LIKE A GOOD IDEA

Carlos Cortez is in his first year of teaching fifth graders. He has been trying to develop some imaginative social studies lessons. Several days ago, he decided that a simulation would be just the thing to get his pupils interested and involved.

At the beginning of the social studies period, he said, "Today we're going to do something different. I'm going to divide you into groups. I want people in each group to identify the name of an explorer and plan this person's trip to the New World. I want everyone to make a presentation to the class at the end of the week."

Carlos had barely gotten these words out when members of the class began shouting out questions:

"What happens if everybody wants to be the same explorer?"

"Do we have to do what the 'real' explorer did, or can we just make stuff up?"

"What if we don't want to be an explorer?"

"Exactly what are we supposed to present to the class?"

"We don't have enough information. When can we go to the library?"

"How come we're doing this, anyway?"

Carlos tried to answer the questions. Then he moved quickly to get members of the class organized into groups. That's when the real fun began. Problems started popping up all over the place. Carlos found himself racing from group to group to settle conflicts and answer questions. Some members of the class did nothing at all. They just sat and talked. It was unclear whether they were unwilling to get to work or were unaware of what they were supposed to be doing. The noise level rose higher and higher. What had seemed a splendid idea a day or two earlier was turning into a disaster.

What Is Your Response?

Take a few minutes to respond to these questions.

1. Why do you think Carlos's plans went awry?
2. What would you have done if you had been in his place?
3. How do you think members of the class felt about the new activity? Why?
4. Was the activity itself a poor choice, or might it potentially have merit?
5. How might better planning have helped Carlos? Specifically, what might he have done before initiating this lesson to increase its likelihood of success?

INTRODUCTION

Skilled professionals perform in ways that make their tasks seem effortless. An artist sitting at an easel creating a beautiful painting gives the appearance of doing something so easy that others may be tempted to pick up a brush and try. Most of us soon become frustrated when attempting tasks that pose few challenges for experts. Our mistake is one of judgment. We see only the public performance of someone who may have spent years perfecting a special ability. The halting, tentative, and not always successful early attempts of today's proficient performer usually were never put on public display.

People who observe skilled teachers often suppose that teaching is easy and that it is something anybody can do successfully. This is not true. Good teachers' performances have been honed by practice, and they are daily sharpened further by careful planning. The preparation that goes into a successful lesson is largely invisible to a casual observer. Novices often fail to grasp the importance of instructional planning because it cannot be seen.

At its heart, teaching is a decision-making process. The success individual teachers enjoy relates directly to the quality of their decisions. During a typical day, researchers have found, teachers make decisions about once every two minutes (Clark & Peterson, 1986). In addition to decisions they make about learning experiences, teachers also decide how to organize and pace content, how to respond to questions, how to react to pupils' behavior, and how to manage paperwork of all kinds.

Further adding to the complexity of the teacher's role is the complexity of the classroom setting. It is a public, multidimensional environment where many things are happening at the same time (Doyle, 1986). This complexity adds pressure to teachers that can cloud teachers' judgment and interfere with their ability to make good decisions.

To cope with these challenges, teachers need to take actions to reduce the unpredictability of the classroom. This can be achieved through good planning. Planning includes careful attention to the following:

- Characteristics of learners
- Nature of content to be taught
- Alternative teaching approaches available
- Availability of resources and materials
- Alternative ways to sequence presentation of material
- Ways to apply basic principles of teaching and learning

AIMS, GOALS, AND LEARNING INTENTIONS

Planning begins with consideration of purposes. Purposes focus on student learning. These vary in terms of their specificity. Many teachers use the following three levels of specificity and generality as they plan learning experiences for pupils in their classes:

- Aims
- Goals
- Learning intentions

Aims

Aims are broad statements that establish a general sense of direction for school programs. They include those general purposes that the public has established for the schools. For example, the public generally expects students who graduate from high school to be informed individuals who are familiar with responsibilities of adult citizenship.

Sometimes aims developed by educators are controversial. This happens because not everyone has the same views regarding the purposes of education. Debates often reflect a clash of philosophies. For example, some people think the primary mission of schools should be to prepare young people to assume vocational roles. They favor practical courses tied clearly to the world of work. Others feel the school's major mission is to transmit academic knowledge that may not necessarily have practical value in the workplace. Public discourse about the purpose of schools helps educators determine what society in general and the local community in particular expect of the schools. (See Figure 12–2.)

Though there are variations from place to place, the following aims for social studies are among those supported in large numbers of American communities (adapted from *History-Social Science Framework for California Public Schools,* 1987):

- Understand the basic principles of democracy.
- Understand what is required of citizens in a democracy.
- Develop social skills and skills of political participation.
- Solve problems and draw conclusions.
- Recognize the sanctity of life and the dignity of the individual.
- Recognize history as common memory.
- Understand world regions and their historical, cultural, economic, and political characteristics.
- Understand the basic economic problems facing all societies.

Goals

Goals are narrower statements of purpose than aims. They indicate specific directions for a given subject or grade level. For example, goals for third-grade social studies help iden-

---

Identify a grade level that interests you. Gather information from people, such as a teacher, a social studies supervisor, and your course instructor, who work at this grade level. You may also want to consult library resources in preparation for your response to these questions:

THINK ABOUT THIS

1. Is there content that your state requires to be taught at this grade level? If so, what are the state content requirements?
2. Are there local content requirements for this grade level? If so, what are they?
3. What topics seem to be typically treated in social studies lessons at this grade level?
4. How are topics typically sequenced throughout the year?
5. What are some ways in which these topics are often subdivided?
6. What important social studies goals can be addressed at this grade level?
7. What key social studies concepts can be taught at this grade level?

Figure 12–2
Mandated content and preplanning questions.

tify the specific material that should be taught at that grade to contribute to the general aim of *producing good citizens.*

Goals frequently are established at the school district level. School boards, curriculum committees, or even textbook selection committees may identify them. Goals often are printed in official school district curriculum guides. The following are examples of goals that might be adopted for the purposes of narrowing a broader aim and identifying more specific instructional responsibilities for teachers:

- Learn basic geographic features of the state.
- Know responsibilities of a citizen.
- Understand that history is an interpretation of past events.
- Grasp basic economic concepts including scarcity, specialization, trade, and economic interdependence.
- Explore relationships of people in homes and schools.
- Gather information from maps.
- Compare lifestyles of people living in different regions.
- Analyze contemporary events.

Goal statements help teachers define general responsibilities they have in working with lessons directed at a particular group of learners (first graders, second graders, and so forth). Goal statements, though, still are rather broad in scope. They must be further refined and made more specific as teacher planning goes forward. Goals represent a distant achievement. The stops along the way must also be considered. These stops include learning intentions.

Learning Intentions

Learning intentions boil down goal statements into a set of specific items a teacher expects a class to learn in a given unit of study. The focus is on what pupils are to learn, not on the activities they may experience or on what the teacher will do. For example, "Read the chapter on the westward movement" is an activity, not a learning intention. A learning intention related to this activity would be, "State some causes of the westward movement." This wording focuses on the new competence pupils should be able to demonstrate as a result of what they have been taught.

Teachers vary in how they write learning intentions. Some are satisfied with quite general statements that suggest little beyond the general kinds of information or skills they want their learners to acquire. Others prefer a format that specifies not only what pupils should be able to do as a result of their exposure to a given block of instruction but also describes kinds of tests they should take and levels of proficiency they should demonstrate when taking them.

Learning intentions suggest kinds of materials pupils need to encounter. In addition, they have implications for the time allotted to specific content. For example, if a learning intention requires pupils to demonstrate only low-level knowledge and comprehension, not as much instructional time will have to be committed as when there is a learning intention that will require them to engage in sophisticated and challenging analyses of complex information.

Learning intentions can also help teachers communicate with parents and others about their instructional intents. Much more is communicated about expectations when parents are told, "Pupils will be expected to state economic differences between the North and South that contributed to the outbreak of the conflict," than when they are simply advised, "The class will be reading about the Civil War."

Learning intentions are especially useful to teachers when they plan units of instruction and lessons for a particular group of learners. For example, in some classes, there are pupils who have limited proficiency in English. For these young people, the teacher might allow ways for demonstrating learning that do not rely heavily on their ability to read English. The teacher might ask them to draw an illustration or orally state a concept instead of taking a more traditional test that would require them to write definitions or match a concept with an appropriate definition.

Some examples of learning intentions for elementary social studies follow:

- Define the roles of different people in the community.
- Point out the regions in the state and describe them.
- State the basic ideas in the Declaration of Independence.
- Demonstrate respect for the opinions of others.
- Describe steps in a procedure that will lead to solution of a problem.
- Define some concepts associated with scarcity.
- Apply generalizations to new problems.
- State questions pertinent to solution of a problem.
- Distinguish between fact and opinion.
- On an essay test, identify at least three advantages and three disadvantages the British had at the time the Revolutionary War began.

INFORMATION NEEDED IN MAKING INSTRUCTIONAL PLANNING DECISIONS

Researchers who have studied instructional planning find that the activity gives teachers a mental picture of what to teach (Clark & Peterson, 1986). This picture often includes routines to be used in setting up and managing the classroom environment, key points to emphasize, the sequence of activities, and probable pupil responses to various parts of the instructional experience. The more detailed and accurate the image that results from planning, the higher the likelihood instruction will yield learning.

Good planning takes into account information from several distinct categories (Armstrong & Savage, 1998). Often the following categories are considered:

- Learners to be taught
- Pupils' expectations and experience
- Specific content to be introduced
- Alternative instructional approaches
- Available resource materials

Knowledge About Learners

Pupils in the schools today are diverse, representing a surprising range of interests, motivations, and abilities even in a single classroom. Knowledgeable teachers appreciate these differences. They plan in ways that will promote the likelihood that as many pupils as possible will learn the new content. Success in one learning task engenders self-confidence. It has few peers as a motivator. Hence, experienced teachers devote considerable time thinking about how their instruction can help each child learn the material.

Pupils' Expectations and Prior Experience

Pupils' personal expectations and prior experiences influence their academic performance. Young people who are confident of their abilities and who believe that learning the material is important react differently to instruction than pupils who lack these characteristics. This issue is particularly of concern in the social studies component of the elementary program. Many pupils, initially at least, do not think social studies content is either important or personally relevant. Because of past experience, some of them expect social studies learning to be boring.

Pupils' attitudes toward social studies are influenced by the kinds of social studies instruction they have received. Some learners may have experienced problems because of their exposure to instruction that failed to take into account their entry level of knowledge. It is imperative that planners not make unwarranted assumptions about what pupils already know. One of the authors once taught a group of pupils who had never seen an ocean. During a lesson, it became apparent that many in the class had the mistaken idea that a person could stand on a Pacific beach, look west, and clearly see the shores of Asia on the other side. Learners who start with misinformation of this magnitude are almost certain to experience difficulties grasping more sophisticated content—a situation with a high likelihood of producing failure, diminished levels of self-esteem, and low opinions of the social studies.

For a variety of reasons, some students have developed a negative view of social studies. This problem is sufficiently widespread that we need to plan all social studies instruction with care. In time, the cumulative effect of well-designed, interesting instruction that involves the learner and takes pupils' backgrounds into account can promote more positive attitudes.

Knowledge About Content

Instructional planning requires teachers to identify specific elements of content that pupils should learn. Listing general topics to be covered will not suffice. Careful plans deal with much more detailed information about key ideas and concepts that will be emphasized.

Knowledge of content to be taught requires more than identifying particular items of information. Lessons develop material in a sequential fashion. Therefore, teachers must think about how new material can best be sequenced to promote learning. Sequencing decisions require careful consideration of the characteristics of the pupils you will be teaching. The sequence of material provided in a textbook may not be appropriate. As a professional, you have an obligation to develop a plan that best responds to the needs of the young people who will be doing the learning.

Knowledge of Teaching Methods

Identifying the instructional approaches you will use is an important part of the planning process. Usually, you will incorporate several techniques within a given instructional sequence. This introduces a variety that can motivate and interest the learners. Also, certain learning intentions may be better served by some instructional techniques than by others.

In identifying specific techniques, consider the characteristics of the pupils, the potential of individual techniques to prompt their interest, the kinds of behaviors suggested by the learning intentions, and the specific nature of the content to be covered. A teacher thinking about preparing an instructional experience focusing on how a bill becomes law might engage in the following kind of thinking:

> Well, I could have them just read about it in the text, but I don't think so. That's pretty dull. Besides, some of these kids aren't good readers. Also, the stuff in the text doesn't give them much feel for the drama of argument and debate that's part of the legislative process. So, that's three strikes against that idea: (1) boring; (2) some of them can't do it; and (3) it will give them an incomplete idea of the process.
>
> Okay, then, how about a simulation? They'll probably like it. More opportunities for them to talk. They always like to talk. It will also give the slower ones a chance to pick up on ideas of some of the more able kids. Finally, it will get them actively involved in debates . . . a pretty good stand-in for the kind of thing legislators do. I think we'll do the simulation.

Knowledge About Available Resources

The kinds of available instructional-support resources strongly influence what teachers can do. As they plan, teachers must know what resources will be available. They need specific information about the availability of equipment (projectors, televisions, video-cassette players, computers, and so forth), appropriate instructional space (rooms with appropriate work spaces, rooms where specific equipment is located, and so forth), learning support resources for pupils (maps, globes, supplementary texts, library books, simulations games, and so forth), and, as needed, human resources (special outside speakers, school librarians, and so on).

Planning resources that teachers often use while designing instructional experiences include district-level social studies curriculum guides and state social studies program frameworks. These documents often provide guidance regarding what content should be taught at each grade level and how it might be sequenced. Sometimes these guides also provide lists of useful instructional support materials and suggestions regarding teaching techniques.

Planning instruction with teams of teachers is an excellent approach to professional development.

ORGANIZING PLANNING INFORMATION

Once you have gathered information about learners, content, alternative instructional techniques, and available resources, you must organize it into a plan of action. Whether this plan is prepared in a careful, formal written form or drafted as a sketchy outline is largely a function of experience. In general, less-experienced teachers benefit from committing more time to the process of organizing planning decisions in a formal way. This helps them to identify areas where more planning specificity is needed.

Instructional planning goes forward at several levels of specificity. More general, long-term planning often results in the preparation of unit plans. Planning focusing on shorter instructional periods takes the form of lesson plans.

Unit Plans

Teachers engage in both long-term and short-term planning. They may develop broad outlines of what they intend to do over an entire instructional year. Such extremely long-term plans need to be broken down into smaller segments that feature more specific information. A term often applied to plans that cover between approximately two and four weeks of instruction is *instructional unit.* An instructional unit describes an organizational scheme for the content to be taught and identifies teaching approaches to be used in introducing material to pupils.

Unit planning typically begins with a consideration of content that state or local authorities require at a given grade level. Once this high-priority, "must-be-included" information is identified, teachers go on to select additional content. In doing so, they weigh alternatives and consider questions such as the following:

- What social science concepts and generalizations relate to this topic?
- How can this topic be tied to pupils' personal goals and interests?
- What skills can be included?
- What values might be emphasized?

Instructional units function as building blocks of the elementary social studies program. It is from units that individual lessons are directed. Completed units also prompt thinking about how content in the social studies can be integrated with information in other subject areas. For example, social studies unit topics can suggest kinds of books pupils might be asked to read as part of their reading lessons. Often it is possible to tie experience from mathematics, science, music, and many other learning areas to content organized in social studies instructional units.

Instructional units must be planned in advance. Often, materials will need to be gathered and special arrangements made. For example, there may be a need to order videotape titles, to get approval for proposed field trips, and to obtain commitments from speakers. As a rough guideline, it is a good idea to plan an instructional unit at least a month before teaching lessons related to it.

Units may be formatted in many ways. Good formats make clear relationships among learning intentions, teaching approaches, and needed materials. Figure 12–3 displays a format that many teachers have found useful.

In planning a unit, teachers must develop specific information about each of the following:

- The grade level for which the unit is intended
- Topic or theme of the unit
- Elements associated with a high-quality social studies program
- Descriptions of opportunities to integrate content
- Identification of prerequisite knowledge
- Specification of learning intentions
- Unit organizational scheme
- Suggested teaching approaches
- Ideas for assessing learners
- Criteria for reviewing the unit

Identifying the Grade Level

Specification of the grade level gives potential unit users important information about the target audience for the described instructional program. Identification of the intended grade level early in unit development serves to remind the developer to keep the proposed instructional program appropriate for learners in the specified grade.

Identifying a Topic or Theme

The topic or theme helps delimit content to be introduced. Good topic titles describe the unit's contents clearly. For example, a title such as, "Family Life in Revolutionary America," provides a better picture of the kind of content to be emphasized in a unit than a less precise alternative, such as "Interesting Happenings in Revolutionary Days."

| Unit Title: |
| Grade Level: |
| Social Science Understandings Emphasized: |
| Citizenship Understandings Emphasized: |
| Problem-Solving Opportunities: |
| Content Integration Possibilities: |
| Prerequisite Knowledge and Skill: |
| Focus Generalization(s): |

Learning Intentions	Teaching Approaches	Materials
Unit Initiation		
Unit Development 1. 2. 3. etc.		
Unit Culmination		

Evaluation Procedures:

Figure 12–3
A format for unit planning.

Including Features Associated with High-Quality Social Studies Programs
Units should include elements that build pupils' understandings in the areas of social science and history, citizenship, and problem solving. To ensure that attention is given to each of these three critical areas, developers consider questions such as the following:

- What will be the citizenship outcomes? What knowledge, skills, values, and decision-making opportunities associated with citizenship will be included?

- What will be the history and/or social science outcomes? What generalizations, concepts, values, skills, and decision-making opportunities associated with history and/or the social sciences will be emphasized?
- What problem-solving opportunities will be provided?

Opportunities to Integrate Content

Social studies instruction can provide an excellent focus for integrating learning from many school subjects. To take advantage of these possibilities, experienced unit developers think about how content from reading, mathematics, science, language arts, music, art, and physical education can be woven into new units.

Identification of Prerequisite Knowledge

Individuals who develop instructional units begin with certain assumptions about pupils who will be taught unit content. Since people other than those who develop instructional units often use them, it is important that assumptions about these pupils be made explicit. This information can help a potential teacher decide whether the unit content might be appropriate for the particular class.

Learning Intentions

As noted earlier in the chapter, learning intentions are succinct statements that specify what pupils will be able to do as evidence that they have mastered unit content. Including learning intentions in unit plans helps teachers keep a clear focus on key instructional priorities.

Learning intentions need to be arranged in an appropriate sequence. Those listed first should identify content introduced at the beginning of the unit. They may tie closely to initial learning activities that are designed to prompt pupils' interest in the general content of the unit. Subsequent learning intentions will focus on the main body of content. The final learning intentions will be broad in scope and will refer to pupils' behaviors, calling on pupils to synthesize, apply, and extend content introduced throughout the unit.

The Organizational Scheme

Units need to be organized so that relationships among their parts are clear. The organizational plan illustrated in Figure 12–3 is one that functions well. An outline or other general unit organizational plan need not be long. Often, three or four pages will suffice. You can keep in a file specific information you will need when teaching unit content (assignments, pictures, artifacts, outline maps, and so forth) and bring it out for use at appropriate times.

Suggested Teaching Approaches

Developers do not need to specify ideas for teaching unit content in instructional units. Teachers will do this when planning individual lessons. What is needed in units is brief ideas that will help teachers as they begin thinking about alternative teaching approaches. The following example is appropriate for use in an instructional unit:

> Role-play the decision to move west by assigning pupils to different roles such as a father, a mother, a sick child, and an elderly grandfather. Discuss the perspective of each of these people. As a class, discuss how each might feel if the family makes a final decision to move west.

This overview indicates the general kind of teaching activity the unit developer has in mind. It leaves specific details regarding introducing the activity, assigning roles, specifying appropriate behavior standards, debriefing questions, and other details to the teacher who will be planning lessons based on the unit.

Sometimes, suggestions for teaching approaches included in unit plans mention needed instructional materials. These might include such things as titles of specific books, names of films, descriptions of maps, and other support resources.

Identifying Assessment Ideas

In this part of the unit plan, developers provide ideas about how to gather and evaluate information related to pupil learning. There may be suggestions recommending the use of approaches including checklists, project critiques, portfolios containing a broad sampling of pupils' work, and formal testing techniques. These ideas are provided as suggestions. Teachers should consider these and other alternatives when unit instruction begins and they prepare specific lesson plans.

Criteria for Reviewing the Unit

When preparing units, it is useful to develop important quality for criteria. These can be used as a quality check before teaching the unit for the first time and can be applied more or less continuously throughout the unit. This kind of systematic and ongoing review is consistent with the idea that units "are never done." They are always being reviewed and revised for the purpose of making them better. Typical quality-check questions include the following:

- Is the whole range of social studies outcomes included?
- Is the material in the unit sequenced logically?
- Is content appropriate for the pupils who will be asked to learn it?
- Are suggested teaching approaches the best that can be devised? Are these approaches consistent with behaviors referred to in the learning intentions?
- Are assessment procedures as good as they can be?

Figure 12–4 presents an entire sample unit plan embodying the characteristics discussed in this chapter.

Lesson Plans

Short-term planning results in the creation of lesson plans, which outline what the teacher and pupils will do during specific lessons. Sometimes these plans cover more than one day. Usually, though, teachers tend to develop plans for what they wish to accomplish during a single day.

The level of detail in individual lesson plans varies. Inexperienced teachers often need to do more detailed planning than teachers who have had many years of successful classroom experience. A rule of thumb is that a lesson plan should include enough detail that a substitute teacher could implement the intended lesson without much difficulty.

Grade Level: 2
Unit Theme: Knowing My Family and Myself

SOCIAL SCIENCE UNDERSTANDINGS

Pupils should begin to acquire several social science and history understandings. They can begin to develop an understanding of change and continuity through the investigation of how their family has changed and how some aspects have remained the same throughout generations. They can begin to develop a simple understanding of the historical approach by gathering data through interviewing others.

Plotting the movement of families can help them begin to understand geographic concepts such as movement, location, and differences between places. An emphasis on sociological concepts such as role, norms, values, and interdependence should be included as the roles of different family members are compared. Economic concepts such as wants, needs, division of labor, money, and employment can be developed as pupils discuss reasons why families might move.

CITIZENSHIP UNDERSTANDINGS

Citizenship understandings can be developed as each pupil realizes that each person in the family has responsibilities to the family. The place of rules and authority in families can also help pupils begin to realize the importance of rules in an orderly society. An appreciation of diversity can be enhanced by making public the wide variety of families in the classroom and the diverse backgrounds of the pupils. Pupils can develop a sense of pride and identity as they explore their cultural and ethnic heritage.

PROBLEM-SOLVING UNDERSTANDINGS

Pupils can begin to learn problem-solving and conflict-resolution approaches as they identify problems and conflicts that individuals have in families. They need to learn the importance of compromise and of taking others into account as they resolve conflicts.

CONTENT INTEGRATION

There are numerous opportunities for content integration in the unit. Reading can be integrated by reading selections of literature that deal with families in different contexts. Numerous opportunities for writing are available as pupils write about their families, write about favorite family events that they remember, and write letters to family members such as grandmothers or aunts. Math can be integrated through counting and adding extended family members. Each family unit can be characterized as a *set*. Music can be integrated by bringing in music that is representative of different eras. Pupils can make some crafts or toys that might have been made or used by grandparents as one way of integrating art. The whole class can put together a quilt or mosaic, with each pupil drawing a picture of his or her family. If these pictures are drawn on heavy paper, they can be taped together to make a mosaic.

HOPED-FOR PREREQUISITE KNOWLEDGE AND SKILL

[Not all pupils will have these characteristics. Instructional approaches must be sufficiently flexible to accommodate special learning needs of individual children.]

- Ability to write simple sentences
- Basic understanding of a map of the world
- Beginning understanding of time and chronology
- Knowledge of such terms as *family, parent, grandparent,* etc.

Figure 12–4
Sample unit.

Unit Outline

Focus Generalizations

- Similarities and differences are to be found among all families.
- Family members are some of the most important people on whom we depend.
- Although families change over time, many practices and traditions related to families continue.

Learning Intentions	Teaching Approaches	Resources
Unit Initiation Identify similarities and differences.	Read selections from the books *Family Pictures* and *Shades of LA: Pictures from Ethnic Family Albums.* Ask pupils how these situations are similar to and different from their families. Ask pupils to identify questions on what they would like to know about different families. List and keep the questions as a reference to use during unit development. Inform pupils that they are going to be studying families, both their own and others from around the world.	Garza, Carmen Lomas, *Family Pictures* (San Francisco, Children's Book Press, 1993). Cole, Carolyn Kozo, and Kathy Kobayashi (eds)., *Shades of LA: Pictures from Ethnic Family Albums* (New York: New Press, 1996). Large piece of chart paper or overhead transparency
Unit Development Define terms.	Introduce the term *ancestors*. Ask if anyone knows what it means. Define the term, provide examples, and share personal examples.	Pictures of families now and long ago. Pictures of individuals from years past.
Locate places on a map.	Send letter home to parents at beginning of unit. Have them identify their ethnic heritage and countries of origin for both mother's and father's side of family. Return this on a 3 × 5-inch card. Introduce a map of the world and point out main features. Choose a few pupils and mark the origin of their ancestors. During the day the others can identify country of origin on a map.	World map, stickers, cards from parents on family origins.
Identify problems. Estimate distances. Construct a grid to help find places on a map.	Review map of the world. Show pupils how to use a simple grid system to locate places on a map. Have a few people identify location of countries when given grid coordinates.	World map, paper for each group to write problems.

Figure 12–4
Sample unit (continued).

Learning Intentions	Teaching Approaches	Resources
	Have pupils estimate which families had to move the greatest distances to get to the local community. Break into small groups and have each group identify problems they think their ancestors might have experienced in moving.	
Construct a graph. Interpret relationships on a graph.	Present own family tree. Discuss various branches of the family tree. Have pupils construct their own family tree. Pose these questions: "What does a family tree tell us about families? Why is this type of chart useful?"	Construction paper, markers, pupil photographs
Identify cause-and-effect relationships.	Discuss some of the reasons immigrants came to America and the problems they faced. List causes for moving under one column and the problems and benefits under another.	Immigrant stories, chart paper with columns labeled *cause* and *effects*.
Gather data through listening.	Invite a parent or grandparent who immigrated to the United States to talk to the class about his or her experience. Have class members identify how the story is like those they have already learned about.	Guest speaker
Identify change and continuity in family customs.	Have pupils interview family members about customs and practices when they were young. In a group session, identify a selection of practices. Have them identify which customs and practices are the same today and which are different. Ask the class, "Why do you think some things stay the same and some things change?" Play and view CD-ROM.	Interview sheets for pupils to take to interview family members CD-ROM: "Seasons and Holidays Around the World"
Identify roles and responsibilities of various family members.	Ask pupils to identify the different jobs people in their family have. List parents, children, etc. Ask, "How are these responsibilities different in different families? Why do you think they are different? What happens if someone doesn't do his or her job?"	

Figure 12–4
Sample unit (continued).

Learning Intentions	Teaching Approaches	Resources
Compare roles and responsibilities of families in different parts of the world.	Show a videotape of a family from another part of the world. Have the class identify the roles and responsibilities of various family members and compare them with those of class members.	Videotape of families around the world
Apply problem solving and conflict resolution.	Have the class share problems that often occur in families. In groups, have class members state how they think these problems might be solved. Discuss how rules might be developed to prevent some problems.	
Culminating Activity Integrate what they have learned from the unit.	Have each class member, together with members of his or her family, develop a picture album of family members doing things together. (The book *Family Pictures* could be used as an example.)	Instruction sheets to go home, construction paper to go home, book: *Family Pictures*
Working together in groups.	Divide the class into work groups to share and discuss the pictures they have developed and begin gluing or taping them to a classroom mosaic or quilt.	Large piece of paper for each group; glue or tape
Review of important ideas. Formulation of generalizations.	After all of the sections of the mosaic have been joined together, review some of the illustrations. Ask class members: "What have we learned in our study of families? What kinds of things can we now say about families?" Review the questions that were identified at the beginning of the unit to see how many of the questions were answered.	Completed classroom mosaic

EVALUATION PROCEDURES

1. Keep a checklist of the participation of individuals and groups on all assignments.
2. Have pupils keep individual portfolios that include information about interviews they have conducted, copies of the stories they have written, copies of pictures they have drawn, and all assignments they have completed. Use contents of the portfolios as a database for making judgments about individual pupils' progress.

Figure 12–4
Sample unit (concluded).

Lesson plans often feature the following categories of information:

- Learning intentions
- Teaching approaches
- Organizing and managing learners
- Adapting instruction to meet needs of special pupils

Learning Intentions

All lessons should focus on a specific learning intention. Some lessons may have more than one. In addition to establishing a focus on what pupils should do as a result of the lesson, the learning intention also provides guidance regarding what kinds of learning materials should be used and what kinds of teaching approaches might be appropriate.

Teaching Approaches

Decisions about instructional approaches reflect the following considerations:

- Entry point for instruction
- Motivating learners
- Procedures to inform pupils about learning intentions and to establish a learning set
- Alternative ways to present lesson content

Determining the Entry Point for Instruction   Identification of an appropriate beginning point for teaching a lesson requires thought about the pupils who will be taught. If they are to succeed, pupils must have certain prerequisite skills and knowledge. The entry point should be selected to help them see connections between what they already know and the new information.

Motivating Learners   Successful lessons prompt and maintain pupils' interest. Planning for motivation requires more than attention to an interesting lesson beginning. It needs to take into consideration specific things you might do to periodically reinforce pupils' motivation throughout the entire time a given lesson is taught. Teachers respond to the following basic questions in planning for motivation:

- How can I gain pupils' attention so they will see a need to learn the content of this lesson?
- What can be done at various places in the lesson to maintain their interest?
- What can I do at the end of the lesson to make sure pupils feel successful and to help them maintain their interest in the subject?

Informing Pupils About the Learning Intention and Establishing a Learning Set   Pupils need to know what is expected of them. For this reason, it is important for the teacher to explain lesson learning intentions to them in language that they can understand. They also need a frame of reference, or *learning set*, to orient them to the new content. This provides a context that will help them to fit new information into what they already know. Often a simple sentence or two can be used to communicate information about both learning intentions and learning sets. Consider this example: "Remember how we have been learning about people in the community who can help us. After today's lesson you'll be able to tell me how a letter carrier, the person who delivers the mail, knows where to deliver letters."

Alternative Ways of Presenting Content   Presentation of new information is the heart of a lesson. Procedures selected for doing this bear directly on what pupils will learn, retain, and transfer to new situations. Decisions about which teaching approaches to use depend on the learning intention of the lesson, the nature of the content, the characteristics of learners in the class, the availability of instructional support materials, and the teacher's experience and skill.

Basic instructional principles guide teachers as they decide how to best transmit content to a specific group of pupils. For example, new content is more likely to be learned when pupils recognize its relationship to what they already know.

Teachers must also consider the time required for a given approach. Attention spans of pupils, particularly those in the primary grades, are short. Successful lessons respond to this reality by including a variety of activities within a single lesson. Learners also retain content better when they process it actively. They need opportunities to see, hear, discuss, and, most important, to apply what they have learned. The needs for variety and active involvement can be accommodated when teachers vary teaching approaches to include such alternatives as reading, demonstration, questioning, modeling, role playing, simulations, and work in cooperative learning groups.

Many teaching approaches require the teacher to make verbal presentations to the class. When this is done, it is important for the teachers' comments to be concise, logically organized, and free from vague and ambiguous terms. Point-to-point transitions must be clear and logical.

Few people remember detailed information the first time that they hear it. Therefore, good lessons feature some *planned redundancy.* This means that teaching methods incorporate opportunities at different points in the lesson for pupils to encounter important content in various examples and activities.

Pacing the lesson should be fairly brisk, but slow enough to allow most of the pupils to achieve success. It is particularly important to allow enough time for practice and application activities. These help pupils to solidify their grasp of new content. Figure 12–5 presents a sample lesson plan designed as discussed in this section.

Organizing and Managing Learners

Some teaching approaches require a change in seating arrangements or in space available for teachers and pupils to walk. When planning lessons, teachers must consider problems in spatial arrangements that might be caused by requirements of specific lessons (e.g., learning centers taking up space ordinarily used for other purposes). This is particularly true when pupils will be required to move from one area to another at some point during the lesson. Unless the room is organized to facilitate quick and easy movement and specific directions are developed that will communicate clearly to pupils what they are to do, important instructional time will be lost.

Lesson Topic _____ Unit Theme _____ Lesson Plan No. _____

Learning Intention(s) _____

_____

_____

New Vocabulary or Concepts _____

_____

Time Allocation	Lesson Sequence	Materials
	Lesson Introduction: Gain attention Stimulate pupil interest Establish learning set Inform pupils of learning intention(s)	
	Presentation of Material: Logical organization Questions Examples/models Checks for understanding Elicit examples of desired behaviors/provide feedback	
	Application/Practice: Guided practice/monitor pupil work Provide corrective feedback Allow for independent practice	
	Lesson Conclusion: Review key ideas Reinforce success Build bridge to next lesson	

Ideas for Adapting Instruction to Respond to Circumstances of Pupils with Special Needs: _____

_____

_____

Teacher Evaluation of Lesson Effectiveness: _____

_____

_____

Figure 12–5
Sample lesson plan format.

Adapting Instruction to Meet Needs of Special Pupils

Today's classrooms enroll a diverse population of young people. Some pupils have special needs that cannot be accommodated by instructional approaches that may be well suited to large numbers of their classmates. For example, in classes you teach, you may well have learners for whom English is a second language and who need help with language-based activities that pose few challenges for native speakers. There may also be pupils who are characterized by various degrees of speech impairment, visual impairment, hearing impairment, mental retardation, learning disability, emotional instability, and other physical and health impairments. Lesson plans need to include some ideas for providing meaningful instruction to individuals in the group whose circumstances demand teaching approaches that differ from those that are appropriate for pupils without these special conditions.

WEB CHECK

Note: Electronic addresses of sites on the World Wide Web change frequently. If the listed URL fails to work, use a standard search engine to locate the new address of the site.

- AskERIC Lesson Plans

  URL—http://ericir.syr.edu/Virtual/Lessons/

  This site provides an extensive array of lesson plans that are organized by major school subjects, including social studies. The provided lesson plans are eminently detailed. In addition, there are links to other Web addresses that feature additional lesson plans. Highly recommended.

- Discovery Channel School

  URL—http://school.discovery.com/

  At this address you will find instructional ideas that tie into programming offered on the Discovery Channel. These are labeled *Classroom Activities*, and they range across a broad array of social-studies-related topics.

- CHCP Golden Legacy Curriculum

  URL—http://ericir.syr.edu.projects/CHCP/

  Material available at this site relates to various topics in Chinese history. Materials are detailed. There is a particular set of materials relating to the former practice of binding women's feet.

- Lesson Plans Library

  URL—http://ed.info.apple.com/education/techlearn/lessonmenu.html

  This site includes links to lesson plans prepared by the Apple K–12 education program that are organized according to their appropriateness for (1) elementary schools, (2) middle schools, and (3) high schools. Within these three major divisions, school subjects including social studies and the organization of lesson plans are discussed.

- Crossroads: A K–16 American History Curriculum

  URL—http://ericir.syr.edu/Virtual/Lessons/crossroads/

  This site includes a variety of elementary social studies materials related to United States history. Materials are divided into sections focusing on elementary schools, middle schools, and high schools.

- NEPTUNES WEB—Oceanography Lesson Plans for Social Studies

  URL—http: www.cnmoc.navy.mil/educate/neptune/lesson/social/social.htm

  At this Web address you will find some interesting lessons prepared under the direction of the Naval Meteorology and Oceanography Command. Some of these lessons are particularly useful for integrating content from science and social studies. Ocean postcards, ocean Morse code, time zones, and migration patterns of the leatherback sea turtle are some of the intriguing offerings available at this site.

- Lesson Plans for the Professional Cartoonists' Index

  URL—http://www.cagle.com/teacher/elementary/lessonplanES1.html

  At this site you will find lesson plans tied to editorial cartoons. In addition to well-developed lesson plans, you have an opportunity to select from a large number of current editorial cartoons. These cartoons provide a focus for the learning activities. Highly recommended.

- CNN Newsroom

  URL—http://cnn.com/CNN/Programs/CNNnewsroom/daily/

  This site provides classroom activity guides to daily programming on CNN. It is possible, too, to select previous calendar dates and retrieve stories and related lesson plans.

- Classroom Materials

  URL—http://www.historychannel.com/class/teach/teach.html

  At this Web address, you will find lessons that tie to programs offered on the History Channel. Topics covered are wide-ranging. For a number of them, related videotapes can be ordered.

KEY IDEAS IN SUMMARY

1. Competent instructional planning is a hallmark of a professional teacher. During the planning process, the teacher establishes priorities for instruction, identifies needed learning materials, considers organizational issues, and makes decisions related to evaluating pupils and programs.

2. Instructional planning begins with a consideration of aims and goals. Aims are broad statements of purpose that describe what society expects of the schools. Goals are related to aims but are much more specific statements. They point out specific directions for people planning instruction for particular subjects and grade levels.

3. Learning intentions focus teacher attention on what pupils should be able to do as a consequence of their exposure to instruction. They are useful to planners of instructional units and lesson plans. They convey to other interested parties the purpose or intent of provided instruction.

4. As they prepare to make instructional decisions, teachers need information related to (1) the pupils to be taught, (2) the content to be presented, (3) alternative instructional methods, and (4) available resources.

5. Long-term planning often results in the development of instructional units. A typical unit organizes instruction for a three- to four-week period of time. Short-term planning often culminates in the development of lesson plans.

6. Lesson plans break down unit plans in more detail. They describe how teachers will meet broader purposes outlined in instructional units. Many lesson plans cover only a single day's instruction. Some lesson plans describe activities that will occur over several days. Among other things, lesson plans provide suggestions about how needs of pupils with special needs will be met.

CHAPTER REFLECTIONS

Directions: Now that you have read this chapter, reread the case study at the beginning. Then, answer these questions:

1. How would you now diagnose the problems Carlos had with his lesson?

2. What planning elements might have helped him avoid the problems?

3. Do you think advance planning would have interfered with his creativity, or would this kind of planning have enhanced it?

4. Describe learning outcomes that might have been included in the unit to which the lesson was related.

5. Suppose you were hired to teach social studies in a district with no social studies curriculum guides. How would you begin to plan your social studies program?

6. Pupils in elementary classrooms have diverse needs. Which need do you feel least capable of accommodating? What might you do to prepare yourself to respond to them more confidently?

7. Educators frequently discuss the issue of motivation. Some people argue that today's pupils are less motivated to do schoolwork than pupils were in the past. Do you agree or disagree? Why or why not?

EXTENDING UNDERSTANDING AND SKILL

1. For a grade level you would like to teach, identify a theme and plan a unit around this theme. Include learning intentions and a selection of different teaching approaches.

2. Write at least two lesson plans for the unit you developed. Describe how parts of your proposed lessons respond to specific content and pupils' specific needs.

3. Motivation should occur not only at the beginning of a lesson but at intermediate points and at the end as well. Describe places in each of your lessons where you will take specific actions to motivate learners.

4. Teach a group of peers a social studies lesson lasting 5 to 10 minutes. Ask them to critique your introduction, your sequencing of activities, and your actions to check for understanding.

5. Describe how you would adapt one of the two lessons you developed in question 2 to respond to the needs of pupils with each of these characteristics:

   • Hearing-challenged

   • Visually challenged

   • Attention deficit

   • Physically challenged

   • Gifted and talented

REFERENCES

ARMSTRONG, D., AND SAVAGE, T. (1998). *Teaching in the secondary school* (4th ed.). Upper Saddle River, NJ: Merrill/Prentice Hall.

CLARK, C., AND PETERSON, P. (1986). Teachers' thought processes. In M. Wittrock (Ed.), *Handbook of research on teaching,* (3rd ed., pp. 255–296). Englewood Cliffs, NJ: Merrill/Prentice Hall.

DOYLE, W. (1986). Classroom organization and management. In M. Wittrock (Ed.), *Handbook of research on teaching* (3rd ed., pp. 392–431). Englewood Cliffs, NJ: Merrill/Prentice Hall.

GARZA, C. L. (1993). *Family pictures.* San Francisco: Children's Book Press.

History–social science framework for California public schools: Kindergarten through grade twelve. (1987). Sacramento, CA: California State Department of Education.

chapter 13

Assessing Learning

This chapter will help you to:

- recognize key features of evaluation,
- describe authentic evaluation,
- explain challenges facing individuals who would like to see more authentic evaluation in the schools,
- suggest how portfolios might be used in authentic assessment programs,
- describe procedures for using informal evaluation techniques,
- point out the strengths and weaknesses of selected formal evaluation techniques,
- explain how evaluation data can be used to assess an instructional program's effectiveness, and
- identify some sites on the World Wide Web that have information of interest to educators who want to broaden their understanding of assessment of pupil learning.

Authentic evaluation	Informal evaluation	Formal evaluation
— Seeks to assess learner behaviors that try to parallel how proficient adults use content in the world beyond the school — Challenges teachers by identifying ways in which learners should demonstrate behaviors and establishing appropriate levels of proficiency	— Teacher observation — Teacher-pupil discussion — Pupil-produced tests — My favorite idea — Headlines — Newspaper articles — Word pairs — Alphabet review game — Mystery word scramble — Anagrams	— Rating scales — Learning checklists — Attitude inventories — Essay tests — True/false tests — Multiple-choice tests — Matching tests — Completion tests

In addition to providing information relating to individual pupil progress, evaluation results also provide insights that are useful for assessing the overall effectiveness of instruction. This information helps teachers as they reflect on what they have done. It helps them identify needed modifications in their teaching approaches.

Figure 13–1
Assessing learning.

Case Study

IF TESTING TAKES TOO MUCH TIME NOW, WON'T "BETTER" FORMS OF TESTING MAKE MATTERS EVEN WORSE?

Phillipa Grandjo, who has taught seventh graders for many years at Miles Standish Middle School, serves as her school's representative on the district's Central Social Studies Curriculum Council. She made these comments recently at a council meeting when the issue of evaluation came up:

> As I look back over my 20 years teaching in this district, I'm struck by how much more time we are asked to spend testing learners today compared with when I started. We have standardized tests. We have some the district has devised. And, in response to some parental concerns, we have even developed a testing program in our social studies department at Miles Standish so we can gather information about content areas that are of particular interest to our own faculty.
>
> All of this testing business takes time—too much time, I think. Every time we stop teaching to administer a test, we deprive people in our classes of opportunities to engage new content. I know that we need to stop to take stock of what our people are learning, but I don't think we need to spend nearly so much time testing.
>
> I'm particularly concerned about all this talk about "authentic assessment." I applaud the intent to develop ways to assess learners that really require them to do the kinds of the things we are attempting to teach them.
>
> For example, if one of our purposes in our social studies lessons is to help our young people develop a clear-headed argument in support of a position, an evaluation that requires us to listen to them do so either orally or in writing makes sense. We certainly shouldn't be administering something like a true/false test and, on the basis of how well a youngster does, making some kind of an inference about his or her logical reasoning powers. That requires a tremendous leap of faith—one that I think goes way beyond what results of a true/false test can tell us.
>
> But the alternative, more "authentic," procedure—I mean the oral exam or essay that calls upon pupils to lay out their logical thought processes—requires an incredible amount of time to administer. It will take even more time away from what we have available to teach new content.
>
> We seem to be caught in a dilemma. Many of us feel that testing already takes too much time. Kinds of tests that don't take too much time to administer, for example true/false and multiple-choice tests, often don't tie closely to kinds of learning we really want to emphasize. But more "authentic" tests will add even more time to the already excessive hours devoted to testing. All of this is very confusing, and I'm not sure what the answer is.

What Is Your Response?

Read over this teacher's comments. Then, respond briefly to these questions:

1. Ms. Grandjo suggests that teachers today spend more time testing learners than they did in previous years. What forces may have led to this change?

2. If teachers are spending more time testing than they used to, is this good or bad? Why do you think so?

3. What does Ms. Grandjo imply that good "authentic" tests can do that are beyond the capability of many more traditional types of teacher-made tests, for example, true/false and multiple-choice tests?

4. Is it possible to develop a testing program that would be authentic but that would not consume excessive amounts of class time? Support your response.

5. How do you suppose other members of the district's Central Social Studies Curriculum Council reacted to Ms. Grandjo's concerns? Why do you think so?

INTRODUCTION

To begin the evaluation process, we must gather information of some kind about pupil performance. Many options are available to us as we consider this task. Today there is increasing interest in using *authentic* measures. These require pupils to engage in sophisticated demonstrations of what they have learned. They are designed to encourage development of thinking and performance skills that are similar in many ways to those characterizing proficient adults. Other, more traditional, assessments often feature the use of informal techniques (relatively open-ended exercises that can be completed successfully by pupils who have mastered the relevant content) or formal techniques (typically structured examinations that feature multiple-choice, true/false, matching, completion, and essay items). Once we have gathered the data, we move on to make judgments about the adequacy of pupils' performances based on these results and on whatever special personal knowledge we have about the young people we teach.

All assessment approaches require us to gather information about pupils before making any judgment about their performance. In this chapter, we introduce authentic assessment approaches and informal and formal data-gathering techniques.

AUTHENTIC ASSESSMENT

All of us have probably heard someone say that "teachers shouldn't teach to the test." The logic behind this view is that most tests sample too narrow a range of what pupils need to know. This problem has been widely recognized by people who support authentic assessment. *Authentic assessment,* also referred to as *performance assessment* (Stiggins, 1994), seeks to provide pupils opportunities to demonstrate what they have learned. That is, they are encouraged to put new knowledge to work in ways that are as similar as possible to how this information is used by proficient adults. Let's consider an example.

Imagine you are teaching social studies to a group of sixth graders. As part of your program, you decide to supplement the regular program on world areas and cultures with lessons focusing on issues facing the local community. Suppose a local zoning board is considering whether a company should be allowed to locate a new plant in an open area bordering a residential neighborhood. Some people in the community are excited about the new plant and the jobs it will bring. Others fear that it will ruin the adjacent residential neighborhood and produce environmental damage.

In a traditional class, we might assign pupils to gather information about contending positions and organize activities such as debates, discussions, and brainstorming sessions to get pupils actively involved in a consideration of these issues. Assessment probably would take the form of an essay item or a series of objective test questions (true/false, multiple-choice, and so forth). Since we're interested in authentic assessment, we will do something different. We might require pupils to give testimony at a simulated hearing of a zoning board. Actual zoning board members or, at least, knowledgeable adults from the community, can be brought in to hear pupils' testimony. We would tell members of our class to organize arguments using the best evidence they can find. They might also be required to turn in a written summary of their position to the person playing the role of chairperson of the zoning board. Evaluation of individuals in this kind of a situation is based on what they are able to demonstrate in a setting that replicates many features of the world beyond the school.

Authentic assessment encourages complex pupil performance and is thought to encourage the development of sophisticated thinking (Wiggins, 1989). This feature differentiates the approach from more traditional testing approaches, for example, multiple-choice tests, which were consistent with a learning theory called *behaviorism* that assumes complex learning is built on small bits of information (such as those assessed by individual multiple-choice items). This view of learning places less emphasis on the context within which pupils learn new material and on how their prior experiences help shape new content as they are learning it (Herman, 1997).

Authentic assessment flows logically out of a *cognitive* orientation to learning. This view emphasizes the context within which new content is learned. It focuses on the interaction between pupils and new material and on a production by learners that evidences their ability to demonstrate new learning in ways that have relevance not just within the school setting but in the world beyond the school. Assessment specialist Joan Herman (1997; p. 9) comments, ". . . the presence or absence of discrete bits of information . . . is not of primary importance in the assessment of meaningful learning. Instead, what is highly valued is how and whether students organize, structure, and use that information in context to solve complex problems." Supporters of this approach believe that it can lead to a significant and relevant emphasis on learning (Spady, 1994). If this is true, pupils' motivation may well be enhanced because their learning tasks bear a real connection to what they see adults doing every day.

Problems in Implementing Authentic Assessment

Though solid logic supports the idea of authentic evaluation, implementing this approach poses certain difficulties. Spady (1994), an expert who has worked with programs featuring authentic evaluation, made these comments about one key challenge: "Reformers from coast to coast agree that measures other than student grades and Carnegie units must be used for determining student and district achievement. But what outcomes *are* and what kinds should be expected . . . are still disputed."

Assessing pupils through observations of their performance is an example of authentic assessment.

In a nutshell, while many people agree that pupils should be expected to demonstrate in sophisticated ways what they have learned, there is by no means widespread agreement as to what form these demonstrations should take or regarding criteria to apply in judging their adequacy. How authentic assessment procedures should be designed, how much money should be committed to their development, and what should be done to ensure that they do not discriminate against certain groups are all issues that continue to be debated in the field (Baker, 1994).

Concerns have also been raised about the long-term effects of an authentic assessment program on teachers' instructional practices. Will teachers limit their instruction to focus exclusively on what students will be required to do on authentic assessment exercises? If this happens, will pupils (supported by their parents) figure out what kinds of behaviors "count" and simply master them for the purpose of scoring well on the tests rather than mastering them in a way that will result in persistent learning? Clear answers to these questions are not yet available.

There are worries, too, that while a good authentic assessment procedure may provide admirable information about a learner's ability to do a *specific* task, the evidence is less clear about how this ability will generalize to different situations. One of the goals of education has always been to assist learners to apply what they have mastered in their lessons to settings outside the school. It is hoped that authentic evaluation approaches will facilitate this transition. However, as is the case with more traditional tests, it is not always clear that assessing proficiency on one real problem necessarily adequately measures a learner's ability to solve a related but somewhat different challenge.

The difficulty is compounded because authentic assessment is relatively time-consuming. As contrasted to a true/false or multiple-choice examination, where several dozen questions covering a broad cross section of content can be included on a single test, an authentic assessment exercise ordinarily allows learners to respond to a much smaller number of questions. Hence, a question arises as to whether the content sampling is truly representative of what has been learned and whether it provides a good indication of learners' mastery of areas of content that are not formally assessed (Herman, 1997).

Long-standing tradition also represents a challenge to those favoring more use of authentic assessment procedures. Parents and other community members have memories of school days featuring essays, short-answer quizzes, and lots of tests with true/false and multiple-choice items. They also are used to seeing grades awarded, according to pupils' performances on these kinds of exams. Authentic assessment represents a departure from these familiar procedures. Because even its supporters admit that there remains much debate about what should go into a high-quality authentic assessment program, some parents and other people in the community are reluctant to support efforts to move away from more traditional evaluation practices.

Another issue has to do with the cost of authentic assessment. Estimates of the cost vary widely, but some work has been done that compares costs of traditional multiple-choice testing of students with authentic assessments. It has been reported that the cost of preparing, administering, and grading hands-on authentic assessment tests is 400 to 500 percent higher than preparing, administering, and grading more traditional multiple-choice tests (Herman, 1997). This cost differential probably ensures that schools will opt for a middle ground that encourages teachers to use both authentic assessment and more traditional kinds of testing in their instructional programs.

By way of summary, it is fair to say that interest in authentic assessment is high. Support for the idea of requiring learners to engage in sophisticated demonstrations of learning continues to grow. Researchers are hard at work on issues associated with establishing quality standards for a variety of authentic assessment approaches (see, for example, Stiggins, 1994). For an example of how authentic assessment might be applied to a social studies assignment, see Figure 13–2.

Portfolios

Many elementary teachers are beginning to use learner portfolios to gather together evidence used in making judgments about pupils' progress. A *portfolio* is a collection of pupil work that covers a specific period of time. Those who like portfolios as part of their authentic instruction and evaluation scheme argue that they provide a way to make evaluation an integral part of the instructional process. Ideally, portfolios are not just a static collection of what pupils have done. Rather, they provide opportunities for learners to organize a sample of their work, write reflective comments in their portfolios as they consider what they have done, and engage in written exchanges with their teacher about their progress and about content issues that interest and concern them. Portfolios provide a developmental profile of learners from the beginning to the end of the school year. Some schools pass them from teacher to teacher. This process allows for a cumulative growth record that spans many years of an individual learner's development.

This example was developed for use in a fourth-grade class. The focus of social studies at this grade level in this state (as in many others) is state history. Look over the following authentic assessment exercise. Think about how it differs from the kinds of things you remember being asked to do as evidence of learning when you were in elementary school.

A STORY BASED ON OUR STATE'S HISTORY

Our state today is different from what it was 50 years ago. Think about some things that have changed. Pick out one thing that is different. Here are some ideas of things that may have changed:

- Schools
- What we eat
- How we spend free time
- How towns and neighborhoods look
- How we get from place to place

Tomorrow, we will be bringing some older people to class. They are people in their 60s, 70s, and 80s. All have lived in our state for many years. Each of you will have a chance to interview these people about the subject you choose. For example, if you choose "changes in schools," you can ask these people about what schools were like when they were children. What did the buildings look like? What were classrooms like? What did people wear? What did they study? What kinds of books did they use? Did they have libraries? These are the kinds of questions a person interested in "changes in the schools" might ask. I want you to write down the ideas you get from these visitors.

On the day after tomorrow, we'll write papers, one to two pages. Each of our papers will tell a story. The story will be about how our subject has changed. A person who chooses "changes in the schools" as a topic, for example, will write a story called, "How Schools Have Changed Over the Past 50 Years." As you prepare to write your papers, I want you to think about two major ideas that might explain why these changes have happened. Then, I want you to develop at least two questions related to each idea. Think about possible answers to these questions and about how these answers might help explain the changes. Before we start writing the papers, I'll give you some examples of what I hope you will do. In your paper, I want to see your ideas, the questions you asked about each, and your conclusions.

Everyone also will have a chance to make an oral report. This will give all of us a chance to learn what you have learned. You will report on the same information included in your paper.

EVALUATION GUIDELINES FOR THE TEACHER

In looking over each pupil's paper, consider whether the pupil did the following:

- Listed two ideas to explain the change
- Developed two questions for each idea
- Used information gathered from talking with the older visitors in responding to the questions
- Included information that suggested an ability to distinguish between fact and opinion
- Based conclusions on evidence that she or he gathered
- Prepared arguments using logical, point-by-point development in both the paper and the oral presentation

Figure 13–2
An authentic assessment assignment.

Portfolios can be configured in many ways. Among features that are often included are:

- Assignments pupils have finished
- Written comments by pupils about content they have learned (or about other relevant issues)
- Written comments by pupils that include their thoughts about and reactions to discussions, speakers, and other instructional events
- Prompt questions written in the portfolio by the teacher
- Written responses by the pupil to the teacher's prompt questions
- Pasted-in materials such as photos, sketches, short articles, drawings, and maps
- Summary statements regarding what has been learned
- Self-evaluation statements regarding parts of the content the pupil now thinks he or she knows well and parts of the content he or she continues to find difficult to understand

These guidelines must be modified so they make sense given the age and sophistication of levels of pupils in a classroom. For example, if you are working with very young children, you might develop a format for portfolios that would include samples of work, anecdotal records, checklists or inventories of important behaviors, responses of pupils to certain questions and requests, and results of screening tests (Grace, 1992). This approach would provide an age-appropriate vehicle for gathering and monitoring information about the development of each child in the classroom.

Portfolio assessment takes time. One recent study found that teachers were committing about 17 hours a month to work with learner portfolios (Herman, 1997). This number would seem high if the only function of the portfolio were to evaluate pupils. However, portfolios function not only as a database for making judgments about learners' progress, but also as an integral part of the instructional program. Hence, teachers who use them believe that the benefits to learners justify the time portfolios require.

INFORMAL EVALUATION

More traditional evaluation often relies on information obtained through use of *informal* techniques. These feature teacher observation of a variety of pupil performances. We use results to identify behavior patterns that suggest whether a child has mastered a given skill or cognitive understanding. Sometimes these pupil responses cannot easily be graded right or wrong. Sometimes, too, informal evaluation sheds light on pupils' attitudes.

Informal evaluation often can be accomplished quickly. For example, if we want to know whether a given pupil can get along with others (an important social skill), casual observation of the pupil's behavior in class and on the playground is usually sufficient. There is no need for a sophisticated test. A simple, dated notation can record the information ("Marta played well at recess and got along well with others in class today, 10/18/98").

Recently, a prospective kindergarten teacher made these comments:

All the kindergarten teachers I've talked to say they spend too much time keeping records. They tell me they feel they must write down "everything" about every child. It seems to me this is a big waste of time. It has to take valuable time away from working with children. Also, I think a really good kindergarten teacher should know the children so well as individuals that there is no need for a formal written record. I mean, if a youngster is slow to learn colors or something else, the teacher should know. I can't understand why so many kindergarten teachers waste so much time on record keeping.

THINK ABOUT THIS

1. If many kindergarten teachers spend a great deal of time on record keeping, why do they do so?
2. Is time spent on record keeping wasted? Explain your view.
3. How might a kindergarten teacher react to this person's comments?
4. If you were to discuss this matter with this person, what would you say?

Figure 13–3
"I don't think good kindergarten teachers need records."

Informal evaluation is nonthreatening and provides information about pupils' "natural" behavior patterns. This is true because much of it takes place without pupils' being aware that it is happening. This is a far different situation from that facing learners confronted with a formal test. Though informal evaluation is used throughout the elementary social studies program, it is used more frequently by teachers of younger elementary school pupils than by teachers of fourth, fifth, and sixth graders. One reason for this is that very young pupils lack the reading and writing skills needed to take formal tests, so their teachers must rely more on informal procedures. Additionally, the social studies program in the early grades is heavily oriented toward developing basic skills and helping pupils to get along well with others. These skills and behaviors are often more easily assessed informally.

Certain cautions must be observed in using informal evaluation techniques. Because these techniques require us to make inferences about pupils based on observing their natural behaviors, sufficient observations must be made to provide a sound basis for judgment.

Additionally, we need a systematic scheme for recording information. Because classes often include large numbers of pupils and because many different kinds of things happen each day, we sometimes find it hard to recall important behaviors of individual pupils. We need a record-keeping scheme that prompts us to take notes about individual behavior patterns close to the time of their occurrence. When we keep careful records and make multiple observations, informal evaluation can provide useful information about each pupil's progress (see Figure 13–3). The subsections that follow introduce common informal evaluation procedures.

Teacher Observation

Teacher observation of pupils is an important informal evaluation tool. Some aims of the elementary social studies program can be assessed in no other way, such as those related to general attitudes and to interpersonal relations skills. For example, "work cooperatively with others" is an objective for kindergarten pupils found in many school districts' social studies curriculum. Obviously, a written test cannot determine how well children have mastered this objective. We must observe children directly to effectively evaluate how well they get along with each other.

Informal evaluation often prompts us to give specific directions to an individual pupil about an attitude, a skill, a desired interpersonal relations behavior, or an item of academic content. Good teacher observation looks for specific behaviors (being polite when others are speaking, sharing, and so forth). We should maintain a brief written record of pupils who are experiencing specific problems so we may note both progress and continuing areas of difficulty.

Teacher-Pupil Discussion

Personal discussions with individual pupils often provide us with insights. These conversations may reveal much about their attitudes, interests, and understandings. Discussions also help us to test the accuracy of our perceptions about how individual learners are feeling and about how well they are mastering social studies content.

There are obvious problems with this approach, however. Time constraints make it difficult to have long discussions with each pupil (Ebel & Frisbie, 1986). Hence, it is not possible to sample individual pupils' learning in this way with a great deal of frequency. Because of this limitation, we have to supplement this approach with other procedures.

Pupil-Produced Tests

This technique is applicable primarily to learners in grades four, five, and six. By the time pupils have progressed this far in school, they typically have taken dozens of teacher-prepared tests and are quite familiar with the common formats of basic test types, such as true/false and multiple-choice.

Many teachers find that having pupils develop their own test items covering studied content provides useful information about what they have learned. Typically, learners focus on what they perceive to have been most important. From this focus, we can determine what pupils have learned from a particular body of content and can identify individuals who have developed mistaken impressions and who need additional work with the material. To make the exercise credible, many teachers incorporate a few pupil-generated items on a subsequently scheduled examination.

My Favorite Idea

A space on the chalkboard or a large sheet of butcher paper is needed for this exercise. To begin, invite pupils to write their "favorite social studies idea" in this space once or twice each week. As a preparation for this activity, provide examples of the kinds of things that pupils might write. ("I would *hate* to have my feet bound like they used to do to girls in China." "I think men here should be forced to wear pigtails like they used to wear in China.") Children should be encouraged to write about whatever has engaged their interest. To personalize the activity, you can ask children to sign their names after their comments.

This exercise yields insights about the kinds of information and attitudes pupils are taking away from social studies lessons. You will often learn things that are worth including in the records kept on individual class members. The technique also provides benefits for learners. It motivates them to think more seriously about their social studies lessons, knowing they will be asked to contribute a "favorite idea."

Headlines

One measure of learning is the ability to summarize accurately. If summaries are accurate, then teachers have grounds for concluding that pupils grasp essential features of the material on which the summary is based. You can test pupils' ability to summarize by asking them to write or state orally possible headlines for newspaper articles about current study topics. Written headlines can be displayed on butcher paper, a bulletin board, or a chalkboard.

Pupil-produced headlines give teachers basic information about how well each learner grasps a subject's essential features. Comments derived from examining each child's headline can be noted in a grade book, on a progress chart, or in some other appropriate manner. Additionally, a review of all of the headlines produced by the class can pinpoint any widespread misconceptions. These can be addressed in follow-up work.

Newspaper Articles

With learners in grades four, five, and six, expand the headline activity to include actually writing a short related newspaper article. To prepare for this activity, introduce pupils to basic formats for newspaper articles and give them guidelines concerning length and kinds of information to include. The content of the articles provides a great deal of evidence about each pupil's level of understanding and can identify learners who need additional help. When a large number of children appear confused about certain issues, the class as a whole can be involved in a clarifying discussion.

Some teachers find it useful to "publish" some of the best articles, distributing them to all class members (and perhaps to other classes), to the principal, and to parents. Copies may be displayed on a bulletin board in the class or in a display area in the hall. The possibility of becoming a "published journalist" is an incentive that motivates pupils to do good work.

Word Pairs

In a word-pairs assessment activity, present pupils with a set of cards on which single words have been written, and ask them to find pairs of cards that go together. Check each learner's work and ask why the child thinks cards in each selected pair are associated. Help individuals who are having difficulty, and maintain records of each pupil's performance. When many learners are making a similar mistake, deal with the issue with the whole class. Conclude the activity with a discussion to reinforce appropriate relationships between words in each correct pair.

As an example, a word-pairs activity focusing on naming leaders and what they lead might use cards, each containing one of the following words:

President	State
Classroom	Teacher
United States	City
Mayor	Governor

We give each learner a complete set of eight cards and ask that these cards be arranged in appropriate pairs. The completed pairs should look like this:

President—United States

Governor—State

Mayor—City

Teacher—Classroom

Alphabet Review Game

The alphabet review game can be used to assess either individuals or groups of learners. This simple exercise provides pupils with a review of basic alphabetizing skills and at the same time reviews currently studied material.

Lead a class discussion to decide what information from the current lesson is the most important. Then, ask learners to find as many important terms as they can that begin with each letter of the alphabet. Pupils are instructed to skip a letter if they cannot find any important terms that begin with it. (For example, relatively few important terms begin with "X.") Set a limit to the time spent on each letter, usually 3 or 4 minutes.

This exercise can be done by pupils working alone or in groups. When groups are used, each group works together to find terms beginning with each letter. Walk around the room to monitor each pupil or group. Often it is desirable to keep records of each learner's progress. As a follow-up activity, lists for each letter can be shared, and pupils can review the meanings of the terms.

Mystery Word Scramble

The mystery word scramble takes advantage of children's love of puzzles. Typically, the exercise focuses on previously introduced key terms. Letters in these terms are scrambled. A definition of the unscrambled term is provided. Pupils look at the definition and try to decide what the word is. As an added feature, you may circle one space in the blanks provided for pupils to copy the correct term. When all terms have been properly unscrambled, the circled letters will spell out a *mystery word*, usually another important social studies term.

Pupils like mystery word scrambles. The exercise provides a way for the teacher to learn about pupils' understanding in a format that minimizes their anxiety. If many learners have

Directions (Answers Are Provided in Parentheses)

The words at the left are real words, but the letters have been mixed up. Arrange the letters to form the correct word. Write the word in the spaces provided. The definition at the right of each mixed-up word will help you decide what the word should be.

tedolingu   Imaginary lines on a globe used to measure   __ __ __ ◯ __ __ __ __ __
            distances east and west   (longitude)

uteltaid   Imaginary lines on a globe used to measure   ◯ __ __ __ __ __ __ __
            distances north and south   (latitude)

reqtuoa   An imaginary line around the globe that   __ __ __ __ __ ◯ __
            separates the northern and southern   (equator)
            hemispheres

mabroteer   A device for measuring air pressure   ◯ __ __ __ __ __ __ __
            on the Earth's surface   (barometer)

hehepsimer A term that means "one half of the   __ __ __ __ __ __ __ __ ◯ __
            Earth's surface"   (hemisphere)

Mystery Word Directions

One letter in each of the above words is circled. Together, these letters form the mystery word. Write the letters in the blanks provided below. The mystery word is defined to the left of the blanks.

__ __ __ __ __   A term used to describe a model of the earth (globe)

Figure 13–4
Sample mystery word scramble exercise.

problems identifying the same terms, these can be featured in a follow-up class discussion. You can easily keep track of each learner's success in identifying the appropriate terms. A sample format for a mystery word scramble is provided in Figure 13–4.

Anagrams

Anagrams are words created by rearranging letters of other words. For example, the word *opus* can be made by using all of the letters of the word *soup*. Anagrams can be used as a means of informal assessment by presenting the exercise to pupils as a puzzle. Many pupils will participate completely unaware that their performance is being observed.

In setting up an anagram exercise, you usually provide the original term plus a definition of another term that can be made using the letters of the original term. Next, encourage pupils to look at the definition and to think of a word that fits it and that uses

---

Directions

Look at the words in capital letters. Then look at the definition. The definition describes a different word from the one at the left, but this new word uses all the letters in the word to the left. Write this new word in the blank provided at the end of the definition.

LEAK   A large body of fresh water completely surrounded by land. _ _ _ _ (lake)

MASTER   A body of running water, such as a river or a brook. _ _ _ _ _ _ (stream)

FURS   The name given to the waves of the sea as they crash on the shore. _ _ _ _ (surf)

DIET   The twice-a-day rising and falling of the level of the ocean. _ _ _ _ (tide)

SALE   The sea animal with flippers that lives along rocky coasts. _ _ _ _ (seal)

LOOP   A small and rather deep body of water. _ _ _ _ (pool)

ALIENS   This refers to something, such as seawater, that contains salt. _ _ _ _ _ _ (saline)

Figure 13–5
Sample anagrams exercise.

all of the letters of the original term. The new terms should relate to content that has been recently studied. Pupil performance on the anagram exercise gives the teacher some indication of how well individual learners have mastered basic terminology.

An example of an anagram exercise for pupils who have recently studied bodies of water and marine life is provided in Figure 13–5.

Other Informal Techniques

These informal observation techniques are only a sample of the many that we can use. Among other techniques are sorting activities of all kinds, which help pupils recognize major categories and items that belong within each category. Some teachers may ask groups of learners to debate issues. The positions introduced during the debates reveal the depth of understanding of individual participants. Crossword puzzles, hidden-word puzzles (puzzles where words are disguised in a seemingly random array of letters), and other puzzles and games are widely used. "What I Learned" diaries are favored by some teachers. The list of possibilities goes on and on.

The decision to use a given procedure should depend on whether, for the specific classroom and circumstances, the answer to this question is "yes": "Will this procedure provide sufficient information for me to judge any given pupil's performance?"

Record Keeping and Informal Evaluation

Informal evaluation techniques generate much useful information. Good record keeping helps teachers make maximum use of this information. There are many ways to record data on pupil performance.

Observing students working in pairs helps a teacher assess cooperative learning and prosocial behavior.

Secondary school teachers often rely exclusively on a grade book to record information about learners' progress. This scheme does not work as well in elementary classrooms. The informal evaluation procedures widely used with younger learners do not lend themselves well to a record reflecting either a numerical score or a letter grade. Instead, much information about pupils is of a "can or cannot" or a "yes or no" nature. For example, one aim of many kindergarten programs is for pupils to know the name of their school and town. The child either does or does not know these facts.

To keep track of pupils' progress in elementary social studies classrooms, many teachers use *daily performance progress checklists.* (Despite the name, teachers do not always update these records daily. Depending on individual circumstances, several times a week may suffice.) These easy-to-use sheets allow the teacher to note quickly how each learner is faring on a limited number of focus competencies. These checklists can be tailored to fit content, and specific notations can be modified to accommodate the needs of the teacher. To record such information, the procedures must allow for frequent observation of small increments of learning that cannot necessarily be described in terms of numerical scores or letter grades. Some teachers find it convenient simply to note whether a pupil has (1) mastered the competency, (2) partially mastered the competency, or (3) not mastered even a part of the competency.

Figure 13–6 illustrates an example of such a daily performance progress checklist. A daily performance record such as shown in the figure is easy to use. It provides a measure of each learner's performance on every area emphasized during a day's lesson. Col-

Kindergarten—Mr. Bianca:
Daily Performance Progress Checklist

Today's Date: _____

Focus Skills

Pupil's Name	Identifies Relative Location (Near, Far)	Recites the Pledge of Allegiance	Names the Days of the Week
Brenda	+	+	+
Erik	+	−	w
Gretchen	−	−	w
Howard	−	w	+
Juan	+	+	+
Karen	+	w	−
Lawrence	w	w	w
Adela	+	+	+
Paul	+	w	w

Key: + The pupil has mastered this competency.
        w The pupil has partially mastered this competency, but more work is needed.
        − The pupil has not even partially mastered this competency.

Figure 13–6
Sample daily performance progress checklist.

lectively, this information can indicate areas of strength and weakness as they exist within the class as a whole.

Periodically, teachers enter this daily information into a cumulative record. A cumulative record form typically includes all grade-level competencies. It summarizes what has been observed about an individual child over time. An example of a social studies cumulative record form for kindergarten is provided in Figure 13–7.

FORMAL EVALUATION

Formal evaluation procedures include teacher-prepared tests and standardized tests. When informal assessment techniques are used, pupils often do not know they are being evaluated. With formal evaluation techniques, learners almost always are aware that they are being tested. As a result, pupils' anxiety is often higher during formal evaluations.

Many kinds of tests qualify as formal assessment instruments. Subsections that follow introduce several that often are prepared by elementary social studies teachers.

Because youngsters in the early elementary grades do not take as many formal examinations (multiple-choice, true/false, and so forth) as do older pupils, it is not practical to keep records in a grade book where little provision is made except for noting numerical scores and letter grades. Though grades will have to be given to youngsters (at least in most school districts), the documentation of young pupils' work is often accomplished more conveniently using a cumulative record form.

A separate cumulative record form is kept for each pupil. Often, these are kept in individual file folders. Periodically, the teacher reviews the information taken from observations of daily performance. (See the daily performance record referenced in the section "Record Keeping and Informal Evaluation.") The teacher typically notes on the cumulative record form those competencies a child has mastered. These forms provide data that can be used to compile information to share with parents during parent-teacher conferences and in formal progress reports from the school.

Formats of cumulative records vary. The following example typifies what you might find in a form designed to show the progress of a pupil in kindergarten-level social studies.

Cumulative Record: Social Studies—Kindergarten

Pupil's Name: _____

Directions

Place a check mark in the blank before each competency the pupil has mastered. Also note the date the check mark was entered.

Area I: History–Social Science—Knowledge, Skills, Values

Check Mark	*Date*	
_____	_____	Understands term *basic needs*
_____	_____	Tells how families meet basic needs
_____	_____	Identifies property as his/hers/mine/ours/yours
_____	_____	Defines *work* and *play*
_____	_____	Names self, school, community
_____	_____	Identifies basic time concepts (minute, hour, day)
_____	_____	Names the days of the week
_____	_____	Identifies relative locations (near, far)
_____	_____	Identifies relative size (large, small)
_____	_____	Identifies basic directions (right, left; up, down)
_____	_____	Identifies safety symbols
_____	_____	Identifies simple road signs
_____	_____	Explains what is meant by *change* and cites examples
_____	_____	Identifies contents of photographs and paintings
_____	_____	Makes inferences from pictures
_____	_____	Notes sequences in multipart events (first, second, and so forth)
_____	_____	Accepts others' right to their own opinions
_____	_____	Identifies major national and state holidays
_____	_____	Recognizes flags of the nation and state
_____	_____	Describes alternative solutions to problems

Figure 13–7
Sample social studies cumulative record form for kindergarten.

Area II: Citizenship-Personal Education—Knowledge, Skills, Values

Check Mark	Date	
_____	_____	Identifies and states reasons for classroom and school rules
_____	_____	Explains consequences of breaking rules
_____	_____	Begins tasks promptly and stays on tasks until they are completed
_____	_____	Volunteers to participate in discussions
_____	_____	Behaves in a way reflecting a grasp of right and wrong behavior
_____	_____	Works cooperatively with others
_____	_____	Participates in group decision making
_____	_____	Demonstrates courteous behavior
_____	_____	Accepts leadership of others when asked to do so
_____	_____	Assumes leadership when asked to do so
_____	_____	Accepts basic idea of accepting decisions of the majority
_____	_____	Listens when others are talking
_____	_____	Takes turns willingly

Figure 13–7 (continued)
Sample social studies cumulative record form for kindergarten.

Rating Scales

Frequently we need to assess learning outcomes beyond those that can be tested using forced-choice examinations such as multiple-choice or true/false tests. For example, some learning objectives may call on pupils to give brief oral summaries of positions, to build models, or to increase their frequency of participation in class discussions. A rating scale can provide information about learners' proficiency in these areas.

Rating-scale preparation begins with identifying a set of focus characteristics. The rater makes judgments about a given pupil's relative proficiency by circling or otherwise marking a point on the scale. The points on a good rating scale refer to specifically defined pupil behaviors. Some rating scales are deficient in this regard. For example, suppose we were interested in the degree to which individual pupils volunteered information during class discussion. A poorly designed rating scale to gather this information is depicted in Figure 13–8.

The rating scale in Figure 13–8 provides an illusion of specificity, but it fails to indicate exactly what each rating point means. As a result, two raters who observed a given pupil might award the learner quite different ratings. In the language of test-design specialists, this rating scale lacks *reliability* (the ability to produce consistent results when applied to similar situations). A better, more reliable rating scale would be one that more specifically identifies meaning of each rating point. Note the specific improvements in the rating scale shown in Figure 13–9.

The ratings in Figure 13–9 are scaled in such a way that two or more raters observing the same pupil would be quite likely to award the learner the same rating. A reliable rating scale can contribute much good information about important categories of pupil behavior.

Figure 13–8
A rating scale with poorly defined rating points.

Circle the appropriate number for each item. The numbers represent the following:

5 = outstanding
4 = above average
3 = average
2 = below average
1 = unsatisfactory

How would you assess this pupil's willingness to volunteer to speak during classroom discussions?

5   4   3   2   1

Circle the appropriate number for each item. The numbers represent the values indicated.

5 = volunteers on 80–100 percent of the occasions when he or she is invited to do so
4 = volunteers on 60–79 percent of the occasions when he or she is invited to do so
3 = volunteers on 40–59 percent of the occasions when he or she is invited to do so
2 = volunteers on 20–39 percent of the occasions when he or she is invited to do so
1 = volunteers on 0–19 percent of the occasions when he or she is invited to do so

How often does this pupil volunteer to participate in classroom discussions?

5   4   3   2   1

Figure 13–9
A rating scale with clearly defined rating points.

Learning Checklists

Checklists share with rating scales the characteristic of measuring behaviors that are not easily assessed through written tests. Learning checklists depend on the teacher's ability to see and record information about behaviors of interest.

Checklists are not as flexible as rating scales, which may offer a continuum that includes many rating points. For instance, the examples in Figures 13–8 and 13–9 allow a user to select one of five rating points. Most checklists, on the other hand, are designed to note only the presence or absence of a given behavior. This is not necessarily a limitation; sometimes "yes" or "no" or "present" or "absent" is all we need.

Measurement specialists Gronlund and Linn (1990) have identified checklist guidelines. The following list draws upon their work:

	Yes	No
Name of pupil: _____		
Distinguishes between *county* and *country.*		
Distinguishes between *county* and *continent.*		
Distinguishes between *country* and *continent.*		
Confuses country and *county,* but not *country* and *continent.*		
Confuses country and *continent,* but not *country* and *county.*		

Figure 13–10
Learning checklist.

- Identify and describe each desired pupil behavior as specifically as possible.
- Add to this list the most common incorrect, or error, behaviors.
- Arrange the list of desired behaviors and incorrect, or error, behaviors in the approximate order one might expect to see them.
- Develop a simple procedure for checking each action as it occurs.

Suppose you were interested in how individual pupils were grasping the distinctions among the concepts *county, country,* and *continent.* (Many learners confuse these concepts.) By listening to pupils' oral comments or by having short interviews with several class members, you could determine how learners were faring with this task, and could record this information about each pupil on a checklist. A sample checklist is shown in Figure 13–10.

All of the checklists, when completed, would provide information not only about each child but also about any misunderstandings that may be widespread throughout the class. This information would tell us to highlight certain points during class discussions.

Attitude Inventories

Not all assessment is directed at obtaining measures of pupils' cognitive achievement. There are times when teachers are interested in learners' attitudes. In such cases, they often use attitude inventories to provide this information.

Attitude inventories call on learners to rate their relative interest in subjects or topics. They are presented with a list of alternatives. Directions tell them to indicate their preferences in rank order. If there are six items, they will indicate their first- through sixth-place preference.

Figure 13–11
An example of an attitude inventory.

Topic: Interest in School Subjects

Directions: Listed below are some of the subjects you will study this year. Look at each. Place a number "1" in the blank before the subject that interests you most. Place a number "2" in the blank in front of your next favorite subject. Continue in this way until you finish with a number "5" in front of the subject you like least.

_____ mathematics
_____ reading
_____ science
_____ social studies
_____ physical education

Suppose you found that at the beginning of the school year members of your class were not particularly looking forward to their social studies lessons. You might try to develop more positive reactions to this part of the school program by involving them in interesting social studies activities throughout the school year. To test the success of your effort, give the inventory on different occasions. Pupils would take it first at the beginning of the year and then again some months later, after they had been exposed to lessons designed to enhance their interest in social studies. A sample attitude inventory is depicted in Figure 13–11.

Many pupils may rank their interest in the social studies program as relatively low when they first complete the attitude inventory. Our hope is that they will rank it higher relative to other subjects later in the year, after they have been exposed to lessons designed to prompt their interest. A higher average rating for the social studies on the second inventory would tell us that our plan to improve learners' attitudes is succeeding.

Essay Tests

Essay tests are much more common in the upper grades than in the middle and lower grades. Few essay tests are used at all with primary-grade learners, who lack the writing skills needed to respond properly. These skills are quite rudimentary even in middle-grade pupils.

Though not appropriate for all elementary learners, essay tests do have a place in the overall school social studies program. Quite apart from their function as an indicator of pupils' academic learning, they contribute to fluency with the written language. With respect to content, essay tests allow learners to assemble bits of information into meaningful wholes (see Figure 13–12).

Essay tests are well suited for such purposes as determining pupils' ability to interpret, compare and contrast, and generalize about given information. Essays help to test more sophisticated kinds of pupil thinking. On the other hand, when assessment focuses on less sophisticated thinking skills (recall of specific names and places, for example), other kinds of tests, including true/false, multiple-choice, and matching, are more appropriate.

The following comments appeared on the editorial page of a local newspaper.

Young people today are poorer writers than they were 50 years ago. Why? It surely cannot be said that our children are not as smart. The explanation is simple. Schoolchildren are no longer compelled to write essays.

Today we have schools filled with electronic scoring devices that encourage teachers to give more and more multiple-choice and true/false tests. These devices doubtless save time. However, they also discourage teachers from giving essay exams that, even today, must be graded by hand. The result is that children are not asked to do much writing, and many of them never learn how.

Mastery of the written language is a hallmark of educated adults. We support the adoption of a school policy that requires elementary teachers to give only essay examinations after grade three. This step may appear radical. However, given the lamentable decline in writing skills, it is one we should take.

THINK ABOUT THIS

1. What problems for teachers would result from adoption of this proposal?
2. What other causes for a decline in pupils' writing proficiency might you suggest, other than the increasing use of objective tests in schools?
3. Would teachers at some grade levels find implementing this proposal more difficult than teachers at other grade levels?
4. If you were asked to respond to the writer of this editorial, what would you say?

Figure 13–12
Needed: More essay tests.

Guidelines for preparing good essay items follow:

- Write a question that focuses on a specific and somewhat limited content area. Essays take time to compose. Not too much content can be covered in the time available for pupils to respond.
- Write questions that encourage pupils to include examples and specific details. Note the differences between items (a) and (b).
  a. What are differences between the northern and southern hemispheres?
  b. Discuss the weather and seasons in the northern and southern hemispheres. State the differences in (1) the months of the year when summer occurs and (2) the months of the year when winter occurs. Also, (3) tell what the relative position of the Earth and sun have to do with these differences.
- Give pupils specific instruction about how much they are expected to write. Usually length is best explained in terms of numbers of paragraphs desired. Even upper-grade learners may have trouble writing a full page on a given question.

Correcting essay items can pose problems. More is involved than simply comparing a pupil's response with answers in a key, as with multiple-choice or true/false tests. While it is more difficult to score essays reliably, certain procedures can make such grading more consistent.

First, we can prepare a sample response to each essay question. This procedure often will reveal potential problems with the language used in the question itself. Our completed response will also identify major points we will want to look for while grading pupil responses. Some teachers list these points separately after they have written their sample responses.

Inexperienced teachers often read one pupil's answers to all questions before going on to the next learner's paper. It is better to read every learner's response to one question at a time. This is desirable because different standards tend to be applied to different questions. If all answers to a given question are read together, there is a better chance that we will apply the same grading standard to each pupil.

Sometimes, the order in which we read essays will make a difference in how we grade them. For example, we may become frustrated when the same mistake appears on paper after paper. Unconsciously, we may grade the papers read later more harshly than those graded earlier. To guard against this possibility, it is wise to read responses several times (when this is practical) and to shuffle the papers so the order is changed with each reading.

Results of essay exams sometimes reveal that expectations for pupils have been set too high. If a review of all answers reveals that many students have missed critical material, this may indicate that they need more instructional time. Grading criteria occasionally have to be adjusted so learners are not punished for not knowing material that the whole class needs to work on.

True/False Tests

True/false tests are widely used in elementary schools. Individual questions can be prepared quickly. Pupils have little difficulty learning how to take them. Because learners can respond to a large number of questions in a limited time, a single true/false test can cover much content. The tests can be corrected quickly. Many schools have machines that electronically score them, provided that learners mark responses on special answer sheets.

Because true/false tests depend on absolute judgments (that is, the answer must actually be *true* or *false* and not something in between), we have to be careful to avoid oversimplifying complex issues.

For example, suppose we asked pupils to respond "true" or "false" to this statement: *The sun set yesterday.* Quite likely our expectation is that learners will respond "true." However, the statement really represents an irresponsible distortion of a complex issue. True, the sun did *appear* to set yesterday, but it did not actually move at all. What happened was that the Earth turned, and, to someone on the Earth, the sun seemed to set.

True/false tests also have been accused of encouraging guessing rather than learning. Critics argue that as a result pupils will sometimes get a higher score than they deserve. Measurement specialists doubt that this is terribly serious, stating that pupils are as likely to guess wrong as to guess right. Overall, guessing is unlikely to raise the score of a pupil who does not know the content.

The following are guidelines for preparing true/false tests:

- Avoid giving unintentional clues. These include use of words such as *all, no,* and *never,* which tend to prompt the answer *false.*
- Approximately half of the questions should be false. True statements are easier to construct. Learners who guess tend to mark *true* more frequently than *false.*
- Every statement should be clearly true or false. "The Yankees are the best baseball team" and similar subjective statements are not appropriate for a true/false test.
- Avoid double negatives in statements. "It is never undesirable to drink milk for breakfast," is a confusing double-negative statement. "Drinking milk for breakfast is recommended by a majority of health authorities," is much less confusing.

When learners' answers are not recorded on electronic scoring sheets, several options are available. Some teachers provide a blank in front of each statement. When providing blanks, we should not allow pupils to enter T for "true" or F for "false." Their printing of these letters sometimes results in a hybrid form halfway between T and F, and we don't know whether the pupil really means to indicate *true* or *false.* We may suspect that the pupil does not know, either.

One remedy for this problem is to require pupils to write out the words *true* and *false.* Some teachers tell pupils to use a + sign for "true" and a 0 for "false." An even better solution is to print the words *true* and *false* to the left of each statement, then direct learners to simply circle their choice.

Better true/false tests probe for understanding. Some of the best require pupils to look at several pieces of information at the same time and to answer related questions. For example, true/false tests can be used to assess pupils' ability to grasp information presented in graphs, tables, and charts. An example of a true/false test that directs learners' attention to a table of information is presented in Figure 13–13.

Multiple-choice Tests

Multiple-choice tests have several advantages. Unlike true/false tests, which give learners only two answer choices, multiple-choice tests provide three, four, or even five options. As a result, they can test pupils' ability to recognize degrees of "correctness." Though the length of individual questions is typically longer than in true/false tests, multiple-choice questions still do not require a great deal of time to complete. Consequently, a given multiple-choice test can cover a fairly large body of content.

Multiple-choice tests reduce the chance that a learner will get a high score as a result of guessing. This is true because there are many more answer options than in true/false tests. As with true/false tests, multiple-choice tests can be scored quickly. Systems are available to score such tests electronically.

There are difficulties associated with preparing and using multiple-choice tests. A good test takes time to prepare. It is not easy to think of good *distracters* (plausible incorrect answers). Also, older learners are often inclined to argue that several options may be correct. Most problems associated with multiple-choice tests can be avoided if we take care when preparing individual questions.

Name_____

**Ages at Which the Average American Man and Woman
Married at Different Times in Our History***

Year	Age of Average Man When He Married	Age of Average Woman When She Married
1890	26	24
1910	25	21
1930	24	21
1950	23	20
1970	23	21

*Source: Data are adapted from *Historical Statistics of the United States, Colonial Times to 1970* (Bicentennial ed., Part 1, p. 19), by U.S. Bureau of the Census, 1975, Washington, DC: U.S. Government Printing Office.

Directions

This is a true/false test. Each statement refers to the table above. Look at the table before you decide on your answer. Circle *true* for true statements. Circle *false* for false statements.

true   false   1. In 1890 the average man was older than the average woman at the time of marriage.

true   false   2. The smallest difference between the age of the average man and the average woman at the time of marriage was in the year 1950.

true   false   3. In 1970, the average man was younger at the time of his marriage than the average man in 1910.

true   false   4. The greatest difference between the age of the average man and average woman at the time of marriage occurred in the years 1930 and 1970.

true   false   5. This chart tells us that men married in 1890 at younger average ages than in 1970.

**Figure 13–13
Sample true/false test.**

The part of the multiple-choice question that introduces the item is called the *stem.* The alternative answers are called the *options.* In a properly prepared multiple-choice item, the stem should provide learners with a context for answering, and should serve a focusing function. Consider these two examples:

1. Washington
    (a) is a common family name in France.
    (b) is the capital of the United States.

(c) is a province of Canada.
(d) is a state on the Mississippi River.
2. The capital city of the United States is called
   (a) Ottawa.
   (b) Washington.
   (c) New York.
   (d) Richmond.

The options provided should be plausible. When some options make no logical sense, pupils will respond to the correct answer as much because of the nonsensical options as because of their knowledge of the content. For example, few pupils would have difficulty responding correctly to this item:
   What is the softest?
   (a) cotton candy
   (b) brick
   (c) steel
   (d) window glass

Stems and options are stated positively in good multiple-choice items. Negatives can be very confusing. Note this example:
   Which is not a statement correctly describing the duties of a governor?
   (a) The job of a governor cannot be said to include the supervision of his or her staff.
   (b) The governor does not serve as a member of the state supreme court.
   (c) The governor is not uninvolved in the affairs of a political party.
   (d) The governor is not absent from ceremonial events.

When preparing multiple-choice items, we need to ensure that each stem has a single correct answer. The correct answer should not be a matter of opinion or judgment. Consider this example:
   The very best chili peppers are grown in the state of
   (a) Arizona.
   (b) Texas.
   (c) New Mexico.
   (d) California.

Obviously, the question of which state has the best chili peppers is a matter of opinion. It is not something that can be adequately tested by a forced-choice test. Matters of opinion and debate are much better handled in essays.

Finally, when preparing multiple-choice questions, we need to exercise care in locating the correct answer. Placement of this answer should vary. There is a tendency for some teachers to select option (b) or (c) as the correct answer in a four-option multiple-choice item. Evidence suggests that pupils who are guessing tend to answer (b) or (c). If too many correct answers are in those two places, these learners may receive higher scores than they deserve.

Matching Tests

Matching tests are especially useful when we want to test pupils' understanding of new terms. A matching test is easy to construct and correct. It can focus learners' attention on important vocabulary terms they will need to know as they continue to work in a given unit of study. Matching tests cannot assess as broad a range of content as either true/false or multiple-choice tests. A matching test focuses exclusively on terms associated with a limited topic area.

Matching tests consist of two columns of information, one containing the definitions, the other containing the terms. Pupils match the definition with the term it describes. A blank is provided before each numbered definition, and a letter of the alphabet precedes each term. Learners are asked to write the letter of the correct term in the blank before its definition.

Measurement specialists prefer to set up matching tests so that definitions are on the left and terms are on the right. This practice encourages the learner to read the definition first and then to look for the term. The definition provides specific clues and makes the search for an appropriate term a relatively focused activity. The alternative arrangement causes pupils to look at individual terms and then to look through all of the definitions. This is less efficient than the preferred format.

It is essential that there be at least 25% more terms in the right column than there are definitions in the left. If there are *exactly* the same number of items in each column, then a pupil who misses one item is forced to miss two. [If the answer for item 1 is (a) and item 2 is (b), and a pupil selects (b) for item 1, the student has by default also missed item 2.] Adding choices makes it possible for the student to miss only one item if one of the additional distracters is chosen.

The entire matching test should be printed on a single page. Teachers sometimes prepare a matching test in which the right-hand column of terms is so much longer than the left-hand column of definitions that the right-hand column goes over to a second page. When this happens, some pupils invariably fail to notice the terms on the second page, and consequently their scores suffer. If length of the terms column is a problem, it is better to split the matching quiz into two separate tests, each of which contains all items on a single page. A properly designed matching test is shown in Figure 13–14.

Completion Tests

Completion tests are easy to construct. They eliminate guessing and can sample a variety of content. However, an individual completion test does not usually cover as much content as either a true/false test or a multiple-choice test. Pupils must write responses in their own handwriting, which is a slower process than noting choices on true/false or multiple-choice forms.

We have to be careful when creating completion items. Unless an item is worded properly, more than one answer may be logically defensible. Attention to the wording of the items can greatly diminish this problem. Consider these two versions of a completion item:

Name_____

Topic: Resources

Directions

This is a matching test. Look at the definitions on the left. Then look at the words on the right. Find the word that matches each definition. Place the letter before the word in the blank in front of its definition. There is only one correct answer for each definition.

_____ 1. Materials people take from the Earth to   a. human resources
            meet needs and wants   b. coal
_____ 2. Resources that cannot be replaced   c. natural resources
_____ 3. The source of fuels such as gasoline and oil   d. technology
_____ 4. Special skills, knowledge, and tools people   e. petroleum
            use to create things to make life better   f. geology
_____ 5. Resources that can be replaced   g. renewable resources
_____ 6. Known supplies of a resource that are   h. nonrenewable resources
            available for use   i. Reserves

Figure 13–14
An example of a properly designed matching test.

- The navigator sailing for Spain whom many consider to be the discoverer of America
  was _____
- The name by which we know the navigator who sometimes is called the discoverer
  of America is _____

The first version has many logical answers. For example, pupils who answered "a man," "a native of Italy," "a Genoan," or even "a sailor" might make a case for the correctness of their answer. The second version provides a better focus. It limits the range of probable answers, as a well-written completion item should do.

There are other problems associated with correcting completion items. Paramount among these is the issue of spelling. Some teachers claim that since the major concern is mastery of content, then logically little attention need be paid to spelling. However, elementary social studies teachers are charged with teaching spelling as well as social studies. They often find themselves in a quandary when dealing with completion-test responses. To take too much off for spelling tends to turn the exercise into a spelling test. To take nothing off for misspelled words may convey to pupils that spelling is important only during the spelling period. This problem can be resolved by fixing the amount to be deducted for spelling errors and informing pupils beforehand.

Another issue we face when correcting completion tests concerns how to handle synonyms. If the correct word for a blank is *hat*, should the word *cap* be accepted? What about *chapeau* or *bandanna?* Answers to these questions are important because doubts as to what constitutes a correct answer can undermine a test's reliability.

Some problems associated with completion items can be solved when a modified version of this test type is used. It features the usual sentences and blanks to be filled in but, in addition, provides a list of words at the bottom of the page. This list includes both answers and distracters. Pupils are told to find the correct word at the bottom of the page and to write it in the blank where it belongs. Since the words are there for pupils to see, they can be held accountable for spelling (simply a matter of correct copying). No synonyms are accepted because learners are directed to use only the words at the bottom of the page. See Figure 13–15 for an example of such a test.

General guidelines for preparing a completion test are as follows:

- Use only one blank per item.
- Place the blank at or near the end of the item. This provides pupils with context clues.
- Avoid using *a* or *an* before the blank. These words will cue pupils to look either for a word beginning with a vowel or for a word beginning with a consonant.
- Avoid placing blanks in statements that have been extracted verbatim from the textbook. Such a practice encourages pupils to focus on textbook wording rather than on textbook content.

USING EVALUATION RESULTS TO IMPROVE INSTRUCTION

Evaluation results have uses beyond the assessment of individual pupil progress. They also help us to evaluate the quality of our instruction. When evaluation results are used for this purpose, scores of all learners are viewed collectively.

Suppose we gave a group of grade-five pupils a test on the general topic of the regions of the United States. The test included 28 items. Seven items focused on each of these subtopics: (1) climate, (2) topography, (3) natural resources, and (4) population characteristics. After analyzing pupils' scores, we found that the following percentages of learners had missed three or more questions in each subtopic area:

climate—10%

topography—12%

natural resources—25%

population characteristics—55%

These figures indicate that class members experienced the most difficulty with content related to population characteristics. Many also missed items associated with natural resources. These results might lead us to provide additional instruction to clear up misunderstandings related to both these topics. Additionally, the next time we teach this content (perhaps the following year to a new class), we might consider reorganizing and improving material relating to areas that test results indicated were problems for our present group of learners.

Name: _____

Test Topic: Climate

Directions

This is a completion test. You are to fill in each blank. Read the words at the bottom of the page. Select the word that belongs in each blank and write it there. You will not use all of the words at the bottom of the page. Each blank has a different correct word; no word at the bottom of the page will be used more than one time.

The four basic elements of climate are temperature, precipitation, air pressure, and

_____ . *The amount of direct sunlight a place receives depends on its* _____ . *Little di-*
  1   2

rect sunlight is received in _____ *latitudes. Places in high latitudes are generally*
                                     3

colder than places in _____ *latitudes. Most of the United States is located in the* _____
                             4   5

latitudes. Land surfaces cool more _____ *than water surfaces. Air temperatures are*
                                        6

_____ *at high elevations than at low elevations. Temperatures are too low for the air to*
  7

hold much _____ *at extremely high latitudes.*
             8

Choose answers from this list:

wind	latitude	low	cooler	dusts
snow	longitude	hotter	slowly	rapidly
moisture	high	middle	clouds	

Figure 13–15
A sample completion test.

Teachers who make systematic use of their evaluation results are in a position to refine their instructional plans rationally. These results tell them what they are doing well and what areas might be presented more effectively another time. Over a period of several years, weak spots in the instructional program can be converted to areas of strength.

WEB CHECK

Note: Electronic addresses of sites on the World Wide Web change frequently. If the listed URL fails to work, use a standard search engine to locate the new address of the site.

- ERIC Clearinghouse on Assessment and Evaluation

URL—**http://ericae.net/main.htm**

At this Web address you will find a tremendous number of links to additional information sources related to assessment. This should be one of your "first stops" in any effort to search out evaluation and assessment information on the Internet.

- Alternative Assessment in the Social Sciences

URL—**http://www.coe.ilstu.edu/jabraun/socialstudies/assessment.main.html**

This site features material developed by the Illinois Goal Assessment Program that provides particularly useful criteria to be used in evaluating learners' performance through authentic assessment approaches.

- Assessment and Evaluation on the Internet

URL—**http://ericae2.educ.cua.edu/intbod.stm**

Dr. Helen Barrett, a faculty member in the School of Education at the University of Alaska, has gathered together a tremendous number of links to websites that provide information related to assessment and evaluation. You will find here references to such topics as action research, alternative assessment, early childhood assessment, fairness in testing, and test construction.

- Authentic Assessment

URL—**http://www.nwrel.org/scpd/sirs/6/cu11.html**

This site includes a number of links to additional websites that feature information about authentic assessment. There are references to topics that include electronic portfolios, evaluating problem-solving processes, self-assessment in portfolios, and creating rubrics.

- Alternative Assessment Database

URL—**http://cresst96.cse.ucla.edu/database.htm**

One of the most important and active university-based centers focusing on assessment and evaluation is the Center for the Study of Evaluation at the University of California at Los Angeles. This site provides links to a number of the Center's products. An outstanding compilation titled *Alternative Assessments in Practice Database User's Manual* can be downloaded from this site.

KEY IDEAS IN SUMMARY

1. Authentic evaluation is designed to encourage learners to master and demonstrate content in ways that are highly similar to how this content is used by proficient adults. The idea is to get away from traditional testing techniques that reward behaviors that, sometimes, have little relevance for the world beyond the school. In using authentic assessment, teachers are challenged both to identify appropriate ways for pupils to demonstrate what they have learned and to establish appropriate standards to use in judging the adequacy of pupils' performance.

2. Portfolios increasingly are used in authentic assessment programs. One of their advantages is that they make evaluation an integral part of the instructional process. Portfolios can be designed in many ways. Among features often included are (a) samples of assignments pupils have completed, (b) written comments by pupils about what they have learned, (c) written comments by pupils about their reactions to instructional events they have experienced, (d) prompt questions written by the teacher, (e) pupil responses to prompt questions, (f) visual materials pasted in by the pupil, (g) summary statements regarding what has been learned, and (h) self-evaluations written by the pupil about his or her mastery of various elements of content.

3. Informal evaluation depends on teachers' observations of many different kinds of pupil performances. Often learners do not even know they are being evaluated. Informal evaluation occurs at all grade levels. Since informal techniques do not require learners to have well-developed reading and writing skills, they are particularly favored by primary-grade teachers.

4. There are many kinds of informal evaluation techniques. Among these are teacher observations, teacher-pupil discussions, pupil-produced tests, "my favorite idea" displays, learner-produced headlines and newspaper articles, word pairs, alphabet review games, mystery word scrambles, and anagrams.

5. Good record keeping is essential if teachers are to derive maximum benefit from informal evaluation procedures. Daily performance checklists keep track of pupils' progress. The teacher may later transfer relevant information to a social studies cumulative record form.

6. Formal evaluation includes tests by teachers and standardized tests prepared by commercial firms. Formal evaluation techniques are more common in the middle and upper grades than in the primary grades because most such procedures require learners to have mastered basic reading and writing skills.

7. Rating scales and checklists provide information about specific pupil behaviors. Rating scales may be used to make judgments about several levels of performance. Most checklists indicate only whether a pupil can or cannot do something.

8. Attitude inventories can be used to provide information about learners' reactions to various school subjects and to various parts of the social studies program. They require pupils to rate their relative interest in alternative selections.

9. Essay tests are most common in the upper grades. They require well-developed writing skills and provide learners with opportunities to put together isolated pieces of information in a meaningful way.

10. True/false tests can cover a broad range of content. Some critics say they encourage guessing. Their use is limited to testing content that can be described in terms of absolutes (something must be clearly true or false).

11. Multiple-choice tests help eliminate pupil guessing while allowing the teacher to sample a wide selection of content. Writing good multiple-choice items, however, is a difficult task that requires considerable time and composing skill.

12. Matching tests are useful for testing pupils' grasp of associations. All material for a given matching test should be printed on a single sheet of paper. Care must be

exercised to design these tests in such a way that a pupil who misses one item does not automatically miss two.

13. Correcting completion tests poses problems for teachers. To what extent should synonyms be accepted? How many misspellings should be tolerated? Some teachers prefer a test that includes a list of words from which pupils are to select their answers. This reduces problems with correction.

14. The evaluation of learning has two important functions. First, it provides a basis for assessing the progress of individual learners. Second, analysis of score patterns of a class can indicate to the teacher areas where instruction was not effective, suggesting areas to review in a class discussion. It can also suggest needed modifications in the teacher's instructional plan when teaching the same content to other pupils.

CHAPTER REFLECTIONS

Directions: Now that you have read this chapter, reread the case study at the beginning. Then, answer these questions:

1. What is meant by *authentic assessment?*
2. Describe some of the problems teachers face in implementing authentic assessment, with particular reference to portfolios.
3. Point out examples of informal evaluation tools often used by elementary teachers to assess pupils' learning of social studies content.
4. What are at least three evaluation procedures? Describe strengths and weaknesses of each.
5. How can results of evaluation be used to improve the social studies instructional program?

EXTENDING UNDERSTANDING AND SKILL

1. Do some reading related to the general topic of authentic assessment. Be especially alert for articles dealing with the use of portfolios in elementary school settings. What problems have teachers encountered in developing more authentic assessments? What kinds of public relations issues have arisen as a result of decisions to implement authentic assessment? What benefits are claimed for this approach? Specifically, what might you do to incorporate authentic assessment into your elementary social studies program? Summarize your answers to these questions in a short paper.

2. Read a textbook on the evaluation of learning. Prepare note cards on three or four formal evaluation techniques not mentioned in this chapter. Orally present these to the class.

3. Review several school social studies textbooks prepared for a grade level you would like to teach. Look at the ends of the chapters. What kinds of tests are provided? Do the books contain other suggestions relating to evaluation? Summarize your findings on a chart. Present it to your instructor for review.

4. Visit someone who teaches a grade level you would like to teach. Ask about the tests used in the social studies program. If possible, bring back samples of formal tests. Present an oral report to the class, and share copies with other students who may have an interest in the same grade level. Take care to point out the number of items on the tests and the tests' several levels of difficulty.

5. Begin a resource file of informal assessment techniques. Gather information from interviews of teachers and professors of education, from professional journals, from evaluation textbooks, and from other sources. Do not include any of the informal techniques mentioned in this chapter. Try to find at least 10 techniques appropriate for assessing pupils' social studies learning at a grade level you would like to teach. Share this material with your instructor and with your class.

REFERENCES

BAKER, E. L. (1994). Making performance assessment work: The road ahead. *Educational Leadership, 51*(6), 58–62.

EBEL, R. L., & FRISBIE, D. A. (1986). *Essentials of educational measurement* (4th ed.). Englewood Cliffs, NJ: Prentice-Hall.

GRACE, C. (1992). The portfolio and its use: Developmentally appropriate assessment of young children. Urbana, IL: ERIC Clearinghouse on Elementary and Early Childhood Education. (ERIC Document Reproduction Service No. ED 351 150).

GRONLUND, N. E. & LINN, R. L. (1990). *Measurement and evaluation in teaching* (6th ed.). Englewood Cliffs, NJ: Merrill/Prentice Hall.

HERMAN, J. L. (1997). Large-scale assessment in support of school reform: Lessons in the search for alternative measures (CSE technical report 446). Los Angeles, CA: University of California, Los Angeles, Center for the Study of Evaluation.

SPADY, W. G. (1994). Choosing outcomes of significance. *Educational Leadership, 51* (6), 18–22.

STIGGINS, R. J. (1994). *Student-centered classroom assessment.* Englewood Cliffs, NJ: Merrill/Prentice Hall.

UNITED STATES BUREAU OF THE CENSUS. (1975). *Historical statistics of the United States, colonial times to 1970* (Bicentennial ed., Part 1.). Washington, DC: U.S. Government Printing Office.

WIGGINS, G. (1989). A true test: Toward more authentic and equitable measurement. *Phi Delta Kappan, 70* (9), 703–713.

chapter 14

Social Studies and the Integrated Curriculum

This chapter will help you to:

- state the rationale for an integrated curriculum,
- define the steps in preparing an integrated curriculum,
- identify how different subjects can be integrated with social studies,
- state how children's literature can be used as an integrating focus,
- define readers' theater,
- plan how to teach study skills appropriate for helping pupils during the prereading, reading, and postreading phases, and
- explain how each of the seven language functions can be integrated into social studies lessons.

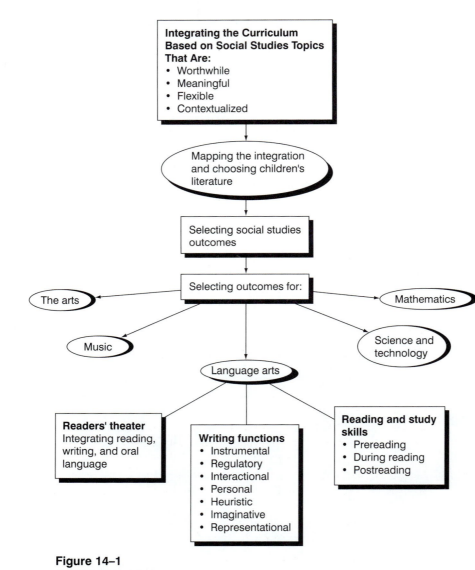

Figure 14–1
Graphic organizer.

Case Study

SHOULD TIME BE DEVOTED IN SOCIAL STUDIES LESSONS TO IMPROVING PUPILS' WRITING SKILLS?

Two fourth-grade teachers recently had this discussion as they sat at a table waiting for a meeting of the district's Central Curriculum Council to start.

"The guidelines we adopted last year calling on us to emphasize development of writing skills are really helpful." The speaker was Loren McPhee, a teacher at Persimmon Creek Elementary School. "Writing ties in particularly well with my social studies lessons. I've found it easy to get students to write about interesting social studies content. They like writing paragraphs about what life was like in the Old West. They're getting much more experience in developing their writing skills than they used to get. I think these people will turn out to be much better writers, given this kind of additional writing practice."

Loren's remarks were directed to Moira O'Roark, a third-grade teacher at Bluff Point Elementary School. After listening politely to Loren, Moira shook her head and said, "I'm sorry, I just don't go along with you on this. This 'writing across the curriculum' business sounds good in theory, but in practice it doesn't make much sense. Every time we ask students to write during a social studies lesson, we are using valuable time. This time could better be used to present new social studies content. It seems to me that writing instruction is something we should do when we are teaching reading and language arts. When we're teaching science, we should concentrate on science. When we're teaching social studies, content that is clearly related to the social studies should be our focus. Too much time spent on writing skills robs pupils of other valuable learning experiences."

What Is Your Response?

Read over these teachers' positions. Then, respond briefly to these questions:

1. "Writing across the curriculum" (the idea that some writing instruction should occur in all subject areas) has many supporters. How do you feel about this idea? On what do you base your opinion?
2. Loren McPhee suggests that writing instruction complements instruction focusing on more traditional social studies content. How can this be? Do you agree with this view?
3. Do you think a directive to include some writing instruction in all elementary subject areas could be implemented more easily in some subjects than others? Explain your answer.
4. Moira O'Roark argues that imposition of a requirement to teach writing while also teaching subjects other than reading and language arts is irresponsible. What is the basis for her position? Do you agree or disagree with it? Why?
5. Suppose you had been present when Loren and Moira were having this discussion. What would you have said if they had asked your opinion?

INTRODUCTION

Traditional school organizational patterns allocate specific time slots to each subject. Reading is taught during the reading time, social studies during the social studies time, and mathematics during the mathematics time. Today this pattern is being questioned. Should pupils be concerned with correct spelling only during the typical Friday spelling test? Should they be concerned with good writing only during language arts? Most teachers would answer with a resounding "No!" We agree. This kind of artificial separation of learning into separate subject matter "boxes" runs counter to how we really experience the world. Many school programs today aim to break down barriers that too often have stood in the way of helping pupils understand interconnections among different kinds of information.

Too much subject-by-subject separation interferes with learning efficiency. This has been recognized by specialists in the teaching of many school subjects (Eisner, 1991). For example, large numbers of mathematics educators have concluded that pupils master basic mathematical facts and operations when they are taught in a context that "connects" them to problems learners see as practical and real. Similarly, reading and language arts educators point out that reading and writing are best taught in the context of "real language," topics that are interesting and significant to pupils. We in the social studies also support the idea that many school experiences should be integrated so that learners see the practical utility of information drawn from many different subject areas.

A recent trend has been to focus on the integration of the curriculum around important and interesting themes or topics. Knowledge is drawn from a variety of subject areas and organized into thematic units (Beane, 1992). To implement this approach, we might choose these themes ourselves or organize them around significant questions asked by our pupils. We believe the concern of the social studies for the experiences and problems of people makes it an ideal subject around which to organize the curriculum. Eisner (1991) points out that the very term *social studies* suggests an integrative approach. Subject areas—for example, art, music, reading, language arts, science, and math—offer alternative ways of learning information, different perspectives, and significant insights into the actions and motivations of people. When we plan lessons that bring these subjects together, we extend learners' critical- and creative-thinking powers and also increase the likelihood that they will see the content as interesting and important.

Developing an integrated curriculum is not easy. Neither does it automatically result in improved learning. An integrated curriculum, if not done with care, can trivialize learning and emphasize unimportant content. If anything, successful curriculum integration takes a good deal more planning and thought than the typical pattern of teaching separate subjects.

An important component of an integrated curriculum is a clear understanding of the learning outcomes. The teacher must have a clear understanding of what the pupils are to learn from the unit. These learning outcomes need to focus on important objectives for each of the subjects that are integrated. In other words, merely including a Civil War song in a music lesson does not mean that the members of the class are learning either significant music or social studies content. We do not assume that students attain important social studies outcomes by simply singing songs, doing art projects, computing math problems, or writing stories that include social studies content. Nor do we quit teaching

There are many opportunities to integrate social studies with art.

reading and writing skills, mathematical operations, or forms of artistic expression and assume that important outcomes are being achieved in these subjects through the study of a social studies unit.

The important point is that we are attempting to achieve important outcomes in several subjects by teaching them in the context of rich themes or topics. This chapter introduces approaches to integrated teaching using the social studies as a source of themes and topics.

CHOOSING APPROPRIATE THEMES

A key task in planning an integrated curriculum is identifying the basic organizational themes. The ones selected should be of high potential interest to learners. If they are not, much of the advantage of the integrated curriculum will be lost.

Begin the planning process by reviewing the curriculum normally taught at the grade level you are teaching. Let's consider a fifth-grade class. In grade five, the focus of the social studies curriculum is usually United States history. You might begin by looking at topics into which the grade-five program frequently is divided, which include the following:

- Native American groups
- Colonization
- Forming a new government

- Growth of a new nation
- Westward expansion
- Sectional conflicts

Next, you might work with pupils to ask questions related to these topics. For example, you might develop questions about how different kinds of people reacted to proposals for a new government. What kinds of people supported these proposals? What kinds of people did not? How might we explain differences in their feelings?

As an approach to developing questions related to these major content topics, sometimes it would be useful to ask pupils to generate questions about present-day issues that are of interest to them. For example, one of the authors recently conducted a discussion with a group of fifth graders who had significant concerns and questions. They wanted to know why people can't get along, why some people act like bullies, why people join gangs, why people pollute the environment, why companies close and people lose jobs, and why earthquakes happen. They were concerned about what the future will be like. These questions raise issues about human behavior and human feelings that often can be tied back to the major content themes.

Such questions can function as foci for integrated units that are not tied specifically to the academic content of the traditional grade-level program. Since social studies has an obligation to promote citizenship education and an appreciation of varying values and perspectives, such lessons have a legitimate role to play in the social studies program.

Successful planning of integrated lessons requires teachers to know the pupils and their concerns well. This is particularly true because of the interest in selecting a learning focus that students will find interesting. There are a few topics that almost all pupils seem to find fascinating. For example, most primary-grade pupils get really excited about dinosaurs. Other topics may have a less general appeal. Some of these will be functions of local conditions. For example, a group of third graders living in western Nebraska may well have different questions and concerns than those living in Chicago.

Blumenfeld, Krajick, Marx, and Soloway (1994) suggest useful guidelines for identifying good focus themes for units. They suggest that questions or topics need to be

- Feasible
- Worthwhile
- Contextualized
- Meaningful

Feasible Themes

A *feasible* theme is one that has a clear potential to lead to successful pupil learning. In considering the issue of feasibility, consider whether pupils have access to the resources they will need in their investigation. Do they have sufficient prerequisite skills and knowledge to successfully complete the task? Instruction centered around themes that are not feasible will undermine pupils' self-confidence. Frustrated pupils often lose interest quickly, and they may resist active involvement in future thematic instruction activities.

In planning for integrated instruction, diagnosing entry-level and performance-level abilities of learners is critical, and materials they will need to complete tasks successfully must be available.

Worthwhile Themes

Themes that are *worthwhile* meet the key test: "importance." Do they have the potential to help pupils understand complex content? Do they allow for consideration of situations that have practical relevance to the lives they and their families live in the world beyond the school? The objective is not to draw on multiple content sources to address trivial issues, but instead to select themes that offer a real possibility of integrating a variety of subjects in ways that truly extend pupils' intellectual, social, and personal development.

Contextualized Themes

Contextualized content relates to real and practical concerns of pupils. If learners regard the topics selected as *phony* or *unimportant,* their motivational levels will plummet. Contextualized learning helps pupils to transfer school learning to outside-of-school tasks. When pupils begin to see the connection between what they are doing in school and in their own lives, their attitude toward their social studies lessons is likely to improve.

Meaningful Themes

Meaningful themes are those that pupils find relevant, interesting, and exciting. An accurate determination of whether a given theme will be seen as meaningful by a particular group of learners requires the teacher to have some knowledge about learners' interests and concerns. It also means that teachers need to act in light of this knowledge to ensure that components of the instructional program relate to what pupils feel is meaningful. Initial interest may wane unless effort is directed toward keeping that interest high throughout all lessons related to the selected theme.

INTEGRATING UNIT CONTENT

Once themes or questions are identified, the subjects of the curriculum need to be integrated. Most of the activity of the school day will revolve around the theme. Spelling words will be ones pupils will be using during lessons related to theme. Similarly, math problems, science investigations, and reading and writing assignments will all be tied to this common focus. However, there may be a theme or topic that is not suited to integrating a particular subject. Do not try to force integration if there are no obvious ties (Shanahan, Robinson, & Schneider, 1995). To attempt to do so can undermine pupil motivation and interest and can lead to distorted understanding of the subject.

**Figure 14–2
Sample graphic
organizer for a
fifth-grade unit.**

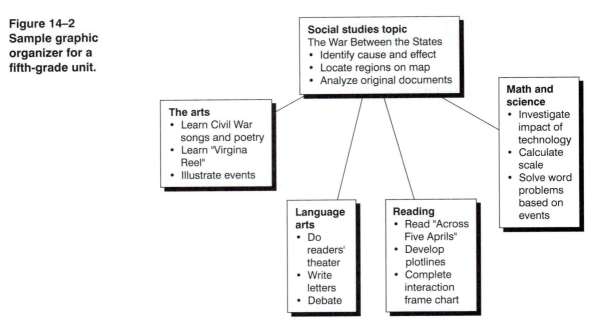

Social studies topic
The War Between the States
- Identify cause and effect
- Locate regions on map
- Analyze original documents

**Math and
science**
- Investigate
  impact of
  technology
- Calculate
  scale
- Solve word
  problems
  based on
  events

The arts
- Learn Civil War
  songs and poetry
- Learn "Virgina
  Reel"
- Illustrate events

**Language
arts**
- Do
  readers'
  theater
- Write
  letters
- Debate

Reading
- Read "Across
  Five Aprils"
- Develop
  plotlines
- Complete
  interaction
  frame chart

Mapping the Integration

One useful technique for planning an integrated unit is to develop a graphic organizer illustrating the connections among the various subjects. The organizer assists in identifying specific lessons to develop. Figure 14–2 is an example of a graphic organizer used in preparation for developing a complete integrated unit for a fifth-grade classroom.

The ideas mentioned in Figure 14–2 are only a beginning. For example, some reading skills might need to be taught to help the pupils comprehend the text. Other books, such as *Harriet Tubman*, by Judith Bentley [Danbury, CT: Franklin Watts, 1990], could also be added. In language arts, the pupils might need to be taught the correct form for writing letters and the oral language skills needed to participate effectively in a debate. In the arts, it would be useful for the pupils to begin to understand how art is used as a communication medium.

Art prints and pictures help convey the tragedy of the war in ways not captured in print. Many songs are available that could be used to teach music concepts as well as provide insight into the feelings of people. Advances in technology helped create some of the strains between the two sections of the country, and technological developments such as the railroads played a large role in determining the outcome. Technological advancements and their impact could be studied, and then extended to a study of the impact of technology on our lives. Finally, the typical math curriculum for the fifth grade could be taught be applying the skills to problems that might have arisen while studying the theme.

A final dimension needs to be added to this pre-unit plan. This involves identification of the ways the content contributes to a theme, such as learning how to get along together.

When the possible connections and a culminating project have been identified, then formal unit planning can begin. It should be noted that there are numerous opportunities for cooperative activities, whole-group activities, inquiry exercises, individualized learning, and the use of technology and media. The unit and lesson planning suggestions presented in Chapter 12 will help you put all of these possibilities together into a coherent plan.

Developing integrated units requires basic understanding of different subject areas and how they relate to the social studies. The following sections suggest how content from different subject areas can be incorporated into social studies–based integrated lessons.

Integrating Units Around Selections of Children's Literature

Many good children's books are useful for teaching social studies material. These books can also become the central focus in an integrated unit (Savage & Savage, 1993). For example, *Carlota,* a story of early California by Scott O'Dell [New York: Dell, 1977], can support integrated instruction focusing on such social studies topics such as war, prejudice, and roles of women.

Possible language arts topics include the use of figurative language and character development. Spanish-language instruction can be included (the book features approximately 125 Spanish words). Mathematics-based word problems can be created from the events in the book, and science experiments relating to weather prediction and adaptations to cold can be planned.

When considering children's books many teachers immediately think of the excellent selection of fiction that is currently available. However, do not overlook the increasing supply of nonfiction literature. Nonfiction literature is no longer confined to biographies of presidents, generals, and sports figures. Excellent books are available on a variety of topics and a variety of individuals representing a diverse spectrum of people and events.

Well-written nonfiction books can be captivating and engaging and do have some important strengths. For example, nonfiction books are about real people and real events. They are not contrived stories, and therefore many students can relate to them in personal ways. The focus on reality helps students begin to view events from different perspectives (Savage & Savage, 1996).

In preparing for a literature-based unit, we begin by identifying the themes or the questions for the integrated unit. Next, we begin our search for selections of children's literature that relate to the theme. Texts such as Donna and Saundra Norton's *Through the Eyes of a Child* [Columbus, OH: Prentice-Hall, 1998] or Masha K. Rudman's *Children's Literature: An Issues Approach* [Boston: Addison-Wesley, 1994] identify good selections of literature related to a variety of themes and issues. Lessons built around children's literature provide a degree of realism and vividness not ordinarily found in other sorts of educational material (Savage & Savage, 1993).

THE ARTS

The objectives of the arts and the social studies are complementary in many ways. Eisner (1991) points out that what pupils learn about a culture is constrained by the forms of representation or the ways they learn about it. If the chief means of learning about a culture is through the written word, this places some limits on what people will learn. Therefore, attention to art, music, and literature helps enlarge understanding as well as make social studies instruction more vivid and interesting to learners.

Works of art can be treated as artifacts that provide revealing glimpses into a culture (Collins & Chandler, 1993). Artwork can capture the mood, the color, the fears, and the joy of a group of people much better than can many written representations. In addition, we can use art in lessons designed to teach children to make inferences. A teacher known to one of the authors begins many of his social studies units with a collection of art prints. The pupils investigate the prints in depth and try to make as many inferences and develop as many questions as they can. These provide a focus for subsequent instruction. Pupils find this to be an exciting activity, and this teacher has experienced great success over the years in using this approach to increase pupils' interest in social studies units.

To gain information from a work of art, a person needs to be artistically literate (Eisner, 1991). This means that we have to provide basic information to our learners about art and art processes. Those of us who have had some formal instruction in art have advantages when we work to develop integrated lessons that include material from the arts. Such lessons do not make contributions only to learners' understanding of social studies content; they also enrich their appreciation for the arts by placing works of art in a particular social, cultural, or historical context (Eisner, 1991). Learners who know this contextual information can derive much more from their art lessons than those who do not.

MUSIC

Much of what has been said about art can be said for music. Music is another source of information about people. Music created by members of a given group gives insight into their values, beliefs, hopes, and fears. It evokes the emotions and communicates aspects of a culture that cannot be communicated in any other way. For example, listening to the song "God Save the South" tells us something about the attitudes of the people living in the South during the Civil War. This kind of a perspective is one we simply cannot expect our learners to get by reading a textbook. Folk songs are particularly good sources of views of the common people. Textbooks rarely devote much attention to this kind of information.

As with art, the goals of music and social studies are complementary. An understanding of culture and social conditions is important in developing a full appreciation of music. Music is created within specific contexts. When learners understand these, they develop more sophisticated understanding of content introduced during music lessons. They can learn that messages and emotions can also be communicated through forms of musical expression such as melody, harmony, and rhythm.

For example, the musical score *Rodeo,* by the American composer Aaron Copland, captures the culture of the American west. The final movement, "Hoe-Down," depicts a tradition that promoted social interaction and unity for ranchers and their families who lived in the west. In addition, the music is useful in helping students learn how rhythmic changes can be used to identify different elements of a story and how tempo changes can be used to capture emotions.*

---

*Thanks to Jenna Hill, teacher, Gauer Elementary School, Anaheim City School District, for this idea.

Music and dance help students learn about other cultures as well as make social studies active and fun.

Abundant tapes, records, and pieces of music that reach far back in history and cross many cultures are available to classroom teachers. In many parts of the nation, groups have preserved a part of their cultural identity through music and dance groups. Many teachers are fortunate enough to have musical talents of their own. This is a great advantage in planning integrated social studies lessons that include some emphasis on music. One of the authors once worked with a teacher who was an accomplished cellist. He captivated his middle school class by beginning many class periods with a short selection of music related to the day's social studies objectives.

MATHEMATICS

More and more, mathematical literacy is becoming an imperative of effective citizenship. We are bombarded daily with massive amounts of data and figures. Much public policy is decided based on such figures. One example is the establishment of monetary policy based on such things as inflation indexes, interest rates, and unemployment rates. Many political campaigns include figures and claims that need to be verified by mathematical analysis. Similarly, consumers need to be prepared to protect themselves in a marketplace that requires a least some mathematical diligence. Daily advertising tries to take advantage of the limited mathematical sophistication of many potential buyers.

A society with a large percentage of mathematically illiterate individuals is in danger of making poor choices that can influence life in profound ways. Mathematical knowledge is relevant to our everyday lives. Mathematics educators are aware of this and have been seeking ways of teaching mathematical operations in applied and meaningful contexts. The social studies are seen as a key area for incorporating these context-based learning experiences.

Teachers have numerous opportunities for teaching mathematical concepts in the social studies. One of the more obvious examples is the teaching of graphs and map scale (see Chapter 11). Understanding the ratio of a map scale is important in order for pupils to compute distances between points on a map.

Another important teaching area is economics. Many economics and mathematics concepts are best taught together. Even in the primary grades, we can use the classroom store to teach concepts such as scarcity, addition, and subtraction. An interesting application in the middle grades is that of using the Consumer Price Index to help pupils understand that the value of a dollar has fluctuated over the years (Savage & Armstrong, 1992).

Figure 14–3 displays the index for the years 1860 through 1998 and instructions for using the index to convert historic prices to current dollar values. Applying this procedure to convert the prices of such items as automobiles in the 1920s to their equivalent cost today is very enlightening and helps destroy the myth that things were much cheaper in times past. See Lesson Idea 14–1 for an example.

Lesson Idea 14–1

SEWARD'S FOLLY

Grade Level:	5–8
Objective:	Pupils will use the formula to convert the purchase price of Alaska to present-day dollars. They will state whether the purchase was a good deal for the United States.
Overview:	Individuals often draw erroneous conclusions based on flawed information. This is especially true when it comes to comparing the cost of particular items over time. The value of the dollar does not stay constant. It changes over time because of inflation and deflation. Most of us appreciate that what the dollar buys today is different from what it would buy only a few years ago. For pupils to understand the real meaning of prices and wages mentioned in texts and other sources dealing with historical information, they need to know how to compute the present-day values of those dollar amounts.
Procedure:	*Learning Set:* Ask the class, "How many of you have heard your parents talk about how cheap things were in the past? Can anyone give us an example?"
	Presentation: Tell the class the following: While it is true that prices of things were different in the past from today, we need to remember that there are other things to consider. For example, although prices may have been lower, people also did not make as much money on their jobs. How can we find out what something really cost in the past? By this I mean, how can we figure out what the item would cost today? To help us do this, the government produces something called the *Con-*

sumer Price Index. This is a table we can use to find out differences in what a dollar would buy in different years. (Pass out copies of the CPI [see Figure 14–3].)

Let me explain this chart to you. When it was first put together, someone had to identify a beginning point we could use in determining how the value of the dollar has changed. The rest of the table tells us whether the dollar was worth more or less at times other than this beginning point. At the present time, the chart is based on what the dollar was worth in the years 1982–1984. The index number assigned for those years is 100. You'll notice that for some other years, the index number is less than 100. This means that something that costs one dollar in 1982–1984 could be purchased for less money in this year. In other years, the index number is more than 100. In these years, it cost more than one dollar to buy what could be had for one dollar in 1982–1984. Notice that no year has an index number of exactly 100.

Let's look at an example. Remember the index for 1982–1984 is 100. When we look at the latest index number for April 1998, we find the number is 162.2. [*Note:* You will probably want to use the latest available CPI number for this exercise.] This tells us that it cost about $1.62 in April 1998 to buy what could be had for $1.00 in the period 1982–1984. Now, let's look at a famous price from our own history.

In the year 1867, the American secretary of state, William Seward, negotiated a deal to buy what is now the state of Alaska. The purchase price was $7,200,000. Many people at the time claimed that this was a terrible waste of money, and they called the purchase *Seward's folly.* Today, we look at that price and think it was incredibly cheap. Today $7 million is not enough money to build even one medium- to-large-sized high school. (If possible, cite a local example.) However, we have to remember that a dollar could buy more in 1867 than it can today. Look again at the index. We find that the index for 1867 is 14. This means that it took only 14 cents in 1867 to buy what cost a dollar in 1982–1984. How much did Alaska cost us in terms of what the dollar was worth in early 1998? Here are the steps we need to follow to get the answer:

1. Note that the index number for 1867 is 14.0. The latest index number for April 1998 is 162.2. We begin by dividing 162.2 by 14.0. What do we get? (11.6)
2. Now, we multiply the original price (the price that Seward paid in 1867) by 11.6. Remember that the original price was $7,200,000. What do we get when we multiply? ($83,520,000). This tells us that the April 1998 dollar equivalent of $7,200,000 1867 dollars is $83,520,000.

Did Seward get a good deal? Most of us would say, "Yes." Although $83 million is a lot of money, it is still a ridiculously low figure to have paid for the wealth and resources of our

largest state. Today, people looking back on what Seward negotiated probably would be more inclined to describe the deal
as *Russia's folly,* not *Seward's folly.*

(For practice, give pupils some other historic prices to convert to present-day equivalents using the index numbers in
Figure 14–3.)

Closure: Ask, "What did we learn today? Why is it important? How can
we apply this information?"

Year	Price Index	Year	Price Index	Year	Price Index	Year	Price Index	Year	Price Index
1860	9.0	1888	9.0	1916	10.9	1944	17.6	1972	41.8
1861	9.0	1889	9.0	1917	12.8	1945	18.0	1973	44.4
1862	10.0	1890	9.0	1918	15.1	1946	19.5	1974	49.3
1863	12.4	1891	9.0	1919	17.3	1947	22.5	1975	43.8
1864	15.7	1892	9.0	1920	20.3	1948	24.1	1976	56.9
1865	15.4	1893	9.0	1921	17.9	1949	23.8	1977	60.6
1866	14.7	1894	8.7	1922	16.8	1950	24.1	1978	65.2
1867	13.4	1895	8.3	1923	17.1	1951	26.0	1979	72.6
1868	13.4	1896	8.3	1924	17.1	1952	26.0	1980	82.4
1869	13.4	1897	8.3	1925	17.5	1953	26.7	1981	90.9
1870	12.7	1898	8.3	1926	17.7	1954	26.9	1982	96.5
1871	12.0	1899	8.3	1927	17.4	1955	26.8	1983	99.6
1872	12.0	1900	8.3	1928	17.1	1956	27.2	1984	103.9
1873	12.0	1901	8.3	1929	17.1	1957	28.1	1985	107.2
1874	11.4	1902	8.7	1930	16.7	1958	28.9	1986	110.4
1875	11.0	1903	9.0	1931	15.2	1959	29.1	1987	115.4
1876	10.7	1904	9.0	1932	13.7	1960	29.6	1988	121.2
1877	10.7	1905	9.0	1933	13.0	1961	30.2	1989	126.0
1878	9.7	1906	9.0	1934	13.4	1962	30.6	1990	133.8
1879	9.3	1907	9.3	1935	13.7	1963	30.6	1991	136.2
1880	9.7	1908	9.0	1936	13.9	1964	31.0	1992	141.9
1881	9.7	1909	9.3	1937	14.4	1965	31.5	1993	145.8
1882	9.7	1910	9.3	1938	13.9	1966	32.4	1994	148.2
1883	9.3	1911	9.3	1939	14.1	1967	33.4	1995	152.4
1884	9.0	1912	9.7	1940	14.0	1968	34.8	1996	156.9
1885	9.0	1913	9.9	1941	14.7	1969	36.7	1997	160.5
1886	9.0	1914	10.0	1942	16.3	1970	38.8	1998	162.2 (Apr)
1887	9.0	1915	10.1	1943	17.3	1971	40.5		

Note: To update table for later years, visit the Consumer Price Index website. The URL is **http://stats.bls.gov/
cpihome.htm.**

Figure 14–3
Consumer Price Index numbers 1860–1998 (April).

CONVERTING OLD PRICES TO NEW USING INDEX NUMBERS

1. Divide the index number of the most recent year by the index number for the historic year. For example, suppose we wanted to find out how much a 1911 price would be in terms of April 1998 dollars. In this case, we would divide the index number for April 1998, 162.2, by the index number for 1911, 9.3. (162.2 ÷ 9.3 = 17.4).

2. We take this figure (17.4) and multiply it by the 1911 price. For example, suppose a small table in a catalog cost $16.00 in 1911. To convert this to an April 1998 price equivalent price, we simply multiply $16.00 by 17.4. This is what we get: $16.00 × 17.4 = $278.40. This latter price is what the table would cost in April 1998 dollars.

GETTING UPDATED CPI INFORMATION

Updated CPI information is available from a number of sources, including the following:

1. *CPI Detailed Report* (monthly). Washington, DC: U.S. Department of Labor, Bureau of Labor Statistics.
2. *Statistical Abstract of the United States* (annual). Washington, DC: U.S. Department of Commerce, Bureau of the Census.
3. *Consumer Price Index Website.* The URL is *http://stats.bls.gov/cpihome.htm*
4. Also, nearly all almanacs have up-to-date CPI information.

Figure 14–3 (continued)
Consumer Price Index numbers 1860–1998 (April).

SCIENCE AND TECHNOLOGY

Science and technology are significant social forces. Any understanding of people and their actions in the past or present requires an understanding of prevailing levels of technology. Today's rapid scientific and technological changes have important, and often unforeseen, consequences for our society (Marker, 1992). This can be disconcerting and can result in a perception that technology is out of control and that individuals are powerless. These feelings often play a role in debates about important public policy, which frequently feature discussions heavily weighted with ethical and values issues, and strengthen a case in support of social studies programs' developing future citizens who have a solid understanding of science and technology (Giese, Parisi, & Bybee, 1991).

Marker (1992) suggests several big ideas or generalizations related to science and technology that need to be taught to elementary youngsters. Among the ideas he suggests are the following:

- Technological changes seldom have an equal impact on all groups in society.
- Technology often changes more rapidly than social institutions.
- In a democratic society, citizens have a right and a responsibility to participate in the development of laws that control the uses of technology.

As a beginning point for teaching elementary school students about technology, we might have them identify ways that technology changes our lives. How has the automobile changed the way people live? How has it made living easier? What problems has it created?

Many science concepts and lessons are easily integrated with social studies lessons. For example, understanding climate patterns requires application of some basic concepts of physics. Integrating science and social studies to understand climate can then be used to teach students some basic scientific concepts as well as social studies concepts, such as patterns of economic activity and their relationship to climate. For example, understanding the social and economic difficulties of settling the nation west of the 100th meridian requires an understanding of climate. In addition, science and social studies both advocate the use of inquiry processes. This makes the two subjects natural partners.

LANGUAGE ARTS

The ability to communicate effectively is an essential skill for any individual. The literacy rate for a democratic society is an important contributor to its stability. Effective communication is often referred to as *communicative competence* (Tompkins & Hoskisson, 1991).

Communicative competence involves two major components: (1) transmitting meaning through speaking and writing and (2) comprehending meaning through listening and reading (Tompkins & Hoskisson, 1991). Because of the importance of communicative competence, school subjects such as reading, spelling, writing, and oral language have been included in the elementary curriculum specifically for the purpose of transmitting these important skills to learners. In recent years, educators have realized that language and communications skills are best learned in genuine, functional, and meaningful communication contexts rather than through contrived lessons and practice exercises (Tompkins & Hoskisson, 1991).

Social studies teachers typically use a variety of print resources. These include textbooks, encyclopedias, almanacs, magazines, and newspapers. Because of the heavy reliance we place on printed materials and because our pupils' success may be strongly influenced by their reading ability, social studies has become a prime candidate for lessons that integrate both reading and writing.

At one time literacy was defined as the ability to read. However, in recent years the definition of literacy has been expanded to include both reading and writing. As with reading, social studies lessons provide numerous opportunities for teachers to support the development of learners' writing. The following subsections provide some general suggestions for integrating reading and writing in our social studies lessons.

Readers' Theater

Readers' theater is an exciting language arts approach that can easily be integrated with social studies. Reader's theater involves two or more pupils reading from a script and using voice and body to portray a scene. Readers' theater presentations are not plays;

hence, little practice is required. Readers' theater promotes the development of oral language. The approach helps pupils learn how to communicate effectively in front of an audience, read critically to identify the emotion and the dynamics of a scene, master effective writing skills as a script is prepared, and develop good listening skills (Laughlin, Black, & Loberg, 1991). Effective readers' theater experiences require pupils to understand the setting of the passage they are presenting. This understanding of context provides a logical tie to the social studies.

One way we implement readers' theater is to assign pupils to select an episode from a book they are reading and to write a script and present it to the class. Historical fiction that has a great deal of dialogue is especially well suited to readers' theater adaptations.

A good way of beginning is to have pupils work in cooperative learning groups. They can select an episode from a book they enjoy. The whole group should read the episode together and discuss what is happening. They might want to discuss the feeling of the characters and how they think the words would sound if spoken. Then they may begin preparing a script by identifying the speaking parts of the different characters. They then can decide who will play each character and practice reading through the script. They can go on to discuss what they can do to make the presentation interesting to the audience. When they are ready, they present their scene to the class.

Laughlin, Black, and Loberg (1991) have developed a number of scripts from a variety of children's books. These scripts can provide models for pupils to use until they feel comfortable enough to develop their own scripts.

In summary, readers' theater includes many of the skills that need to be developed in a total language arts program. In addition, it is an exciting way for young people to learn social studies content. Pupils enjoy good readers' theater both as active participants and as listeners.

Reading and Study Skills

A key part of helping pupils learn how to read and comprehend social studies material is helping them master basic reading and study strategies. These strategies provide pupils with a set of tools they can apply across subject areas. In developing study and reading strategies, we need to know something about how the human brain functions.

Our brain does not act as a camera that passively records its exposure to reality. Instead, it actively looks for patterns that can be organized and transformed into storable information. The way the brain does this has an important bearing on how well a person retrieves information and uses it later. Pupils can be taught to monitor the way they organize and store information and, thus, improve their learning from printed material. They need special help during three important reading stages:

- Prereading stage
- Reading stage
- Postreading stage

Instruction during the *prereading stage* is designed to help pupils discover a personal purpose for reading and establish a scheme to organize information they will be learning as they read. Teachers can assist in this process by relating new information from the reading assignment to previously mastered material. The teacher can also tell his or her pupils what they will be expected to do after completing their reading to demonstrate that they understand what they have read.

During the *reading stage,* learners read the assigned material. Teachers monitor them to spot individuals who may have difficulty understanding what they are reading. This monitoring involves questioning pupils about what they are reading and encouraging them to think about the content. Teachers can sometimes ask pupils to develop questions of their own that can be answered using the content from the reading assignment, and teachers can encourage pupils to take notes focusing on major points.

During the *postreading stage* pupils are encouraged to reflect on and evaluate what they have read. Often this can be done by discussing one or more of the major ideas introduced in the reading assignment. The effort here is to involve the entire class in the postreading discussion so as to identify and help individuals who may still be experiencing difficulty.

Prereading Techniques

Prior experiences help readers fit what they read into meaningful patterns. When people are lacking any experiential base related to what they read, they may find the information difficult to understand, and they may fail to grasp certain important ideas.

In elementary social studies classes, pupils often become frustrated when asked to read about people and places that are totally unfamiliar to them. Prereading techniques are designed to provide a frame of reference for pupils that will help them better grasp information introduced in prose materials. The objective is to help pupils establish a link between what they already know and what they will be reading as part of a learning assignment. Two techniques that teachers have found useful are the *structured overview* and *ReQuest.*

The Structured Overview.   A structured overview provides pupils with a graphic or pictorial display illustrating relationships among concepts that will be featured in a reading assignment. Pupils should be involved in developing the overview. You may ask them to brainstorm what they know or think they know about the topic to be read. You also may inquire about experiences they have had that might help them understand the subject to be studied.

Suppose a group of fifth graders were assigned to read material on the westward movement. You might begin by asking them to think about the general issue of moving. What are things people have to think about when deciding whether to move or to stay where they are? What must they think about after the decision to move has been made? Responses to such questions can be graphically organized into a structured overview. An example is provided in Figure 14–4.

Pupils use the structured overview diagram as they begin their reading. They are invited to add components to it as needed. The overview suggests things for them to think about as they read. It gives purpose to the activity, and it helps them fit new information into an orderly pattern and make sense out of what they read. The structured overview can also play a role during postreading. Its categories provide a framework you can use to discuss and debrief content with your pupils.

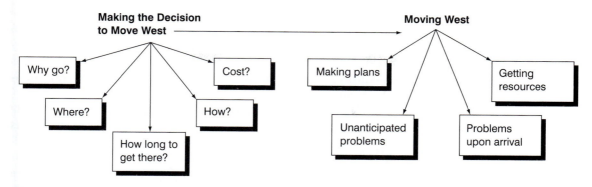

Figure 14–4
Structured overview for the westward movement.

ReQuest.   ReQuest stands for "reciprocal questioning" (Manzo, 1969). It involves both teacher and pupils in asking and answering questions related to a prose selection. Learners' active participation in framing questions helps them draw on prior knowledge related to new content to be introduced in the reading assignment. It also helps them to see relationships between their own interests and topics to be covered in the reading. Questions guide pupils toward appropriate content once they begin working on the assignment.

These steps are followed in the ReQuest technique:

- The teacher and pupils read together the first sentence of a reading assignment.
- The teacher closes his or her book while pupils keep theirs open. Pupils are invited to ask the teacher any question they wish that relates to the first sentence. The teacher answers the questions as accurately as possible. If one sentence is not enough to stimulate questions, another sentence or two may be read. During this phase the teacher may guide the general direction of learners' questions.
- The pupils close their books. The teacher asks questions. These questions are designed to help pupils recall information from their own experience that may help them understand content introduced in the reading material.
- Procedures outlined in steps 1, 2, and 3 may be repeated several times. When the teacher senses that pupils are ready, he or she asks, "What do you think you will be reading about in the rest of this material?" This question helps learners develop expectations that can help them better understand what they will be reading.

Techniques During Reading

As they read, pupils need to know how to recognize important information and make connections among the ideas presented. Many elementary school learners have difficulty distinguishing between important and unimportant content. Many also have problems identifying relationships among important elements. Two techniques that can be used to help learners are *visual frameworks* and *multipass reading*.

Visual Frameworks.   Visual frameworks help pupils organize content from material they read. Many teachers have tried to help learners organize material by teaching them to outline what they have read. Some pupils find outlining to be very tedious. Often they fail to appreciate its value in helping them grasp new content. Younger elementary pupils often lack outlining skills. The visual framework approach overcomes some of the difficulties with content outlining.

The number of purposes that might be established for reading a prose selection of only two or three paragraphs is enormous. Some assignments might require learners to focus on a specific category of facts. Others might require them to identify certain cause-and-effect relationships. Still others might ask pupils to make predictions of future trends based on information introduced in the reading assignment. See Lesson Idea 14–2 for a sample comparing two teachers' use of the same text material for different purposes.

It is clear that an assignment asking learners to focus on certain kinds of facts requires them to look at the reading content differently from when they are asked to identify cause-and-effect relationships. To assist pupils in developing an appropriate approach to their reading assignments, it makes sense for us to explain the nature of the task clearly. Then additional assistance can be provided through visual frameworks. These are devices that will help learners *see* which elements of content they should focus on. They also provide a means for taking good notes on the reading.

Lesson Idea 14–2

SPANISH COLONIZERS AND THE CARIBBEAN

Grade Level:	5
Objective:	Pupils will identify the relationship between specific items of information using a visual framework.
Overview:	This lesson plan is somewhat different in that it displays how visual frameworks will vary according to the purposes of the teacher. This illustration supposes that two teachers had very different purposes in mind when they assigned their pupils to read exactly the same material. Teacher One wants the pupils to identify which islands were discovered by which explorers. Teacher Two wants pupils to identify how the settlers tried to meet their need for workers and what happened as a result.
Procedure:	*Learning Set:* Display a picture or a brochure of a cruise ship visiting one of the Caribbean islands. Ask the pupils what they know about cruise ships and why people like to visit the Caribbean islands. Tell them that today they are going to read about some of the first people who took a "cruise" to the islands, the Spanish explorers.
	Presentation: Give each pupil a copy of the visual framework. Tell members of the class that they should fill in the blank spaces as they read. When they have completed their reading, have the class discuss what they read.

Visual Framework for Teacher One

Topic: The Islands and Spanish Explorers

Explorers		*Islands Discovered*
Columbus	⟶	_____
_____	⟶	Cuba
_____	⟶	Puerto Rico
_____	⟶	Jamaica

Visual Framework for Teacher Two

Topic: Finding Workers

Why were workers needed? _____

Actions		*Results*
First:_____	⟶	_____
Second:_____	⟶	_____
Third:_____	⟶	_____

The Reading Passage:

Christopher Columbus first landed on San Salvador Island. This happened in 1492. San Salvador is one of the islands that today we call the Bahamas. Later, Columbus went on to discover many Caribbean islands. He set up a fort on one of the biggest islands, Hispaniola.

Another famous Spanish explorer was Nicolas de Ovando. In 1502, he was sent to become governor of Hispaniola. He brought many colonists with him. The colonists tried to make money in two ways. Some of them tried farming. Some of them tried mining. One of their biggest problems was finding people to do the hard work.

One thing the early Spanish colonists tried was to make slaves of the Indians. This did not work. The Indians died when they were forced into slavery. At first, the Spanish tried to solve the problem by capturing Indians from other islands. But many of these Indians died, too. Later, slaves were brought from Africa.

After all of these things were tried, there were still not enough people to do the work. Many of the original colonists from Spain gave up on Hispaniola. They moved to other islands of the Caribbean. Some of these colonists were led to the island of Puerto Rico. This happened in 1509. The Spanish leader who led them there was Juan Ponce de León. This happened in 1508. Another leader, Juan de Esquival, took another group to Jamaica in 1509. Spanish settlers reached the largest Caribbean Island, Cuba, in 1514.

When the class has had a chance to complete the visual framework, review the findings with learners by completing a

	copy of the framework on an overhead projector. Add details and additional questions as they are brought up in class.
Closure:	Review the visual framework constructed by the class. Ask what was learned and how such a framework can be used to help them remember information.

Visual frameworks can take many shapes. Some teachers help their pupils to work out their own frameworks. Whether developed by the teacher alone or with some active participation by pupils, visual frameworks help learners master content assigned in required reading.

Multipass Reading.   Multipass reading encourages readers to go over the same material several times, approaching the reading with a different purpose each time. The purpose of the first pass is to help learners develop a framework for the content and to relate it to what they already know. This is accomplished quickly. During this phase, we encourage learners to skim the content, note major chapter divisions, and glance at the illustrations.

Once pupils have completed the first pass, we ask general questions, such as the following:

- What is this chapter or section about?
- What do we already know about these events?
- How is the chapter organized? What comes first, second, and so forth?
- What kinds of photos or illustrations did you see? Why do you think they might have been included?

The second pass through the material helps pupils to identify major ideas. During this pass, learners read major headings, subsection headings, and the first sentences of paragraphs. Most writers include the major ideas of their paragraphs in the first one or two sentences. When pupils read only the first sentence of each paragraph, they are able to pick up a surprising amount of key information. Even slow readers find they can learn a good deal about the content when they follow this procedure.

After learners have completed the second pass, we ask questions such as these:

- What are the main ideas you found?
- Are these ideas similar to or different from those you already knew?
- What additional information do you need to find out whether the ideas you read about are true or false?

During the third pass, learners look for specific details. At this point they typically have a good idea of how the content is organized. This allows them to find needed details relatively quickly. Often this phase concludes with specific questions, such as the following:

- What do people in Ethiopia eat?
- How are their houses different from ours?

- Is the climate there in summer different from ours?
- What different things are taught in school to boys and girls?

The final pass is for review. Pupils quickly read the entire assignment from beginning to end. This last pass helps individuals who may have missed important information to fill in the gaps.

Teachers who have not used multipass reading sometimes wonder about how much time it takes. The technique is not so time-consuming as one might suppose. Some of the passes are completed very quickly. Once pupils have developed a general feel for how content is organized, even reading for details does not require a great deal of time. The higher rates of comprehension that often result with this technique save time later. Less time is needed for reteaching and review.

Postreading Techniques

What teachers do after learners have completed reading assigned material has an important influence on pupils' comprehension of the information. We need to help pupils relate new information to what they have learned previously.

Small-group activities are particularly useful during the postreading stage. Sharing information with other learners stimulates pupils to reflect on and react to what they have read. Also, the setting allows group members to benefit from the thinking processes of pupils who have successfully grasped the new content. This experience often helps pupils who are not well informed about what they have read to recognize and use approaches employed by more successful pupils. Approaches often used during postreading include *graphic postorganizers* and *interaction frames.*

Graphic Postorganizers. Graphic postorganizers represent an extension of the structured overview approach introduced previously. The basic differences center on timing and on who is responsible for preparing the material. Structured overviews are prepared before reading takes place and are prepared jointly by pupils and their teacher. Pupils develop graphic postorganizers after they have completed reading the assigned material. The outcome is the development of a graph of the main ideas and supporting information.

In preparing learners to develop graphic organizers, divide the class into groups of four to six members each. Each group is provided with two packs of index cards. Each pack is a different color.

To begin the activity, tell class members that first they are to use the note cards in only one of the packs. ("When we start, use only the pink cards. We will use the green ones later.") Pupils are instructed to individually identify as many different major ideas or concepts from the reading as they can. ("Let's think about what we have read. First of all, take several pink cards. Quietly, write on the cards as many major ideas from the reading as you can recall. Write only one idea on each card.")

After pupils have completed writing on their cards, move on to the next phase of the activity. This requires members of each group to share their main ideas with the rest of the group. Each group then develops a master set of cards containing the group's major ideas. As this phase unfolds, you sometimes will need to establish a ground rule about the maximum number of major ideas each group will be allowed to have. The purpose of the exercise is for learners to identify the truly important ideas. Pupils sometimes indiscriminately identify both important and unimportant ideas. If you sense that this is happening, you might require each group to agree on no more than five or six major ideas. ("Some ideas you have identified probably are more important than others. As a group, I want you to identify no more than six major ideas. If you have more than six, discuss the ideas in your group. Then, decide which six are the most important.")

Next, ask pupils to place the cards containing their main ideas face up on the table. If there are important relationships among some of the major ideas, they should place these cards side by side. ("Now, put the cards with your major ideas on the table. Lay them so they are facing up. If some of these ideas are closely related, put those cards close together.")

At this point, instruct pupils to take cards from the second packet. ("All right, now I want each of you to take several of the green cards.") Ask them to look at the cards with the major ideas (the pink cards) and think about facts and other pieces of information from the reading that are related to each main idea. Have them write one fact or one item of information on each green card. ("Look at your major ideas. Your reading presented quite a bit of information about each one. I want you individually to write down some information about the major ideas on the green cards. Write only one piece of information on each green card. Also, make a note about the specific major idea it relates to.")

When this phase concludes, give pupils time to discuss the specific information on the cards and the main idea to which it is related. Each group then arranges the cards with the specific information under the main ideas to which they refer (under the pink cards).

A graphic layout of major ideas and supporting information results from this activity, with one set of cards representing major ideas and the other representing supporting information. All groups are asked to make a chart, displaying their organization, on either a large piece of paper or an overhead transparency.

The activity concludes with each group displaying its chart. A final discussion focuses on similarities and differences in major ideas and supporting information from each chart. Conclude by discussing any ideas that may have been missed by the groups.

Interaction Frames.   Interaction frames help learners work with social studies content that refers to interactions among individuals or groups. For example, pupils in many fifth-grade classrooms read about the conflict between Roger Williams and the Puritan leaders of the Massachusetts Bay Colony. The interaction frame procedure is particularly useful in helping learners grasp positions of contending parties in such situations. Interaction frames are organized around four key questions:

- What were the goals of the various individuals or groups?
- What actions did they take to accomplish these goals?
- How did the individuals or groups get along?
- What happened as a result of contacts between and among these individuals or groups?

Ask pupils to think about what they have read as they respond to these questions. Then start the interaction frame lesson by identifying the specific people or groups that will be the focus of the activity. Organize learners into groups, and have each group de-

Figure 14–5
Sample interaction frame
chart.

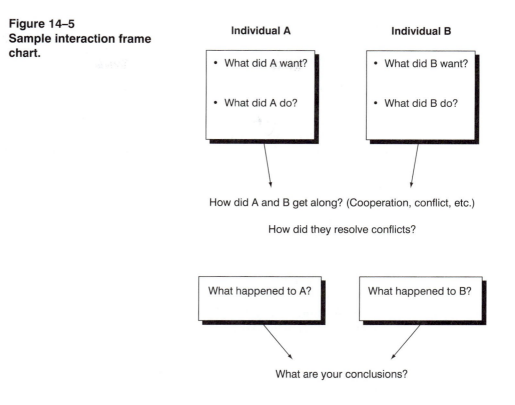

Individual A

- What did A want?

- What did A do?

Individual B

- What did B want?

- What did B do?

How did A and B get along? (Cooperation, conflict, etc.)

How did they resolve conflicts?

What happened to A?

What happened to B?

What are your conclusions?

velop answers to the four key questions. Each group shares its responses as part of a general class discussion. Pupils may construct a summary interaction frame chart based on the discussion. A model for such a chart is provided in Figure 14–5. Often it is useful to provide copies of this chart to the class to reinforce understanding.

Writing and the Social Studies

In recent years, concerns about pupils' writing skills have paralleled worries about their reading abilities. As with reading, teachers have been encouraged to provide opportunities for pupils to write in all of their major elementary school subjects. Social studies lessons often present an excellent context for our learners to develop and refine their writing abilities.

Researchers report that languages reflect and reinforce the cultures of their speakers (Halliday, 1973; Halliday & Hasan, 1989). One implication of this finding is that language instruction should tie clearly to pupils' use of language in natural settings (Halliday, 1973). There are many opportunities to do this in the context of social studies instruction. Halliday (1973) has identified seven basic functions of language:

- Instrumental
- Regulatory
- Interactional

- Personal
- Heuristic
- Representational
- Imaginative

These functions provide a framework for planning writing activities that are closely tied to social studies lessons.

Instrumental Function

The instrumental function of language, sometimes referred to as the *I want* function, concerns how people use language to meet their needs. For example, people write to apply for jobs, to place orders for goods and services, and to invite others to visit. You can involve your pupils in social studies–related instrumental writing by having them do such things as the following:

- Writing letters requesting information from government agencies
- Writing to invite special guests to the classroom
- Writing a class request to the principal
- Completing mock job applications or loan applications
- Writing captions to accompany collages of pupil-assembled pictures illustrating personal wants and needs

Regulatory Function

This function concerns tasks that control behavior or provide information about how a task should be performed. It is sometimes called the *do as I tell you* function. Road signs, directions for constructing or repairing something, and printed collections of traffic laws illustrate the regulatory function of written language. You can give pupils experience with regulatory writing through activities such as these:

- Writing to friends out of town inviting them to visit and giving them directions to the pupil's home
- Pretending that a trek over the Oregon Trail has just been completed, writing to friends in the East telling them what they should bring, and providing them with other directions about "moving west"
- Writing rules for the classroom or the school or for the care of pets or materials
- Writing suggestions to the principal about needed new rules
- Preparing written directions for such things as building a log cabin, making candies, or engaging in a traditional craft

Interactional Function

This function, sometimes called the *me and you* function, includes communications that seek to improve the quality of interpersonal relations. Social studies activities consistent with this function include the following:

- Writing to a friend to visit the classroom
- Preparing and sending thank-you notes to special guests

- Creating personal holiday greeting cards to be sent to specific people
- Writing regularly to a pen pal in another state or country
- Playing the role of an explorer and writing an imaginary letter to a member of the explorer's immediate family back home

Personal Function

This type of communication is used to express their personal feelings or ideas and to explore personal meanings. Letters to the editor, reaction statements, and poetry are examples of writing in this general category. The personal function is sometimes called the *here I come* function. The following examples illustrate ways you can involve pupils in personal writing:

- Writing letters to the editor in reaction to something printed in a news or editorial column
- Writing an account of a personally experienced event
- Preparing and sending a letter to a public official expressing a personal opinion about a controversial issue
- Writing a poem to express feelings about something studied in a social studies lesson
- Keeping a personal diary
- Preparing a time capsule that includes items of interest to class members along with explanations of some of their personal beliefs

Heuristic Function

The heuristic function of language, sometimes referred to as the *tell me why* function, has to do with seeking or gathering information. People exercise this function when they take notes or develop questions they want to have answered. The following examples illustrate possible applications of heuristic writing in the elementary social studies classroom:

- Writing down questions to be asked after study of a particular social studies topic, or to ask a guest speaker
- Keeping note cards with information about a topic that is being studied
- Taking notes while listening to a speaker
- Keeping minutes at a meeting
- Writing down hypotheses to explain a puzzling situation after considering relevant data

Representational Function

The representational function of language concerns the use of language to transmit information. It is sometimes referred to as the *I've got something to tell you* function. The following examples suggest possible uses of representational writing in elementary social studies classes:

- Maintaining an imaginary diary for someone who was present at an important historical event
- Writing a short history of the local community

- Preparing a classroom newspaper or newsletter
- Labeling items on a map and writing accompanying explanations
- Developing lists of major ideas to be included in oral reports
- Writing an account of a past event based on an oral history interview
- Writing a report of information learned on a field trip

Imaginative Function

This is a creative, *let's pretend* function of language. When using it, individuals allow their minds to wander in unpredictable ways. Possibilities for including imaginative writing in the social studies program include the following:

- Writing stories to complete a "what would happen if . . . ?" question
- Writing a play or television script about something studied in a social studies lesson
- Writing song lyrics about a topic studied in a social studies lesson
- Inventing and writing novel solutions to important social problems such as drug abuse and air pollution
- Preparing a written account describing what life might be like 50 years from now
- Preparing political cartoons referring to current topics and issues

These seven functions are all part of a comprehensive writing program. Teachers too often restrict social studies writing activities to those related to the representation function. We need to encourage other kinds of writing. Over time, this kind of training improves the sophistication of pupils' writing skills. These skills make them more effective communicators, not only in their social studies classes but in other settings as well.

WEB CHECK

Note: Electronic addresses of sites on the World Wide Web change frequently. If the listed URL fails to work, use a standard search engine to locate the address of the site.

- Music Education Resources

  URL—**http://www.geocities.com/Athens/Delphi/3528/**

  This site has links to a variety of musical topics. There are outstanding links to sources of information related to such issues as (1) folk and world music, (2) music education, (3) music curriculum and standards, (4) music-related professional groups, (5) classical music, and (6) music technology
- The Mudcat Café—A Magazine Devoted to Blues and Folk Music

  URL—**http://www.mudcat.org/folksearch.html**

  This is a digital tradition folksong database that contains over 6,000 folksongs, sung by artists such as Muddy Waters, Leadbelly (Huddie Ledbetter), and John Lee Hooker.

- Poetry and Fiction of the War Between the States

  URL—**http://www.erols.com/kfraser**

  This site includes poetry and music from both sides of the Civil War. Separate links lead you to sections titled Confederate poetry, Union poetry, and music of the war.

- Taking Stock

  URL—**http://www.santacruz.k12.ca.us/~jpost/projects/TS/TS.html**

  This site describes a simulated stock market activity for learners in grades 5 through 12. There are links that provide extensive information about activities designed to improve learners' abilities in mathematics, persuasive writing, and research.

- Consumer Price Index (CPI) website

  URL—**http://stats.bls.gov/cpihome.htm**

  At this site, you will be able to download historic and contemporary information from the Consumer Price Index. Data are updated regularly, and this is an excellent place to get the most current CPI data. There is also excellent information here about how the CPI is calculated. The answers to frequently asked questions are also a useful resource for finding responses to issues that may puzzle pupils.

- National Council of Teachers of Mathematics

  URL—**http://www.nctm.org/**

  This is the home page of NCTM, the National Council of Teachers of Mathematics. The site includes many articles on the topic of teaching mathematics.

- Weather Unit

  URL—**http://faldo.atmos.uiuc.edu/WEATHER/weather.html**

  This is an interactive unit that integrates math, science, reading, writing, social studies, art, music, and drama.

- Ben Franklin: Glimpses of the Man

  URL—**http://sln.fi.edu/franklin/rotten.html**

  This site is sponsored by the Franklin Institute in Philadelphia. Information is available here about Ben Franklin the scientist, economist, musician, philosopher, statesman, and printer.

- Writing and Reading Across the Curriculum Resources

  URL—**http://www.indiana.edu/~eric rec/bks/wac.html**

  This site includes numerous links to sites with practical suggestions for implementing approaches to teaching writing and reading across the curriculum. There are specific links to sites about applying these ideas to school social studies programs.

- Cinderella Project

  URL—**http://www-dept.usm.edu/%7eengdept/cinderella/cinderella.html**

  There are excellent materials here related to the many versions of the Cinderella story found in various parts of the world.

KEY IDEAS IN SUMMARY

1. Integrating the curriculum so that subjects are taught in the context of learning about an important topic or theme helps pupils understand the relatedness of subjects and is more consistent with the way the world is organized.

2. Teachers have available several methods of choosing themes. One approach involves a review of topics normally taught at a particular grade level, identifying important topics or themes. Teachers can survey pupils for their interests and concerns and then use those issues as a focus for thematic instruction. Topics that are selected should be feasible, worthwhile, contextualized, and meaningful.

3. A useful device for identifying the ways that content can be integrated is to draw a semantic map or graphic organizer that illustrates the relationships among different topics. This graphic can then be used to guide unit development.

4. Children's literature selections are excellent sources around which to build integrated lessons. After reviewing social studies topics and identifying themes, teachers can select high-quality works of children's literature that fit the emphasized themes. Specific skills in different content areas that need to be taught can then be selected and taught in the context of the reading.

5. Social studies goals and the goals of many other curriculum areas are complementary. Learning about those subjects enhances social studies understanding and helps pupils attain objectives in that specific curricular area. Eisner (1991) makes the point that what individuals learn about a culture is influenced by the types of representations they use when learning. Therefore, if the arts, music, math, and science are used to learn about another culture, the types of representations increase, and this helps the individual obtain more understanding.

6. Language arts and social studies are especially compatible subjects. The goal of language arts is to develop communicative competence. Competence is enhanced when the language arts are taught in the context of meaningful and functional experiences.

7. Readers' theater is an especially strong dimension of the language arts that can be integrated with social studies. Pupils identify selected incidents from the social studies or from children's literature. They then write a script of the incident and present it to the class. This involves the four main language processes: reading, writing, speaking, and listening.

8. Reading materials are widely used as information sources in elementary social studies classes. This suggests a need for social studies teachers to be concerned about learners' reading abilities. It makes sense to integrate some reading development activities into social studies lessons.

9. Specific plans for assisting pupils to learn from prose materials can be developed for each of the three major stages of the reading process. These stages are (1) prereading, (2) reading, and (3) postreading.

10. Teachers are concerned with developing pupils' writing as well as reading skills in social studies lessons. Writing activities can be organized under seven major functions of language: (1) instrumental, (2) regulatory, (3) interactional, (4) personal, (5) heuristic, (6) representational, and (7) imaginative.

CHAPTER REFLECTIONS

Directions: Now that you have read this chapter, reread the case study at the beginning. Then, answer these questions:

1. How would you now respond to the question of whether writing activities should be emphasized in social studies lessons?
2. Give some examples of where you think it would be particularly appropriate to integrate the teaching of mathematics, science, and other traditional school subjects with social studies.
3. In what ways could reading and writing activities be included so that time is not taken away from more traditional social studies content?
4. What are specific examples of social studies activities consistent with each of the writing functions?

EXTENDING UNDERSTANDING AND SKILL

1. Review a chapter of a social studies text designed for use at a grade level you would like to teach. List possible themes that could be used as a focus for integrating a unit involving several different subjects.
2. Prepare a graphic organizer illustrating how several different subjects might be studied in the context of a theme or a question.
3. Read a work of children's literature. Brainstorm various ways that subjects might be taught using this book as a focus.
4. Experiment with multipass reading. Choose a chapter in a book that is unfamiliar to you. Read the chapter several times using the multipass technique described in this chapter. How effective was it for you? Do you think it took a significantly longer period of time to read the material this way? Do you think it enhanced your comprehension?
5. Identify a topic you might teach to learners in the middle or upper grades. Identify appropriate writing activities that could be developed for at least three of the seven functions of language discussed in the chapter.

REFERENCES

BEANE, J. A. (1992). The middle school: The natural home of integrated curriculum. *Educational Leadership, 95,* 9–13.

BLUMENFELD, P., KRAJICK, J., MARX, R., & SOLOWAY, E. (1994). Lessons learned: How collaboration helped middle grade science teachers learn project-based instruction. *Elementary School Journal, 94* (5), 539–551.

COLLINS, E., & CHANDLER, S. (1993). Beyond art as product: Using artistic perspective to understand classroom life. *Theory Into Practice, 32* (4), 199–203.

EISNER, E. (1991). Art, music and literature within social studies. In J. Shaver (Ed.), *Handbook of Research on Social Studies Teaching and Learning* (pp. 551–558). Englewood Cliffs, NJ: Merrill/Prentice Hall.

GIESE, J., PARISI, L., & BYBEE, R. (1991). The science-technology-society theme and social studies. In J. Shaver (Ed.), *Handbook of Research on Social Studies Teaching and Learning* (pp. 559–565). Englewood Cliffs, NJ: Merrill/Prentice Hall.

HALLIDAY, M. A. K. (1973). *Explorations in the functions of language.* London: Edward Arnold.

HALLIDAY, M. A. K., & Hasan, R. (1989). *Language, context, and text: Aspects of language in a social-semiotic perspective* (2nd ed.). New York: Oxford University Press.

LAUGHLIN, M., BLACK, P., & LOBERG, M. (1991). *Social studies readers' theater for children: Scripts and script development.* Englewood, CO: Teacher Ideas Press.

MANZO, A. V. (1969). ReQuest; A method for improving reading comprehension through reciprocal questioning. *Journal of Reading, 13* (2), 123–126, 163.

MARKER, G. (1992). Integrating science-technology-society into social studies education. *Theory Into Practice, 31* (1), 20–26.

NORTON, D. (1995). *Through the eyes of a child: An introduction to children's literature.* Englewood Cliffs, NJ: Merrill/Prentice Hall.

RUDMAN, M. (1993). *Children's literature: An issues approach* (3rd ed.). New York: Longmont.

SAVAGE, M., & SAVAGE, T. (1993). Children's literature in middle school social studies. *Social Studies, 84* (1), 32–36.

SAVAGE, M. K., & SAVAGE, T. V. (1996, Fall). Achieving multicultural goals through children's nonfiction. *Journal of Educational Issues of Language Minority Students, 17,* 25–37.

SAVAGE, T., & ARMSTRONG, D. (1992). Were things really so cheap in the "good old days?" *Social Studies, 83* (4), 155–159.

SHANAHAN, T., ROBINSON, B., & SCHNEIDER, M. (1995). Integrating curriculum: Avoiding some of the pitfalls of thematic units. *Reading Teacher, 48,* 718–719.

TOMPKINS, G., & HOSKISSON, K. (1991). *Language arts: Content and teaching strategies.* Englewood Cliffs, NJ: Merrill/Prentice Hall.

chapter 15

Social Studies and Technology

This chapter will help you to:

- describe several technologies that can be integrated within elementary social studies lessons,
- suggest specific ways computers can be used to enhanced instruction in the elementary social studies classroom,
- explain potential classroom uses of the World Wide Web,
- point out how existing technologies such as videotapes, videodiscs (laser discs and the new DVD technology) might be incorporated into social studies lessons, and
- speculate about how emerging technologies, for example, programmable personal digital assistants (PDAs), may influence elementary social studies instruction.

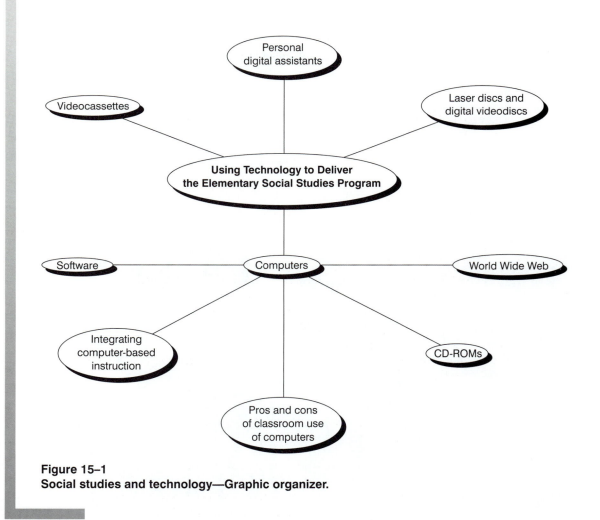

Figure 15–1
Social studies and technology—Graphic organizer.

Case Study

CD-ROMs AND TRADITIONAL LIBRARY RESEARCH

This exchange took place between Henry Duforge and his friend Francelle Dupuis, during a party at the home of another friend.

"So how's the wonderful world of grade four education?" asked Francelle. "Let's see, you're about halfway through your second year now. Right?"

"That's right," Henry replied. "Basically, things are fine. The kids are super. The other teachers have been great, and my principal has been really supportive. I'm having trouble getting some of the parents up to speed, though."

"What do you mean?"

"Well, Francelle," Henry replied, "these parents got out of school years before anyone dreamed there would be personal computers in classrooms. Many use them at work, but hardly any of these parents have an idea about what we can do with computers in the schools. As a result, some of them don't quite understand what I'm trying to teach."

"Give me an example," said Francelle.

"Well, when you and I were in school, we did a lot of work in the library, right? When we had to find some specialized information, we didn't really have a choice. It was go to the library and look at the card catalog or ask the librarian for help. A lot of my kids' parents remember library work, and they don't understand that, for the most part, library assignments just aren't necessary anymore."

"Why not?" inquired Francelle.

"Because we now have these great computers equipped with high-speed CD-ROM drives. We've got CD-ROM disks containing huge volumes of information. They are easy to store in the classroom. They allow kids to find specific information quickly. And they represent an up-to-date technology that young people today need to know about."

"Have you tried to explain this to your parents?"

"Well, Francelle, I have," replied Henry. "A few of them nod their heads, but many of them think their kids are 'just playing' when they are working with computers. They don't see the computer as a tool for doing serious work. I know lots of them would be happier if their kids came home and announced that they had been doing work in the library."

"To tell you the truth," Henry went on, "I'm a bit worried. I'm afraid some parents may think that I am not seriously trying to teach important content and improve the thinking skills of their children."

What Is Your Response?

After reading the conversation between Henry and Francelle, respond briefly to these questions:

1. Do parents' personal experiences during their school years influence their expectations about their children's teachers?
2. Is there a bias in this country in favor of educational innovation, or is there a bias in favor of traditional ways of doing things? Explain your answer.

3. Do teachers have an obligation to familiarize pupils with the latest technology, or is this simply faddism, an emphasis on something that may be forgotten in a few short years?

4. Some critics have charged that schools are extremely slow to adapt to change. Is this accurate? What leads you to your conclusion?

5. If you were Francelle, what specific advice would you pass on to Henry?

INTRODUCTION

Jodie McCracken told her mother she was going up to her room to work on her social studies speech. Her assignment was to compare and contrast typical daily experiences of 10-year-olds in two quite different parts of the United Kingdom, London and the Shetland Islands (north of Scotland). From her backpack, she extracted the portable CD-ROM unit provided by the school. She inserted the tiny CD-ROM disk, connected the unit to a color monitor, and began scanning for appropriate information.

Quickly she located information she needed. On the monitor, digitized images depicting a typical day of a young resident of the Shetland Islands played out, accompanied by a sound commentary. Jodie looked, listened, and took notes. At the end, she was invited to ask specific questions. Answers to many of them were built into the memory of the CD-ROM program. Where answers were not immediately available, the monitor suggested World Wide Web addresses Jodie might query. This same general sequence reoccurred as Jodie sought information about a typical day of a young resident of London.

After working with the portable CD-ROM, Jodie briefly used a computer to log onto the Internet. She directed queries to several of the Web addresses that had been recommended as she watched and listened to the CD-ROM and gathered additional information.

Now she was ready to put the elements of her presentation together. She sat down at her computer and developed a basic speech outline. She went back to the CD-ROM and identified some of the graphics she would like to include to support her talk. In addition, she included several graphics she had found when she visited some of the recommended websites. During her presentation, she would have access to a large monitor that presented information from a computer with a connection to the Internet and a fast CD-ROM drive. She would "call up" appropriate visual clips to support her points. As an experienced user of technology, Jodie felt her presentation would be a good one.

* * *

Does this all seem a bit far-fetched? Will technology really change how young people go about the business of gathering, organizing, learning, and presenting information? A few fortunate schools already have the kinds of equipment needed to support this kind of pupil work. It is likely that in the years ahead many others will be able to support the kinds of technologies Jodie used. Though some places will embrace these changes more rapidly than others, evidence mounts that technology is playing an ever-larger role in education.

Technology, especially as reflected in content available on the World Wide Web, promises to play an especially key role in reshaping social studies curricula. Social studies education specialist C. Frederick Risinger (1998), points out that "even a casual Web surfer will note that social studies/social science content, broadly construed, seems to dominate the Internet" (p. 148). Indeed, the volume of information itself poses a problem. Teachers sometimes are frustrated by the time required to sort through huge numbers of websites to identify specific documents or other information they wish to use. Some school districts, including the Montgomery County Public Schools in Maryland, are dealing with this problem by developing websites of their own with carefully selected links to good social materials that can be used by teachers as they plan units and lessons (Thomas, Creel, & Day, 1998).

Given all the technology-related activity today, a logical question is: "Does it help children learn?" This question is still being investigated. However, some research is starting to be reported that lends support to those who want to accelerate the rate at which new technologies are being incorporated into school programs. A large, well-designed study sponsored by the Center for Applied Special Technology (1996) looked at the performance of fourth and sixth graders in schools in seven large urban school districts. Children were divided into two groups: an experimental group and a control group. Pupils in both groups studied a common subject—civil rights. Both the experimental group and the control group were invited to use computers, but only the experimental group was permitted to take advantage of on-line resources on the Internet. Researchers found that pupils in the experimental group performed significantly better than pupils in the control group in terms of their ability to (1) present their work, (2) describe a civil rights issue, (3) offer a complete explanation (who, what, where, why, how), (4) bring together different points of view, and (5) turn in a complete project.

Findings such as those reported in this study and a general belief that exposing learners to new technologies makes sense are leading to a proliferation of technology-based curricular materials. For example, in a recent textbook adoption in California, of the eight programs that were considered, only two included a traditional text for pupils. *Seven of the eight books packaged learning experiences in formats depending on one or more of these technologies: videodiscs, computer software, videotapes, and audiotapes.*

Technology has led to the development of a number of parent-school communication systems. Educational Telephone, a Tennessee-based company, allows teachers to leave messages with parents about absences, homework, or other topics. Parents can also call in for recorded messages about school events. A typical system holds as many as 500 thirty-second messages. Homework Hotline is another parent-school communication system. It features recorded messages in multiple languages and is proving particularly useful in schools enrolling large numbers of pupils who speak languages other than English at home (Stearns, 1993).

Technology is now available that allows individual school districts to create their own CD-ROM disks. This is making it possible to tailor the curriculum to meet special needs. For years, teachers working with pupils in schools on the White Earth Reservation in northern Minnesota wanted materials focusing on the culture of the Ojibway Native American culture. With money from a grant, a Native American researcher who was an expert both on the Ojibway and in technology teamed up to produce a CD-ROM disk. It includes complete lesson plans for teachers and self-guided lessons for pupils that focus on the Ojibway language, history, and culture.

These developments hint at the kinds of changes that implementation of new technologies may bring to our classrooms. Change is so rapid that it is hazardous to guess exactly

Learning how to search for information on the computer has become an important social studies tool.

how technologies will change programs in schools. One high-growth area is the World Wide Web of the Internet. Today, between one-third and one-half of the nation's schools have Internet access, and this number continues to grow. Expenditures for electronic instructional materials increased by 20 percent in the last years of the 1990s, reaching a figure in excess of $1 billion annually (Mendels, 1997). The federal government through the Technological Literacy Challenge Fund has set aside money to send to the states for the purpose of helping schools upgrade their instructional-support technology.

The potential for technology to change not only school programs but also the way all of us lead our lives invites social studies educators to engage learners in consideration of important new issues. Peter Martorella (1997), a prominent national leader in social studies education, suggests lessons focusing on questions such as:

- If computers allow more of us to work alone rather than in groups, how will our lives be changed as members of this new, "degathering" society?
- If much information presently found in school classrooms and libraries becomes available to everyone with access to the World Wide Web, should we continue to invest public funds in new school buildings?
- Not all information contained in books and print material is considered appropriate for learners of all ages. If there is a nearly unlimited volume of information of all kinds available electronically (through the Internet and other means), should there be guidelines restricting access of some learners to some of this information?

If so, what should these guidelines be, who should decide on them, and how should they be enforced?

These questions hint at the range of fascinating new issues that can engage pupils' interest in today's and tomorrow's social studies classrooms. The new electronic technology promises not only to serve as an aid to our instruction but also to be a focus of policy questions that will engage our entire society in the years ahead.

COMPUTERS IN THE SCHOOLS

The number of computers in schools has soared over the past 15 years. Early on, teachers had problems integrating computer-based instruction into their programs because insufficient machines were available. Today, some elementary schools have large numbers of computers in each classroom. Many other schools have large, well-equipped computer rooms that are staffed by teachers trained to help pupils master computer-based lessons.

The availability of computers in the schools has increased for several reasons. Perhaps the most important has been the public demand that they be made available for learners' use. Many people believe that the future growth of our economy depends on innovative applications of technology. Employers in the future may be even more insistent than they are today that employees be fluent computer users. Large numbers of parents want to be sure their children leave school with these skills.

The huge demand for computers in this country and throughout the world has resulted in economies of scale in their manufacture. Prices have come down dramatically. A computer that might have sold for thousands of dollars in the early 1980s can be had today for a few hundred dollars. As a result, schools have been able to buy more of them for classroom use.

In recent years, there have been great improvements in the quality of educational software. This has been true in elementary social studies as well as in other areas of the school curriculum. Consequently, teachers today are more inclined than previously to incorporate computer-based lessons into their programs.

Finally, computers today are much more compact than they used to be. Early word processors were about the size of an upright piano. Today, much more powerful computers take up only a modest amount of space on a tabletop or desktop. Notebook and sub-notebook computers, including hard disks with enormous storage capacities, are small enough to fit easily into a briefcase. The physical space required for computer-based instruction is much less today than it was when the first units came on the market.

Software

Social studies–related software supports a variety of instructional approaches including simulations, case studies, drill and practice, and basic information review. In addition, some software provides learners with easy access to needed background information. For example, there are programs that include complete encyclopedias, gazetteers, and atlases that pupils can use in searching out data they need to complete assignments.

Large numbers of vendors today sell software designed for use in elementary school classrooms. The following firms are among those with especially large inventories of social studies materials:

Tom Snyder Productions
80 Coolidge Hill Road
Watertown, MA 02172

Davidson and Associates, Inc.
P.O. Box 2961
Torrance, CA 90509

Mindscape
88 Rowand Way
Novato, CA 94945

Broderbund
P.O. Box 6125
Novato, CA 94948

Forest Technologies
514 Market Loop, Suite 103
West Dundee, IL 60118

MECC
6160 Summit Drive North
Minneapolis, MN 55430-4008

Queue, Inc.
338 Commerce Drive
Fairfield, CT 06432

In addition to special social studies–related software, generic word processing, database management, and spreadsheet software also can play a role in elementary social studies classes. Table 15–1 illustrates a computer-generated spreadsheet that can be used to improve learners' proficiency in making inferences. Note that the column headings in Table 15–1 show very different annual rates of population increase for New Zealand and Jordan. The chart illustrates how these rates are reflected in actual (and projected) populations for each country from 1989 through 2002. This kind of a spreadsheet is easy to generate and can help pupils develop conclusions about the impact on populations over time of different annual growth rates.

CD-ROMs

CD-ROM stands for "compact disk-read only memory." This powerful technology allows for integration and management of tremendous quantities of digital, audio, and visual information. A CD-ROM disk holds as much information as 1,500 floppy disks. Pupils and teachers using CD-ROM have access to sound, text, and visuals of all kinds. Full motion video can even be encoded and played back interactively. The technology has the potential to provide social studies teachers with extraordinary flexibility in planning and delivering instruction.

Table 15–1

A completed spreadsheet showing the impact of different rates of population increase on populations of two countries.

Year	New Zealand (annual rate of natural increase = 0.08%)	Jordan (annual rate of natural increase = 3.60%)
1989	3,397,000	3,031,000
1990	3,424,000	3,140,116
1991	3,451,392	3,253,160
1992	3,479,003	3,370,273
1993	3,506,835	3,491,603
1994	3,536,890	3,617,301
1995	3,565,185	3,747,524
1996	3,593,706	3,882,435
1997	3,622,456	4,022,203
1998	3,651,436	4,167,002
1999	3,680,647	4,317,014
2000	3,710,102	4,472,426
2001	3,739,782	4,633,433
2002	3,769,699	4,800,236

CD-ROM is among the most rapidly expanding technologies in the schools. Several reasons account for this trend. First, many computers now being purchased by schools feature a built-in CD-ROM drive. This means the capability to use the technology comes with the machine and is not something that must be purchased as an expensive add-on.

Second, an increasing number of CD-ROM titles have been developed specifically to support school instruction. Many of these go beyond the supplementary materials (electronic encyclopedias and so forth) that were featured on many early CD-ROMs. More and more CD-ROM titles are curriculum-based. That is, they treat the actual subjects that are being taught in school.

Third, CD-ROM equipment that allows individual schools to produce CD-ROM disks of their own to meet unique local needs is coming down in price. (Recall the earlier mention of a successful effort to produce a CD-ROM curriculum program for learners who are members of the Ojibway Native American group.) Many districts have special populations for whom few relevant learning materials are available. CD-ROM technology provides a mechanism to create and distribute learning experiences that respond to special local needs.

How is CD-ROM technology helping teachers today? Here are two examples. Because of today's emphasis on including pupils with special needs in regular classrooms, elementary teachers must be prepared to respond instructionally to pupils with varying personal conditions. For example, many elementary classrooms include learners with severe hearing impairments. Educators have long recognized that deaf and severely hearing-impaired learners need many visual representations of new concepts to help them learn. The tremendous storage capacity of a CD-ROM disk makes thousands of images available. One interesting project called *StreetSigns* focuses on the preparation of a CD-ROM program that will be an American Sign Language Dictionary. Visual images will facilitate translation between sign language and English equivalents.

In today's elementary classrooms, individual pupils may have family ties to the Dominican Republic, the Philippines, Haiti, Mexico, Vietnam, and many other countries around the world. CD-ROM disks are available that allow pupils to easily retrieve information about these lands. This permits individuals to learn about and take pride in their roots and the entire class to develop a greater appreciation for the multicultural characteristics of our country.

An interesting program with a multicultural perspective is called *Ethnic Newswatch.* This application of CD-ROM technology features the full text of 100 ethnic newspapers published in the United States. Learners who use it have an opportunity to see how current events are perceived by different cultural groups and can promote sensitivity to the diversity that is a special American strength.

Several compilations of good current CD-ROM titles are available. Two useful ones are the *CD-ROM Buyer's Guide and Handbook,* from Eight Bit Books, Online, Inc., 462 Danbury Road, Wilton, CT; and *Only the Best,* from ASCD, Technology Resource Center, 1250 N. Pitt Street, Alexandria, VA 22314.

The World Wide Web of the Internet

The Internet is a connection of over 5,000 electronic networks that embraces every continent on the planet (Dyrli, 1993). Telecommunications technology allows individual computer users to tap into an incredible array of information sources. Data can be easily sent and received along this "electronic highway." Special browsers, such as Netscape Communicator or Microsoft Internet Explorer, make it easy to locate specific information.

Only in recent years has access to the Internet become easily available to individuals and schools and relatively inexpensive. Many schools now have Internet access. This allows teachers and pupils to access information to documents, updated news releases, paintings, photos, political analyses, research reports, and an incredible supply of other information. Internet access, too, allows for almost instantaneous person-to-person communication between individuals at separate geographic locations.

World Wide Web sites with information that is especially useful for planning elementary social studies lessons are diverse and numerous. See the Web Check section at the end of the chapter for some examples.

Integrating Computer-based Instruction

Computer-based instruction works best when it is not a stand-alone procedure. Computer learning should be integrated both with learning in other subject areas and with other instructional techniques used to introduce social studies content. Such integration promotes the development of cumulative learning experiences that have more total impact on learners' development.

Ties with other subjects make especially good sense because computer software in these other areas often is designed to develop competencies with relevance for the social studies. For example, many mathematics programs help learners to become more proficient in working with information depicted graphically. It is clear that an ability to learn from graphical displays of information is also critically important in the social studies.

A teacher recently made these comments:

> I'm tired about hearing technology enthusiasts talk nonstop about how much more pupils can learn from computers than textbooks. I'm not against computers, but I think some claims for what they can do are exaggerated.
>
> What we get from people pushing for more computers are examples of the finest computer programs used in responsible ways by talented teachers. These are invariably contrasted to the worst possible use of textbooks by teachers whose instructional skills could only be charitably rated as mediocre.
>
> This is the reality as I see it: There are outstanding instructional programs utilizing computers, and there are terrible instructional programs utilizing computers. We should stop this nonsense about computer technology being superior to textbook technology in any absolute sense. Neither is inherently good or bad. We need the best example of both in our schools, and we need outstanding teachers who can take advantage of what each has to offer our young people.

THINK ABOUT THIS

1. How do you react to this teacher's position?
2. If you agree that computers should be promoted to educators in ways that avoid negative comparisons with other technologies, how might you make a case supporting their use?
3. Do you believe any instructional technology can overcome a teacher's lack of proficiency?

Figure 15–2
Are computers better than textbooks?

Integration of computer-based instruction with other methods used to introduce social studies content is also important. If there is no real link between what pupils do when they work with computers and what they do when other instructional techniques are used, they may well view their computer time as a recreational diversion with little real connection to the academic social studies program. Many teachers find it useful to select software that ties closely to academic content also being treated in other ways. For example, for studying a social studies unit on the American Revolution, learning experiences requiring the use of the textbook, learning centers, special library resources, and other materials provide an excellent context for a computer simulation of some aspect of the revolutionary experience.

Computers and Schools: Some Pros and Cons

Our economy depends more on technology with each passing year. Consequently, many parents have come to believe that their children must have a thorough grounding in using computers, and these parents—often supported by members of the business community—have successfully lobbied school boards for more computers in the schools.

Evidence is overwhelming that computer use in schools is increasing. Yet, despite their presence in school, there is no universal agreement that computers should be extensively used in educational programs. Arguments on both sides of this issue continue.

Some Arguments for More Extensive School Use of Computers

Exposure to computer use provides learners with numerous personal benefits. These skills have high transfer value. For example, expertise in computer use gained in a social studies lesson may enable the learner to use skills, such as word processing, to increase performance levels in language arts or in other areas where writing is required. Basic computer competence acquired in the elementary grades may facilitate learning in a number of areas when pupils go on to secondary school. Finally, the computer provides a direct link to the real world of the employment marketplace.

Computer programs can be developed that respond well to special needs of individual pupils. The possibility exists of delivering instruction in ways that can help larger numbers of learners succeed. For example, programs may include features that provide pupils with immediate feedback when they respond to questions related to an assignment. Because immediate feedback helps learners identify their mistakes quickly, it contributes to overall learning efficiency. Research has revealed that computer-assisted instruction can reduce the instructional time necessary for students. The prospect of increasing instructional efficiency is especially attractive in a content-crowded subject such as social studies.

Some Cautionary Arguments About School Use of Computers

Enthusiasm for school use of computers has grown so widespread that some school officials may have installed them quickly in their buildings to avert a public relations disaster. The tendency of some school districts' public relations materials to emphasize the number of computers available for school use suggests the political capital to be gained by schools with high-profile computer-based learning programs.

In some cases, computers have been purchased before teachers have been trained adequately in their use. Further, though instructional programs have improved tremendously in recent years, some of the available software is not good. For example, some simple (if not simplistic) programs are nothing more than electronic versions of pupil workbooks. Little learning difference should be expected when the only change made is that pupils type answers into a blank on a computer screen rather than write them on a blank in a printed workbook. This kind of computer use raises serious cost-benefit questions. Dollar-conscious critics of school programs might well ask why a $500 computer is needed to replace a $5 workbook.

Certain characteristics of computers impose limitations. For example, many computers in schools are not portable. Notebook and subnotebook computers represent a tiny fraction of the computers purchased for use in schools. The typical school computer does not begin to approach the portability of the typical textbook. Further, computers, particularly when subjected to heavy use, break down. The schools, to keep them up and running, must hire specially trained technicians.

VIDEOCASSETTES

Videocassette technology is widely used in elementary schools. Nearly all schools have the necessary playback equipment. Social studies materials catalogs feature a large number of titles appropriate for use with elementary school pupils.

Videocassettes have largely replaced 16-mm films. This has happened because of cost. Sixteen-millimeter films are expensive. A half-hour color film may cost more than $500; many videocassettes are available for less than a tenth as much. Tight instructional budgets stretch further with videocassettes than with 16-mm films.

Videocassettes are easy to store; a single shelf may hold several dozen. The playback equipment is simple to use. Most units require the operator to do little more than turn on a switch and insert the cassette. The cassette containers are durable, and the playback system itself places little stress on the film. These features make it possible for videocassettes to last many years, given reasonable care.

In addition to playing prerecorded videocassettes, many teachers use videocassette equipment to record information of their own choosing. For example, in social studies classes, some teachers make video recordings of pupils working in groups, engaging in role-playing activities, and participating in simulations. Portable equipment can be taken into the field to make permanent audio and video records of field trip experiences.

LASER DISCS AND DIGITAL VIDEODISCS

On a laser disc, a laser beam is used to store and retrieve information. As the disc turns, the beam senses information that has been stored and converts it to audio and visual signals. Since only a beam strikes the disc surface, no physical wear occurs when the disc plays. Hence, laser discs, unlike traditional phonograph records, do not wear out as a result of abrasion from the playback needle.

The sound reproduction quality of laser discs can be superb when signals are played back through a good speaker system. This feature makes them much prized in music programs, where faithful reproduction of sound is important. Today, relatively few laser discs for elementary school social studies have been developed specifically for the purpose of providing concert-quality sound.

GTV, an extremely high-quality social studies program that relies heavily on laser disc technology, has been developed with the support of the National Geographic Society. This interactive American history program is designed for use in grades 5 through 12. There are two full hours of available video divided into 40 segments that last from three to five minutes each. Users can identify which segments they want and can sequence them. Learners can be involved in sequencing decisions. The program allows them to pursue a common theme across a number of selected segments, to develop short programs to support content in the text, and to otherwise get directly involved in decisions involving selection and organization of information. A word processing feature allows either teacher or pupils to write scripts to accompany the visual stories. For information about GTV, write to National Geographic Society, Department GTV, Washington, DC 20077-9966.

Digital video disc, or DVD, is an exciting new videodisc technology. DVD discs are small five-inch platters that look like ordinary compact discs. They store huge quantities of information. The images from DVD discs are much sharper than those of more familiar laser discs. Sound quality is superb. A single disc can hold more than two hours of video. A variety of separate sound tracks can be included. In time, this feature may prove particularly attractive to teachers of English as a second language as well as to others with pupils who are still struggling to master English. It will make it possible for the teacher to select from one of several languages to accompany narration of the video information on the DVD disc. The enormous capacity of DVD discs also makes it possible to store several versions of a program. For example, a version of a film with some language that may be inappropriate for younger elementary programs can coexist on the same disc as another version with uncut, adult vocabulary.

There are plans to begin producing DVDs that will be played in personal computers, probably in drives that will allow use of both DVDs and conventional CD-ROM discs. This will allow full motion film to be viewed on computer screens. It also will allow for links to the World Wide Web. Supporters of DVD technology believe it represents an important step toward a completely integrated video-, audio-, and Internet-based information system. DVD equipment is just now becoming widely available for home use. Relatively few schools now have it, but the technology seems destined to play an important role in instructional programs in the years ahead.

PERSONAL DIGITAL ASSISTANTS (PDAs)

Personal digital assistants (PDAs) bring together multiple technologies in a device small enough to be held in the hand. Some units now on the market contain functions that not too long ago would have had to be accommodated by as many as seven different technologies—clipboards, memo pads, telephones, file cabinets, fax machines, E-mail transmission and reception systems, and typewriters.

The potential for PDAs to establish wireless ties to the Internet and to other points of access to the fast-emerging information superhighway may make it possible for pupils to gather and exchange information from almost any location. The wireless feature involves an arrangement whereby PDAs will be able to access cellular telephone networks. Cellular telephones, which have made it possible for people to use phones from automobiles or planes or to dial a friend or business associate while walking down the street, allow for wireless, over-the-air transmission of information. Availability of cellular phone facilities is expanding rapidly, as is the number of users. By the year 2005, it is estimated that there will be 60 million subscribers to cellular services in the United States alone (Santelesa, 1994).

PDAs offer the possibility that children in the future will have a handheld device they can take back and forth to school that will provide them instant access to a whole world of information. This has enormous potential implications for educators. For example, to-

Advances in technology continue to create exciting new ways for students to explore the world.

day's teachers often are constrained to provide instruction that can be supported by resource materials available at their own schools, or at least by resources available in their school district. PDA technology can make available to pupils everywhere information that today is either not available at all or available only to learners in affluent school districts. Further, these devices offer the possibility of establishing frequent and personal links between pupils in different parts of the country and, indeed, in different parts of the world. Obviously, this portends a future in which learners will be able to have many more direct contacts with people from cultures different from their own than is possible today.

PDAs, so far as schools are concerned, are devices of the future. They are only now coming to market in large numbers. Prices remain high. However, if observed market patterns hold true, prices will fall rapidly as production levels increase and additional vendors begin bringing competitive models to the market. It is estimated that when PDA prices fall below $300, the market for these devices will explode. PDAs may then begin to appear in the schools in large numbers.

WEB CHECK

Note: Electronic addresses of sites on the World Wide Web change frequently. If the listed URL fails to work, use a standard search engine to locate the new address of the site.

- Recommended Software

  URL—**http://link.ci.lexington.ma.us/WWW/Shelley/recsoft/index.html**

  This site, maintained by the Lexington, Massachusetts, Public Schools, includes extensive reviews of software titles that have been recommended for use in the schools. There is a large social studies section.

- SuperKids Educational Software Review

  URL—**http://www.superkids.com/aweb/pages/reviews/socstud1/sw_sum1.shtml**
  This site provides reviews of social studies software titles. New materials are reviewed each month. Titles are reviewed by parents, teachers, and kids. Results are reported separately for reviewers in each category.

- SchoolWorks: Social Studies

  URL—**http://esi.cuesta.com/c/@KvoNEb8q_nZxY/product.html?code@H-SS0312**

  This site provides a description of and ordering information for SchoolWorks: Social Studies, a program available through the Educational Software Institute of Omaha, Nebraska. The program contains information about western hemisphere countries and includes databases, lesson plans, worksheets, activities, assessment devices, and reports.

- Social Studies

  URL—**http://www.summit.k12.oh.us/site/Curriculum/socialstudies.htm**

  This site, developed by the Summit County, Ohio, Education Service Center, includes links to a variety of materials of interest to social studies teachers. One link connects users to extensive information about social studies software.

- Technology and Learning Online

  URL—**http://www.techlearning.com/**

  This is the home page of *Technology and Learning,* a journal that publishes material related to technology and teaching. An outstanding feature is its software review search engine. This enables users to search for reviews of software related to a number of elementary school subjects, including social studies. Another useful feature of this site is the capability it provides visitors to search for grant opportunities related to technology and education. Highly recommended.

- K–12 Curriculum, Curriculum Software—Social Studies

  URL—**http://ed.info.apple.com/education/techlearn/sp/socstsoft.html**

  Material at this site includes a listing of social studies software titles that are organized into categories including (1) simulation software, (2) historical software, and (3) reference software. The site is maintained by Apple Computer, Inc.

- William K. Bradford Publishing Company On-Line K–12 Software Catalog

  URL—**http://www.wkbradford.com/subjsoci.htm**

  Material at this site consists of social studies software that is available from the William K. Bradford Publishing Company. An internal search engine allows users to locate titles appropriate for use in (1) elementary social studies programs, (2) middle school social studies programs, or (3) secondary social studies programs.

- Resources for Educators

  URL—**http://www.intel.com/intel/educate/teacher/links/**

  This site, which is operated by Intel Corporation, gathers together a huge number of links to resources of interest to classroom teachers. These links allow quick access to professional organizations, ERIC Clearinghouses, specialty Internet publications, technologically related teaching approaches, and a host of other areas with some ties to the theme of technology and education. We highly recommend this site, particularly as a "first visit" to the Web in search of technology-related information.

KEY IDEAS IN SUMMARY

1. New technologies are playing increasingly important roles in elementary social studies and in other parts of the elementary curriculum. New technologies increase options of teachers as they plan to help students gather, organize, manipulate, and think about new information.

2. Computers are now well established in schools. Many now feature CD-ROM as well as floppy disk drives. Development of the Internet gateway to the information superhighway makes it possible for computers in schools to link to thousands of information sources through the World Wide Web. Technology is also facilitating improved parent-school communication links. A number of systems are now in place that provide parents with information about homework assignments, upcoming school events, and other matters. In the future, personal digital assistants (PDAs), handheld devices that blend many sophisticated technologies, may allow pupils literally to carry around a world's worth of information.

3. Personal computers are now available in most schools. In social studies programs, word processing capabilities allow pupils to write and edit reports easily. Databases allow them to make sophisticated comparisons and contrasts. Electronic spreadsheets have many applications in social studies lessons, including the potential to allow teachers and pupils to engage in sophisticated "what if" speculations. Large numbers of software vendors have programs focusing on such social studies–related topics as (1) simulations and role-playing exercises, (2) geographic information, (3) profiles of events and people from history, and (4) general lesson reference material.

4. Many new computers being sold to schools include CD-ROM drives. Also, there has been a tremendous expansion in the number of CD-ROM disks developed specifically to support instruction in the social studies and other traditional subjects. CD-ROM allows students to access and manipulate enormous quantities of information. Also, equipment is now available that allows local school districts and schools to develop CD-ROM disks of their own. This capability has the potential to allow instructional programs to be developed that are uniquely suited to special characteristics of learners at a particular place.

5. More and more social studies lessons are being built around information sources available from the World Wide Web of the Internet. The vast array of information that is instantaneously available makes it possible for children and teachers in even the remotest area to be in touch with the world.

6. Computer-based instruction has been found to be most effective when it is not introduced as a stand-alone procedure. It works best when integrated as a regular part of the instructional program, much as textbooks have traditionally been used.

7. Though computers seem destined to be permanent features of public schools, pros and cons of their use continue to be debated. People who enthusiastically support early introduction of computers in schools often make economic arguments. They argue that technological proficiency of the workforce is essential if we are to be economically competitive with other nations in the future. Supporters also point to the great improvements that have been made in the quality of software designed for classroom use. On the other hand, some argue that certain school leaders have been interested in buying more computers as a public relations gimmick than as a sincere effort to help learners. They point out that some teachers have had little training in their use and that, at least in some instances, computers are used as little more than expensive equivalents of old-fashioned workbooks.

8. Videocassettes have tended to replace 16-mm films in school programs. They are less expensive than 16-mm films, and numerous titles are available to support lessons in the social studies and other curricular areas. The technology is very user-friendly. Individual cassettes last a long time, given reasonable care. Videocassette equipment is also available that allows teachers to record activities of their own pupils in the classroom or on field trips.

9. Videodiscs use laser beams to store and retrieve information. Because there is no direct contact with the surface of the disc, videodiscs do not easily wear out. They have the potential to store thousands of units of visual and graphic information that can, depending on the design of the system, be modified to meet specific learning needs. Digital videodiscs (DVDs)—the newest videodisc technology—are as small as conventional CD-ROM discs. They have an enormous information storage capability. In time, DVD technology may tie together a wide variety of audio-, visual-, and Internet-based information to produced a truly integrated and complete information system. Schools are just beginning to purchase DVD equipment. However, this technology promises to spread rapidly in the schools throughout the next decade.

10. Personal digital assistants (PDAs) are just now coming to the consumer market in large numbers. They still are expensive and, experts believe, probably won't represent a mass-purchase item for schools and for individuals who must watch expenditures carefully until prices drop considerably from present levels. This price drop is anticipated sometime before the end of the century. PDAs integrate a large number of other technologies into small handheld units. They offer the possibility that someday teachers and learners may have constant access to quantities of information barely imaginable today.

CHAPTER REFLECTIONS

Directions: Now that you have read this chapter, reread the case study. Think about other topics and issues raised in the chapter. Then, answer these questions:

1. What are some reasons that professionals working in schools have not always eagerly embraced new technologies?

2. What can the newer electronic technologies help teachers do?

3. Today there is much talk about an electronic information superhighway that will enable people everywhere to connect through computer access to the World Wide Web. What changes will this information highway produce in how elementary social studies programs are delivered in the future?

4. You learned in the chapter that some school districts are using CD-ROM technology to produce instructional programs to serve pupils when relevant instructional materials are not available. Can you think of some pupils you teach who are in this situation and for whom special instructional programs might be developed within district-produced technology programs involving CD-ROMs, DVDs, PDAs, or other options?

5. Suppose you had access to equipment for making videocassette recordings of your pupils. What kinds of things might you record? What would you do with this information? How would it help your pupils, and how would it help you improve your instructional program?

6. Traditionally, schools have lagged behind many private-sector enterprises in using new technologies. What might be done to encourage schools to be leaders rather than followers in the adoption of innovations?

7. Suppose PDAs were available to each pupil in your class. What kinds of social studies lessons might you develop to take advantage of this technology?

EXTENDING UNDERSTANDING AND SKILL

1. Reports of how technology is being used to support instruction in social studies classes often are published in the journals *Social Education* and *The Social Studies*. Review the last three years of each publication for articles focusing on classroom applications of technology. Prepare a report for members of your class.

2. CD-ROM technology is rapidly becoming available in the nation's elementary schools. At the same time, many more CD-ROM titles are being produced that may be useful for teaching elementary social studies. Review such sources as the annual catalog of Social Studies School Services (10200 Jefferson Boulevard, Room 1, P.O. Box 802, Culver City, CA 90232-0802). Prepare a list of CD-ROM titles suitable for use in elementary social studies programs and where they can be ordered. Share the list with members of your class.

3. With a group of three or four others, do some reading about the Internet. Make a panel presentation to your class on possible ways that linking school computers to the Internet might enhance the elementary social studies program.

4. Assume that you are in a school with computers and that this school has software titles you wish to use with pupils. Develop a lesson plan that incorporates use of computer technology as one of your approaches to involving pupils in mastering the new material. Ask your instructor to critique your plan.

5. Use an Internet search engine to locate material on the World Wide Web that could help you teach social studies lessons. Compile a list of at least 20 websites (include the electronic addresses or URLs). Distribute this material to members of your class, and explain specific kinds of information available at each site and why you think it would be helpful to you.

REFERENCES

CENTER FOR APPLIED SPECIAL TECHNOLOGY. (1996). *The role of online communications in schools: A national study.* Peabody, MA: Center for Applied Special Technology.

DYRLI, O. E. (1993). The Internet: Bringing global resources to the classroom. *Technology and Learning, 14*(2), 50–58.

MARTORELLA, P. H. (1997). Technology and the social studies: Which way to the sleeping giant? *Theory and Research in Social Education, 25*(4), 511–514.

MENDELS, P. (1997, December 12). Private report maps out growth in electronic teaching aids. *Cybertimes* (*New York Times* on the Web). URL: **http://www.nytimes.com/librar/cyber/week/122097education.html.**

RISINGER, C. F. (1998). Separating wheat from chaff: Why dirty pictures are not the real dilemma in using the Internet to teach social studies. *Social Education, 62*(3), 148–150.

SANTELESA, R. (1994). PDAs here, there, and everywhere. *Computer Shopper, 14*(3), 201–208.

STEARNS, P. H. (1993 special edition, October). History comes alive. *Electronic Learning, 13,* 8–9.

THOMAS, D. F., CREEL, M. M., & DAY, J. (1998). Building a useful elementary social studies website. *Social Education, 62*(3), 154–157.

chapter 16

Social Studies for Limited-English-Proficient Learners

This chapter will help you to:

◆ state the need for altering social studies instruction to accommodate limited-English-proficient pupils,

◆ identify the potential problems that limited-English-proficient pupils have in learning social studies,

◆ apply sheltered instruction (Specially Designed Academic Instruction in English) to social studies,

◆ list principles of language development to consider when planning lessons, and

◆ define specific instructional approaches useful for teaching limited-English-proficient pupils.

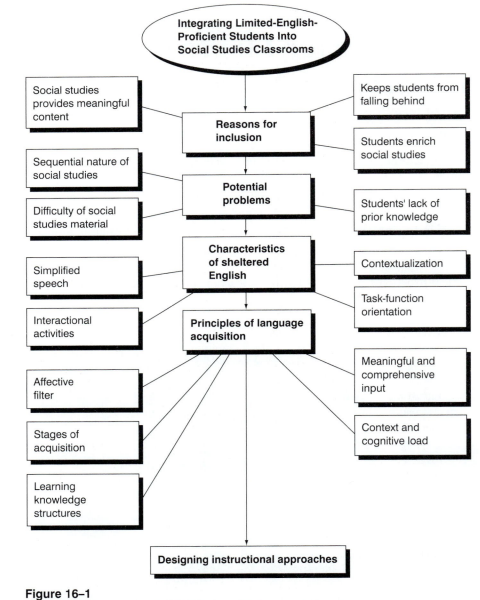

Figure 16–1
Social studies and limited-English-proficient students.

Case Study

SHOULD YOU ALTER INSTRUCTION FOR LIMITED-ENGLISH-PROFICIENT PUPILS?

John Taylor wearily made his way to the Wednesday afternoon faculty meeting. The first two weeks had been busier than he could have imagined. Most of all he worried about how to prepare lessons that would meet the needs of the diverse group of fourth graders assigned to this, his first class.

He had some pupils who had difficulty reading, some who appeared to be gifted, and some mainstreamed special education pupils. Nearly 40% of his class had a primary language other than English. Some of them communicated quite well, while others had limited comprehension. He knew a bit of Spanish, so that helped with some of the pupils. However, he also had pupils whose primary languages were Korean and Vietnamese. As he thought about how difficult it was to help all of these youngsters and how much preparation time he was spending, he concluded that the last thing he needed was another meeting. However, as he was learning, meetings of all kinds were just part of the job.

He entered the library, found a seat near the rear, and prepared to take notes. Mrs. Quesada, the principal, announced that the district was continuing to experience an influx of students from a variety of cultures. The newest wave included large numbers of Romanians who were settling within the attendance boundaries of the school. As a result of these demographic shifts, and in response to pressure from the state department of education, the school board was requiring all teachers to attend a series of workshops focused on the topic of teaching limited-English-proficient pupils. Furthermore, the board had decided that all nontenured teachers would have to obtain bilingual teaching credentials as a condition of continued employment. The district would pay the cost of the required training. This unexpected news prompted some immediate complaints.

"Wait a minute—I've got enough to do without attending another series of meetings!" retorted one veteran teacher.

"I agree," said another. "Plus, I disagree with the whole concept. People who come to the United States should be prepared to learn English and to learn it quickly! We should not be required to disrupt the learning of all pupils to accommodate the language needs of these students. They should be placed in a total-immersion English program until they learn English well enough to enter our classrooms!!"

"You're absolutely right," asserted another. "If we went to another country, we would not expect to be taught in English. We would be expected to learn the language of our host country." These remarks led some in the room to nod in agreement; others frowned and shook their heads disapprovingly.

"I think we are forgetting something," one teacher remarked. "Our concern ought to be providing success for all pupils. It will not do anyone any good to ignore the learning needs of these kids who come to school with poor English language skills. If we don't help them, they'll fail, become alienated, and drop out. It's our responsibility to do what it takes to prevent this from happening."

John was surprised at the strength of convictions on both sides of the argument. As the debated raged around him, he became increasingly confused. He wasn't sure about his own feelings about this issue that others in the room were debating so passionately.

What Is Your Response?

Read this case carefully. Then respond briefly to these questions:

1. Do you think that regular classroom instruction should be altered to facilitate teaching limited-English-proficient pupils?
2. Should pupils first acquire proficiency in English before studying content areas such as social studies? Why or why not?
3. Do you think that accommodating the needs of these pupils interferes with the learning of other pupils? Why or why not?
4. What specific things can be done to aid the learning of these pupils?
5. What problems do you think you might encounter in trying to teach these pupils social studies?

INTRODUCTION

The number of pupils who have a primary language other than English has increased dramatically over the past few years. These pupils are generally referred to as *limited-English-proficient* learners. Other terms often used are *English learners, English language learners, non-native English speakers,* and *second language learners* (Peregoy & Boyle, 1997). Some people object to *limited-English-proficient* as a pejorative term and prefer the term *English learner.* However, since we are all lifelong English learners and because *limited-English-proficient* is a common term used by the government for classification purposes, we will use the term *limited-English-proficient* in this chapter for the purpose of clarity. We by no means intend the term to imply anything negative or demeaning.

Statistics on the increase of bilingual students in schools suggest that it is probable you will have limited-English-proficient pupils in your classroom. These young people will not be able to deal with social studies content in the same way as do pupils with well-developed English communication skills. What problems may they experience in learning social studies content? What will you do? You cannot ignore these pupils and deliver lessons as if they were not present. That some teachers fail to respond to the needs of these young people is evident in the sad reality that children from non-English-speaking backgrounds drop out of school at nearly twice the rate of individuals with English-speaking backgrounds (Garcia, 1994).

To help these young people catch up and keep up with their English-speaking peers, schools must deliver programs that assist them in mastering academic content at the same time that they are learning to be more proficient users of English (Early, 1990). Their needs must be met and appropriate learning experiences provided if they are to grow toward productive citizenship. There is evidence that well-planned school programs and sensitive teachers can support the personal and academic development of language-minority pupils (Garcia, 1994). For example, teaching English through content-area instruction facilitates both the acquisition of English and academic achievement.

Pupils need two types of language proficiency to succeed in content-area classes. One of these focuses on the development of *basic interpersonal communication skills*. This kind of language proficiency allows pupils to participate in everyday conversation in informal situations. This is what they use to communicate on the playground, in the store, or elsewhere to convey their needs. The second type of language proficiency is termed *cognitive/academic language proficiency*. This kind of language expertise allows pupils to understand and communicate in classroom discussions where the contextual clues are reduced and where unique terminology is used. It usually takes pupils whose first language is not English several years to acquire a cognitive/academic language proficiency as good as that of a native speaker of English. Sometimes teachers make the mistake of assuming that because a pupil has developed a fairly high degree of basic interpersonal communication skill, he or she also possesses a high level of cognitive/academic language proficiency.

Social studies lessons are especially useful vehicles for helping pupils develop both interpersonal communication and cognitive/academic language proficiency. The study of culture is a major ingredient in language acquisition programs. Those pupils who are receiving assistance in bilingual programs or limited-English-proficient programs will have experiences that tie closely to their social studies lessons. For example, learners who spend part of the day in bilingual classrooms often are able to use content from their social studies classes in assigned conversational exercises. There are many opportunities for regular classroom teachers and bilingual teachers to engage in cooperative planning of experiences that can benefit youngsters who are working to become more proficient in English.

The social studies curriculum gives learners from different cultures an opportunity to share their native culture and history with peers. Pupils from different backgrounds become resources who can help all pupils in the class learn important social studies content and values. These pupil-to-pupil exchanges enrich content understanding and at the same time help individuals to develop self-respect and pride in their cultural heritage. This is what is referred to as *additive bilingualism*. Additive bilingualism occurs when individuals learn a new language with little or no pressure to reduce their first language and culture. *Subtractive bilingualism* occurs when there is pressure to replace or demote the first language and culture. Students who experience additive programs have a more positive self-concept than those who experience subtractive programs (Baker, 1996). Thus the social studies program provides an excellent context for the development of a sound second-language learning program.

Another advantage of social studies lessons for limited-English-proficient pupils is the opportunity these lessons provide for them to learn and understand basic American cultural values and beliefs. This kind of learning helps them sort through the mysterious behavior of others in the classroom and keeps them from making embarrassing mistakes. As teachers, we need to make sure that this new understanding does not come at the expense of their home culture.

POTENTIAL PROBLEMS FOR LIMITED-ENGLISH-PROFICIENT LEARNERS IN SOCIAL STUDIES

There are several potential problems for limited-English-proficient learners in social studies classes. One problem is that social studies is a "language-bound" content area. Teachers tend to rely on written and oral language to convey concepts, ideas, and key points. For this reason, social studies can be a challenging area of the curriculum for pupils and teachers. It is not just the amount of reading that creates problems. The type of reading also contributes to the difficulty. Much required social studies reading is expository in style and filled with abstract concepts and unfamiliar terms and names (Short, 1994).

Language problems represent just one difficulty that limited-English-proficient learners face. These students also often encounter difficulties having to do with:

- Differing cultural backgrounds
- Lack of adequate content background
- Lack of connection with the content-organization pattern used in many social studies curricula
- Some social studies content

Cultural Conflict

If we are unaware of sociocultural factors in play in our classrooms, it may be difficult for our limited-English-proficient pupils to succeed (Garcia, 1991). Anthropologists define *culture* as the attitudes, values, beliefs, and traditions shared by a group of people. Culture gives direction to life and helps people make sense out of their environment (Garcia, 1991). It influences how people perceive themselves and others and exerts a powerful influence on the way they behave. Initially, all pupils, regardless of race, creed, or social class, come to school as culturally whole individuals with a language, a set of values, attitudes, beliefs, and knowledge (Garcia, 1991). We need to understand the cultural heritage of our learners so we can develop activities and interaction patterns that are consistent with their values and beliefs.

Limited-English-proficient pupils often find the predominant classroom culture different and strange. They may be unaware of the rules and social conventions that guide social interactions (King, Fagan, Bratt, & Baer, 1992). For example, a Vietnamese student related to one of the authors the embarrassment and confusion she felt when her teacher did not understand her name or how to pronounce it. The result was a barrier that hindered her learning and progress.

These learners may not understand cultural expectations regarding how students are supposed to relate to the teacher and to other students in the class. As a result, they may find themselves in a situation of cultural conflict where what they have learned in their primary culture is contrary to what we, as teachers, expect of them. They may become confused and embarrassed. A frequent response to this situation is withdrawal and a refusal to participate, the opposite of what they need if they are to progress in learning the language. It is imperative that we understand the cultural backgrounds of our pupils and that we use this information to plan culturally congruent instruction.

Expected sociolinguistic interaction in the classrooms often creates difficulties for limited-English-proficient children. These difficulties may even persist after students have acquired basic competence in communication. For example, many classroom environments feature a rapid pace of instruction and an emphasis on individual performance and competition. Students from different cultural backgrounds may not be responding because they have been taught that they are to speak only when spoken to, and they are waiting to be invited to speak. Other students might have cultural perspective that considers answering questions in this way as an offense. They may see pupils who raise their hand frequently as attempting to make others appear ignorant (Peregoy & Boyle, 1997).

We need to strive for *culturally congruent* instruction. This kind of instruction builds on pupils' cultural and linguistic strengths. Abundant evidence exists that learners who receive instruction consistent with the norms of their home culture will have better learning opportunities (Au & Kawakami, 1994).

Lack of Social Studies Background

Prior knowledge is an important component in learning. New knowledge must be related to previous learning if it is to be meaningful. Many limited-English-proficient pupils lack the prerequisite knowledge to succeed when new lessons are introduced. For example, limited-English-proficient youngsters whose families have come to the United States as immigrants may not have had previous instruction in some topics that are featured in most U.S. social studies programs. When this is the case, these young people have no conceptual base they can use as a foundation when we, as teachers, introduce new information. Teachers need to be particularly careful to diagnose entry-level understandings of their limited-English-proficient pupils.

In addition to lacking formal instruction in topics familiar to most American learners, recent immigrants to this country may know little about traditions and events that become part of the shared cultural heritage of people who have lived here for some time. We often make references to these traditions and events assuming that everyone will understand these illustrations. For example, students may have no understanding of Thanksgiving or of the Pilgrims. Using this familiar American experience as an illustration may be confusing and mystifying to pupils from another culture. An example of this situation happened to one of the authors when he moved to Texas. One of his sons had some difficulty in class on the history and geography of Texas because the teacher and the other students made assumptions about famous people and places that were familiar to native Texans but were unknown to him. Imagine how much more difficult it is for a child who comes from another culture and who speaks another language!

Finally, even those limited-English-proficient learners who have previous experience in American schools may have difficulty because of an inadequate understanding of central concepts taught in classes they have attended (King, Fagan, Bratt, & Baer, 1992). Research indicates that it takes from five to seven years for limited-English-proficient pupils to achieve a level of language proficiency that is on a par with pupils who speak English as their first language (Short, 1994; Cummins, 1981). Because young children develop verbal fluency in social conversation fairly rapidly, we may assume that our limited-English-proficient youngsters' level of English comprehension is higher than it really is. Therefore, even though these pupils have been exposed to certain ideas and concepts in previous years, there is no assurance that they have been adequately understood. This point reinforces the need to monitor carefully what our limited-English-proficient pupils really know. We need to be cautious that we do not assume comprehension in content areas simply because the individual appears to be proficient in interpersonal communication.

Sequential Nature of the Curriculum

Social studies curriculum and social studies texts generally follow a regular sequence of topics. They assume pupils have been continuously enrolled in American schools. For example, nearly every school in the United States teaches U.S. history in the fifth grade. It is assumed that pupils have already received specific instruction about the local community and the state in previous school years. The cumulative nature of the elementary social studies curriculum often creates problems for limited-English-proficient pupils (King, Fagan, Bratt, & Baer, 1992). These difficulties are especially serious for limited-English-proficient pupils in middle schools and high schools.

For example, the *History–Social Science Framework for California* includes the study of U.S. history and geography in grades 5, 8 and 11. In grade 5, the content stops with westward expansion, giving some attention to linking the past with the present. Grade 8 includes a summary of what was learned in grade 5 and expands the content to the study of industrial America up to World War I. The 11th-grade curriculum then begins with the Progressive Era and moves to the present. It is not surprising that students entering California's schools from other countries who missed either the 5th- or the 8th-grade program often experience difficulty when they encounter the 11th-grade program. For teachers, this suggests a need to think beyond the limits of the prescribed grade-level content when working with limited-English-proficient learners. We have to be sure these young people have access to key ideas that they will need to succeed as they progress through the entire school program.

Difficulty of Social Studies Materials

Another major problem relates to the nature of the material often used in social studies classrooms. Unfortunately, many social studies classes do not include hands-on or manipulative activities that often can enhance comprehension for limited-English-proficient pupils (Short, 1994). Although there are pictures in most social studies books, they tend to depict events or famous people. Typically they do not supply concrete references needed by limited-English-proficient pupils.

In addition, social studies lessons often include specialized terminology that can create confusion. For example the term *strike* as used in a social studies lesson on labor relationships is very different from *strike* as used in describing a battle or a baseball game. Similarly, pupils may have a different understanding of a term or an event from that assumed by the teacher. For example, a pupil coming from another country with a different form of government might have a different interpretation of the term *democracy* from U.S. natives.

Reading material used in social studies creates difficulties for limited-English-proficient pupils. The typical expository style compresses huge volumes of information into a short selection. This results in a heavy concept load that makes comprehension difficult for pupils who do not have highly developed reading skills (Perez & Torres-Guzman, 1992). In addition, much prose material is not written in ways that stimulate high levels of interest.

* * *

In summary, limited-English-proficient pupils encounter many problems as they seek success in the social studies. Most of these can be overcome if teachers are sensitive to their needs and work hard to judge entry-level understanding, monitor progress carefully as lessons develop, and adjust lessons to respond to special characteristics of our limited-English-proficient learners.

SHELTERED INSTRUCTION (SDAIE) IN THE SOCIAL STUDIES

Limited-English-proficient pupils come from enormously varied backgrounds. They trace their ancestry to different countries. Languages they speak at home are diverse. It is not uncommon for school districts to have pupils in their district with 20 or 30 different first languages. It is simply not possible for school districts to employ teachers who are proficient in all of these languages. Therefore, the idea of providing instruction in the first language until the pupil is ready to be mainstreamed into an all-English classroom is not feasible. One response to this situation is what has been termed *sheltered instruction.* Recently some individuals have come to prefer the term *specially designed academic instruction in English,* or SDAIE, as a more precise term. This type of instruction is based on the work of Krashen (1982). It refers to instruction that provides access to the core academic curriculum, opportunities for English-language development, and opportunities for social integration in the classroom (Peregoy & Boyle, 1997). In summary, it seeks to make instruction across the curriculum more comprehensible to the limited-English-proficient pupil. There are four basic elements of sheltered instruction:

- Simplified speech
- Contextualization
- Task-function orientation
- Interactional activities

Simplified speech refers to speaking clearly with controlled vocabulary and sentences of reduced syntactic complexity. *Contextualization* is the extensive use of visuals, body language, and other techniques that provide nonverbal clues to the learner. *Task-function orientation* refers to relating new information to everyday life and to concrete experiences. Thus, language is used in helping students deal with concrete tasks and not in abstract or contrived academic exercises. This is intended to make the language useful and meaningful. *Interactional activities* are those that provide opportunities for pupils to interact with others and use the new language they are acquiring. This requires that the student feel safe enough to use the language without fear of embarrassment. The emphasis is placed on the content of what the student is saying rather than on correct language usage.

Sheltered instruction in social studies provides pupils with concrete examples of abstract ideas and concepts. Extensive use of *realia,* that is, pictures, charts, graphs, and nonverbal behavior, supplements words. The content emphasizes practical application of ideas and concepts. Numerous opportunities are provided for limited-English-proficient pupils to work in groups where they can talk and discuss things with a minimum amount of risk. When you talk to pupils in a sheltered instructional situation, carefully avoid overuse of unfamiliar idiomatic expressions, and repeat key words and ideas often. Speak as clearly and slowly as possible. When preparing new prose material, carefully control sentence length and take care to ensure that other elements that can contribute to comprehension problems are eliminated.

The next section introduces basic principles associated with successful programs that focus on second language learning in the content areas.

PRINCIPLES OF SECOND LANGUAGE LEARNING IN CONTENT FIELDS

Understanding some of the basic principles of language acquisition can help create classroom learning environments where both limited-English-proficient and native English-speaking pupils can be successful. Subsections that follow introduce examples of principles for preparing lessons in content areas such as the social studies for classes that include limited-English-proficient pupils.

The Affective Filter

A key element in providing a classroom environment where second language learning is enhanced is the *social-emotional component.* This is what experts in language acquisition call the *affective filter.* The affective filter refers to the combination of the affective variables of self-concept, motivation, anxiety, and fear that can facilitate or block language learning. The climate of the classroom interacts with these variables to raise or lower the affective filter. It is hypothesized that when the affective filter is high or when there is a great deal of anxiety or threat, a pupil has trouble processing information that would be comprehensible if the affective filter were lower.

The affective filter differs from pupil to pupil. Young people who have a positive self-concept and are motivated to learn English tolerate more anxiety and generally move quite quickly through the early stages of language development. On the other hand, those filled with anxiety or fear struggle and may become frustrated as they attempt to learn the new language.

For the teacher of limited-English-proficient pupils, this implies that the classroom climate needs to be a safe and an encouraging one. Teachers need to use positive reinforcement and celebrate pupils' successes. They must be careful when correcting pupils so that the student does not develop a fear of ridicule or failure. Teachers and English-proficient pupils in the classroom need to model acceptance and encourage linguistically different learners.

Meaningful and Comprehensible Input

This principle is a part of the concept of sheltered instruction. It directs us to present material to limited-English-proficient pupils in ways that are meaningful and comprehensible; that is, the content and presentation must be relevant and important to the pupil. Many of us recall our frustration when we were beginning the study of a foreign language. Sometimes, instruction we received was ineffective because we were asked to learn phrases that were relatively unimportant and that we could not imagine ourselves using in the normal course of our lives. This kind of language instruction contrasts with how young children first learn a language. They begin by mastering words and phrases that are important and meaningful to them. This pattern has implications for teachers planning social studies lessons, particularly for classes enrolling limited-English-proficient pupils. One of the major tasks is to find ways to relate social studies content to the experiences and lives of the pupils. Social studies lessons that are abstract or that deal with topics remote from their everyday lives will do little to help limited-English-proficient pupils learn either English or social studies content.

In addition to being relevant to pupils' lives, learning materials that are comprehensible to limited-English-proficient pupils must be selected with care. Language that is too abstract or too technical will not be understood and will not lead to improvement. New information that pupils can comprehend builds carefully on what they already know. This implies a need for teachers to carefully diagnose entry-level understandings of their learners.

Social studies material can also be made more understandable when we provide numerous clues to meaning. For example, we can use pictures, graphs, charts, and concrete objects to illustrate key points. Multiple reinforcements of information help to shore up pupil understanding.

Stages of Language Acquisition

Understanding the stages of language development helps us plan and implement meaningful and comprehensible material. The following stages are based on what has been termed the *natural approach* to language development (Terrell, 1981):

- Preproduction
- Early production
- Emergence of speech
- Intermediate fluency

Preproduction

This is the beginning stage of receptive language acquisition. This stage often is found among people from non-English-speaking countries who have recently arrived in the United States. The name of the stage is based on the idea that even though these individuals may know a few English words, they are too shy to respond and generally prefer to remain silent. They may point to items, use gestures such as nodding, or use other actions to communicate with others. Somewhat later, they may respond with "yes" or "no" or with single words in their primary language or in English. It is normal for this stage to last for six months or longer. You need to recognize that it is normal for pupils in this stage to be reluctant to speak, and you should not place undue pressure on them to do so. Speaking will emerge naturally.

At this stage, people focus their attention almost exclusively on aural comprehension. They observe gestures and try to make sense out of the input by using context clues. They guess about the meaning of vocabulary words.

You can assist pupils at this stage by using contextualized language. Gestures, realia, or pictures provide contextual clues that can help them find the meaning of what was spoken. You need to speak at a slow rate and to articulate words clearly. Short, simple directions and questions such as, "Point to the _____ ," or "Is this a _____ ?" are useful in helping determine the comprehension of pupils at this stage. It is also a good idea to write key words on the board and to emphasize them in oral presentations.

Early Production

At this stage, individuals begin to try limited production of the language. They are starting to develop basic interpersonal communication skills. They can communicate with short verbal statements that may be memorized to fit certain contexts. The result is that these attempts to produce language contain many mistakes of pronunciation and word usage. These individuals may have a receptive vocabulary of about 1,000 words but can produce only about 10% of these. This stage may last from six months to one year.

Progress of these pupils is facilitated when you introduce them to written words and phrases that they find meaningful. They should not be ridiculed because of their misuse of language. Modeling correct usage is an appropriate way to provide correction. The purpose is to help lower the affective filter of these young people so they are not afraid to attempt communication in their new language. Patterned language usage and the use of contextual language is critical. Graphic organizers, story maps, and language experience charts are all helpful to these pupils as they seek meaning in the language they hear.

Emergence of Speech

At this stage, individuals begin to feel more comfortable with the language and are more willing to attempt to speak sentences and participate in conversations. There is a noticeable expansion of comprehension. They have now broadened their receptive vocabulary to about 7,000 words, with about 10% production. They still need help in continued vocabulary development and in the development of their basic interpersonal communication skills. This stage tends to last for about one year.

Because learners are more confident about their ability to use the new language at this stage than at earlier stages, there are fewer worries about undermining their self-image when correcting their mistakes. At this stage, it makes sense to direct correction efforts to improving their levels of comprehension. Some sensitivity remains regarding the ability to pronounce all words in the new language correctly, and you have to be careful about drawing too much attention to this kind of difficulty. Graphic organizers are still useful in helping pupils discover meaning in a text.

Pupils who have arrived at this stage of language proficiency can begin to participate in group writing activities and in reading literature they select themselves. The major task is to provide as many opportunities as possible for these pupils to use English in a variety of contexts. They need to be encouraged to participate in discussions and conversations and challenged to respond to questions that require them to make fairly lengthy verbal responses.

Intermediate Fluency

It often takes pupils three or four years to arrive at intermediate fluency. At this stage, individuals engage in everyday conversations with ease. However, pupils may be reluctant to speak in front of large groups. They still make some mistakes and, although there appears to be a high degree of fluency, comprehension of content in academic areas such as social studies may be a problem. At this stage, pupils have developed a fairly high level of development in the language domains of listening and speaking. However, they still need assistance in achieving native-like fluency in reading and writing. They can engage in extended discourse and can give oral reports. They can benefit from working with peers on activities requiring reading and writing. These pupils often enjoy using their new communication skills in small groups. Teachers are able to challenge these youngsters with tasks requiring quite sophisticated thinking skills. Correcting mistakes can be done in a much firmer manner than in previous stages.

Even at this stage, pupils' level of language proficiency in some areas is likely to fall short of that of native speakers of English. Because many of these pupils speak the language well, sometimes there is a tendency for teachers to confuse verbal fluency with total mastery of the language. When this happens, these pupils' needs may be overlooked, and they may not get the kind of special assistance they need to ensure that they comprehend the academic content of lessons. You need to remember that these pupils are being asked to learn content presented in a language in which many have not yet attained native speakers' fluency.

Context and Cognitive Load

The four stages of language acquisition emphasize the importance of context in helping limited-English-proficient pupils comprehend lessons presented in English. Cummins (1981) identified the context and the cognitive demands of a message as two important variables that teachers need to consider when communicating with individuals with limited language abilities. He used these two variables to construct a four-cell matrix that is useful in determining the type of tasks and instruction that can be provided to pupils (see Figure 16–2).

Quadrant A includes language that is used in a clear context and that is relatively undemanding cognitively. This includes the basic interpersonal communication skills that an individual needs for simple communication with others. Activities such as buying lunch, getting materials, following simple directions, and drawing a picture fall into this category. These would be appropriate for individuals in the early stages of language acquisition. The social studies content provided for individuals at this level would need to be very basic, concrete, and embedded in classroom and school activities and should not extend much beyond comprehension of key vocabulary.

Figure 16–2
Varying context and
cognitive load.

Source: From "The Role
of Primary Language
Development in Promoting
Educational Success
for Language Minority
Students," in *Schooling
and Language Minority
Students: A Theoretical
Framework,* by J. Cummins,
1981, Los Angeles:
California State University,
Evaluation Dissemination
and Assessment Center.

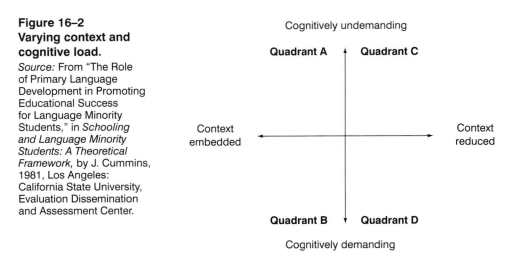

Quadrant B of the matrix includes activities that are still very context-dependent but that are more demanding cognitively. In other words, the lessons need to include many clues provided in a concrete manner so that pupils can comprehend the message yet requiring more sophisticated thought processes beyond recall or repeating language patterns. Examples might include social studies lessons accompanied by concrete objects, pictures, graphs, story webs, games, dramatization, or building projects. These kinds of learning experiences are appropriate for pupils in the phase when speech emerges. They need intellectually demanding instruction but with clues presented to assist their search for meaning. It is important to remember that more cognitively demanding material is generally more interesting and challenging to the pupils. Therefore, you need to try to move to this type of instruction as soon as possible. However, it is important that the cognitive demands not be so high as to raise the affective filter to a level where progress is blocked.

Quadrant C indicates those types of activities that are not too intellectually demanding and are also relatively free of context clues. A good example might be talking on the telephone, where there is no context to help the individual sort out the meaning of the message even though the message might be a simple one. Following written directions might be an example of a classroom activity. Unless accompanied by a chart or a diagram, there are few clues to help the limited-English-proficient pupil sort out the meaning of the message. This type of instruction is appropriate for those pupils who have made considerable progress in the speech-emergence phase and who may have reached intermediate fluency.

Quadrant D includes those types of activities and tasks that have reduced numbers of context clues and that are cognitively demanding. This includes activities such as reading the textbook, taking a test, and listening to a speaker or a lecture. Pupils who can function at this level have achieved quite a high level of literacy in English. Most of the typical social studies activities can be conducted with minimal regard for the special comprehension needs of these pupils. Individuals at this level have arrived at a level of cognitive/academic language proficiency.

When designing social studies instruction, diagnose the stage of language acquisition of the limited-English-proficient pupils in the class. The matrix can then be used to determine the types of activities that might be most appropriate for them.

Types of Knowledge Structures

Mohan (1986) proposed a framework that can be used when deciding what types of activities to provide for limited-English-proficient pupils. His framework is based on the idea that knowledge is structured similarly from situation to situation. If pupils learn types of knowledge that apply to certain situations, then they can transfer this to different content areas to enhance their comprehension of the content. Mohan also states that these knowledge structures have certain common linguistic features that set them apart. These features facilitate transfer of learning from one language to another. Finally, Mohan points out that six key visual organizers representing particular knowledge structures can help learners organize and simplify content. They are:

- Description
- Sequence
- Choice
- Classification
- Principles
- Evaluation

In working with individual learners, we can frame questions related to each of these categories.

Description
This knowledge type requires pupils to observe, identify, locate, or describe persons, objects, settings, or events. The types of questions you can ask in this category relate to issues such as who, what, where, and how many? Key visuals are pictures, slides, diagrams, maps, and drawings.

Sequence
This knowledge type requires pupils to organize things in order, note changes over time, follow steps in directions, or note recurring cycles. Questions you might ask in this category include, "What happened first? What was next? What was the order?" Key visuals that can help pupils understand issues associated with sequence are flow charts, timelines, and filmstrips.

Choice
Pupils are required to make decisions, select from alternatives, propose alternatives, and take action in this knowledge type. Some questions you might ask related to choice include, "What are the alternatives? What would you do? What other choices could be made? What would be the consequences?" This type of knowledge is consistent with the types of strategies discussed in Chapter 10, "Developing Prosocial Behavior." Key visuals for displaying relationships are flow charts and decision trees.

Classification

Pupils identify common attributes and group and define items with common characteristics in this knowledge type. It is very much like concept formation, described earlier. Among questions about classification are, "What things go together? How are these items alike? How are these items different? In what other ways could these things be grouped?" Key visuals include charts, webs, tables, and semantic maps.

Principles

This knowledge type requires pupils to explain, predict, interpret data, formulate hypotheses, test hypotheses, apply information, and note cause and effect. It is consistent with the interpretation of data and the inquiry approaches introduced earlier. Questions we might ask related to principles include, "How do you explain that? What caused that? Why do you think it happened that way? What do you think would happen if . . . ? How could you apply this to problems?" Key visuals that can facilitate mastery are Venn diagrams, cycle charts, and data retrieval charts.

Evaluation

This knowledge type requires pupils to make a judgment about the worth or relative strength of something. Questions that you might ask include, "Which is the best choice? What criteria would you use to judge the worth of this? Which one is right?" Key visuals useful for displaying this type of thinking are rating scales, grids, and rank ordering.

Some of these knowledge types are easier for pupils to master than others. This has implications for planning learning experiences for limited-English-proficient learners. For example, content related to *description, sequence,* and *classification* often is not so complex as content related to other knowledge categories. For this reason, we might opt to focus on content of this kind when preparing lessons for pupils at the early-production stage of acquiring English. Lessons focusing on more demanding content, associated with categories such as *principle formulation* and *evaluation,* need to be reserved for limited-English-proficient pupils who have developed to fairly advanced levels of English usage and comprehension. When we take care to match knowledge types to limited-English-proficient pupils' individual levels of English facility, we improve the prospects that they will master the content. This is important because every academic success learners experience has the potential for enhancing their self-image and motivating them to learn more.

SUCCESSFUL INSTRUCTIONAL PRACTICES FOR TEACHING LIMITED-ENGLISH-PROFICIENT LEARNERS

Researchers have identified several common characteristics of classrooms that are successful in helping limited-English-proficient pupils achieve success. In these classes there is great emphasis on functional communication from teacher to learner and from learner to learner. These classrooms tend to be organized around a theme and to have an integrated curriculum. There is a great deal of pupil collaboration on almost all activities, with a minimal amount of individual work. Finally, there is an informal and almost familial atmosphere (Garcia, 1994). Instructional practices that relate to these characteristics include cooperative learning, multimedia and concrete experiences, and language experiences.

Cooperative learning approaches facilitate inter- action between students and lead to improved language usage.

Cooperative Learning

Cooperative learning approaches are strongly recommended for limited-English-proficient pupils. Cooperative learning maximizes the opportunities for pupils to interact with each other and to use language in a nonthreatening environment. Pupils who might otherwise be silent because of embarrassment are more likely to communicate in a small group. Elementary school pupils can be quite inventive in communicating with those with very limited English. In cooperative groups, they are able to help the limited-English- proficient pupil comprehend what is happening in the classroom. The group rewards serve as strong incentives for limited-English-proficient pupils. This approach helps them avoid the fear of failure and provides them with opportunities to succeed in spite of their language difficulties.

Multimedia and Concrete Experiences

Because many social studies ideas are communicated in written form and are abstract, concrete experiences and different types of media are important aids to pupil learning. This is particularly true when you work with limited-English-proficient pupils, who of- ten are challenged both by the difficulty of abstract content and by the necessity to learn in a language they do not yet know well.

Many social studies concepts can be conveyed through the use of pictures. A good pic- ture file including pictures of objects and scenes is an extremely useful tool for teaching social studies to all pupils. Maps, globes, artifacts, and filmstrips are useful as well. There are particular advantages in using filmstrips with classes that include limited-English- proficient pupils. The narrative that accompanies most filmstrips can be rewritten to ac- commodate the pupils' stage of language acquisition. In this way pupils get pictures to accompany the English, which reinforces the content being introduced visually and pro- vides additional practice in reading English.

It is also useful to make audiotapes of classroom discussions, and make them available to pupils. Pupils can replay these tapes as many times as needed to comprehend the material. Pupils can stop the tape and ask the teacher if they do not understand the meaning of a word or a phrase. Sometimes other pupils in the class can listen with them and provide clarification.

Flashcards and sentence strips are also useful supplements. Important names, dates, concepts, and terms can be written on flashcards. The key vocabulary and concepts can then be previewed at the beginning of the lesson and reviewed periodically during the lesson. Sentence strips with key phrases or ideas can also be developed. For example, if you were teaching a fifth-grade class that included limited-English-proficient pupils, you could prepare flashcards featuring names of various explorers. You might review these with the limited-English-proficient pupils before the lesson. During the lesson, you could display appropriate flashcards when introducing each explorer, which would provide a visual reference for the spoken word and enhance comprehension.

Another activity based on flashcards is to have the pupils develop word banks of commonly used or imperfectly understood terms. These terms can then be addressed specifically in developing comprehension. As the pupils continue to develop their language fluency, they can keep adding to the word bank. Not only does this help them review and learn new terms; it provides them with a visible record of their progress.

Field trips provide pupils with concrete experiences. Visits to stores, parks, factories, and the local neighborhood forge a link between everyday tasks and language acquisition. Other concrete activities for social studies classes include construction of social studies projects such as models, dioramas, and murals. Dramatizing events and role-playing represent still other approaches to embedding social studies content in contexts pupils will view as "real." For example, the principle of taxation without representation is commonly included in fifth-grade lessons. However, this is an abstract idea that may be difficult for a second-language learner to grasp. Acting out a dramatization where individuals are required to pay a fee with no opportunity for input or discussion can make the idea concrete and help pupils grasp the meaning.

Language Experiences

Most pupils have a natural desire to communicate. Communication is essential in building the language skills of limited-English-proficient pupils. However, many limited-English-proficient pupils are embarrassed and fearful about sharing. In other words, they have a high affective filter. Lessons need to encourage communication in the classroom (King, Fagan, Bratt, & Baer, 1992). Two approaches that can foster this kind of communication are semantic mapping and guided writing.

Semantic Mapping
Semantic mapping encourages visual representation of connections among ideas. One way that semantic mapping can be used is to present the pupils with a topic or an idea. They then brainstorm to generate associations with the topic. Next, ask them to organize these associations into a graphic that serves as an advance organizer for the material presented. Once the pupils have completed their study of the content, they revise their map.

The process of eliciting a visual framework that can be used in comprehending the content, the chance to participate and exchange ideas with others, and the revision of the visual framework during and after the lesson aid overall comprehension and are extremely useful to limited-English-proficient pupils (Reyes & Molner, 1991).

Lesson Idea 16–1

ALTERING A LESSON TO ACCOMMODATE LIMITED-ENGLISH-PROFICIENT PUPILS

Original Lesson

Grade Level: 4

Objectives: Pupils will use cardinal directions to indicate the relative location of places on a map.

Overview: An understanding of cardinal directions helps individuals to orient themselves. Proficiency in the skill of using cardinal directions is needed for pupils to determine the relative and absolute location of places.

Procedure: *Learning Set*   Ask the class, "How many of you have asked someone for directions on how to get somewhere?" Allow them to share stories of problems with unclear directions. Tell them, "Today we are going to learn about something called *cardinal directions.* These can help you learn how to find places on maps and help you give better directions to people."

Presentation   Show the class a compass. Ask if anyone knows what it is and how it is used. Illustrate how to find north using the compass. Inform them that north is one of the cardinal directions. Show them the compass rose on a wall map. Inform them that the compass rose tells the direction that north is on the map. Place the map on the floor of the classroom and orient to north using the compass and the compass rose. Ask the class if they know what direction is the opposite of north. Introduce them to the concept of *south.* Point out the direction *south* on the map. Tell them there are two other cardinal directions. If they are facing north, the direction to their right is east and the direction to their left is west. Have them identify those directions on the map.

For guided practice give them a few questions orally. Examples might be, "What direction is Chicago from New Orleans? What direction is Los Angeles from New York?"

When it appears that they understand the concept, give them a worksheet that asks them to identify the direction of one place on the map when they are traveling from another.

Closure: Ask, "What did we learn today? How is understanding cardinal directions useful?"

Altered Lesson

Grade Level:	4
Objectives:	Pupils will use cardinal directions to indicate the relative location of places on a map.
Overview:	An understanding of cardinal directions helps individuals to orient themselves. Proficiency in the skill of using cardinal directions is needed for pupils to determine the relative and absolute location of places.
Procedures:	*Learning Set* Take the class outside during the middle of the day. Have them note their shadows. Show them a compass and ask if anyone knows how it is used. Use the compass to show them that at about noon their shadow points roughly to the north.
	Presentation Return to the classroom and find north using the compass. Give pupils a card with *north* printed on it and have them place the card on the north wall of the classroom. Show them a wall map and point out the compass rose. Tell them that the compass rose tells the map reader which direction is north on the map.
	Take the map off the wall and orient it on the floor of the classroom. Ask which direction is opposite of north. Provide one of the pupils a card with *south* printed on it. Have a pupil place the card on the south wall of the classroom. With the map on the floor, call on individual pupils to stand at one place on the map and then walk either north or south. For example, "John, Where is Los Angeles on our map? Please stand on Los Angeles. Now walk north from Los Angeles." "Maria, find Chicago on the map. Walk south from Chicago." Call on some of the limited-English-proficient pupils to perform the task.
	Introduce east and west by giving two students cards labeled *east* and *west*. Have the pupils place the cards on the appropriate walls. Repeat the exercise of walking from one point to either east or west. Then mix the directions and have them walk in one of the four cardinal directions.
	Have the class work in groups using a map to identify the relative locations of places listed on the map.
Closure:	Ask, "What did we learn today? How is understanding cardinal directions useful?" Call on limited-English-proficient pupils and check for understanding by giving students such directions as, "Juan, point to the north."

Guided Writing

Guided writing promotes generation of ideas in an oral context and integration of reading and writing in social studies. It is a technique that appears to be effective for older elementary limited-English-proficient pupils (Reyes & Molner, 1991). The procedure begins with brainstorming and a discussion of what pupils in the class already know about a topic. The outcome of this discussion is a brief outline or web of the topic. Following this discussion, assign learners to groups and ask each group to write a short piece following the outline or web. Working together gives limited-English-proficient pupils an opportunity to share as well as to observe the connection between spoken and written vocabulary. After students have completed these short written assignments, quickly read and analyze these initial drafts. Then return them to the groups with a checklist containing suggestions they can incorporate into a more polished second draft.

Next, ask pupils to read material on the topic using the guides or outlines to help their comprehension. After they discuss the material together in their groups, have them write a third draft of the paper including the new material and ideas they learned from the reading. This helps the limited-English-proficient pupils comprehend the reading and see the connection between the four language arts processes of speaking, reading, writing, and listening.

At later stages of language development, pupils can be encouraged to keep content journals, wherein they write down information and questions about the content they are learning. This helps the pupil communicate with the teacher on a one-to-one basis in written form. These journals are useful to the teacher in quickly identifying misconceptions or "fuzzy" understanding of a content.

*   *   *

In conclusion, we can do many things to help limited-English-proficient pupils attain success in the classroom. The satisfaction of seeing growth and learning among limited-English-proficient pupils makes the additional effort worthwhile.

WEB CHECK

Note: Electronic addresses of sites on the World Wide Web change frequently. If the listed URL fails to work, use a standard search engine to locate the new address of the site.

- TESOL

  URL—**http://www.tesol.edu/index.html**

  This is the home page for TESOL, Teachers of English to Speakers of Other Languages, Inc. TESOL is the leading national organization for educators with an interest in helping improve the English-language proficiency of people who are nonnative speakers of English. There are excellent links at this site to other Web locations with information that can help teachers who teach learners for whom English is a second language.

- National Clearinghouse for Bilingual Education

  URL—**http://www.ncbe.gwu.edu/**

  The National Clearinghouse maintains this site for bilingual education with funds provided by the U.S. Department of Education's Office of Bilingual Education and Minority Languages Affairs. It contains much information of interest to teachers who work with learners who are not native speakers of English. There are also numerous links to other relevant websites. Highly recommended.

- Cross-Age Tutoring

  URL—**http://cisl.ospi.wednet.edu/CISL/Strategies/CRSAGETUTR.html**

  This site includes an extensive listing of ERIC Document Reproduction Service documents and articles in educational journals that focus on approaches to assisting limited-English-proficient pupils by using cross-age tutoring techniques. Links are provided to these items. Many can be downloaded.

- Welcome to ESL Net!

  URL—**http://esl.net/**

  Seattle-based ESL Net is an information source for materials of all kinds on English as a second language. There are also direct links to schools with strong ESL programs.

- Language Development Strategies

  URL—**http://www.lalc.k12.ca.us/laep/smart/Sunrise/lang.html**

  As the title of the site implies, material here focuses on a number of strategies for assisting limited-English-proficiency learners. Information is provided that relates to (1) English language development, (2) second-language acquisition, and (3) self-image and multicultural learning. There are also sample English language development lessons.

KEY IDEAS IN SUMMARY

1. The rapid increase in the number of limited-English-proficiency (limited-English-proficient) pupils in public schools has increased the need for teachers who know how to meet their needs. Teaching them in content areas such as social studies allows them to progress academically while they are acquiring a new language. Teaching content areas has been found to facilitate language acquisition.

2. Two types of language proficiency are important for pupils to succeed in content area instruction. The first is basic interpersonal communication skill. This proficiency allows pupils to interact with others and to communicate their needs and usually develops in a relatively short time. The other type of proficiency is cognitive/academic language proficiency, which allows pupils to understand a subject when the context clues are reduced and when unique vocabulary is present. It usually takes an individual several years to reach this level.

3. Social studies is an appropriate subject for limited-English-proficient pupils because it has the potential for providing meaningful learning experiences. Teaching in this area of the elementary curriculum allows these pupils to use their own backgrounds as resources for lessons and to engage in instructional experiences that can help them become more proficient users of English.

4. There are potential problems for limited-English-proficient pupils in social studies classes. Some social studies teachers introduce print material that may be too difficult for some limited-English-proficient pupils. Further, many of these youngsters lack previous background in social studies content, often because they have not attended U.S. schools in earlier years when content was introduced. Furthermore, teachers erroneously assume that everyone in their present grade level already knows this content.

5. Sheltered instruction is an approach designed to make content instruction more comprehensible to limited-English-proficient pupils. Sheltered instruction involves simplified speech, providing a context for the instruction, focusing on a task-function relationship, and providing for numerous interactional activities.

6. When teaching limited-English-proficient pupils, teachers should attempt to reduce the anxiety and fear of the pupils and provide input that is meaningful and comprehensible.

7. The four stages of language development are (1) preproduction, (2) early production, (3) emergence of speech, and (4) intermediate fluency. An understanding of the characteristics of each of these stages helps teachers design successful lessons for limited-English-proficient pupils.

8. Varying the contextual clues present and the cognitive complexity of communication is important in providing comprehensible input for pupils at the different stages of language acquisition.

9. Certain knowledge structures are similar across situations. These knowledge structures have common linguistic features. Key visuals that fit with each knowledge type can be used to provide context clues for learning. Teaching these knowledge structures to limited-English-proficient pupils facilitates their learning across content areas. The knowledge structures that can be taught are (1) description, (2) sequence, (3) choice, (4) classification, (5) principles, and (6) evaluation.

10. Successful instructional practices for limited-English-proficient pupils involve the use of cooperative learning, multimedia and concrete experiences, and semantic mapping and guided writing procedures.

CHAPTER REFLECTIONS

Directions: Now that you have read this chapter, reread the case study at the beginning. Then, answer these questions:

1. How would you respond to the statements of the teachers in the faculty meeting?

2. What is your position on the inclusion of limited-English-proficient pupils in social studies classes? Do you believe that altering instruction for limited-English-proficient pupils interferes with the other pupils' learning?

3. What else do you think you need to learn to be able to meet the needs of limited-English-proficient pupils?

4. Have your ideas about teaching limited-English-proficient pupils changed as a result of reading this chapter? If so, what specific ideas or perspectives have changed?

EXTENDING UNDERSTANDING AND SKILL

1. Identify those elements of a classroom that have the potential for creating cultural conflict for pupils from different cultures. State how you think instruction in social studies might be made more culturally congruent for pupils from other cultures.

2. Check the credential (teacher certification) requirements for the state where you reside. Are requirements designed to prepare teachers for teaching limited-English-proficient pupils? If so, what is required? If not, what do you think should be done?

3. Visit an elementary school and see what is done to provide for the learning needs of limited-English-proficient pupils. Use the ideas presented in this chapter to evaluate the school you visit and to identify areas where improvement might be needed.

4. Imagine that you are teaching at the grade level of your choice and that a new pupil who speaks almost no English has been enrolled in your class. What specific things could you do to help the pupil learn the social studies content for that grade? Give specific suggestions, and provide your rationale for them.

REFERENCES

ASSOCIATION FOR SUPERVISION AND CURRICULUM DEVELOPMENT (1994). *Update* (Vol. 36, No. 5.). Alexandria, VA: Association for Supervision and Curriculum Development.

AU, K., & KAWAKAMI, A. (1994). Cultural congruence in instruction. In E. Hollins, J. King, & W. Hayman (Eds.), *Teaching diverse populations: Formulating a knowledge base* (pp. 5–23). Albany, NY: State University of New York Press.

BAKER, C. (1996). *Foundations of bilingual education and bilingualism* (2nd ed.). Philadelphia, PA: Multilingual Matters, Ltd.

CUMMINS, J. (1981). The role of primary language development in promoting educational success for language minority students. In California State Department of Education (Ed.), *Schooling and Language Minority Students: A Theoretical Framework* (p. 12). Los Angeles: California State University, Los Angeles Evaluation and Assessment Center.

EARLY, M. (1990, October). Enabling first and second language learners in the classroom. *Language Arts, 67,* 567–575.

GARCIA, E. (1994). Attributes of effective schools for language minority students. In E. Hollins, J. King, & W. Hayman (Eds.), *Teaching diverse populations: Formulating a knowledge base* (pp. 93–103). Albany, NY: State University of New York Press.

GARCIA, R. (1991). *Teaching in a pluralistic society: Concepts, models, strategies* (2nd ed.). New York: HarperCollins.

KING, M., FAGAN, B., BRATT, T., & BAER, R. (1992). Social studies instruction. In P. Richard-Amato & M. Snow (Eds.), *The multicultural classroom* (pp. 287–299). White Plains, NY: Longman.

KRASHEN, S. (1982). *Principles and practice in second language acquisition.* Oxford: Pergamon.

MOHAN, B. (1986). *Language and content.* Reading, MA: Addison-Wesley.

PEREGOY, S. F., & BOYLE, O. F. (1997). *Reading, writing, and learning in ESL.* New York: Longman.

PEREZ, B., & TORRES-GUZMAN, M. E. (1992). *Learning in two worlds: An integrated Spanish/English biliteracy approach.* New York: Longman.

REYES, M., & MOLNER, L. (1991). Instructional strategies for second-language learners in the content areas. *Journal of Reading, 35* (2), 96–103.

SHORT, P. (1994). The challenge of social studies for limited-English-proficient students. *Social Education, 58* (1), 36–38.

TERRELL, T. (1981). The natural approach in bilingual education. In California State Department of Education (Ed.), *Schooling and language minority students: A theoretical framework* (pp. 117–146). Los Angeles: California State University, Los Angeles Evaluation and Assessment Center.

name index

subject index